Fast Track to SCSI
A Product Guide

Fujitsu Microelectronics, Inc.
Integrated Circuits Division

Prentice Hall, Englewood Cliffs, New Jersey 07632

This document is published by the Publications Department, Integrated Circuits Division;
Fujitsu Microelectronics, Inc.,
3545 North First Street, San Jose, California, 95134–1804; U.S.A.

Printed in the U.S.A.

Edition 1.0

Published by Prentice-Hall, Inc.
A Division of Simon & Schuster
Englewood Cliffs, New Jersey 07632

The publisher offers discounts on this book when ordered in bulk quantities. For more information, write:

Special Sales/College Marketing
College Technical and Reference Division
Prentice-Hall
Englewood Cliffs, New Jersey 07632

Printed in the United States of America
10 9 8 7 6 5 4 3 2 1

ISBN 0-13-307018-2 {C}

ISBN 0-13-307000-X {PBK}

Prentice-Hall International (UK) Limited, *London*
Prentice-Hall of Australia Pty. Limited, *Sydney*
Prentice-Hall Canada Inc., *Toronto*
Prentice-Hall Hispanoamericana, S.A., *Mexico*
Prentice-Hall of India Private Limited, *New Delhi*
Prentice-Hall of Japan, Inc., *Tokyo*
Simon & Schuster Asia Pte. Ltd., *Singapore*
Editora Prentice-Hall do Brasil, Ltda., *Rio de Janeiro*

CONTENTS

CONTENTS (Continued)

CONTENTS (Continued)

CONTENTS (Continued)

CONTENTS (Continued)

Figures

CONTENTS (Continued)

Figures (Continued)

Tables

Acknowledgements

The American National Standards Institute, Inc. has generously granted permission to use material from their copyrighted book:

American National Standard for information systems –
small computer system interface (SCSI). New York: American National Standards
Institute, 1986.
(ANSI X3.131–1986)

This document provided source material for Chapter 1 of this book. Exact reprints from the ANSI document include the following:

Figures 1–1, 1–2, 1–3, 1–4, 1–5, 1–6, 1–7, 1–8, and

Tables 1–1, 1–2, 1–4, 1–6, 1–7, 1–8, 1–9, 1–10, and

Appendix A: – 4.7 SCSI Bus Timing

Tables 1–3 and 1–5 are based on tables in the ANSI document.

Copies of this standard may be purchased from the American National Standards Institute at 1430 Broadway, New York City, NY 10018.

Preface

This book has been written to present an overview of the SCSI concept, a criteria for SCSI's use, and an explanation of vendor-unique (Fujitsu's) design features for a SCSI Protocol Controller. You will find that the book covers the general (and generic) SCSI design information in the first two chapters and continues with specific product information on Fujitsu's SPC line of products. A brief synopsis of the chapter contents follows:

Chapter 1

THE SCSI–I CONCEPT

The Small Computer System Interface or SCSI*, is fast becoming the popular industry standard for an interface. In the next few years there will be tremendous growth in the SCSI market place. Many of today's peripherals have a SCSI interface, and of the new and emerging peripherals, many will be introduced with a SCSI interface to meet the needs of this established market base. Currently, SCSI is probably the closest thing to a universal interface in the computer industry. For system and peripheral designers, SCSI is an option that must be considered prior to the start of the design cycle.

Development of the Small Computer System Interface

In the late 1970s, Shugart Associates began a program to develop an intelligent interface for its new line of disk drives. The interface was to be a device-independent parallel bus. The architecture was based on IBM's Input/Output (I/O) channel architecture, used in the 1960s and 1970s on IBM mainframe computers and intelligent peripherals. The new interface was called the Shugart Associates Standard Interface or

*Pronounced scuzzy

SASI*. The development and design was successful and Shugart began to manufacture drives with it.

In November of 1981, Shugart Associates and NCR petitioned the Intelligent Peripherals Committee of the American National Standards Institute, Inc. (ANSI) to adopt SASI as the working document for an Intelligent Peripheral Interface Standard. In February of 1982, the ANSI subcommittee X3T9.2 was formed and began work on the Shugart Associates Standard Interface. The first order of business was to choose a name that did not contain a reference to a corporation; Small Computer System Interface (SCSI) was chosen. The word "small" however, is not an indication of the performance or size of the interface. Today, the SCSI bus is used in systems ranging from personal computers, work stations and minicomputers, to mainframes and super computers with maximum transfer speeds in the range of 4 to 5 megabytes per second. In all these environments, the SCSI bus is a widely accepted interface standard.

In response to increasing requests for higher speed and performance, the current SCSI bus specification is being reviewed and revised to include future needs for a universal interface. Currently, a SCSI-II specification has been defined and should be ratified sometime in 1990. The anticipated SCSI-II specification incorporates all the standards of the SCSI-I specification; thereby making all SCSI-I peripherals compatible with SCSI-II. The SCSI-II bus provides for 8-bit, 16-bit or 32-bit wide data transfers and for transfers up to 10 megabytes per second(8-bit bus width). Depending on bus width, the new specification allows up to 40 megabytes-per-second transfers. These added capabilities to the SCSI-II specifications will carry the use of these standards well into the next century.

Today, I/O speed is an important factor in overall system throughput; and SCSI is fast—and getting faster. Another important factor of SCSI is its flexibility and versatility. The variety of devices that can be used on the bus is growing and is limited only by the peripheral designer's imagination. The list of peripherals available with SCSI interfaces is extensive: hard disk drives, removable disk drives, Bernoulli™ disks, floppy disk drives, scanners, plotters, printers, LANs, CD-ROMs, WORMs, modems, 9-track tape drives, 8 mm tape drives, cassette tape drives, video equipment, and many more.

---

*Pronounced sassy

™Bernoulli is a trademark of IOmega.

Basic Principles

When you review the ANSI specification you will find that the SCSI concept is both detailed and subtle. The first element of the SCSI design is that SCSI is a bus, not a direct connection between two peripherals. The SCSI bus can be shared by many devices, thereby increasing bus flexibility and utilization, and it has both a *physical* and a *logical interface*. The *physical interface* includes the cables, connectors, and the timing and voltage relationships of the electrical signals. The *logical interface* is the communication protocol, the bus sequences and phases, the message system, the commands, the data transfer mode, etc. It is important to remember the *logical* and *physical* structure of SCSI, if you are to understand the elements of the interface.

The devices connected to the SCSI bus are known as either INITIATORs or TARGETs. An INITIATOR is a device that initiates or requests a device on the bus to perform a SCSI operation. A TARGET is the object of a request. Some devices can function both as an INITIATOR and a TARGET, but usually a device is either one or the other. Computers and host systems are usually configured as INITIATORs. Peripherals, such as disk or tape drives, are usually TARGETs.

SCSI Bus Configurations

The SCSI bus can be configured in three basic arrangements: (1) Single INITIATOR/Single TARGET, (2) Single INITIATOR/Multiple TARGET, and (3) Multiple INITIATOR/Multiple TARGET.

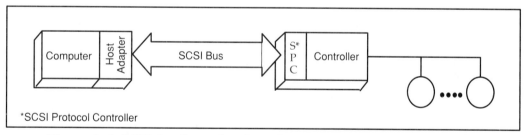

Figure 1–1. SCSI Configuration for a Single INITIATOR/Single TARGET

(1)   Single INITIATOR/Single TARGET

The single INITIATOR/single TARGET configuration implies that there is only one host connected to one peripheral. This was probably the most common configuration in the early days of SCSI, since few SCSI peripherals were available. Many simple SCSI systems operate in the single INITIATOR/single TARGET configuration. An example of a simple SCSI system is a personal computer with a SCSI host adapter connected to a SCSI hard disk drive.

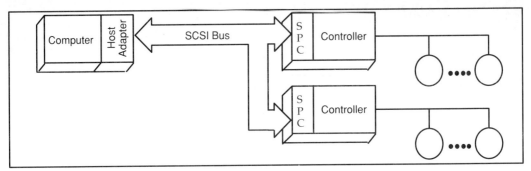

Figure 1–2. SCSI Configuration for a Single INITIATOR/Multiple TARGET

(2)   Single INITIATOR/Multiple TARGET

The single INITIATOR/multiple TARGET configuration is the prevelant arrangement today. This configuration can take advantage of some of the more powerful SCSI features, such as arbitration and reselection, that permits peripheral-to-peripheral transfers and overlapped I/Os. Again, the example could be a personal computer with two or more SCSI hard disk drives, or a hard disk and a CD-ROM drive, etc.

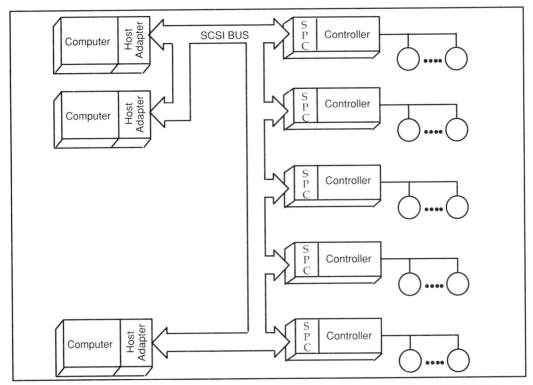

Figure 1–3. SCSI Configuration for a Multiple INITIATOR/Multiple TARGET

(3)   *Multiple INITIATOR/Multiple TARGET*

This is by far the most powerful configuration and one that can fully maximize bus performance. The multiple INITIATOR/multiple TARGET configuration can provide such functions as host-to-host communication, peripheral-to-peripheral data transfer, and multi-threaded and concurrent operations to peripherals (multi-tasking). This configuration is usually found in high-end systems, but with proper software support, this configuration could support low-end systems as well.

It is important to remember that the SCSI bus is electrically compatible in any of the above configurations. Software and host system throughput, not the protocol, are the factors that may limit compatibility.

The SCSI Interface

The small computer system interface, SCSI, is a local I/O bus that can be operated at data rates up to five megabytes per second. The interface provides host computers with a device-independent method to access a class of devices.

ANSI defines several device classes. One class is for direct access devices, (hard disk drives, removable cartridge drives, floppy drives, etc). Device classification allows the system designer to develop generic software that will function with one or more device classes. Designs using generic software allow the system to be easily expanded by adding disk and tape drives, printers, and communications devices, but without modifying generic system hardware and software. SCSI also allows for non-generic features and functions to be added through vendor-unique fields and commands.

The SCSI protocol is based on the logical structure of the bus, rather than the physical characteristics of the interface devices. For example, the SCSI host does not have to know how many heads, cylinders and sectors a disk drive has to access it. If SCSI system software is developed to support direct access devices, the user should be able to access any hard disk drive connected to the bus without any software modification and regardless of its capacity, speed, physical characteristics or manufacturer.

SCSI Physical Characteristics

The ANSI SCSI-I specification defines the physical characteristics of the SCSI bus (cable) that includes: cables (bus), drivers, connectors, signals, terminators, and timings. The SCSI bus consists of 18 signals, one termination power, and multiple grounds. SCSI devices are connected together in a daisy-chain fashion making the signals common to all devices. Each end of the cable must be terminated with the characteristic impedance of the bus.

SCSI Cable/Driver Combinations

Two cable/driver combinations, single-ended and differential, (and the criteria to determine which combination is needed) are specified in the ANSI SCSI-I standard. The single-ended cable/driver is used for short distances (up to a maximum of six meters). A typical single-ended connection would be one between internally mounted peripherals inside a cabinet. The differential cable/driver is used for greater distances (up to a maximum of 25 meters). A typical differential connection would be one between a mainframe and a bank of peripherals contained within their own cabinet.

Two cable types, single-ended and differential, (corresponding to the two driver techniques) are also defined in the ANSI SCSI-I standard. These cables can either be shielded or unshielded. For unshielded flat or twisted pair ribbon cable, a characteristic impedance of 100 ohms +/− 10 percent is recommended. For a shielded cable, a characteristic impedance of 90 ohms is recommended. To minimize cable reflections, cables within a SCSI system should be of the same type (not mixed). Cables can have a significant effect on system performance. The maximum speed and drive capability of the bus will depend upon the quality of the cable. A minimum conductor size of 28 AWG is needed to minimize noise and ensure proper power distribution.

(1)   *Single-Ended Cable*

A single-ended cable is made of either a 50-signal flat ribbon cable or 25-signal twisted pair cable. Excluding ground signals, each SCSI signal occupies one wire within the cable. The single-ended cable is used with single-ended drivers/receivers only.

(2)   *Differential Cable*

A differential cable is made of either a 50-signal ribbon cable or a 25-signal twisted pair cable. Excluding ground signals, each SCSI signal is differential and will occupy two wires within the cable. The differential cable is used with differential drivers/receivers only.

SCSI Connectors

Three types of connectors for SCSI-I are defined in the ANSI SCSI-I standard. The first is a 50-pin non-shielded connector (arranged as two rows of 25 pins on 0.1 inch centers) that is used primarily to connect to a ribbon or flat type of cable. The second connector is a shielded version of the first connector (with the same pin assignments) that is typically used for connections to devices within a cabinet. The third connector is a shielded 50-pin D-shell type connector used for connections to a twisted wire pair of cable. Connections between devices outside a cabinet to devices within a cabinet, use the third connector type.

See Table 1–1 and Table 1–2 for pin assignments of shielded and unshielded connectors.

Table 1–1. Single-ended Pin Assignments

Signal[1]	Even Pin Numbers[2]
–DB (0)	2
–DB (1)	4
–DB (2)	6
–DB (3)	8
–DB (4)	10
–DB (5)	12
–DB (6)	14
–DB (7)	16
–DB (P)	18
GROUND	20
GROUND	22
GROUND	24
TERMPWR	26
GROUND	28
GROUND	30
–ATN	32
GROUND	34
–BSY	36
–ACK	38
–RST	40
–MSG	42
–SEL	44
–C/D	46
–REQ	48
–I/O	50

Notes: [1]The minus sign next to the signals indicates active low.

[2]All odd pins, except pin 25, shall be connected to ground. Pin 25 should be left open.

(Some products designed prior to the generation of this standard connected this pin to ground.)

Table 1–2. Differential Pin Assignments

Signal Name	Pin Number		Signal Name
SHIELD GROUND*	1	2	GROUND
+DB (0)	3	4	–DB (0)
+DB (1)	5	6	–DB (1)
+DB (2)	7	8	–DB (2)
+DB (3)	9	10	–DB (3)
+DB (4)	11	12	–DB (4)
+DB (5)	13	14	–DB (5)
+DB (6)	15	16	–DB (6)
+DB (7)	17	18	–DB (7)
+DB (P)	19	20	–DB (P)
DIFFSENS	21	22	GROUND
GROUND	23	24	GROUND
TERMPWR	25	26	TERMPWR
GROUND	27	28	GROUND
+ATN	29	30	–ATN
GROUND	31	32	GROUND
+BSY	33	34	–BSY
+ACK	35	36	–ACK
+RST	37	38	–RST
+MSG	39	40	–MSG
+SEL	41	42	–SEL
+C/D	43	44	–C/D
+REQ	45	46	–REQ
+I/O	47	48	–I/O
GROUND	49	50	GROUND

Note: *SHIELD GROUND is optional on some cables. (Implementors note: some shielded flat ribbon cables use pin 1 as a connection to the shield.)

Bus Signals

The SCSI bus consists of 18 signals (excluding grounds and termination power), nine data signals and nine control signals. The nine data lines constitute a 9-bit (8 data bits, 1 parity) bi-directional DATA BUS. The nine control lines are used to indicate the various phases of the bus protocol and to control the flow and direction of the DATA BUS. Some of the control lines are controlled by the INITIATOR and some are controlled by the TARGET.

When the SCSI signal is in the active state, it is *true, asserted* and *active*. When the SCSI signal is in the inactive state, it is *false, negated* or *inactive*. SCSI signals may be either active or inactive. In all cases, the signals must be driven in the active state. The inactive state cannot drive a signal, but it allows the bus terminators to pull up the signal to the voltage level of the inactive state. This pull-up is done when OR-tied or open-collector drivers are used. The signal can also be driven into the inactive state by using three-state drivers. Noise margins and signal rise-times can be improved by driving the signals active; i.e., allows a faster data transfer.

Signal Definitions

The ANSI SCSI-I specification defines the SCSI bus signals as follows:

DB0–DB7, DBP (DATA BUS)

The DB0 through DB7 and DBP signals form the DATA BUS, eight for data and one for parity. These signals are bi-directional and can be driven or sensed by both the TARGET and the INITIATOR. DB0 is the least significant bit and DB7 is the most significant. DBP is the ODD parity bit. The data bus is used for transferring data between the TARGET and the INITIATOR and for device priority selection during the ARBITRATION phase, with DB7 being the highest priority bit and DB0 the lowest.

Use of the DBP parity signal is optional and it can be enabled or disabled depending upon the system configuration. The parity bit is not valid during the ARBITRATION phase.

BSY (BUSY)

The busy signal is an OR-tied signal that can be driven active by any device wishing to gain access to the bus. This signal is driven by an INITIATOR to begin an ARBITRATION/SELECTION action, or by the TARGET during an ARBITRATION/RESELECTION action. When active, this signal indicates that the SCSI bus is in use.

SEL (SELECT)

The SELECT signal is used by the INITIATOR to select a TARGET during the SELECTION phase and by the TARGET to select an INITIATOR during the RESELECTION phase.

C/D (CONTROL/DATA)

The C/D signal is driven by the TARGET and indicates the type of information passing over the DATA BUS, either control or data. Control information is indicated when this signal is asserted, active, or true.

I/O (INPUT/OUTPUT)

The I/O signal is driven by the TARGET and indicates the direction of data flow over the DATA BUS. An active, asserted, or true signal indicates that data is flowing into the INITIATOR; i.e., the INITIATOR is reading from the DATA BUS and the TARGET is writing. An inactive signal indicates that the INITIATOR is writing to the DATA BUS and the TARGET is reading.

The I/O signal is also used to indicate if a SELECTION or RESELECTION operation is taking place. When the I/O is negated or inactive, an INITIATOR is selecting a TARGET; when it is asserted, a TARGET is reselecting an INITIATOR.

MSG (MESSAGE)

The MSG signal is driven active by the TARGET and indicates that a message phase is occurring.

REQ (REQUEST)

The REQ signal is driven active by the TARGET and indicates a request to the INITIATOR for data transfer over the DATA BUS. The data transfer request is acknowledged with the REQ/ACK handshake.

ACK (ACKNOWLEDGE)

The ACK signal is driven active by the INITIATOR and indicates an acknowledgement of the REQ/ACK data transfer handshake to the TARGET.

ATN (ATTENTION)

The ATN signal is driven active by the INITIATOR and indicates the ATTENTION condition to the selected TARGET.

RST (RESET)

The RST signal is an OR-tied signal that can be driven active by any device on the bus and indicates a RESET condition.

The BSY and RST signals are the only signals required to be OR-tied. The mandatory OR-tied condition requirement allows these signals to be simultaneously driven active by several devices. Signals other than the BSY and RST signals can be driven using either OR-tied, open collector drivers or three-state drivers.

Signal Sources

Signal sources, or originators, are either the INITIATORs or TARGETs. As indicated in Table 1–3, some signals are INITIATOR originated only, some are TARGET originated only, and some are both INITIATOR originated and TARGET originated.

Table 1–3 shows the devices that are permitted to drive each signal during a specific bus phase.

Table 1–3. Signal Sources

Bus Phase	Signals[1,4]				
	BSY (Notes 1,2,3,4)	**SEL** (Notes 1,4,5,6)	**C/D, I/O MSG, REQ** (Notes 1,4)	**ACK/ATN** (Notes1,6)	**DB (7-0, P** (Notes 1,4,6,7)
BUS FREE	None	None	None	None	None
ARBITRATION	All	Winner	None	None	SCSI ID
SELECTION	I&T	INITIATOR	None	INITIATOR	INITIATOR
RESELECTION	I&T	TARGET	TARGET	INITIATOR	TARGET
COMMAND	TARGET	None	TARGET	INITIATOR	INITIATOR
DATA IN	TARGET	None	TARGET	INITIATOR	TARGET
DATA OUT	TARGET	None	TARGET	INITIATOR	INITIATOR
STATUS	TARGET	None	TARGET	INITIATOR	TARGET
MESSAGE IN	TARGET	None	TARGET	INITIATOR	TARGET
MESSAGE OUT	TARGET	None	TARGET	INITIATOR	INITIATOR

Notes: 1. None: The signal shall be released; that is, not be driven by any SCSI device. The bias circuitry of the bus terminators pulls the signal to the false state.

2. All: The signal shall be driven by all SCSI devices that are actively arbitrating.

3. I&T   The signal shall be driven by the INITIATOR, TARGET, or both, as specified in the SELECTION phase and RESELECTION phase.

4. TARGET: If the signal is driven, it shall be driven only by the active TARGET.

5. Winner: The signal shall be driven by the one SCSI device that wins ARBITRATION.

6. INITIATOR: If this signal is driven, it shall be driven only by the active INITIATOR.

7. SCSI ID: A unique data bit (the SCSI ID) that shall be driven by each SCSI device that is actively arbitrating; the other seven data bits shall be released (i.e., not driven) by this SCSI device. The parity bit (DB (P)) may be undriven or driven to the true state, but shall never be driven to the false state during this phase.

Single-ended SCSI Bus Signals

SCSI signals within single-ended cables shall be terminated into a resistive load with 220 ohms connected to +5 volts and 330 ohms connected to ground at each end of the cable. See Figure 1–4 for the single-ended bus terminator arrangement. All signals on the bus will be driven using open-collector or three-state drivers.

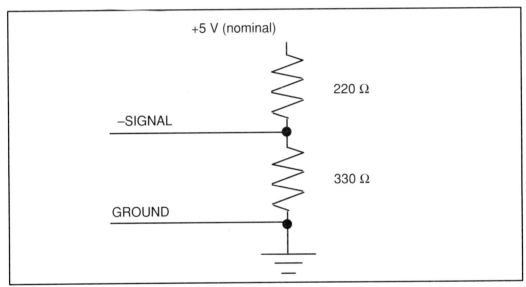

Figure 1–4. Termination for Single-ended Devices

Each **output signal** driven by a SCSI device shall conform to the following output characteristics:

> Signal asserted = 0.0 volts DC to 0.4 volts DC
> Minimum drive = 48 milliamps sinking at 0.5 volts DC
> Signal negated = 2.5 volts DC to 5.25 volts DC

The inactive or negated signal state is achieved when the terminating resistors pull up an open-collector or three-state output.

Each **input signal** received by a SCSI device shall conform to the following input characteristics:

Signal asserted = 0.0 volts DC to 0.8 volts DC
Maximum input load = –0.4 milliamps at 0.4 volts DC
Signal negated = 2.0 volts DC to 5.25 volts DC
Minimum input hysteresis = 0.2 volts DC

Differential SCSI Bus Signals

A differential signal consists of two lines, +SIGNAL and a –SIGNAL. A signal is considered active, asserted, or true when the +SIGNAL is more positive than the –SIGNAL and a signal is considered inactive, negated, or false when the –SIGNAL is more positive than the +SIGNAL. Each signal shall be terminated as shown in Figure 1–5.

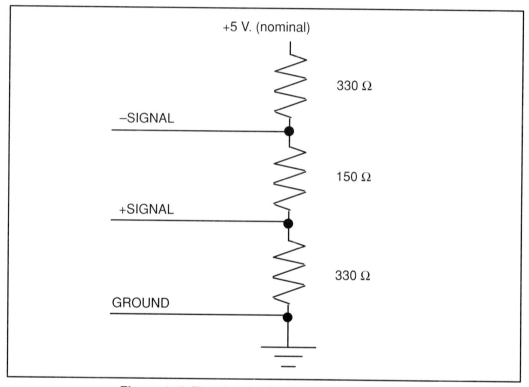

Figure 1–5. Termination for Differential Devices

Each **differential output signal** driven by a SCSI device shall conform to the Electronic Industries Association (EIA) RS-485-1983 specification and will have the following output characteristics.

V_{OL} = 2.0 volts at maximum I_{OL} = 55 milliamps
V_{OH} = 3.0 volts at I_{OH} = –55 milliamps
V_{OD} = 1.0 volts with common–mode voltage ranges from –7.0 volts DC to +12.0 volts DC

Each **differential input signal** received by a SCSI device shall conform to the EIA RS-485-1983 specification and will have the following input characteristics:

$I_I = \pm 2.0$ milliamps maximum

$V_{ID} = -5.0$ volts DC to $+12.0$ volts DC

$V_{IH} = 35$ millivolts hysteresis, minimum

Termination Power

As an option, it is possible for a SCSI device to provide power to the bus to energize the bus terminators. This option is used to supply power to terminators that are local to a device that is currently in a powered-off state, but still connected to the SCSI bus.

Bus Timing

Designers need to know the SCSI bus timing requirements to verify that the SCSI device they have chosen meets or exceeds the signal requirements given in ANSI X3.131–1986. Timing information from ANSI's X3.131–1986 specification will be found in Appendix A. For more detailed electrical and timing information, consult the ANSI specification. The discussions in this chapter, and throughout this book, reference only SCSI devices that meet the X3.131–1986 delay-time measurements.

SCSI Logical Characteristics

SCSI devices are classified into two logical types, INITIATOR and TARGET. The INITIATOR requests a TARGET device to perform a SCSI operation; i.e., the INITIATOR initiates, the TARGET performs. A SCSI device can be classified as either an INITIATOR or a TARGET type, or as both types. If the SCSI device is both an INITIATOR and a TARGET, it can only operate as one or the other during any one complete SCSI operation.

The SCSI bus can connect up to eight physical devices and each of the eight devices can control (as an INITIATOR) up to eight sub-devices (inclusive), called logical units or LUNs. If needed, the bus can be expanded to handle more devices. Each bus device must have a unique bus address, in the range of 0 through 7, and each LUN also has an address ranging from 0 through 7. Bus devices are prioritized by their bus address. (The higher the numeric value of the address, the higher the priority of the device. For example, address 7 is higher priority than address 3.)

The SCSI bus can have a logical connection between two devices while they are physically disconnected from the bus. For example, an INITIATOR sends a command to a TARGET to read data. While it is collecting the data to be read, the TARGET is physically disconnected from the bus and, later, it is reconnected to the INITIATOR to complete the transaction. During the disconnect, each device considers itself connected to the other. This characteristic allows high bus utilization because, while the selected INITIATOR and TARGET devices are disconnected from the bus, the bus is available for other devices to use. This technique can only be implemented when ARBITRATION and RESELECTION are supported.

SCSI Bus Phases

A typical SCSI operation is composed of a series of bus phases: ARBITRATION, SELECTION, RESELECTION, and DATA TRANSFER. These bus phases control and qualify the data flow over the bus.

The ARBITRATION phase sequence allows an orderly and simultaneous contest for the bus by multiple SCSI devices with the highest priority device winning control of the bus.

A SELECTION phase allows an INITIATOR to select one specific TARGET to perform an operation. A physical path is also established between the devices at this time.

The RESELECTION phase allows a TARGET to select an INITIATOR, re-establish the physical path and complete a previously requested operation.

The DATA TRANSFER phases allow data bytes to flow between the INITIATOR and TARGET over the physical DATA BUS.

A message system allows communication between the INITIATOR and TARGET during an operation. These messages allow the devices to manage error detection, data transfer retries, transfer speed selection, data path and data buffer management and more.

Bus Phase Descriptions

The following descriptions explain the bus phases in terms of logical signals. The SCSI bus protocol can operate in up to eight distinct phases; they include the control and data qualification phases:

1.   BUS FREE
2.   ARBITRATION
3.   SELECTION
4.   RESELECTION

and the information transfer phases:

5.   COMMAND
6.   DATA
7.   STATUS
8.   MESSAGE

The SCSI bus can only be in one phase at any given time. The current phase determines the type of operation and information that is being transferred between the INITIATOR and the TARGET at that time.

BUS FREE Phase

The BUS FREE phase indicates when the SCSI bus is in an idle state and is available for use by the SCSI devices.

The BUS FREE phase occurs when no SCSI devices are active on the bus; i.e., the bus is released or inactive and available. No signals are being driven by any device during this period. Any device needing the bus can acquire it by asserting the BSY signal.

When SEL and BSY are both false (inactive) for more than the bus settle delay, any SCSI device attempting access shall detect the BUS FREE phase. After detecting the BUS FREE phase, the SCSI device will release all SCSI bus signals within a bus clear delay time.

ARBITRATION Phase

The ARBITRATION phase allows multiple SCSI devices to simultaneously contest for ownership of the SCSI bus. All bus devices connected to the bus can be involved in the ARBITRATION. Devices that want to be INITIATORs can ARBITRATE for the bus before going to the SELECTION phase and TARGET devices can ARBITRATE before going to the RESELECTION phase.

The ARBITRATION phase is optional. SASI and non-arbitrating devices cannot participate in the ARBITRATION phase. However, devices that do not implement the ARBITRATION phase can access the bus.

In a single-TARGET/single-INITIATOR environment, a non-arbitrating device has direct access because there is no competition. When the non-arbitrating devices share a bus with arbitrating devices, they can gain control of the bus only when an arbitrating device is not attempting to gain control.

Systems that do not implement the ARBITRATION phase cannot support the RESELECTION phase or the multiple-INITIATOR multiple-TARGET and single-INITIATOR multiple-TARGET configuration and cannot perform peripheral-to-peripheral transfers. It is recommended that new designs implement the ARBITRATION phase to make the system more powerful and flexible and, at the same time, allow compatibility with non-arbitrating devices.

A SCSI device can attempt to gain control of the SCSI bus as either an INITIATOR or a TARGET during the ARBITRATION phase. The ARBITRATION phase can only be entered from the BUS FREE phase.

To acquire control of the SCSI bus, a device must first wait for the BUS FREE phase to occur, then arbitrate for the bus by asserting the BSY signal and driving the DATA BUS signal that corresponds to its prioritorized SCSI ID. (The SCSI ID is a single-bit value that correlates to the device's SCSI bus address. The numeric value of the SCSI address is the numeric name of the DATA BUS signal that must be asserted; i.e., a device with bus address 7 must assert the DB7 signal, a device with bus address 6 must assert the DB6 signal, etc.) The device may not arbitrate for the bus if the bus is not in the BUS FREE state at the time of ARBITRATION. If the bus is not in the BUS FREE state, it means that other devices are already using, or trying to acquire, the bus. Therefore, the device seeking ARBITRATION has missed the arbitration window.

The device with the highest SCSI ID, having won the ARBITRATION, now asserts the SEL signal. The SEL signal indicates that the DATA BUS is now busy. When the DATA BUS is busy, all other losing devices (those devices that did not win the arbitration) release their SCSI IDs and return to the wait-state until the BUS FREE phase occurs again.

SELECTION Phase

The SELECTION phase allows an INITIATOR to select a TARGET device to perform a SCSI operation. This phase may be entered either from the BUS FREE phase or following the ARBITRATION phase, depending upon the system configuration. In order to distinguish this phase from the RESELECTION phase, the I/O signal is negated during the SELECTION phase. This phase is not optional; it must be supported for correct bus operation.

In systems where the ARBITRATION phase is not implemented (single-INITIATOR only systems), the SELECTION phase is entered after the INITIATOR detects the BUS FREE phase. The INITIATOR then asserts its own SCSI ID and the TARGET SCSI ID on the DATA BUS and the SEL signal.

In systems where the ARBITRATION phase is implemented, the SCSI device winning the ARBITRATION asserts its own SCSI ID and the TARGET SCSI ID on the DATA BUS and negates the I/O signal to indicate it is operating as an INITIATOR. The INITIATOR then deasserts the BSY signal and begins looking for a response from the TARGET (TARGET asserts BSY).

In both arbitrating and non-arbitrating systems, the TARGET will know that it has been selected when the BSY and I/O signals are negated and the SEL and its SCSI ID bit are asserted for at least one bus settle delay.

Once the TARGET has been selected, it can inspect the DATA BUS to read the BUS ID of the selecting INITIATOR. After reading the BUS ID, the selected TARGET immediately asserts the BSY signal (within a selection abort time) for the correct operation of the timeout procedure. The selected TARGET will not respond to the

INITIATOR if a parity error is detected (only applicable in systems that implement the parity checking option), or if more than two SCSI ID bits are asserted on the DATA BUS.

RESELECTION Phase

The RESELECTION phase allows a TARGET to disconnect from the bus when it encounters unusual time-consuming events. (The seek operation in disk drive is an example of an operation that requires a relatively long period of time to complete.) Once the TARGET completes the time consuming task, it may select an INITIATOR, physically reconnect the bus, and then continue with the operation that was interrupted by the disconnect.

Only systems that implement the ARBITRATION phase are capable of supporting the RESELECTION phase. This phase is optional and does not have to be supported for correct operation of the bus.

The RESELECTION phase can only be entered after using the ARBITRATION phase. After acquiring the bus, the winning device asserts both the BSY and SEL signals. The device asserts its own SCSI ID and the INITIATOR SCSI ID on the DATA BUS, and asserts the I/O signal to indicate it is operating as a TARGET. The TARGET then deasserts the BSY signal and begins to look for a response from the INITIATOR (INITIATOR asserts BSY within a selection abort time).

The INITIATOR acknowledges to the TARGET that it has been reselected, and asserts its own SCSI ID bit and I/O and SEL signals. At this time, the INITIATOR also inspects the DATA BUS to read the BUS ID of the selecting TARGET and asserts the BSY signal. The INITIATOR must assert the BSY signal when it has been reselected, or the TARGET will drive the bus into the BUS FREE phase. The INITIATOR will not respond if a parity error is detected (this can only occur in systems that implement the parity checking option) or if more than two SCSI ID bits are asserted on the DATA BUS.

When the reselected TARGET detects the BSY signal asserted by the INITIATOR, the TARGET will also assert the BSY signal and negate the SEL signal. When the INITIATOR detects the negated SEL signal, it negates its BSY signal. The BSY signal is held active by the TARGET (OR-tied) until the TARGET is ready to release the bus. When the bus is released, TARGET negates the BSY signal.

Information Transfer Phases

The information transfer phases are used to control and pass data over the DATA BUS. The COMMAND, DATA, STATUS, and MESSAGE phases constitute the information transfer phases. Each transfer phase is defined by a combination of the three control lines, C/D, I/O and MSG, for a possibility of eight different states. The TARGET device drives these signals during a SCSI operation. See Table 1–4 for a list of information transfer states. The ASYNCHRONOUS and SYNCHRONOUS modes of data transfer referred to in the information transfer phase descriptions are detailed in the Transfer Methods Section, page 20.

Table 1–4. Information Transfer States

Signal*			State Name	Direction of Transfer	Comment
MSG	C/D̄	I/Ō			
0	0	0	DATA OUT	INITIATOR to TARGET	Data Phase
0	0	1	DATA IN	INITIATOR from TARGET	Data Phase
0	1	0	COMMAND	INITIATOR to TARGET	Data Phase
0	1	1	STATUS	INITIATOR from TARGET	Data Phase
1	0	0	RESERVED**		
1	0	1	RESERVED**		
1	1	0	MESSAGE OUT	INITIATOR to TARGET	Message Phase
1	1	1	MESSAGE IN	INITIATOR from TARGET	Message Phase

Notes:* 0 = False, 1 = True

** = Reserved for future standardization.

DATA OUT Phase

The TARGET requests the INITIATOR in the DATA OUT phase to send a number of data bytes over the DATA BUS. The DATA OUT phase is indicated by the TARGET driving the C/D, I/O, and MSG signals inactive. The SCSI command previously sent to the TARGET determines the number of bytes that can be received by the TARGET. The DATA OUT phase can use either the ASYNCHRONOUS or SYNCHRONOUS method of data transfer. The ASYNCHRONOUS transfer is the default unless otherwise specified.

DATA IN Phase

The TARGET requests the INITIATOR in the DATA IN phase to receive a number of data bytes over the DATA BUS. The DATA IN phase is indicated by the TARGET driving the I/O signal active, and the C/D and MSG signals inactive. The number of bytes to be sent are determined from the SCSI command previously sent to the TARGET. The DATA IN phase can use either the ASYNCHRONOUS or SYNCHRONOUS method of data transfer. The ASYNCHRONOUS transfer is the default unless otherwise specified.

COMMAND Phase

The TARGET requests commands from the INITIATOR in the COMMAND phase. The command phase is indicated by the TARGET driving the C/D signal active and the I/O and MSG signals inactive. The COMMAND bytes specify the type of operation the

TARGET is to perform. The COMMAND phase must use the ASYNCHRONOUS method of data transfer.

STATUS Phase

The TARGET requests the INITIATOR in the STATUS phase to send status information over the DATA BUS to the TARGET. The STATUS phase is indicated by the TARGET driving the C/D and I/O signals active, and the MSG signal inactive. The STATUS phase must use the ASYNCHRONOUS method of data transfer.

MESSAGE OUT Phase

The TARGET requests the INITIATOR in the MESSAGE OUT phase to send a number of message bytes over the DATA BUS, under the following conditions.

The MESSAGE OUT phase is entered only when the INITIATOR has indicated to the TARGET that it has message bytes to send. The INITIATOR asserts the ATTENTION signal and indicates the TARGET is ready to receive these bytes.

The MESSAGE OUT phase is indicated by the TARGET driving the C/D and MSG signals active and the I/O signal inactive.   CTRL, MSG, output

The TARGET device determines when, and if, it will assert the MESSAGE OUT phase. As indicated in the ANSI SCSI-I specification, the TARGET is not required to go into the MESSAGE OUT phase at any time during a SCSI operation. The MESSAGE OUT phase must use the ASYNCHRONOUS method of data transfer.

MESSAGE IN Phase

The TARGET requests the MESSAGE IN phase to send a number of data bytes over the DATA BUS to the INITIATOR. The MESSAGE IN phase is indicated by the TARGET driving the C/D, I/O and MSG signals active. The MESSAGE IN phase must use the ASYNCHRONOUS method of data transfer.

Data Transfer Methods – Asynchronous and Synchronous

Data passing over the DATA BUS is always qualified by the REQ/ACK handshake. The handshake is used to ensure a reliable transfer of data between the INITIATOR and TARGET. The SCSI bus can support two methods of transfer, ASYNCHRONOUS and SYNCHRONOUS. A discussion of both these methods follows.

Asynchronous Transfer

The ASYNCHRONOUS data transfer allows one byte of data to pass over the bus for each REQ/ACK handshake. The direction of the transfer is controlled by the use of the I/O signal by the TARGET. When I/O is asserted, data is transferred from the TARGET to the INITIATOR. When I/O is negated, data is transferred from the

INITIATOR to the TARGET. Before sending data to the INITIATOR, the TARGET drives the C/D and MSG signals to their desired values and assert the I/O signal to indicate the bus phase.

When data is sent to the INITIATOR, the TARGET drives the DATA BUS to its desired value and asserts the REQ signal. The TARGET must hold the data on the DATA BUS until the TARGET senses the asserted ACK signal. When the INITIATOR senses the REQ signal is asserted, it reads the DATA BUS. The INITIATOR indicates to the TARGET that it has accepted the data by asserting the ACK signal. When the TARGET detects that the ACK signal is asserted, it can change, release, or continue to drive the data bus, and then negate the REQ signal. When the INITIATOR detects the negated REQ signal, it negates the ACK signal. This completes the transaction. The TARGET may continue to transfer more data by repeating this handshake or it can change the I/O, C/D, and MSG signals to go to another phase. The TARGET must not change the I/O, C/D, and MSG signals during the handshake. See Figure 1–6 for a timing diagram of this sequence.

Before receiving data from the INITIATOR, the TARGET must drive the C/D and MSG signals to their desired values, and negate the I/O signal to indicate the bus phase. To receive data from the INITIATOR, the TARGET asserts the REQ signal. When the asserted REQ signal is detected, the INITIATOR drives the DATA BUS to its desired value and asserts the ACK signal. The INITIATOR must hold the data on the DATA BUS until the TARGET negates the REQ signal. The DATA BUS is read when the TARGET senses the ACK signal has been asserted. The TARGET indicates to the INITIATOR that it has accepted the data by negating the REQ signal. When the REQ signal is negated, the INITIATOR can change, release, or continue to drive the data bus, and then negate the ACK signal. This completes the transaction. The TARGET may continue to transfer more data by repeating this handshake, or it can change the C/D, I/O, and MSG signals to go to another phase. During the handshake, the TARGET must not change the C/D, I/O, and MSG signals. See Figure 1–6a and Figure 1–6b for a timing diagram of this sequence (1–6a – sending, 1–6b – receiving).

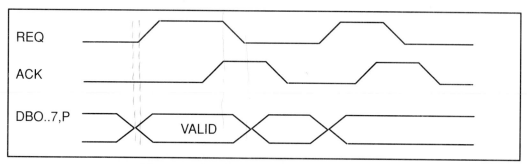

Figure 1–6a. Asynchronous Handshake
(One byte of data per each handshake – Sending)

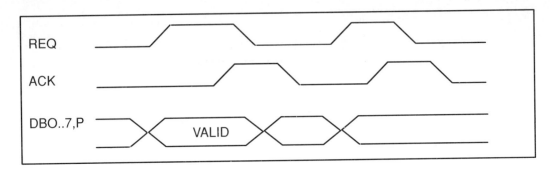

Figure 1–6b. Asynchronous Handshake
(One byte of data per each handshake – Receiving)

Asynchronous Bus Conditions

The SCSI bus supports two asynchronous conditions, the ATTENTION condition and the RESET condition. Either of these conditions can alter the phase sequence of a SCSI operation.

ATTENTION Condition

The ATTENTION condition informs the TARGET that the INITIATOR has a message for the TARGET. The INITIATOR can cause the ATTENTION condition by asserting the ATN signal at any time, except during the ARBITRATION or BUS FREE phases.

The TARGET may choose to ignore or respond to the ATTENTION signal. If the TARGET responds, it will go into the MESSAGE OUT phase and will begin to transfer the message. If the message is longer than one byte, the INITIATOR will keep the ATN signal asserted. Whether or not the TARGET responds to the ATTENTION condition, the INITIATOR can negate the ATN signal at any time, (except when the ACK signal is asserted during the MESSAGE OUT phase). When the ACK signal is asserted during the MESSAGE OUT phase, it indicates that more message bytes are to be sent. Typically, the INITIATOR negates the ATN while the REQ signal is asserted, and the ACK signal is negated during the last REQ/ACK handshake of the MESSAGE OUT phase.

RESET Condition

The RESET condition causes all SCSI devices to release the bus and go to the BUS FREE phase. This condition can occur at any time and takes precedence over all other operations on the bus. The RST signal is an OR-tied signal (meaning any device can assert this signal).

Synchronous Transfer

The SYNCHRONOUS data transfer is a system option and is only supported during the DATA IN and OUT transfer phases, and then only after the INITIATOR and TARGET have agreed on a transfer rate and REQ/ACK offset through the message system.

The SYNCHRONOUS transfer allows higher speed transfers to take place because every byte passing over the DATA BUS does not need the REQ/ACK handshake. Without repeated REQ/ACK handshakes, the propagation delays associated with each stage of the handshake are reduced.

The REQ/ACK offset is defined as the number of REQ pulses that a TARGET can send before it must receive at least one ACK pulse from the INITIATOR. If the number of REQ pulses sent exceeds the number of ACK pulses received by the REQ/ACK offset, the TARGET will not send another REQ pulse until an ACK pulse is received. The data transfer phase is considered completed when the number of ACK pulses received equals the number of REQ pulses sent. See Figure 1–7 and Figure 1–8 for diagrams of the synchronous data transfer handshake.

Synchronous Bus Conditions

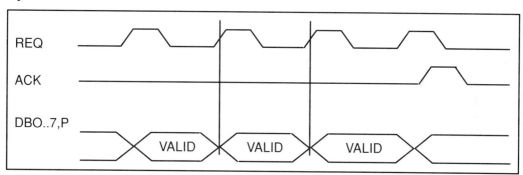

Figure 1–7. Synchronous Handshake – One

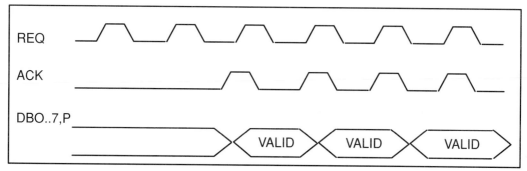

Figure 1–8. Synchronous Handshake – Two

Pointer Concept

The SCSI architecture provides for data path management with a system of memory pointers within the INITIATOR. There are two sets of pointers and each set contains three pointers. These three pointers are used to point to the

(1)   command block

(2)   data block and

(3)   status byte

within the INITIATOR's memory.

One set of the pointers is known as the current or active pointers and the second set of pointers as the saved pointers. The current set of pointers manages the data flow for the currently active command between an INITIATOR and a TARGET that are physically connected on the bus. The saved set of pointers manages each pending command between an INITIATOR and TARGET, whether or not they are physically connected to the bus. (A pending command is any command issued to a TARGET from the INITIATOR. It is possible for an INITIATOR to have more than one pending command; e.g., it can issue multiple commands to a number of TARGETS.)

The current set of pointers is used by the TARGET to reach into the INITIATOR's memory. The TARGET can have the INITIATOR manipulate the pointers by sending SCSI messages.

The saved set of pointers always point to active commands within the INITIATOR. The assignment of a saved set of pointers for an active command is as follows:

(1)   The saved command pointer points to the beginning of the command block.

(2)   The saved status pointer points to the location of the status byte.

(3)   The saved data pointer points to the current position (within the data area) where the next data transfer will take place.

The INITIATOR will save the position of the current data pointer when it receives the SAVE DATA POINTER message from the TARGET. The INITIATOR will load the current pointers (COMMAND, STATUS, and DATA) from a specific set of saved pointers when the TARGET issues a RESTORE POINTERS message. The set that gets loaded depends on the identity of the TARGET issuing the message. When a TARGET reselects an INITIATOR, the INITIATOR will automatically load the current set of pointers from the appropriate saved set. When a TARGET device disconnects from the bus, the INITIATOR stores the current pointers into a saved pointer set, whether or not a SAVED DATA POINTER message was issued. It is important to realize that an INITIATOR can have many commands active or pending to different TARGET devices. The INITIATOR should maintain a saved set of pointers for each pending command.

Anytime a physical path is established between an INITIATOR and a TARGET, the INITIATOR must ensure that the active pointers are equal to the saved pointers for that particular TARGET and LUN.

An INITIATOR that does not support DISCONNECT/RESELECT only needs to maintain one set of active pointers; it does not have to maintain any stored pointers.

Message System

The message system allows the INITIATOR and TARGET to communicate in order to manage the data flow and physical path between both devices. All SCSI devices are required to support the COMMAND COMPLETE message, but for increased flexibility, it is recommended that most of the optional, non-extended messages should also be supported.

SCSI devices must indicate to each other that they can support more than the COMMAND COMPLETE message. The INITIATOR indicates to the TARGET that it can support additional messages by asserting the ATN signal during the SELECTION phase. The TARGET indicates that it can support other messages by responding to this ATTENTION condition with a MESSAGE OUT phase immediately after the SELECTION phase. In response to the MESSAGE OUT phase, the first message sent by the INITIATOR should be an IDENTIFY message. The IDENTIFY message selects a specific LUN (logical unit number) for the selected TARGET and indicates whether or not the INITIATOR can support the DISCONNECTION/RESELECTION sequence.

After the RESELECTION phase, the TARGET requests a MESSAGE IN phase and sends the IDENTIFY message to the INITIATOR, thereby re-establishing the physical path with the TARGET's LUN. In some special circumstances, the INITIATOR may send an ABORT or BUS DEVICE RESET message immediately after the SELECTION phase. See Table 1–5 for a list of mandatory and optional messages.

Table 1–5. Mandatory and Optional Messages

Code	Type*	Description	Source
00H	M	COMMAND COMPLETE	TARGET
01H	O	EXTENDED MESSAGE	INIT or TARG
02H	O	SAVE DATA POINTER	TARGET
03H	O	RESTORE POINTERS	TARGET
04H	O	DISCONNECT	TARGET
05H	O	INITIATOR DETECTED ERROR	INITIATOR
06H	O	ABORT	INITIATOR
07H	O	MESSAGE REJECT	INIT or TARG
08H	O	NO OPERATION	INITIATOR
09H	O	MESSAGE PARITY ERROR	INITIATOR
0AH	O	LINKED COMMAND COMPLETE	TARGET
0BH	O	LINKED COMMAND COMPLETE WITH FLAG	TARGET
0CH	O	BUS DEVICE RESET	INITIATOR
0DH–7FH	R	RESERVED	
80H–FFH	O	IDENTIFY	INIT or TARG

Note: *M = Mandatory,　O = Optional,　R = Reserved

Single-Byte Message Definitions

COMMAND COMPLETE 00H, (Mandatory).

The TARGET sends a COMMAND COMPLETE message to the INITIATOR to indicate that a command or linked command has been executed and that the status bytes have been sent to the INITATOR. When the TARGET determines that this message has been successfully received, it releases the BSY signal and goes to the BUS FREE phase.

This message does not indicate the success or failure of the command execution; the received status byte must be examined in order to determine either condition.

EXTENDED MESSAGE 01H, (Optional).

An EXTENDED MESSAGE is the message sent from the TARGET or INITIATOR as the first byte of a multiple byte message. This is, technically, not a single byte message; see extended messages.

SAVE DATA POINTER 02H, (Optional).

The TARGET sends a SAVE DATA POINTER message to direct the INITIATOR to save the active data pointer, in the saved data pointer area, for the currently attached TARGET and LUN.

RESTORE POINTERS 03H, (Optional).

The TARGET sends a RESTORE POINTERS message to direct the INITIATOR to load the saved pointer set (COMMAND, STATUS, and DATA) into the active pointer set for the currently attached TARGET and LUN. The COMMAND and STATUS pointers will point to the beginning of the command and status area. The DATA pointer will point to the last position of the SAVE DATA POINTER message that was received, or to the beginning of the data area if no SAVE DATA POINTER message was received.

DISCONNECT 04H, (Optional).

The TARGET sends a DISCONNECT message to inform the INITIATOR that the physical path between them is about to be broken. The DISCONNECT message implies that the TARGET will issue a RESELECT sequence at a later time in order to reestablish the physical path and complete the current command for this TARGET and LUN.

A catastrophic error condition will occur if the INITIATOR detects the BUS FREE phase without the first receiving a DISCONNECT or COMMAND COMPLETE message.

The TARGET may issue multiple DISCONNECT commands in order to complete a long data transfer. If the TARGET does issue multiple DISCONNECT commands, then the SAVE DATA POINTER message will be issued before the DISCONNECT message.

INITIATOR DETECTED ERROR 05H, (Optional).

The INITIATOR sends an INITIATOR DETECTED ERROR message to the TARGET indicating that a parity error, or possibly other information transfer error, has occurred. The TARGET may retry the operation by restoring the current pointers and repeating the same phase sequence.

ABORT 06H, (Optional).

The INITIATOR sends an ABORT message to the TARGET to abort the current operation. The TARGET clears all results of the pending command for the LUN connected to this INITIATOR and goes to the BUS FREE state. The TARGET does not go to the STATUS phase or issue a COMMAND COMPLETE message before releasing the bus.

MESSAGE REJECT 07H, (Optional.)

Either the INITIATOR or the TARGET can send the MESSAGE REJECT to indicate that neither the INITIATOR nor the TARGET supports or can act upon the last message received. When the MESSAGE REJECT is sent, the INITIATOR must assert the ATN signal before it negates the ACK signal, during the REQ/ACK handshake of the message that is being rejected. Multiple byte messages should be received completely before the INITIATOR begins to perform the reject sequence.

A TARGET sends the MESSAGE REJECT by first going to the MESSAGE IN phase, and then going to the next MESSAGE OUT phase, if there is any. This TARGET initiated procedure allows the INITIATOR to absolutely determine which message has been rejected.

The MESSAGE REJECT must be implemented if any other optional messages are to be supported.

MESSAGE PARITY ERROR 09H, (Optional).

The INITIATOR sends a MESSAGE PARITY ERROR to inform the TARGET that a parity error occurred during the reception of the last message. The INITIATOR must assert the ATN signal before negating the ACK signal for the REQ/ACK handshake of the message. When the TARGET detects the asserted, it goes to the MESSAGE OUT phase to receive the message that incurred the MESSAGE PARITY ERROR.

LINKED COMMAND COMPLETE 0AH, (Optional).

The TARGET sends the LINKED COMMAND COMPLETE message to indicate to the INITIATOR that the execution of a linked command has been completed and its status has been sent. The INITIATOR will update the current command, status, and data pointers to the initial state for the next command to be sent. The last command in a sequence of linked commands will terminate with a COMMAND COMPLETE message.

LINKED COMMAND COMPLETE WITH FLAG 0BH, (Optional).

The LINKED COMMAND COMPLETE WITH FLAG message, similar to the LINKED COMMAND COMPLETE message, is sent when the flag bit is set to one in the command block of the most recently executed linked command.

BUS DEVICE RESET 0CH, (Optional).

The INITIATOR sends the BUS DEVICE RESET command to the TARGET to clear all pending commands from all INITIATORS. The TARGET immediately goes to the BUS FREE phase after this message.

IDENTIFY 80H to FFH, (Optional).

The INITIATOR or TARGET sends the IDENTIFY message to establish a physical path between a specific TARGET LUN and an INITIATOR.

This message is generally used by devices that support the DISCONNECT/ RESELECT sequence during a command. If the DISCONNECT/RESELECT option is not supported, the INITIATOR establishes a physical path to a specific TARGET LUN by placing the LUN address in the command block.

The INITIATOR will attempt to send an IDENTIFY message immediately after the SELECTION phase (to select a specific LUN). The INITIATOR can also indicate to the TARGET that it will support the DISCONNECT/RESELECT sequence during this command. The sequence is supported by setting bit 6 to one.

The TARGET will go to the MESSAGE IN phase immediately after the RESELECT phase and indicate which LUN is reconnected to the INITIATOR. The INITIATOR performs an implied RESTORE POINTERS message when it receives the LUN information. The RESTORE POINTERS is performed before the INITIATOR acknowledges that it has successfully received a message.

Extended Message Definitions

The extended messages consist of more than one byte. The first byte (of an extended message) indicates that the message is an extended one. Generally, extended messages are used to set up the conditions for a SYNCHRONOUS DATA TRANSFER. Table 1–6 lists the currently defined extended messages for SCSI-I.

Table 1–6. Extended Messages

Subcode	Type*	Description	Source
00H	O	MODIFY DATA POINTER	TARGET
01H	O	SYNCHRONOUS DATA TRANSFER REQUEST	INITIATOR and TARGET
02H	O	EXTENDED IDENTIFY	INITIATOR and TARGET
03H–7FH	R	RESERVED	
80H–FFH	V	VENDOR UNIQUE	

Note: *M = Mandatory,   O = Optional,   R = Reserved

MODIFY DATA POINTER 00H, (Optional).

The MODIFY DATA POINTER message from the TARGET directs the INITIATOR to modify its current data pointer by adding the two's complement contained within the message. The two's complement allows the TARGET to perform pointer arithmetic on the INITIATOR's data pointer

SYNCHRONOUS DATA TRANSFER REQUEST 01H, (Optional).

The INITIATOR and TARGET exchange a pair of SYNCHRONOUS DATA TRANSFER REQUEST messages to establish the parameters for a SYNCHRONOUS DATA transfer. This message is usually sent when either the INITIATOR or TARGET recognize that a negotiation is needed. The parameters are retained by each device until a hard RESET condition or a BUS DEVICE RESET message has been received. This message will establish the REQ/ACK offset and the transfer period (in multiples of 4 nanoseconds). The INITIATOR or the TARGET can start the message exchange at their discretion.

EXTENDED IDENTIFY 02H, (Optional).

THE INITIATOR or TARGET can send the EXTENDED IDENTIFY message to establish a physical path between a specific LUN and sub-LUN, and the INITIATOR. This message must be sent in conjunction with the IDENTIFY message. The EXTENDED IDENTIFY message is used to select expanded logical units within a TARGET. Up to 256 sub-logical units can be specified. Therefore, each TARGET (with a maximum of 8 LUNs and up to 256 sub-LUNs) has a total of 2048 addressable units on a single TARGET.

SCSI Commands

SCSI commands are sent from the INITIATOR to a TARGET to request that a specific operation take place between both devices. Commands are grouped by category or group code and may cause device specific actions to take place; that is, the same command code may cause different operations to occur within different device types.

The following is a description of the structure of SCSI commands and a definition of the fields used within those commands.

Command Structure

A SCSI command is a multi-byte data structure known as a command descriptor block or CDB. The first byte of a CDB always contains an operation code that has both a command code and a group code. Table 1–7 shows the operation code structure.

The command code is a 5-bit value that defines the type of operation that the TARGET will perform. The group code is a 3-bit value that catorgorizes the operation codes into eight groups.

Table 1–7. Operation Code

Bit Byte	7	6	5	4	3	2	1	0
0	Group Code			Command Code				

The group code specifies the length and type of the CDB. There are 32 command codes for each group, for a total of 256 unique commands.

> Group 0 – six byte CDB
> Group 1 – ten byte CDB
> Group 2 – reserved
> Group 3 – reserved
> Group 4 – reserved
> Group 5 – twelve byte CDB
> Group 6 – vendor unique (any size CDB)
> Group 7 – vendor unique (any size CDB)

Table 1–8, Table 1–9, and Table 1–10 show the CDB structure for typical Group 0, 1, and 5 commands.

Table 1–8. Typical Command Descriptor Block for Six-Byte Commands

Bit Byte	7	6	5	4	3	2	1	0
0	Operation Code							
1	Logical Unit Number			Logical Block Address (if required)				(MSB)
2	Logical Block Address (if required)							
3	Logical Block Address (if required)							(LSB)
4	Transfer Length (if required)							
5	Control Byte							

Table 1–9. Typical Command Descriptor Block for Ten-Byte Commands

Bit Byte	7	6	5	4	3	2	1	0
0	Operation Code							
1	Logical Unit Number			Reserved				RelAdr
2	Logical Block Address (if required)							(MSB)
3	Logical Block Address (if required)							
4	Logical Block Address (if required)							
5	Logical Block Address (if required)							(LSB)
6	Reserved							
7	Transfer Length (if required)							(MSB)
8	Transfer Length (if required)							(LSB)
9	Control Byte							

Table 1–10. Typical Command Descriptor Block for Twelve-Byte Commands

Bit Byte	7	6	5	4	3	2	1	0
0	Operation Code							
1	Logical Unit Number			Reserved				RelAdr
2	Logical Block Address (if required)							(MSB)
3	Logical Block Address (if required)							
4	Logical Block Address (if required)							
5	Logical Block Address (if required)							(LSB)
6	Reserved							
7	Reserved							
8	Reserved							
9	Transfer Length (if required)							(MSB)
10	Transfer Length (if required)							(LSB)
11	Control Byte							

Command Bytes

In the second byte of every CDB, the three-bit location is defined as the logical unit number (LUN) of the TARGET. Systems that do not support the optional IDENTIFY message can place the address of the desired LUN in this location. If the TARGET supports the IDENTIFY message, it will use the LUN defined within the message and ignore the LUN bits within the CDB.

Many commands require a logical block address that is contiguous (starting from block 0 to the last block on the device) to access data. Group 0 commands provide space for a 21-bit logical block address. Groups 1 and 5 commands can specify a 32-bit block address.

The number of bytes within a logical block is device specific. (The INITIATOR may retrieve the block size through the READ CAPACITY or MODE SENSE command.) Some devices allow the logical block size to be modified, usually with the MODE SELECT command.

The relative address bit within groups 1 and 5 CDB changes the definition of the logical block address to a two's complement logical displacement that is added to the last accessed logical block on a device. This feature is only permitted when using linked commands.

Many commands specify a transfer length indicating the number of bytes or blocks to be transferred. The definition of the command being executed specifies whether bytes or blocks of bytes should be transferred; usually blocks are specified. Group 0 commands use a single byte to specify the transfer length for a value of 1 to 256 bytes, or blocks, to be transferred. A transfer length of 0 indicates the maximum amount of 256. Groups 1 and 5 use 2 bytes to specify a transfer length for a range of 1 to 65,535 bytes or blocks. For groups 1 and 5, a length of 0 specifies that no data will be transferred.

The last byte of the CDBs for groups 0, 1, and 5 is always the control byte. This byte is used to control the linking of command blocks. Setting bit 0 to one indicates that this command is one in a group of linked commands. Multiple commands to be executed by a particular TARGET and LUN may be linked together and sent to the TARGET without going to the BUS FREE phase between each command. This feature avoids the overhead of going through the SELECTION phase for each command and can only be invoked once, at the start of the sequence. Linked command support is a system option and does not have to be supported by either the INITIATOR or TARGET. When a TARGET that does not support linked commands receives a linked command, it will return a CHECK CONDITION status and set its sense key to ILLEGAL REQUEST. The TARGET will send a LINKED COMMAND COMPLETE at the completion of each command.

If bit 1, the flag bit, of the control byte is set to one along with the link bit, then the TARGET will send a LINKED COMMAND COMPLETE WITH FLAG message at the completion of each linked command. The flag bit should not be set without the link bit being set.

SCSI Status Phase

At the completion of each command, the TARGET will drive the bus into the STATUS phase and will send a status byte to the INITIATOR (to indicate whether the command failed or succeeded without error). When the TARGET receives a BUS DEVICE RESET, an ABORT message, or a hard RESET, the TARGET will go to the BUS FREE phase and will not issue a status byte.

SCSI Status Codes

A SCSI status code is an 8-bit value with four bits for defining the standard status code, three bits for defining vendor unique usage, and one reserved bit. See Table 1–11 for the bit placement of the status byte.

Table 1–11. Status Byte

Bit Byte	7	6	5	4	3	2	1	0
0	Reserved	Vendor Unique		Status Byte Code				V

Status Byte Bit Values

00H	– GOOD
02H	– CHECK CONDITION
04H	– CONDITION MET/GOOD
06H	– Reserved
08H	– BUSY
0AH	– Reserved
0CH	– Reserved
0EH	– Reserved
10H	– INTERMEDIATE/GOOD
12H	– Reserved
14H	– INTERMEDIATE/CONDITION MET/GOOD
16H	– Reserved
18H	– RESERVATION CONFLICT
1AH	– Reserved
1CH	– Reserved
1EH	– Reserved

GOOD 00H

The TARGET returns a GOOD status when it has successfully completed the command.

CHECK CONDITION 02H

The TARGET returns a CHECK CONDITION status whenever an error or abnormal condition occurs during the execution of a command. The TARGET sets the sense data bytes indicating the reason for the command failure. The INITIATOR issues a REQUEST SENSE command as the next command to this TARGET to retrieve the sense data bytes.

CONDITION MET/GOOD 04H

The TARGET returns the CONDITION MET/GOOD status whenever a search condition has been satisfied. The REQUEST SENSE command can be used to retrieve the logical block address of the search condition.

BUSY 08H

The TARGET returns the BUSY status when it is busy and unable to accept a command from the INITIATOR. The INITIATOR retries the command at a later time.

INTERMEDIATE/GOOD 10H

The TARGET returns a INTERMEDIATE status at the successful completion of a linked command, except for the last command in the chained command list. Returning any status other than INTERMEDIATE for a linked command breaks the chain of linked commands. If an error or abnormal condition takes place, the TARGET returns a CHECK CONDITION or RESERVATION CONFLICT status.

RESERVATION CONFLICT 18H

The TARGET returns an RESERVATION CONFLICT status whenever an attempt is made to access a reserved logical unit or an extent within a logical unit.

Chapter Summary

This chapter has presented SCSI's historical background and basic design classifications. SCSI bus configurations, physical characteristics, and signals were discussed. SCSI's two logic types (INITIATOR and TARGET), SCSI's operation, bus phases, modes of transfer (ASYNCHRONOUS and SYNCHRONOUS), message system, and a brief review of the command structure were presented. For greater details on these subjects, please refer to ANSI's SCSI standard (see Acknowledgements).

Chapter 2

THE SCSI-I SYSTEM OPERATION

Introduction

The flexibility of SCSI has made it the interface of choice for a growing number of computer systems ranging from high-powered mainframes to ultra low-cost PC compatibles. The unique ability of SCSI to interface multiple peripherals of various functionality to a computer through a single port means improved I/O efficiency (resulting in lower cost), smaller form factors, improved durability, and more reliable products.

To understand how SCSI improves system flexibility, it is important to first understand how SCSI interacts with the two pieces of hardware it ties together, the system bus and the peripheral controller (sometimes called a device controller).

First of all, SCSI does not replace the device or peripheral controller. It does move it from the computer enclosure to an embedded position in the peripheral itself. The SCSI interface control circuitry is contained in the peripheral in front of the device controller. It communicates with another SCSI controller that resides in the computer in the form of a host adapter add-in card or as dedicated circuitry embedded on the CPU motherboard. (Note: Peripheral-to-peripheral and host-to-host communications are also possible with SCSI).

Figure 2–1 illustrates a non-SCSI system with dedicated peripheral (device) controller cards located in the chassis of the computer. These add-in cards are specific to the peripheral they control. Typically, each peripheral added to the system means another card added to the computer. Since the computer has a limited amount of space available for the add-in cards, the system is physically limited by the number of back plane slots available. In many of the new desk-top PCs that number is three, and for laptops it may be one or even zero.

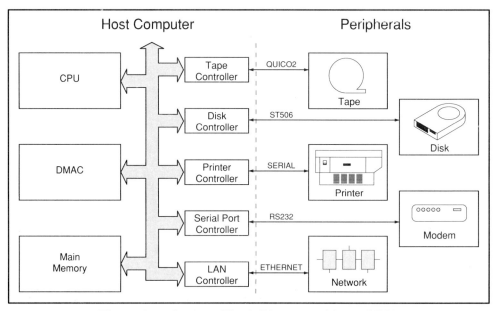

Figure 2–1. System Block Diagram without SCSI

In Figure 2–2 the SCSI host adapter is the only add-in card required to connect the computer to a variety of peripherals. It is theoretically possible to displace all of the controller cards with a single SCSI host adapter or embedded SCSI interface on the motherboard. Most SCSI systems in use today are already connecting two or three peripherals to the computer via the SCSI port and this number is increasing as more and more SCSI-based peripherals become available.

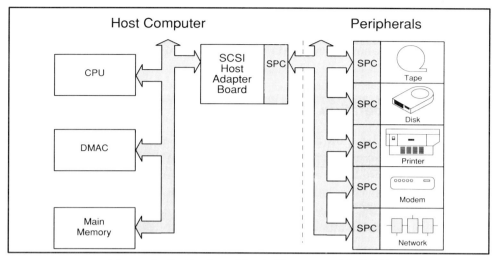

Figure 2–2. System Block Diagram with SCSI

The SCSI Protocol Controller (SPC)

In the early stages of SASI and SCSI, the interface protocol was implemented using general purpose microcontrollers (i.e., Intel®'s 8048) or microprocessors (i.e., Zilog Z80). This approach relied heavily on firmware (software that is embedded in ROM and is not user controllable), which is typically much slower in performing the same functions than hardware. As the SCSI standard neared ratification in the mid 1980s, however, it became apparent to the integrated circuits community that dedicated SCSI controller ICs would soon become viable products.

The first SCSI controller implementations performed only the most rudimentary portions of the protocol such as the REQUEST/ACKNOWLEDGE handshake between the INITIATOR and the TARGET. These SCSI controller implementations were still highly firmware intensive.

The next generation of the SPCs featured state machine logic that relieved the firmware of a significant amount of the protocol overhead. It is these products that are still in widespread use today, although newer SPCs with embedded microprocessor characteristics are beginning to find their way into higher performance applications.

The state-machine-based SPCs are capable of performing bus and phase monitoring, transfer byte counting, command and message sending/receiving, and controlling all the required signals to communicate across the SCSI bus in strict accordance with the ratified SCSI I standard.

®Intel is a registered trademark of Intel Corporation.

In order to fully realize the extent and complexity of the logic required to
implement ea _____ understand a typical
operating seq

[handwritten:]
PHASES
• CONTROL/ DATA QUALIFICATION

A Typical S

1. BUS FREE   *auto made*

Figure_____ 2. ARBITRATION _____ ng activity of a typical SCSI
operation. A___ 3. SELECTION — *init only* SPC can assume the role of
an INITIATO 4. RESELECTION mple presents the SPC in an
INITIATOR ___ • INFO TRANSFER — *all by target* RBITRATION and the
DISCONNE___ GET will support the
ATTENTION 5. COMMAND ___) COMPLETE.

This e 6. DATA pletion of a READ
command se 7. STATUS y type of peripheral: a disk
drive, tape ___ 8. MESSAGE

Each s _____ as a corresponding letter on
the timing diagrams shown in Figure 2–3 and Figure 2–4.

SCSI Bus Phase Sequences

A   BUS FREE PHASE. The BUS FREE phase is indicated when no SCSI control signals
are asserted; i.e., the SCSI bus is available and any INITIATOR can attempt to gain
control of the bus.

B   ARBITRATION PHASE. One or more INITIATORs may attempt to ARBITRATE for
control of the SCSI bus. Each INITIATOR drives BSY and places its SCSI ID bit on
one of the 8 bits of the data bus and, at the same time, each INITIATOR reads the
remaining 7 bits of the DATA BUS to determine which one is the highest priority
device on the bus. The highest priority bus device wins the ARBITRATION and
continues to drive the BSY line active and the SEL signal active. All other devices
participating in the ARBITRATION release BSY and their SCSI ID bit when SEL
become active.

C   SELECTION PHASE. The INITIATOR that wins the ARBITRATION drives both
SEL and BSY active. When SEL and BSY are active, the winning INITIATOR
releases the BSY signal, drives the TARGET's ID bit and its own ID bit active on the
DATA BUS, and drives the I/O signal INACTIVE, thereby indicating the
SELECTION phase. The INITIATOR will continue to drive the SEL line until the
TARGET drives the BSY line active. During the SELECTION phase, the INITIATOR
may drive the ATN line active to indicate that it wants to go to the MESSAGE OUT
phase immediately after the SELECTION PHASE.

D   ATTENTION CONDITION. The INITIATOR causes an ATTENTION CONDITION by asserting the ATN signal during the SELECTION phase and while the SEL signal is still asserted, thus indicating that it wants the TARGET to go to the MESSAGE OUT phase immediately after the SELECTION phase.

E   MESSAGE OUT PHASE. The TARGET drives the C/D and MSG active and the I/O inactive to indicate the MESSAGE OUT phase. The INITIATOR sends the IDENTIFY message out to indicate which logical unit of the TARGET is to be selected and if the INITIATOR will support the DISCONNECT/RESELECT operation.

F   COMMAND PHASE. The TARGET asserts the C/D signal and negates the I/O and MSG signals to indicate the COMMAND phase. The INITIATOR responds by sending the command bytes to the TARGET. (The bytes will be transferred using the REQ/ACK handshake.) In this example the command is a 6-byte READ command.

G   When the TARGET has determined that it needs to do a disconnect operation to best utilize the SCSI bus, it asserts the C/D, I/O and MSG signals indicating the MESSAGE IN phase. When the INITIATOR reads the DISCONNECT message from the TARGET, the message byte is enveloped with the REQ/ACK handshake.

H   After sending the DISCONNECT message, the TARGET goes to a disconnected state, leaving the sequence in the BUS FREE phase by releasing all asserted signals.

The TARGET remains in the disconnected state until it is ready to continue with the data transfer. The INITIATOR also remains in the disconnected state until the TARGET reselects it.

I   ARBITRATION PHASE. The TARGET goes into the ARBITRATION phase to gain control of the bus in order to begin the RESELECTION operation. The TARGET drives the BSY signal and its SCSI ID active during ARBITRATION.

J   RESELECTION PHASE. The TARGET asserts its SCSI ID, and the ID of the INITIATOR it wishes to RESELECT on the DATA BUS, and then drives the SEL and I/O signals active and releases BSY. The INITIATOR detects that it has been reselected when the SEL, I/O and its SCSI ID bit are asserted and BSY is inactive.

The reselected INITIATOR indicates its detection (of the reselection) to the TARGET by asserting the BSY signal. At this time, the TARGET drives the BSY signal active and releases SEL, thus indicating the end of the RESELECTION phase. When the reselected INITIATOR detects the SEL signal going inactive, it releases the BSY signal. However, BSY will still be held active because the TARGET is driving it. This transfer of control is necessary because it allows the TARGET to regain control of the BSY signal and control the usage of the bus.

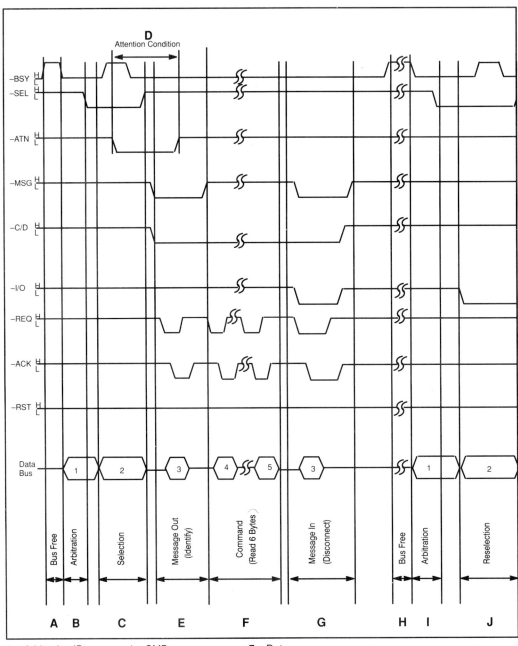

1 = Arbitration IDs   4 = CMD_1 7 = $Data_{N-1}$
2 = INIT ID and Target ID   5 = CMD_N 8 = $Data_N$
3 = MSG   6 = $Data_1$ 9 = Status

**Figure 2–3. SCSI Bus Phase Sequence
(A through J)**

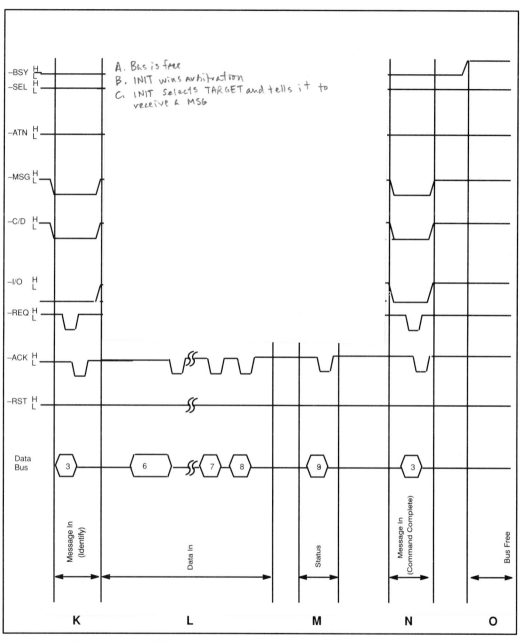

A. Bus is free
B. INIT wins arbitration
C. INIT selects TARGET and tells it to receive a MSG

Figure 2–4. SCSI Bus Phase Sequence
(K through O)

1 = Arbitration IDs   4 = CMD_1 7 = $Data_{N-1}$
2 = INIT ID and Target ID   5 = CMD_N 8 = $Data_N$
3 = MSG   6 = $Data_1$ 9 = Status

K   MESSAGE IN PHASE. The TARGET drives the C/D, I/O and MSG signals active to indicate the MESSAGE IN phase and its wish to send a message to the INITIATOR. The TARGET places the message byte on the DATA BUS and asserts the REQ signal to indicate the beginning of a REQ/ACK handshake.

The INITIATOR responds by completing the REQ/ACK handshake and reading the message bytes.

The message sent from the TARGET is the IDENTIFY message to identify which logical unit (LUN) as the TARGET is reselecting the INITIATOR.

L   DATA IN PHASE. The TARGET indicates the DATA IN phase by driving the I/O signal active and the C/D and MSG signals inactive. The TARGET then places the first byte of the data to be transferred on the DATA BUS and begins the REQ/ACK handshake. Upon receipt of the byte, the INITIATOR completes the REQ/ACK handshake. The TARGET continues to transfer bytes, as described, until all requested data bytes have been transferred.

M   STATUS PHASE. The TARGET indicates the STATUS phase by asserting the C/D and I/O signals and negating the MSG signal. The TARGET then places the status byte, representing the status for this operation, on the DATA BUS and begins the REQ/ACK handshake. The INITIATOR reads the status byte and completes the REQ/ACK handshake.

N   MESSAGE IN PHASE. The TARGET asserts the C/D, I/O, and MSG signals indicating the MESSAGE IN phase. The TARGET places the message byte on the DATA BUS and begins the REQ/ACK handshake. The INITIATOR reads the message byte and completes the REQ/ACK handshake.

In this example, the operation is complete and the message to the INITIATOR will be the COMMAND COMPLETE message. This message implies that the transaction is finished between the INITIATOR and TARGET.

O   BUS FREE PHASE. After sending the COMMAND COMPLETE message the TARGET releases all asserted signals to indicate the BUS FREE phase. Both the INITIATOR and TARGET will, physically and logically, disconnect from the bus and the bus will be available again, ready for another transaction.

Most of the SPCs are equipped with a set of commands that are used to communicate messages and status to other SCSI devices. Some SPCs link commands together so that one instruction from the controlling CPU will result in several commands being executed across the SCSI bus. The obvious advantage is fewer CPU interrupts. The disadvantages are less apparent but very real and very critical depending on the implementation. The commands that are linked together are commands that are typically executed consecutively in a SCSI exchange. However in less than typical conditions, the linked command may actually result in additional overhead.

Take for example an error condition that occurs while a link command is in process (it is not at all unusual to encounter error conditions in SCSI). If the SPC does not have a mechanism for reporting where in the sequence the error occurred, then the error finding routine will require the MPU to backtrack through the sequence to locate the error. This is time consuming and cumbersome and may result in offsetting the overhead savings that the link command is designed to offer.

The SCSI Driver

The SCSI driver is firmware that ties the controller and the SCSI interface together. In a peripheral environment, the driver connects the controlling MPU to the SCSI interface hardware. In the host computer, the SCSI driver connects the operating system to the SCSI interface hardware.

Although the state-machine-based SPC with its low level commands and low level pricing are the predominant choice for most of today's SCSI designs, the introduction of SPCs with high level command processing capabilities has created a stir in the industry. The benefits of these high level products are reduced software overhead and fewer MPU interrupts. There is, however, a growing misconception that because the chips are more intelligent with regards to protocol handling, the designer need not be as familiar with the subtleties of the SCSI.

The flaw in this line of thinking is that chip designers cannot always anticipate all the conditions that can potentially be encountered. In addition, even with the high level command structure there are still many decisions affecting the implementation that are left to be configured by the firmware developer. Proper implementation requires the designer to know what will occur on the bus and in the chip when a high level command is being processed.

In addition, some conditions may render the high level command structure inefficient. For example, an error condition may require the designer to locate the point of occurrence of the error, correct it, and complete the exchange using low level commands. Obviously a thorough knowledge of protocol is required under such circumstances.

Appendix E in this book offers examples of a driver that is designed to show operation of the Fujitsu SPCs under MS DOS operating system. The routines shown are not necessarily limited to use in the DOS environment but do reflect the limitations of a non-multitasking operating system. A UNIX or OS/2 driver might be more complex. The examples document the volume of code required to set up and execute the critical sequences encountered in a typical SCSI exchange.

Conclusion

To select a SCSI protocol controller, the designer must determine the performance limitations of the product that the SPC will be designed into and the system level limitations that may be controlled by the designer. In particular, it is important to identify special or unusual conditions that may affect the system in question. It is these special situations that should be carefully considered when evaluating the capabilities of a particular SPC.

Chapter 3

FUJITSU'S FAMILY OF SCSI PROTOCOL CONTROLLERS

Fujitsu's first SCSI Protocol Controller (SPC) was introduced to the marketplace in 1985, only three years after the formation of the ANSI subcommittee. The first member (core) of Fujitsu's SPC was the MB87030* that was developed to fill the need of every configuration and to operate at every performance level described in the ANSI SCSI-I standard.

Physical and Logical Characteristics

All Fujitsu SCSI Protocol Controllers (SPCs) are generic and can be used in a variety of SCSI subsystems (disk drives, printers, PCs, workstations, etc.). Easily interfaceable to X86 and 68XXX, Fujitsu SPCs provide the best cost and performance solutions available and meet all the physical and electrical characteristics outlined in the ANSI specified SCSI-1 standard.

*Replaced in 1989 by the MB87035

Software and Firmware

The logical characteristics (described in Chapter 1) are determined by the firmware, and all Fujitsu SPCs, in any configuration, allow complete use of all SCSI features. To achieve complete implementation, all Fujitsu SPCs have been designed with a common architecture: 16 directly addressable byte-wide registers and an 8-byte, first-in first-out (FIFO) that easily handles timing requirements between a system bus and the SCSI bus. The "open architecture" of the registers allows the user complete flexibility to program the SPC to the desired application.

Accessed via a unique 4-bit address (A3 to A0), the register set is laid out in a logical and straightforward manner to simplify the job of firmware design. Many critical functions such as arbitration, phase sensing handshake, and data transfer count are all handled in hardware. Thus software overhead and development time are reduced while performance is increased.

Interrupt Modes

Fujitsu SPCs can be driven using hardware interrupts or they may operate in a polled mode with interrupts disabled. An implementation requiring a combination of polled and hardware interrupts can also be accommodated.

In addition to multiple interrupt modes, there are four operating modes. Three of the operating modes function as transfer modes and the fourth as a diagnostic mode.

Operation Modes

(1)   *The Manual Transfer Mode* has control of the SCSI bus signals; i.e., direct control of the REQ/ACK handshake. The designer will find this operating condition useful for testing and debugging software and hardware.

(2)   *The Program Transfer Mode* (for automatic data transfers) is designed for non-direct memory access (DMA) transfers with complete hardware handshake. This mode is useful for short data transfers.

(3)   *The DMA Mode* (also for automatic data transfers) is used for large block transfers. On-chip DMA interface logic simplifies hardware connection to commercially available DMA controllers.

(4)   *The Diagnostic Mode* is designed to simulate events on the SCSI bus. This mode can be used to check the software and the SPC hardware interface without actually connecting it to the SCSI bus.

Single-ended and Differential Drivers

The Fujitsu SPC family consists of four general-purpose controllers. These controllers products can be grouped into two product categories, asynchronous and synchronous (data transfer method). Within each of these groups there is a version with on-chip, single ended drivers and a version optimized for differential drive (to be used with off-chip drivers).

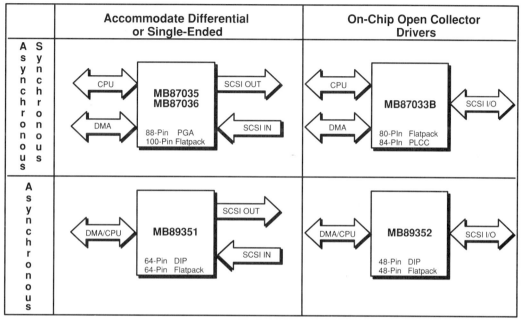

Figure 3–1.   Bus Structures in Relation to Chip Features

The optimization for differential drive consists of the separation of SCSI Out and SCSI In ports (see Figure 3–1). If these buses were combined, three-state logic would be required between the driver/receiver and the SPC to support the arbitration feature of SCSI. (See the following reference.)

According to the ANSI X.131-1986 document defining SCSI, when SCSI devices arbitrate for control of the SCSI bus, each must assert its individual ID bit (bits 0 through 7 are available with bit 7 awarded the highest priority). While asserting one bit, the SPC must concurrently read the other seven lines to determine if arbitration was won or lost. Simultaneous assertion of one bit, while reading others, necessitates the use of three-state logic (situated between the SPC and the driver LSIs) if one bus is used to receive and send the ID bits.

The complexity and added connections required for differential drivers make the addition of three-state logic significant. Fujitsu SPCs eliminate the need by allowing the SPC to read incoming IDs on the SCSI In bus while asserting the ID bit on the SCSI Out bus.

In a single-ended environment the number of connections is relatively low, so using three-state logic does not add a significant amount of logic to the board. Those SPCs that contain on-chip single-ended drivers feature a single SCSI I/O port and on-chip three-state circuitry.

Functional and Operational Descriptions

The Fujitsu SPCs are based on a common architecture so the functional and operational descriptions of the registers found in Chapters 5 and 6, respectively, apply to all products (except where noted).

Fujitsu's SPCs

MB87033B

The MB87033B is intended for high performance systems requiring synchronous data transfer. The MB87033B includes on-chip single-ended drivers that allow direct connection to a single-ended SCSI bus. Separate control buses and data buses permit the microprocessor unit (MPU) to monitor the SPC during high-speed synchronous-burst data transfers.

MB87035/36

The MB87035/36 is very similar in functionality to the MB87033B and is designed for high performance applications. The primary difference between the two products can be found in the way they interface with the SCSI bus. The MB87035/36 is designed to interface with external differential driver circuits without drivers on-chip (found on the MB87033B) and features a split SCSI input and SCSI output bus structure to eliminate the need for three-state logic between the SPC and the driver.

MB89351

The MB89351 is a low cost SPC that features most of the functionality found in the MB87033B and MB87035/36 products. The MB89351 is capable of data transfers of up to 3 MB/sec in asynchronous mode, but it does not support synchronous transfers. The synchronous logic has been removed from this device to reduce die size and cost. The elimination of the synchronous function also eliminates the need for a split control and data bus structure. (The split bus is only required during high speed synchronous burst transfers.)

The MB89351 SCSI bus interface is developed from the MB87035/36 and is designed for use with external differential drivers.

MB89352

This device is functionally the same as the MB89351, but it has single-ended drivers on-chip. Because the device is used only in single-ended applications, the SCSI In and SCSI Out buses are combined.

More detailed product information and complete specifications for Fujitsu's SPCs can be found in the Product Profiles in this book, Chapters 7 through 10.

Table 3–1 highlights the unique features of each Fujitsu SPC.

Table 3–1.   Fujitsu's SPC Features

Feature	MB87033B	MB87035/36	MB89351	MB89352
Single-Ended Driver/Receiver	On Chip	External	External	On Chip
Differential Driver/Receiver	No	External	External	No
Synchronous Transfer	Yes	Yes	No	No
Transfer Byte Counter	28-bit	28-bit	24-bit	24-bit
Arbitration Fail Interrupt	Yes	Yes	No	No
Attention Condition	—	Yes	—	—
Detect Interrupt	Yes	Yes	No	No
FIFO Full/Empty Interrupt	No	Yes	Yes	Yes
Interrupt Signal Line Count	2	2	1	1
MPU Bus Parity Generator	Yes	Yes	Yes	Yes
DMA Bus	Separate from CPU Bus	Separate from CPU Bus	Common with CPU Bus	Common with CPU Bus
Addressable Registers	16, ea. Byte-wide	16, ea. Byte-wide	16, ea. Byte-wide	16, ea. Byte-wide
Process	CMOS	CMOS	CMOS	CMOS
Package	QFP-80P	PGA-88P	SDIP-64P	DIP-48P
	LCC-84P	QFP-100P	QFP-64P	QFP-48P

The product line shown above has progressed in an evolutionary, not revolutionary, manner. There is a product designed specifically for each and every SCSI configuration. This complete offering allows the user to select the part that is most cost effective for the application. Should the requirements of the application change over time, then it is a simple and economical process to migrate within the product family and select a product that is better suited to meet the cost and/or performance requirements of the new application.

Chapter 4

FUJITSU'S SPC ARCHITECTURE

Architecture

Fujitsu's SPCs share a common architecture of 16 directly addressable registers. The open architecture approach was required because, in 1985, the typical SCSI implementation had yet to be clearly defined. There were questions about the viability of the two available driver technologies – differential or single-ended. The differential driver was technically superior, and it offered sharper signals and the capability to transmit over a longer length of cable; but the single-ended driver was less expensive and required less board space. Another key consideration was the transfer method, synchronous versus the slower asynchronous method. In view of the concerns and issues concerning the SCSI SPC, Fujitsu decided to provide a product that would accommodate every facet of the SCSI.

Therefore, Fujitsu's first SPC, the MB87030, had an open architecture. This open architecture allowed designers to select the features that were most appropriate for their application and market requirements. As these needs became better defined, Fujitsu has been quick to respond with new chip designs that retain the basic architecture of the MB87030 and include the latest requirements.

The architectural overview offered in this chapter applies to all Fujitsu's SPCs, except where noted.

Logic Blocks

The block diagram shown in Figure 4–1 is composed of the following seven logic blocks:

(1)   Internal register block

(2)   MPU interface control block

(3)   Bus phase control block

(4)   Arbitration and selection sequence control block

(5)   Transfer sequence control block
a.   Synchronous SPCs
b.   Asynchronous SPCs

(6)   Transfer byte counter block

(7)   Data buffer register block

Description and Operation of Logical Blocks

1.   Internal Register Block

The register block is made up of 16 directly addressable registers that are designed to perform timing, counting, and protocol management. Details on register functionality can be found in Chapter 5.

2.   MPU Interface Control Block

The MPU Interface Control Block selects a specified internal register and controls a read/write operation. This is done to report the result status of the SPC's internal operation and the detection of an error, if encountered.

3.   Bus Phase Control Block

The bus phase control block generates a specified bus phase for SCSI and controls its sequence of execution. This block also supervises SCSI status and responds to the bus phase being executed, if necessary.

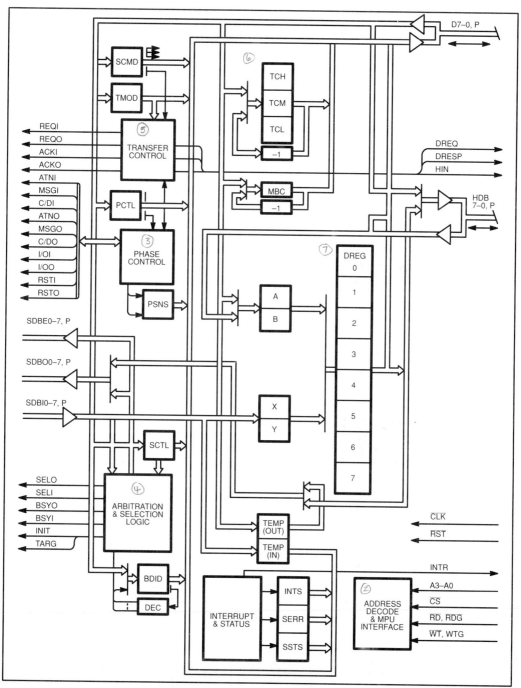

Figure 4–1. Functional Block Diagram of Fujitsu's SPCs

4. Arbitration/Selection Sequence Control Block

The sequence control block executes the ARBITRATION phase with the SCSI-specified timing and obtains permission to use the SCSI bus. Then it carries out the SELECTION/RESELECTION phase and checks the response from the selected and reselected device. This block also detects the SELECTION/RESELECTION phase on the SCSI bus and checks the bus device ID specified in the internal register against that specified on the SCSI data bus. If this block finds that the SPC has been selected by another SCSI bus device, it executes the response sequence for the SELECTION/RESELECTION phase.

5a. Transfer Sequence Control Block for Synchronous SPCs

This sequence control block controls the DATA IN/OUT, COMMAND, STATUS, and MESSAGE IN/OUT phases to be executed in SCSI. The following two modes are available for execution of these transfer phases:

(1)   *Manual Transfer Mode*

In Manual Transfer Mode, the MPU interface is used for transferring data and sending, receiving, and checking the REQ/ACK signals on the SCSI bus.

(2)   *Hardware Transfer Mode*

In Hardware Transfer Mode, the SPC controls the SCSI transfer sequence according to the transfer mode and transfer byte count specified in the internal registers and reports the end result of transfer.

In the synchronous mode transfer operation, a maximum of 8-byte offset is available for the DATA TRANSFER phases. The hardware transfer mode is subdivided into two modes according to the data routing:

a)   *Program Transfer Mode*

Data is routed via MPU interface in the following data paths:
SCSI ↔ Data buffer register ↔ Data bus lines D7 to D0 and DP.

b)   *DMA Mode*

Data is routed using DREQ and DRESP signals for DMA control in the following data paths:
SCSI ↔ Data buffer register ↔ Data bus lines HDB7 to HDB0 and HDBP.

5b. Transfer Sequence Control Block for Asynchronous SPCs

This sequence control block controls the DATA IN/OUT, COMMAND, STATUS, and MESSAGE IN/OUT phases to be executed on the SCSI bus. The following two modes are available for execution of these transfer phases:

(1)   *Manual Transfer Mode*

In Manual Transfer Mode, the MPU interface is used for transferring data and sending, receiving, and checking the REQ and ACK signals on SCSI.

(2)   *Hardware Transfer Mode*

In Hardware Transfer Mode, the SPC controls the SCSI transfer sequence according to the transfer mode and transfer byte count specified in the internal registers and reports the end result of transfer.

In the asynchronous mode transfer operation, the REQ and ACK signals are controlled by the interlock protocol. The hardware transfer mode is subdivided into two parts according to the following data routing:

a)   *Program Transfer*

Data transfer between the MPU and SCSI is executed using DREG. The DREG status is acknowledged by the MPU with one of the following methods.

- The MPU reads the SSTS register at any time and controls data transfer according to the results.

- INTR (interrupt signal) is sent to the MPU to acknowledge that the DREG needs data or has data as a result of reading from or writing in SCSI.

b)   *DMA Transfer*

In this mode, the SPC executes data transfer with the MPU via DMAC by sending the DREQ signal.

When requesting memory access, the SPC makes the DREQ signal active.

During an input operation, the DREQ is sent when the SPC internal data buffer register contains data received from SCSI. During an output operation, the DREQ is sent when all bytes specified by the transfer byte counter have not yet been fetched and the internal data buffer contains empty bytes.

DREQ is not a 1-byte transfer request. DREQ is kept active while the SPC is in the state described above.

The $\overline{\text{DACK}}$ signal may be kept active if the response can be continuously issued. It does not have to be pulsed for each byte (for synchronous SPCs).

6. Transfer Byte Counter Block

The transfer byte counter indicates the number of bytes to transfer to or from SCSI for hardware transfer mode operation. It is 24 bits long. The MB87033B and MB87035/36 transfer byte counter is 28 bits long. Except for execution of a special transfer operation (padding), the transfer byte counter is decremented by one each time one byte of data is transferred on SCSI. The transfer byte counter is also used as a timer for supervising the waiting time for a response to be returned from the selected SCSI bus device during execution of the SELECTION and RESELECTION phase. The three 8-bit registers, TCH, TCM, and TCL, make up the 24-bit counter.

7. Data Buffer Register Block

The data buffer register block is used in the execution of a Hardware Transfer Mode operation in SPC. It has a capacity of eight bytes, and operates on the FIFO principle for each byte.

In an input operation (from SCSI to SPC), data received from SCSI is loaded into the buffer register. In the DMA mode, the transfer request signal (DREQ) is generated to the external buffer memory. Data can also be read out from this buffer register in the program transfer mode.

In an output operation (from SPC to SCSI), data supplied from the MPU interface (program transfer mode) or external buffer memory (DMA mode) is loaded into the buffer register and then sent to SCSI. In this case, a maximum of eight bytes of data is prefetched into the SPC. The eight byte FIFO appears as a single register (DREG) to the MPU interface.

In an input operation, the byte locations holding valid data are selected in succession for reading out. In an output operation, the empty byte locations are selected in succession for writing in.

Chapter 5

FUNCTIONAL DESCRIPTION OF FUJITSU'S SPC REGISTERS

This chapter discusses the functional operation of Fujitsu's SPC and offers a comprehensive explanation of the Fujitsu SPC register set. The descriptions appear in order of the individual hex address code for the subject register. Each register (an abbreviation) and hex address appear in bold type on the upper right hand corner of the first page of each section to help in quickly finding the register description.

The registers discussed in this chapter apply to all Fujitsu SPCs, except where noted. Those features that are unique to a specific SPC are covered in the Product Profile for that SPC. (Please check Table of Contents for pages.)

Internal Register Addresses

Fujitsu has assigned a unique address to each internal register with each specific register identified by the configuration of address bits A0 to A3. Table 5–1 shows the internal register addresses.

Table 5–1.   Internal Register Addressing

CS	A3	A2	A1	A0	OP	Register Name	Mnemonic
0	0	0	0	0	R W	Bus Device ID	BDID
0	0	0	0	1	R W	SPC Control	SCTL
0	0	0	1	0	R W	Command	SCMD
0	0	0	1	1	R W	Transfer Mode	TMOD
0	0	1	0	0	R W	Interrupt Sense Reset Interrupt	INTS
0	0	1	0	1	R W	Phase Sense SPC Diagnostic Control	PSNS SDGC
0	0	1	1	0	R W	SPC Status —	SSTS
0	0	1	1	1	R W	SPC Error Status —	SERR
0	1	0	0	0	R W	Phase Control	PCTL
0	1	0	0	1	R W	Modified Byte Counter —	MBC
0	1	0	1	0	R W	Data Register	DREG
0	1	0	1	1	R W	Temporary Register	TEMP
0	1	1	0	0	R W	Transfer Counter High	TCH
0	1	1	0	1	R W	Transfer Counter Middle	TCM
0	1	1	1	0	R W	Transfer Counter Low	TCL
0	1	1	1	1	R W	External Buffer	EXBF

Bit Assignments for Internal Registers

Table 5–2 shows the bit assignment for each internal register. When accessing an internal register (read/write), remember the following:

(1)   The internal register block includes read-only and write-only registers.

(2)   Some registers serve two functions depending on whether the register is being written to or read.

(3)   A write to a read-only register is ignored.

(4)   If a write-only register is read out, the data and parity bit are undefined.

(5) At bit positions indicating "——" for a write, Table 5–1 and Table 5–2 indicate either 1 or 0, and may be written.

Table 5–2. Internal Register Bit Assignment

HEX Address	Name (Mnemonic)	OP	7 (MSb)	6	5	4	3	2	1	0 (LSb)	P
0	Bus Device ID (BDID)	R	SCSI Bus Device ID								'0'
			#7	#6	#5	#4	#3	#2	#1	#0	
		W						SCSI Bus Device ID			
								ID4	ID2	ID1	
1	SPC Control (SCTL)	R	Reset and Disable	Control Reset	Diag Mode	ARBIT Enable	Parity Enable	Select Enable	Reselect Enable	INT Enable	P
		W									
2	Command (SCMD)	R	Command Code			RST Out	Inter-cept xfer	Transfer Modifier			P
		W						PRG Xfer	'0'	Term. Mode	
3	Transfer Mode (TMOD)	R	Sync. Xfer	Max. Transfer Offset			Min. Transfer Period		'0'	Xfer Counter Expand	P
		W		4	2	1	2	1			
4	Interrupt Sense (INTS)	R	Selected	Reselected	Disconnected	Command Complete	Service Required	Time Out	SPC Hard Error	Reset Condition	P
		W	Reset Interrupt								—
5	Phase Sense (PSNS)	R	REQ	ACK	ATN	SEL	BSY	MSG	C/D	I/O	P
	SPC Diagnostic Control (SDGC)	W	Diag. REQ	Diag. ACK			Diag. BSY	Diag. MSG	Diag. C/D	Diag. I/O	—
6	SPC Status (SSTS)	R	Connected INIT	TARG	SPC Busy	Xfer in Progress	SCSI RST	TC=0	DREG Status FULL	EMPTY	P
		W	—								—
7	SPC Error Status (SERR)	R	Data Error SCSI	SPC	'0'	'0'	TC P-Error	Phase Error	Short Period	Offset Error	P
		W									
8	Phase Control (PCTL)	R	Bus Free Interrupt Enable	Arbitration Interrupt Enable	Attention Condition Interrupt Enable	Reset Condition Interrupt Mask	'0'	Transfer Phase			P
		W						MSG Out	C/D Out	I/O Out	

Continued on following page

Table 5–2. Internal Register Bit Assignment (Continued)

HEX Address	Name (Mnemonic)	OP	7 (MSb)	6	5	4	3	2	1	0 (LSb)	P
9	Modified Byte Counter (MBC)	R	Extended Transfer Counter				Bit 3	MBC 2	1	0	P
		W	Bit 27	Bit 26	Bit 25	Bit 24	0				
A	Data Register (DREG)	R	Internal Data Register (8 Byte FIFO)								P
		W	Bit 7	6	5	4	3	2	1	0	
B	Temporary Register (TEMP)	R	Temporary Data (Input From SCSI)								P
			Bit 7	6	5	4	3	2	1	0	
		W	Temporary Data (Output to SCSI)								P
			Bit 7	6	5	4	3	2	1	0	
C	Temporary Counter High (TCH)	R	Transfer Counter High (MSB)								P
		W	Bit 23	22	21	20	19	18	17	16	
D	Temporary Counter Mid (TCM)	R	Transfer Counter Middle (2nd Byte)								P
		W	Bit 15	14	13	12	11	10	17	8	
E	Temporary Counter Low (TCL)	R	Transfer Counter Low (LSB)								P
		W	Bit 7	6	5	4	3	2	1	0	
F	External Buffer (EXBF)	R	External Buffer								P
		W	Bit 7	6	5	4	3	2	1	0	

BDID
Address
#0

BDID Register – Bus Device Identifier Register

OP	7 (MSb)	6	5	4	3	2	1	0 (LSb)	P
R	Bit Significant Bus Device ID								
	#7	#6	#5	#4	#3	#2	#1	#0	'0'
W	———					SCSI Bus Device ID			———
						ID4	ID2	ID1	

Register Function

The BDID register is used to store the SPC's SCSI bus address and bus ID number. The bus ID number can be one of eight numbers (0 – 7) and will determine a device's priority level with number 7 being the highest priority.

Write Operation (Bits 2 to 0)

The BDID register specifies the SCSI bus address of the SPC (ID) as a three-bit binary number. This setting must be completed before resetting the SCTL register's bit 7 (Reset and Disable). Bits 2 to 0 are cleared during a power-on reset only.

Read Operation

The BDID register indicates the SCSI physical device ID of the SPC. The SCSI physical device address is decoded from the values of bits 2 to 0 as specified in a write operation to the BDID register described above. One of the bits is a 1, the others are all 0s. The SCSI bus usage priority is assigned in descending order from bit 7 to bit 0. Using a bus device ID indicated in this register, the SPC executes the ARBITRATION phase. Also, if a SELECTION and/or RESELECTION phase occurs, the value of the SCSI data bus is checked against the contents of this register to see whether the SPC has been selected/reselected or not. If a match occurs, the SPC will automatically respond to the SELECTION and/or RESELECTION

Examples: Writing hex 03 to this register will result in hex 08 being read.

Writing hex 07 to this register will result in hex 80 being read.

SCTL
Address
#1

SCTL Register — SPC Control Register

OP	7	6	5	4	3	2	1	0	P
	(MSb)							(LSb)	
R	Reset and	Control Reset	Diag Mode	ARBIT Enable	Parity Enable	Select Enable	Reselect Enable	INT Enable	P
W	Disable								

Register Function

The SCTL register controls the SPC modes and operating conditions.

Bit 7:   Reset and Disable

Bit 7 generates a reset instruction to the internal registers and control circuits of the SPC. When this bit is 1, the SPC is reset and disconnected from SCSI (disabled). Execution of the hardware reset ($\overline{\text{RST}}$ input = 'L') causes this bit to be set to 1. To enable the SCSI operation, bit 7 must be set to 0.

Bit 6:   Control Reset

The data transfer control circuit is reset when this bit is 1. Even if the control reset is executed while the SPC is connected to the SCSI bus, the SPC maintains the connection with SCSI. In fact, this bit should be used for resetting the data transfer control circuit while SPC is connected to the SCSI bus. More specifically, it should be used when an error is indicated by bit 1 (SPC Hardware Error) of the INTS register during execution of the SCSI transfer phase or when a timeout occurs before completion of Transfer command execution (supervised by the MPU program). Bit 1 (SPC Hardware Error) of the INTS register and Bit 1 (offset error) of the SERR register are also cleared by this bit.

> *Note:*   *This reset function initializes the SPC's transfer control circuits when the SPC serves as an INITIATOR. The first byte should be transferred in manual mode after resetting since the REQ signal may be active during control reset.*

Bit 5:   Diagnostic Mode

When bit 5 is 1, the SPC enters a diagnostic mode and is disconnected from SCSI. The diagnostic mode allows pseudo-execution of the SCSI operation using the SDGC register (explained later).

Bit 4:   Arbitration Enable

Bit 4 indicates whether the ARBITRATION phase is executable in SCSI or not.

1   – ARBITRATION phase executable

0   – ARBITRATION phase nonexecutable

With this bit set to 1, the Select command causes the SPC to execute the ARBITRA-TION phase. If the SPC wins the arbitration, it executes the SELECTION/RESELECTION phase. With this bit set to 0, the Select command causes the SPC to execute the SELECTION phase without the ARBITRATION phase. As long as bit 4 is 0, the SPC will not respond to a reselection request from other SCSI bus devices. No response is made even if bit 1 (Reselect Enable) of this register is set to 1.

> *Note:*   *Remember that bit 4 must be set correctly before clearing bit 7 (Reset and Disable) of the SCTL register. Note also that this bit should not be changed in other than a diagnostic mode after clearing bit 7 of the SCTL register.*

Bit 3:   Parity Enable

Bit 3 indicates whether the parity of data received from the SCSI data bus is to be checked or not.

1   – Parity of the data received from the SCSI data bus is checked.

0   – Parity of the data received from the SCSI data bus is not checked.

Regardless of the value of this bit, the parity of the data to be sent to the SCSI data bus is ensured. Also, the parity of the data on the SPC internal data bus is always checked.

> *Note:*   *While the SPC is connected with SCSI, this bit should not be changed.*

A parity check is carried out in the following cases:

(1)   When checking an ID value placed on the data bus upon detection of the SELECTION/RESELECTION phase in SCSI, detection of a parity error causes no response to the SELECTION/RESELECTION phase. This occurs even if the SCSI bus device ID has matched.

(2)   If a parity error is detected in a data byte, when data is received from SCSI in an input transfer sequence, the relevant parity bit value is corrected and the data byte with the corrected parity is sent to the MPU/DMA data bus.

Bit 2:   Select Enable

1   – The SPC responds as a TARGET device to the SELECTION phase in SCSI.

0   – The SPC does not respond to the SELECTION phase in SCSI.

> *Note:*   *If the SPC has already detected the SELECTION phase during an attempt to set this bit to 0, the SPC responds to the SELECTION phase as a TARGET device. In this case, the 0 setting is effective for the subsequent SELECTION phase (with no response).*

Bit 1:   Reselect Enable

1   – SPC responds as an INITIATOR to the RESELECTION phase in SCSI.

0   – SPC does not respond to the RESELECTION phase in SCSI.

> *Note:*   *If SPC has already detected the RESELECTION phase during an attempt to set this bit to 0, SPC responds to the RESELECTION phase as an INITIATOR. In this case, the 0 setting is effective for the subsequent RESELECTION phase (with no response).*

Bit 0:   Interrupt Enable

Bit 0 serves as a mask for enabling/disabling the hardware interrupt (INTR) output from the SPC.

1   – Interrupt enabled

0   – Interrupt disabled

A hardware interrupt due to a RESET condition detected in SCSI cannot be masked.

Regardless of the value of this bit, an interrupt event is always indicated in the INTS register. This allows poll-mode operation when the hardware interrupt (INTR) is disabled.

SCMD
Address
#2

SCMD Register — SPC Command Register

OP	7 (MSb)	6	5	4	3	2	1	0 (LSb)	P
R W	Command Code			RST Out	Inter-cept Xfer	Transfer Modifier			P
						PRG Xfer	'0'	Term. Mode	

Register Function

The SCMD register is used for issuing a command to the SPC. Writing into this register causes the SPC to initiate the command specified with bits 7 to 5.

Bit 7 to 5:   Command Code

Bit 7	6	5	Command
0	0	0	Bus Release
0	0	1	Select
0	1	0	Reset ATN
0	1	1	Set ATN
1	0	0	Transfer
1	0	1	Transfer Pause
1	1	0	Reset ACK/REQ
1	1	1	Set ACK/REQ

Bit 4:   RST Out

If bit 7 (Reset and Disable) of the SCTL register is 0, setting bit 4 to 1 asserts the SCSI RST signal. When bit 4 is set to 1, a command being executed or waiting for execution in the SPC is cleared and all signals to SCSI other than RST are deactivated. To ensure the SCSI timing requirements, the MPU must maintain this bit at 1 for more than 25 microseconds.

> *Note:*   If the RST signal is received from the SCSI bus with this bit set to 0, the operation sequence is as follows:
>
> (1)   A command being executed or waiting for execution in the SPC is cleared.
>
> (2)   All signals to the SCSI bus are deactivated.
>
> (3)   An interrupt condition (non-maskable) is generated.

Whenever bit 7 (Reset and Disable) of the SCTL register is 0, the SPC always accepts the RST signal from the SCSI bus.

Bit 3:   Intercept Transfer

Bit 3 specifies the special data transfer mode. It is valid only when SPC serves as an INITIATOR.

This bit should be set to 1 together with the Set ATN, Set ACK/REQ, or Bus Release command. (Bus Release command has no effect when the SPC is connected with SCSI as an INITIATOR.) This bit should be reset together with the Reset ACK/REQ command. (When two or more bytes are transferred using the Set ACK/REQ and Reset ACK/REQ commands, this bit must be reset on issuance of the Reset ACK/REQ command for the last byte.) With bit 3 of SCMD register set to 1, executing manual transfer (MPU-controlled transfer using the Set ACK/REQ and Reset ACK/REQ commands) does not change the contents of the eight-byte data buffer register in the SPC. Therefore, if a TARGET changes bus phase (i.e., it changes to MESSAGE IN during execution of the DATA OUT phase), this intercept transfer mode makes it possible to optionally restart the DATA OUT phase at the end of the interrupting phase. The phase change during transfer execution is reported by a "service required" interrupt. To execute this intercept transfer mode, bit 3 of SCMD register must be set to 1 prior to the resetting of an interrupt (an interrupt must be reset after bit 3 is set to 1). Even when the intercept transfer mode is not used, bit 3 may be specified for resetting a "service required" interrupt. In this case, bit 3 must be set/reset together with the Bus Release command. For more details, see the description of bit 3 (Service Required) of the INTS register.

Bits 2 to 0:   Transfer Modifier

Bits 2 to 0 are used as a field for specifying the execution mode of the information transfer phase. A value must be set in this field when the Transfer command is issued. If any of the following commands are issued during execution of the Transfer command, the value in this field must not be changed.

(1)   Set ATN

(2)   Transfer Pause

(3)   Reset ACK/REQ

Bit 2:   Program Transfer

1   – Data are transferred between the MPU and the data buffer register in SPC.

0   – Data are transferred in the DMA mode in which the SPC signals a transfer request to the external buffer memory.

Bit 1:   Unused

Bit 1 must always be set to 0.

Bit 0:   Termination Mode

Bit 0 provides different functions depending on the SPC operating mode. When SPC serves as an INITIATOR, bit 0 specifies the following operations:

1   – Even after the transfer byte counter reaches 0 during execution of the Transfer command, data transfer will continue if the REQ signal arrives from a TARGET within the same phase. If an output operation is in progress, all 0 bits (with a parity bit set to 1) are transmitted as data. During an input operation, the received data is ignored. But parity is checked if it is enabled (Parity Enable). The above data transfer is referred to as padding transfer, which is effective only when the DATA IN or DATA OUT phase is executed. Padding transfer is executed only within SPC, and a transfer request is not signaled to the external buffer memory even if the DMA transfer mode is specified.

Padding transfer is maintained until a TARGET changes the bus phase. In the padding transfer mode, if the Transfer command is issued with the initial value of the transfer byte counter set to 0, execution of padding transfer is started with the first byte. To carry out an output operation in this case, the TEMP register must be set to X'00' prior to issuance of the Transfer command.

0   – Transfer command execution terminates when the transfer byte counter reaches 0. The Transfer command must be reissued to receive the next REQ signal from a TARGET.

When the SPC serves as a TARGET, bit 0 specifies the following operations:

1   – If a parity error is detected in the received data during execution of the
     Transfer command for input, the current transfer sequence is immediately
     stopped to terminate Transfer command execution.

0   – Even if a parity error is detected in the received data during execution of the
     Transfer command for input, the current transfer sequence continues until
     the transfer byte counter reaches 0.

Command Functions

Fujitsu SPCs feature a set of commands that are designed to minimize software
overhead. Notice that the command may serve different functions depending on whether
the SPC is operating in the Initiator or the Target mode and that some commands are
functional in one mode only (Initiator or Target).

For a clear account of how these commands are designed to interact with events
occurring on the SCSI bus, please refer to Figure 5–1.

Bus Release command

When the SPC acts as a TARGET, the Bus Release command instructs a transition to
the BUS FREE phase. During execution of the information transfer phase, the Transfer
Pause command must be issued to halt the data transfer operation prior to this command.
Otherwise, the SCSI bus sequence is not ensured. The Bus Release command may also be
used to cancel the Select command waiting for the bus to become free. Note that the Bus
Release command is ignored if the SPC has already started the ARBITRATION or
SELECTION phase.

Select command

The Select command requests the SELECTION/RESELECTION phase to be started.
It shall be issued only when the SPC is not connected with SCSI. When the SPC receives
this command, it carries out the following operation upon detection of the BUS FREE
phase.

(1)   *When bit 4 (Arbitration Enable) of the* SCTL *register is set to 1:*

After the BUS FREE phase has been detected, the SPC executes the
ARBITRATION phase to try to obtain bus usage permission. If the SPC
has lost the arbitration, the Select command terminates its execution. If
the SPC has won the arbitration, the SPC executes the SELECTION or
RESELECTION phase. The SELECTION phase is executed when bit 0
(I/O Out) of the PCTL register is set to 0, and the RESELECTION
phase is executed when it is set to 1.

(2)   *When bit 4 (Arbitration Enable) of the* SCTL *register is set to 0:*

After the BUS FREE phase has been detected, the SPC executes the
SELECTION phase.

Before the select command is issued, the following settings must be made in either
of the above cases:

(1)   *PCTL register*

Specify the phase to be executed at bit 0 (I/O Out).

0 — SELECTION phase to be executed
1 — RESELECTION phase to be executed

Note that whenever bit 4 (Arbitration Enable) of the SCTL register is
set to 0, the SELECTION phase is executed regardless of the value of
bit 0 in the PCTL register.

(2)   *Set ATN command*

Issue the Set ATN command if it is required to assert an ATN signal at
the SELECTION phase.

(3)   *TEMP register*

In the TEMP register, specify a value to be sent to the SCSI data bus
during execution of the SELECTION/RESELECTION phase.

(4)   *TCH and TCM register*

Specify a response (BSY signal) waiting supervisory time for execution
of the SELECTION/RESELECTION phase. The supervisory time T_{SL}
should be calculated as follows:

Assuming that the value of

TCH and TCM is N (MSB: TCH; LSB: TCM):

When

N does not equal 0, $T_{SL} = (N \times 256 + 15) \times T_{CLF} \times 2$.

When

N equals 0, T_{SL} = infinite.

Where

T_{CLF} is a cycle time of the clock signal supplied to the $\overline{CLK}$ pin of the
SPC.

(5)   *TCL register*

Specify a period of time (T_{WAIT}) from the moment when both BSY and SEL signals become inactive on SCSI (upon detection of the BUS FREE phase) to the moment when the SPC initiates the ARBITRATION/SELECTION phase. Parameters (X'00') to (X'OF') can be specified in the TCL register.

The average value can be derived using the following equation:

$$T_{WAIT} = [(T_{CL}) + 6] \times T_{CLF} \text{ to } [(T_{CL}) + 7] \times T_{CLF}$$

Where

(T_{CL}) equals the set value in the TCL register.
T_{CLF} equals the cycle time of the clock signal supplied to the $\overline{CLK}$ pin of the SPC.

Table 5–3 lists the recommended values for the TCL register.

Table 5–3.   TCL Register
Recommended Values for Use of Select Command

T_{CLF} (ns)	T_{CL}	T_{WAIT} (average) (ns)
124 – 180	$(04)_{16}$	1,250 – 1,980
140 – 200	$(03)_{16}$	1,260 – 2,000

In ARBITRATION phase execution by the Select command, the bus device identifier (ID) which is sent to the SCSI data bus is the value specified in the BDID register. The following equation can be used to obtain the period of time (T_{ARB}) required from the moment when the arbitration is started (BSY signal assertion) to the moment when the bus usage priority is examined:

$$T_{ARB} = 32 \times T_{CLF}$$

Where

T_{CLF} indicates a cycle time of the clock signal supplied to the $\overline{CLK}$ pin of the SPC.

After the SELECTION/RESELECTION phase execution is started, a time-out interrupt occurs if no response is acknowledged within the supervisory time specified in the TCH and TCM registers. When a time-out interrupt occurs, the SPC holds the current execution state of SELECTION/RESELECTION phase for SCSI. However, until the time-out interrupt condition is reset, the SPC executes "no operation" to the response from the bus device being selected. Either of the following procedures can be used for a time-out interrupt:

(1)   *Restart of SELECTION/RESELECTION phase.*

After specifying a new supervisory time in the TCH, TCM and TCL registers, reset the time-out interrupt condition. Then, the SPC will restart the SELECTION/RESELECTION phase in progress. At this time, changing the TEMP register contents can alter the value being sent to the SCSI data bus. New supervisory time T_{SL} is specified as follows:

Assuming

TCH, TCM and TCL value to be N (MSB: TCH, LSB: TCL);

$$T_{SL} = N \times T_{CLF} \times 2 \ (N \neq 0)$$

Where

T_{CLF} indicates a cycle time of the clock signal supplied to the $\overline{CLK}$ pin of the SPC.

(2)   *Termination of SELECTION/RESELECTION phase.*

When a time-out interrupt occurs, the values of TCH, TCM and TCL registers are 0. Resetting the time-out interrupt condition in this state causes the SPC to deactivate all signals to SCSI and terminate the SELECTION/RESELECTION phase unless the BSY signal is returned. If the BSY signal is returned when the interrupt condition is being reset, then the SPC executes the normal sequence to complete the Select command. To reset a time-out interrupt condition, set bit 2 of the INTS register and TCM registers, and the time-out interrupt will not occur. However, the above time-out interrupt resetting procedure must be carried out to terminate the SELECTION/RESELECTION phase in progress. If the SPC recognizes a response from the selected/reselected device during the SELECTION/RESELECTION phase execution, the SPC executes an interface sequence to serve as an INITIATOR (SELECTION phase) or TARGET (RESELECTION phase). When the Select command is issued, the SPC status is indicated in the SSTS register. Figure 5–1 shows the status transitions.

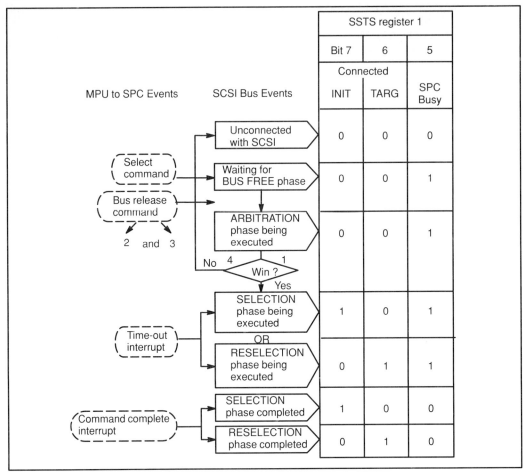

Figure 5–1.   Status Transition in Select Command Execution

Notes: [1] Check the SPC status after the elapsed time (shown below) following issuance of the Select command:

    (1) If Arbitration Enable bit is set to 0 the minimum waiting time is $22 \times T_{CLF}$ (Clock cycle)

    (2) If Arbitration Enable bit is set to 1 the minimum waiting time is $(55 + \text{Set value in TCL}) \times T_{CLF}$

[2] The Select command waiting for BUS FREE phase can be canceled using the Bus Release command. However, if the bus becomes free simultaneously with the issue of the Bus Release command, the Select command remains valid to execute the ARBITRATION and SELECTION/RESELECTION phases. The MPU program must make sure that the Select command has been canceled after more than four clock cycles from the time the Bus Release command (write to SCMD register) was issued.

[3] This particular use of the bus release command should not be implemented when using the MB87030 and MB87031 SPCs.

[4] If the SPC loses the arbitration, the Select command terminates automatically (a command complete interrupt does not occur). In this case, note that the register contents are unpredictable. When issuing the Select command again, be sure to specify the relevant value (see (5)), TCL register. *The MB87033B can be configured to issue a command complete interrupt if the SPC loses the arbitration.*

Set ATN command

The Set ATN command is valid only when the SPC is acting as an INITIATOR. If this command is issued prior to the Select command, the ATN signal is sent to SCSI during the execution of the SELECTION phase. If the Set ATN command is issued while the SPC is connected with SCSI as an INITIATOR, the ATN signal is sent to SCSI immediately. When the parity checking for the SCSI data bus is enabled and the SPC detects a parity error in the data received from SCSI (during execution of the input transfer operation in hardware transfer mode), the ATN signal is sent automatically to SCSI regardless of the Set ATN command (see Figure 5–2). The assertion of ATN signal is retained until the condition described in the following subsection, Reset ATN command, is satisfied. However, the ATN signaling condition held in SPC by the Set ATN command issued prior to the Select command is cleared if one of the following conditions is met:

(1)   The Select command is canceled by the Bus Release command.

(2)   A selected/reselected interrupt occurs before execution of the SELECTION phase.

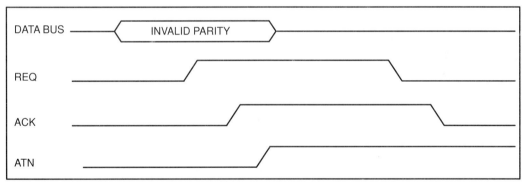

Figure 5–2.   ATN Signal Generation in Data Transfer

Reset ATN command

The Reset ATN command is used to reset the ATN signal being sent to SCSI. **If the SPC generates an ATN signal (due to a parity error in the received data) during execution of the Hardware Transfer Mode operation, do not issue this command to reset the ATN signal until execution of the current Transfer command is complete.** Also, to reset the ATN signal in manual transfer mode, execute the Reset ATN command before the

ACK signal is sent to SCSI. In the following cases, the SPC will automatically reset the ATN signal without the Reset ATN command:

(1)   On occurrence of a disconnected interrupt.

(2)   On sending the last byte during execution of the MESSAGE OUT phase in hardware transfer mode (see Figure 5–3).

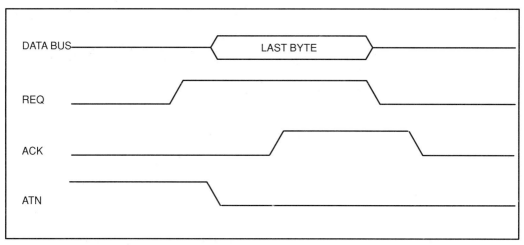

Figure 5–3.   ATN Signal Resetting in MESSAGE OUT Phase

Transfer command

The Transfer command executes the following information transfer phases in SCSI:

(1)   DATA IN/OUT phase.

(2)   STATUS phase.

(3)   COMMAND phase.

(4)   MESSAGE IN/OUT phase.

The transfer operation initiated by this command is referred to as a hardware transfer operation, the sequence of which is controlled by the SPC. Before issuing the Transfer command, be sure to set up the following:

(1)   Transfer byte counter (TCH, TCM, TCL)
        Set the byte count of the data to be transferred (MSB: TCH, LSB: TCL)

(2)   Bits 2 to 0 of the PCTL register.
        Set a pattern indicating the phase to be executed.

(3)   TMOD register.
        Set detailed transfer mode.

When the SPC serves as a TARGET, it executes the information transfer phase specified in the PCTL register and terminates the Transfer command when any of the following conditions are encountered:

(1)   Completion of transfer of the number of bytes specified in the transfer counter.

(2)   Receipt of the Transfer Pause command.

(3)   Detection of a parity error in the received data during an input operation with bit 0 (Termination Mode) of the SCMD register set to 1 (when the parity checking is enabled).

When the SPC serves as an INITIATOR, it starts the transfer operation as follows:

(1)   If the REQ signal is received before the Transfer command is issued, the SPC compares the phase requested by the SCSI with that specified in the PCTL register at receipt of this command. Then, if they match, the SPC starts the transfer operation.

(2)   If the REQ signal has not been received when the Transfer command is issued, the SPC will wait to execute this command. When the phase specified in the PCTL register matches that requested by SCSI on receipt of the REQ signal, the SPC will start the transfer operation. In the above phase comparison, if a phase mismatch occurs, the Transfer command is nullified, and the SPC generates a service required interrupt. On occurrence of this interrupt, check the PSNS register for the phase requested by the SCSI bus, and issue the Transfer command again or carry out manual transfer.

When the SPC serves as an INITIATOR, Transfer command execution terminates when any of the following conditions is encountered:

(1)   In other than the padding transfer mode, when the transfer of data of the byte count specified in the transfer byte counter is completed.

(2)   When another information transfer phase is requested by the TARGET.

(3)   In the padding transfer mode, when another information transfer phase is requested by the TARGET.

(4)   When disconnected interrupt occurs.

Transfer Pause command

The Transfer Pause command prematurely halts a hardware transfer operation initiated by the Transfer command when the SPC serves as a TARGET. (Note that the Transfer Pause command cannot be used when the SPC serves as an INITIATOR). On receipt of this command, the SPC performs the following:

(1)   Stops sending another REQ signal to SCSI (in an input operation).

(2)   Stops sending a transfer request (DREQ) signal to the external buffer memory (in a DMA mode output operation).

Note: *For an output operation in program transfer mode, a write to the data buffer register is not allowed after this command has been issued.*

Finally, the hardware transfer operation terminates when the internal data buffer register in the SPC becomes empty.

Set ACK/REQ command

The Set ACK/REQ command is used to set ACK or REQ signals for SCSI during execution of manual transfer. When the SPC acts as an INITIATOR, this command causes the ACK signal to be sent. When SPC acts as a TARGET, it causes the REQ signal to be sent. In manual transfer mode, data is transferred via the TEMP register. In this case, the pattern (type) of the information transfer phase to be executed must be preset in bits 2 to 0 of the PCTL register. During execution of manual transfer, the transfer byte counter remains unchanged. Figure 5–4 and Figure 5–5 show the manual transfer procedures.

Reset ACK/REQ command

The Reset ACK/REQ command is used to reset the ACK or REQ signals to the SCSI bus. When the SPC acts as an INITIATOR, this command resets the ACK signal. When the SPC acts as a TARGET, it resets the REQ signal. Use this command for execution of manual transfer. See Figure 5–4 and Figure 5–5 for the manual transfer procedures. Also, reset the ACK signal for the last byte in the MESSAGE IN phase of the hardware transfer mode. In the MESSAGE IN phase, the end of the Transfer command is reported with the ACK signal for the last byte being asserted. The MPU program checks the validity of the received message first, then issues this command. In this case, the ATN signal, if necessary, may be sent out using the Set ATN command prior to this command.

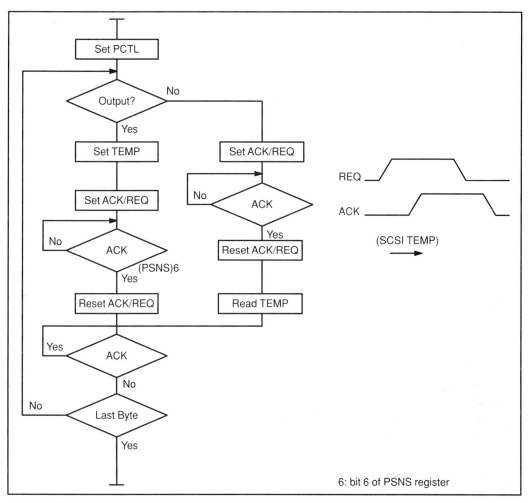

Figure 5–4.   Manual Transfer Procedure (SPC serving as a TARGET)

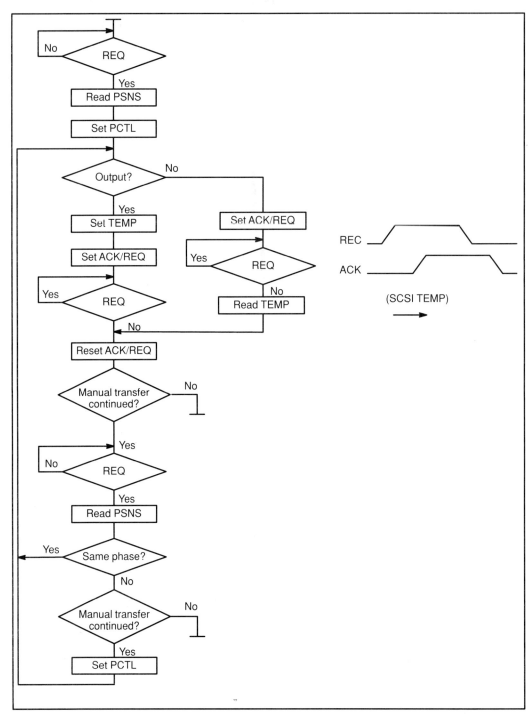

Figure 5–5.   Manual Transfer Procedure (SPC serving as an INITIATOR)

Command Termination Report

(1)   *Immediate commands.*

The following are immediate type commands which terminate operations immediately after being issued. For these commands, the SPC does not report termination.

a)   Set ATN

b)   Reset ATN

c)   Set ACK/REQ

d)   Reset ACK/REQ

(2)   *Interrupt commands.*

For the following commands, an interrupt occurs at the end of execution. The interrupt cause is indicated in the INTS register.

a)   Select

b)   Transfer

(3)   *Non-interrupt commands.*

The following commands terminate with different timings depending on the SPC operation being executed. Check the termination status according to the status information in the SSTS register.

Termination Status (SSTS Register)			
	Bit 7 INIT	Bit 6 TARG	Bit 5 SPC Busy	Bit 4 Xfer in Prg.
Transfer Pause	0	1	0	0
Bus Release [1]	0	0	0	0

Note: [1] If a selected/reselected interrupt condition is detected immediately after termination of the Bus Release command, an interrupt occurs and either the INIT or TARG bit is set.

Command Issuance Timing

Issuance of a command requires a write to the SCMD register. The SPC synchronizes a write to the SCMD register with a clock supplied from the $\overline{\text{CLK}}$ pin, and then starts executing the command specified at bits 7 to 5. Figure 5–6 shows the command execution timing. When issuing commands successively, leave an interval between them for more than the sync-loss period (four clock cycles) in the SPC.

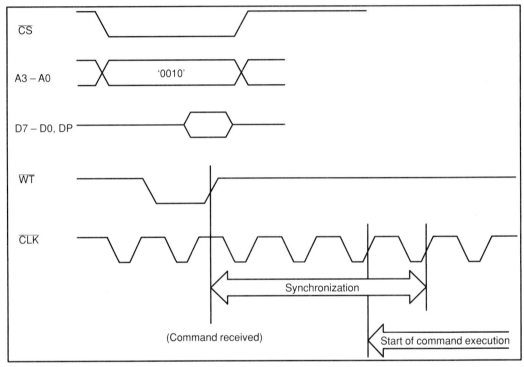

Figure 5–6. Command Execution Timing

TMOD Register for Synchronous Protocol Controllers

TRANSFER MODE REGISTER

OP	7 (MSb)	6	5	4	3	2	1	0 (LSb)	P
R/W	Sync. Xfer	MAX. Transfer Offset			MIN. Transfer Period		'0'	Transfer Counter Extend	P
		4	2	1	2	1			

Register Function

The TMOD Register is used exclusively for setting up and executing synchronous data transfers.

Bit 7:   Synchronous Transfer

1   – Indicates that the DATA IN/OUT phase is executed in synchronous transfer mode. The COMMAND, STATUS, and MESSAGE IN/OUT phases are executed in asynchronous transfer mode regardless of this bit value.

0   – Indicates that the DATA IN/OUT phase is executed in asynchronous transfer mode.

Bit 6 to 4:   Maximum Transfer Offset

Bit 6	Blt 5	Bit 4	Maximum Offset Value
0	0	0	8
0 – 1	0 – 1	1 – 1	1 – 7

Bits 6 to 4 indicate a maximum value of the REQ/ACK offset to be used in synchronous transfer mode.

When the SPC serves as a TARGET, it sends the REQ signal in advance within the specified maximum offset value. When the SPC serves as an INITIATOR, it can receive the REQ signal and input data within the specified maximum offset value. If the maximum offset value is exceeded in reception of the REQ signal, an error condition is detected at bit 0 (Transfer Offset Error) of the SERR register.

Bit 3 and 2: Transfer Period

Bits 3 and 2 indicate a parameter for determining the minimum repeat cycle of the REQ and ACK signals in synchronous transfer mode. Specify a period between the trailing edge of the REQ (ACK) signal and the leading edge of the next REQ (ACK) signal in multiples of a clock signal cycle (T_{CLF}) supplied at the $\overline{CLK}$ pin of the SPC. Figure 5–7 shows an example of a transfer period setting. In synchronous transfer mode, the REQ (ACK) signal pulse width (Typical) equals a cycle of the clock signal (T_{CLF}) supplied to the $\overline{CLK}$ pin.

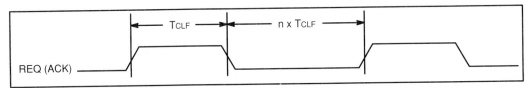

Setting Examples: Maximum Transfer Rates					
Bit 3	Bit 2	'n' Number of Cycles	10 MHz T_{CLF} = 100 ns	8 MHz T_{CLF} = 125 ns	6 MHz T_{CLF} = 166 ns
0	0	1	5.00 MBps	4.00 MBps	3.01 MBps
0	1	2	3.33 MBps	2.67 MBps	2.01 MBps
1	0	3	2.50 MBps	2.00 MBps	1.51 MBps
1	1	4	2.00 MBps	1.60 MBps	1.21 MBps

Figure 5–7. Transfer Period Setting

Bit 0: Transfer Counter Extend

1 – Sets the length of the Transfer Byte Counter as 28 bits.

0 – Sets the length of the Transfer Byte Counter as 24 bits.

If this bit is set to 1, it is necessary to specify the MBC register bits 7 through 4 (TCE), when SELECT and TRANSFER commands are issued.

Transfer Mode Setting

The TMOD register determines the parameters for the DATA IN/OUT phase. So it follows that when the SPC is used in the TARGET mode, all settings to this register are completed prior to the time when the TARGET is ready to initiate the DATA IN/OUT phase.

When the SPC is operating in the INITIATOR mode, ensure that proper setting of the TMOD register is complete prior to the INITIATOR initiating the DATA IN/OUT phase.

Condition A:

Following completion of the SELECTION phase, when the MESSAGE phase occurs and prior to the COMMAND phase, follow this instruction:

Instruction: **TMOD register should be set prior to the Initiator issuing the TRANSFER command.**

Condition B:

Following completion of the SELECTION phase, when the COMMAND phase occurs and prior to the MESSAGE phase, follow this instruction:

Instruction: **The TMOD register should be set prior to resetting the ACK signal to receive the last byte in the MESSAGE IN phase (before issuing the Reset ACK command) when a synchronous data transfer message is transmitted at the end of the COMMAND phase.**

Condition C:

Following a RESELECTED interrupt, follow this instruction:

Instruction: **Set the TMOD register before issuing the Reset ACK command in the MESSAGE IN phase (IDENTIFY message).**

INTS Register – Interrupt Status Register

OP	7 (MSb)	6	5	4	3	2	1	0 (LSb)	P
R	Selec–ted	Resel–ected	Discon–nected	Command Complete	Service Required	Time Out	SPC Hardware Error	Reset Condi–tion	P
W	Reset Interrupt								—

Register Function

The INTS register is used to indicate the cause of an interrupt and reset it. An interrupt issued by the SPC (INTR pin) can be masked by bit 0 (INT Enable) of the SCTL register (except an interrupt whose cause is indicated at bit 0 [RESET condition]). To clear an interrupt, set 1 at the corresponding bit position in this register. Note that only the interrupt condition specified by 1 for that bit is reset. The bit positions having zeros remain unchanged (corresponding interrupt conditions are maintained). In this register, two or more interrupts may be reset at the same time.

Bit 7: Selected Interrupt

Bit 7 indicates that the SELECTION phase in SCSI has resulted in the SPC being selected by another bus device (INITIATOR). When the SELECTION phase is detected, the SPC checks the contents of the SCSI data bus. If the following conditions are satisfied, the SPC executes a response sequence on SCSI, then generates a selected interrupt.

(1)   The ID specified in the BDID register is selected.

(2)   Not more than two bits are set on the SCSI data bus (excluding the parity bit).

(3)   When parity checking is enabled, the parity bit value is correct.

In the SELECTION phase, the TEMP register holds the value of SCSI data bus. The SPC serves as a TARGET from the occurance of this interrupt until the Bus Release command is issued or the RESET condition is detected in SCSI. During this period the SPC asserts the BSY signal to SCSI. Before issuing the Bus Release command, be sure to reset the cause of this interrupt.

Bit 6: Reselected interrupt

Bit 6 indicates that the RESELECTION phase in SCSI has resulted in the SPC being reselected by another bus device (TARGET). When the RESELECTION phase is detected, the SPC checks the contents of the SCSI data bus. If the following conditions are satisfied, the SPC executes a response sequence on SCSI, then generates a reselected interrupt.

(1)   The ID specified in the BDID register is selected.

(2)   Not more than two bits are set on the SCSI data bus (excluding the parity bit).

(3)   When parity checking is enabled, a parity bit value is correct.

In the RESELECTION phase, the TEMP register holds the value of the SCSI data bus. The SPC serves as an INITIATOR from when this interrupt occurs until the disconnected interrupt occurs or the RESET condition is detected in SCSI. Before starting the transfer operation in SCSI, be sure to reset the cause of this interrupt. If the disconnected interrupt is indicated together with the reselected interrupt, reset both of these interrupts simultaneously.

Bit 5: Disconnected interrupt

Bit 5 indicates that the BUS FREE phase has been detected in SCSI when bit 7 (Bus Free Interrupt Enable) of the PCTL register is set to 1. Also, when the SPC serves as an INITIATOR, bit 5 indicates transition to the BUS FREE phase in SCSI. After this interrupt condition has occurred, the next SELECTION/RESELECTION phase may be executed in SCSI. However, the SPC does not respond to SCSI until this interrupt condition is reset. If the disconnected interrupt condition is detected during hardware transfer (Transfer command) execution with the SPC serving as an INITIATOR, the SCSI operation stops, but the SPC internal transfer sequence continues until one of the following events is encountered:

(1)   The internal data buffer register becomes empty in an input operation.

(2)   The data prefetch sequence to the internal data buffer register is completed in an output operation.

When a disconnected interrupt occurs, check the SSTS register to confirm that the transfer operation has been completed.

Bit 4: Command Complete Interrupt

Bit 4 indicates that the Select command/Transfer command operation has been completed.

(1)   Completion of Select command.

This interrupt indicates that the SPC has acknowledged a response (BSY signal) from the selected bus device in SELECTION/RESELECTION phase execution. It indicates that the SELECTION /RESELECTION phase has been completed in SCSI. The SPC serves as an INITIATOR after the SELECTION phase has been executed, and it serves as a TARGET after the RESELECTION phase has been executed.

(2)   Completion of Transfer command (when the SPC serves as a TARGET).

This interrupt indicates that the number of bytes transferred equals the byte count specified in the transfer byte counter. Or, in an input operation with bit 0 (Termination Mode) of the SCMD register set to 1, this interrupt indicates transfer stop due to parity error being detected in the data received from SCSI. In either case, this interrupt occurs after a check that the ACK signal for the REQ signal of the last byte is inactive on SCSI during asynchronous mode transfer. This interrupt also occurs after a check that the number of ACK signals received matches the number of REQ signals transmitted during synchronous mode transfer.

(3)   Completion of Transfer command (when the SPC serves as an INITIATOR).

When padded transfer mode is not specified, this interrupt indicates the byte count specified in the transfer byte counter has been completed. When padding mode transfer is performed, this interrupt indicates that the current transfer operation has been terminated due to another transfer phase requested in SCSI. In this case, the service required interrupt occurs at the same time. In the MESSAGE IN phase, this interrupt occurs while the ACK signal to the last byte is held active. Before resetting this interrupt, be sure to issue the Reset ACK/REQ command.

Bit 3: Service Required Interrupt

This interrupt indicates a request for MPU program intervention and occurs only if the SPC serving as an INITIATOR is put in either of the following conditions:

(1)   SPC has received the Transfer command, but cannot start the transfer operation because the transfer phase specified by bits 2 to 0 of the PCTL register does not match the one requested in SCSI.

(2)   The SPC has stopped the current hardware transfer operation (Transfer command) because of a request for another transfer phase in SCSI. In this case, the transfer operation in SCSI stops immediately, but the SPC internal transfer sequence continues until one of the following events is encountered:

> a) Input operation.
>   The internal data buffer register becomes empty.
>
> b) Output operation.
>   The data prefetch sequence to the internal data buffer register is completed.

Therefore, when this interrupt occurs, read out the SSTS register and check whether the SPC internal transfer operation is completed. If the service required interrupt occurs during an output operation, the data prefetched in the SPC internal data buffer register may remain in the data buffer register (not sent to SCSI). To determine how to handle the remaining data (up to eight bytes), see the interrupt processing procedure described below. When the service required interrupt occurs, the MPU program examines a transfer phase request from SCSI and executes the transfer operation using one of the following procedures. (Figure 5–8 and Figure 5–9 show examples of interrupt processing procedure.)

(1)   *Hardware transfer*

The MPU program specifies the transfer phase pattern requested by SCSI as indicated by bit 2 to 0 of the PCTL register, and reissues the Transfer command.

(2)   *Manual transfer*

If this interrupt occurs during an output operation, the remaining data in the SPC internal data buffer register may have to be preserved. In this case, with bit 3 (Intercept Transfer) of the SCMD register set to 1, perform manual transfer and reset the interrupt. When the interrupted original transfer phase (output) is requested again after manual transfer following the above given procedure, the suspended transfer operation can be restarted and the transfer of the remaining data held in the data buffer register can be completed.

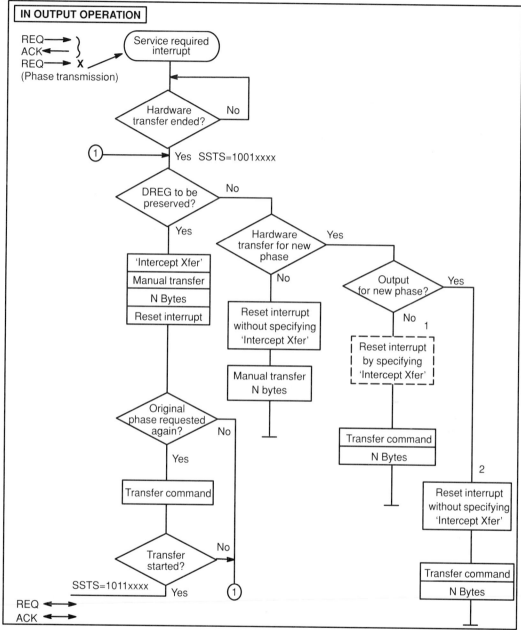

Figure 5–8.   Service Required Interrupt Processing Procedure (Output)

Notes: [1]An interrupt need not always be reset. The interrupt is reset automatically when the Transfer command starts hardware transfer.

Notes: [2]If the interrupt is reset, the data prefetched in the internal data buffer register (before a change of phase is detected) is lost.

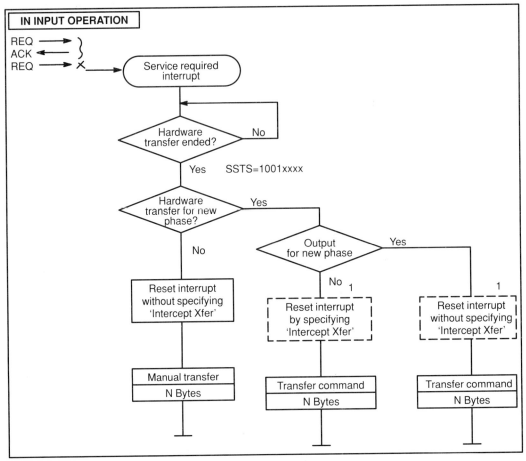

Figure 5–9. Service Required Interrupt Processing Procedure (Input)

Note: [1]An interrupt need not always be reset. The interrupt (service required) is reset automatically when the Transfer command starts hardware transfer.

Bit 2: Time-out Interrupt

This interrupt indicates that the selected bus device has not responded within the predetermined supervisory time after the SPC initiates the SELECTION/RESELECTION phase. (See Select command in SCMD register for details of the supervisory time setting procedure and the interrupt processing procedure.)

Bit 1: SPC Hardware Error Interrupt

This interrupt indicates that the SPC has detected one of the following error conditions in the SERR register:

(1)   TC parity error

(2)   Phase error

(3)   Short transfer period

(4)   Transfer offset error

See the SERR register for details of these errors. When this interrupt occurs, the SPC does not stop the operation being executed (for any error cause). Since the normal operational sequence and end report cannot always be guaranteed in this case, the MPU program must be used for SPC control and bus phase control of SCSI.

Figure 5–10, Figure 5–11, and Figure 5–12 show examples of error control procedures.

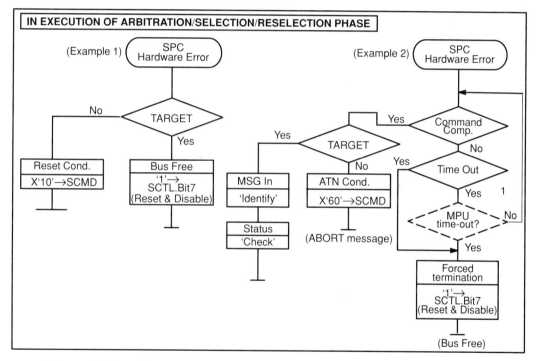

Figure 5–10.   Example of Control Procedure for SPC-Detected Error (1)

Note: [1]Normal SPC time-out supervision cannot always be guaranteed. Be sure to perform time supervision using the MPU program.

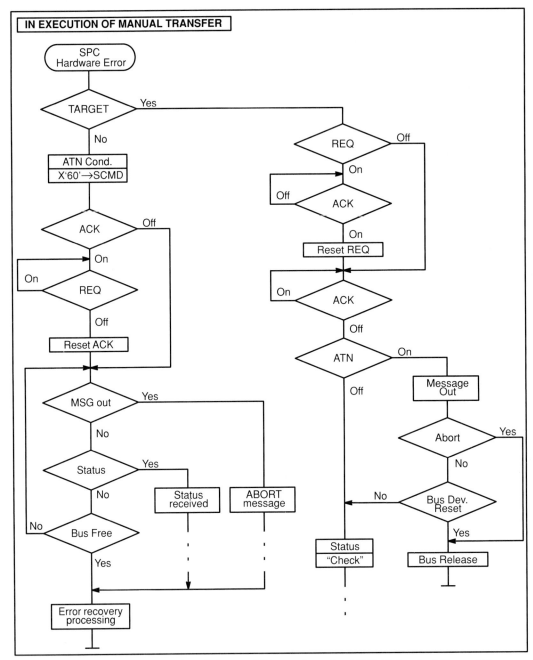

Figure 5–11. Example of Control Procedure for SPC-Detected Error (2)

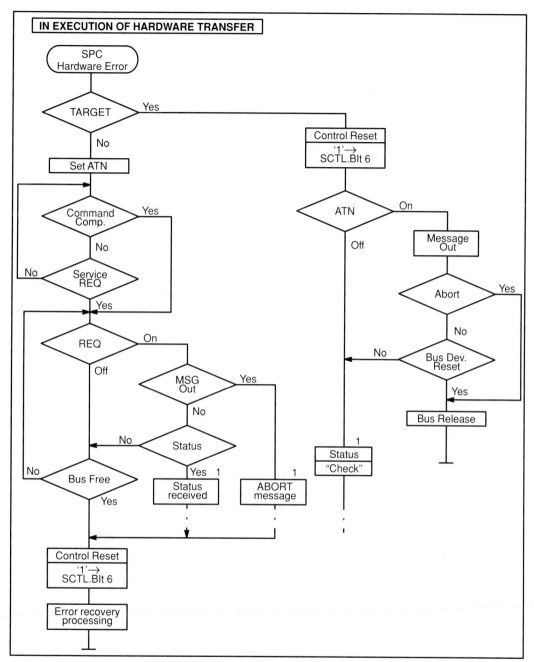

Figure 5–12. Example of Control Procedure for SPC-Detected Error (3)

Note: [1]Execute by manual transfer.

Bit 0: Reset Condition Interrupt

This interrupt indicates that the RESET condition has been detected in SCSI. Note that this interrupt cannot be masked. The reset condition persists for an unpredictable period of time. After making sure that bit 3 (Reset In) of the SSTS register becomes 0, the MPU must reset this interrupt condition. The reset condition interrupt may occur regardless of whether the SPC is connected with SCSI or not. When the SPC is connected with SCSI, occurrence of this interrupt causes the SPC to immediately deactivate a signal being sent to SCSI. Then the SPC proceeds to the BUS FREE phase. When the SPC is executing a command, occurrence of this interrupt causes the SPC to terminate its operation and reset its internal state. However, the following internal registers hold the control information unchanged:

(1)   BDID register

(2)   SCMD register

(3)   PCTL register

(4)   SCTL register

(5)   TMOD register

(6)   Transfer byte counter

Until this interrupt is reset, the SPC's internal reset state is maintained even if the RESET condition is released in SCSI. Therefore, the SPC does not respond even when a new bus phase (e.g., SELECTION) is executed in SCSI.

PSNS/ SDGC
Address #5

PSNS Register – Phase Sense Register

OP	7 (MSb)	6	5	4	3	2	1	0 (LSb)	P
R	REQ	ACK	ATN	SEL	BSY	MSG	C/D	I/O	P

Register Function

The phase sense register is used to determine the status of the SCSI and can be read out at any time. When bit 5 (Diagnostic Mode) of the SCTL register is set to 0, the PSNS register indicates the control signal status on SCSI (input signals to the SPC).

Read Operation

Bit	Signal	SPC input pins
7	REQ	REQI
6	ACK	ACKI
5	ATN	ATNI
4	SEL	SELI
3	BSY	BSYI
2	MSG	MSGI
1	C/D	C/DI
0	I/O	I/OI

A read from this register is allowed at any time, regardless of the SPC condition. Bit 5 (ATN) of this register indicates the ATN signal status on SCSI. When the SPC serves as a TARGET, receipt of the ATN signal is indicated in this register but does not have any effect on other operations. The MPU program examines the ATN signal status in sequence and responds to the ATTENTION condition from SCSI at the following times.

(1)   When a selected interrupt occurs.

(2)   When the RESELECTION phase has been completed.

(3)   When the Transfer command has been completed.

(4)   During execution of the Transfer command.

When the ATN signal is detected, the Transfer Pause command can halt the transfer operation for transition to the MESSAGE OUT phase.

(5)   During execution of manual transfer.

When bit 5 (Diagnostic Mode) of the SCTL register is set to 1, the PSNS register indicates the status of control signals sent from the SPC to SCSI. In the pseudo SCSI operation using the SDGC register, the PSNS register can be used to check the SCSI control signal status.

PSNS/ SDGC
Address #5

SDGC Register – SCSI Diagnostic Control Register

OP	7 (MSb)	6	5	4	3	2	1	0 (LSb)	P
W	Diag REQ	Diag ACK	Xfer enable[1]	—	Diag BSY	Diag MSG	Diag C/D	Diag I/O	—

Note: [1]This feature is available only for the MB89351/352 parts.

Register Function

The SDGC register is used to operate the SPC in the diagnostic mode (with bit 5 Diagnostic Mode of the SCTL register set to 1). To simulate the SCSI operation, the SDGC register bits are used as having alternative SCSI control signal lines. In diagnostic mode, the SDGC register is used to check SPC internal operation. The Diagnostic Mode stops signaling to the physical SCSI bus and nullifies input signals from the SCSI bus except the data bus signals. The SPC internal operation can be performed in the ordinary manner. To check SPC internal operation, the MPU can manipulate the SDGC register bits to generate input signals to and from SCSI.

The following bus phases can be simulated:

(1)   BUS FREE

(2)   ARBITRATION (Always win)

(3)   SELECTION (For INITIATE operation)

(4)   RESELECTION (For TARGET operation)

(5)   Information transfer (Input data manipulation not allowed in an input operation).

Bit 5 is used as an enable bit for issuing an interrupt signal (INTR) when the SPC FIFO needs servicing (feature available on MB89351/352 devices). During a SCSI input operation, an interrupt will occur when the SPC has data to be read. During a SCSI output operation, an interrupt will occur when the SPC needs a byte to be written into the FIFO. Bit 5 can be SET/RESET during NORMAL and DIAGNOSTIC mode of SPC operation. This bit is write only; it will be read back as '0' regardless of its setting.

Initialization

The SPC is in the reset state when the input to $\overline{RST}$ pin is low (hardware reset) or bit 7 (Reset and Disable) of the SCTL register is set to 1. SPC-SCSI operation is disabled until the SPC reset state is released. The MPU program releases the reset state after initializing the SPC internal registers. The following SPC internal registers remain unchanged even in the SPC reset state.

(1)   BDID register

(2)   TMOD register

(3)   Transfer byte counter

(4)   SCMD register

(5)   PCTL register

(6)   TEMP register (for sending)

When the power is turned on, the contents of these internal registers are unpredictable even though hardware reset ($\overline{RST}$ input = low) is executed. After $\overline{RST}$ input is released, the MPU program initializes the SPC as shown in Figure 5–13.

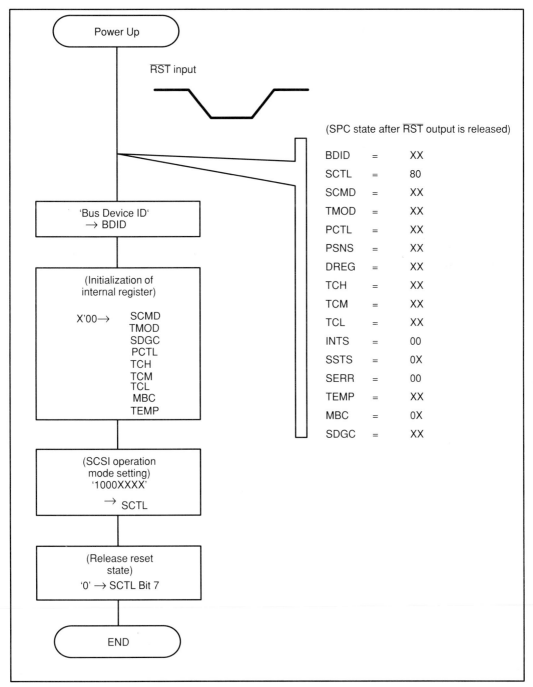

Figure 5–13.   SPC Initialization (at power-up)

SSTS
Address
#6

SSTS Register – SPC Status (Register)

OP	7 (MSb)	6	5	4	3	2	1	0 (LSb)	P
R	CONNECTED INIT	TARG	SPC Busy	Xfer in Progress	SCSI Reset In	TC=0	DREG FULL	Status EMPTY	P

Register Function

The SSTS register indicates the SPC internal status, which can be read out at any time.

Bit 7 and 6:   Connected (INIT, TARG)

These bits indicate the connecting status between the SPC and SCSI bus.

Bit 7: INIT	Bit 6: TARG	State
1	0	SPC serves as an INITIATOR: (1) During execution of the SELECTION phase and after its completion. (2) After a reselected interrupt.
0	1	SPC serves as a TARGET: (1) During execution of the RESELECTION phase and at its completion. (2) After a selected interrupt.
1	1	Undefined

Bit 5:   SPC Busy

Bit 5 indicates that a command is being executed or is waiting to be executed.

Bit 4:   Transfer in Progress

Bit 4 indicates that a hardware transfer operation is being executed or the SCSI is requesting an information transfer phase.

Bit 3:   SCSI Reset In

Bit 3 indicates that the SCSI RST signal is active.

Bit 2:   TC = 0 (Transfer Counter Zero)

Bit 2 indicates that the transfer byte counter (TCH, TCM, TCL) has reached 0.

Bits 1 and 0:   DREG Status (Full, Empty)

These bits indicate the status of the internal data buffer register. When executing a hardware transfer operation in program transfer mode, determine the data buffer register access timing by using these bit values.

Bit 1: FULL	Bit 0: EMPTY	Data Buffer Register Status
0	0	Holds 1 to 7 bytes of data
0	1	Empty
1	0	Holds 8 bytes of data, leaving no free space
1	1	Undefined

SPC Status

SPC status is represented by combinations of status bits 7 to 4 of this register. Table 5–4 lists the combination of these bits and SPC status.

Table 5–4.   SPC Operating Status Indications

SSTS Register				SPC Operating Status
Bit 7: INIT	**Bit 6: TARG**	**Bit 5: SPC Busy**	**Bit 4: Xfer in Progress**	
0	0	0	0	SPC is not connected with SCSI. SPC does not hold a command waiting to be executed.
0	0	1	0	SPC is not connected with SCSI. SPC holds the Select command, which is waiting for BUS FREE phase or SPC is executing ARBITRATION phase.
0	1	0	0	SPC serves as a TARGET. No operation is being executed in SCSI or manual transfer is being executed.
0	1	1	0	SPC is executing RESELECTION phase on SCSI.
0	1	1	1	SPC serves as a TARGET. Hardware transfer operation (Transfer command) is being executed.
1	0	0	0	SPC serves as an INITIATOR. No operation is being executed in SCSI or manual transfer is being executed.
1	0	0	1	SPC serves as an INITIATOR. Although SPC has received a REQ signal from SCSI, it is not ready to start transfer operation because no Transfer command has been issued or transfer phase does not match.
1	0	1	0	SPC is executing the SELECTION phase on SCSI.
1	0	1	1	SPC serves as an INITIATOR. Hardware transfer operation (Transfer command) is being executed.

SERR
Address
#7

SERR Register – SPC Error Status Register

OP	7 (MSb)	6	5	4	3	2	1	0 (LSb)	P
R	Data Error		'0'[1] Xfer out[2]	'0'	TC Parity Error	Phase Error	Short Xfer Period	Xfer Offset Error	P
	SCSI	SPC							

Notes: [1]Only on Asynchronous Protocol Controllers (MB89351/352).
Notes: [2]To be reset (including the INTR signal) to satisfy the data request by writing or reading to the SPC FIFO (DREG).

Register Function

The SERR register provides details of an error detected in the SPC. An SPC hardware error interrupt occurs if an error is indicated at any bit from 3 to 0.

Bits 7 and 6:   Data Error

These bits indicate that a parity error has been detected in the transferred data during transfer phase execution in SCSI. Table 5–5 lists the data error indication bit patterns and the relevant SPC operations. When changing the transfer phase in SCSI, these error indication bits must be reset.

Bit 5:   Xfer Out

When bit 5 of SDGC is equal to 1 in program transfer mode, the interrupt signal (INTR) is output for a data request. This bit is a flag indicating the data request.

In the MPU, this bit is referenced in the interrupt routine to perform data transfer according to the data requests.

Table 5–5. Data Error Indication Bit Patterns in Transfer Phase

Bit 7	Bit 6	
Data Error		SPC Operations
SCSI	SPC	
0	0	No parity error was detected in the transferred data.
0	1	During execution of an output operation in hardware transfer mode, a parity error was detected in the data to be sent to SCSI.
		The parity is checked regardless of the value of bit 3 (Parity Enable) of the SCTL register. The erroneous data (parity bit value) is corrected and then sent to SCSI.
1	1	A parity error was detected in the data received from SCSI during an input operation
		The parity is checked only when bit 3 (Parity Enable) of the SCTL register is set to 1. After an error is detected, the parity bit is corrected. If the SPC serving as an INITIATOR detects this error during hardware transfer execution, it generates an ATN signal to SCSI. (See Figure 5–2) In this case, the MPU program must reset this error condition before the ATN signal is reset.
		If the SPC serving as a TARGET detects this error during hardware transfer execution, it follows the specification at bit 0 (Termination Mode) of the SCMD register. See SCMD register for details.
1	0	Undefined

Bit 3: TC Parity Error

Bit 3 indicates that a parity error occurred while the transfer byte counter (TCH, TCM, TCL) was being decremented.

Bit 2: Phase Error

When the SPC serves as an INITIATOR, the transfer phase has been changed in SCSI during hardware transfer mode operation (service required interrupt occurs). In this case, bit 2 indicates that:

(1)   The new phase is a synchronous transfer mode DATA IN phase.

(2)   The REQ signal has been received two or more times before the MPU program completed interrupt processing and issued the Transfer command for the new phase. In this case, the SPC cannot receive data and return the ACK signal normally.

Bit 1: Short Transfer Period

Bit 1 indicates that the REQ/ACK signal (input signal to REQI/ACKI pin) has a cycle exceeding the specified input range (see Figure 5–14). If this error occurs, the transfer sequence executed by the SPC is not guaranteed.

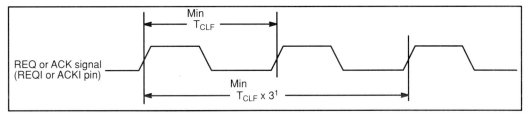

Figure 5–14. Specified Input Cycle of REQ/ACK Signal

Note: $^1T_{CLF}$: A cycle of the clock signal supplied to SPC.

Bit 0: Transfer Offset Error

Bit 0 indicates that one of the following errors has been detected during synchronous transfer mode. (The offset value referred to below denotes the REQ/ACK maximum offset value specified in the TMOD register).

(1)   When SPC serves as a TARGET.

- The number of ACK signals received exceeds that of REQ signals transmitted.

- The number of REQ signals transmitted exceeds the offset value (SPC malfunction).

(2)   When SPC serves as an INITIATOR.

- The number of REQ signals received exceeds the offset value.

- The number of ACK signals transmitted exceeds that of REQ signals received (SPC malfunction).

If this error occurs, the transfer sequence executed by the SPC is not guaranteed.

Error Reset

To reset an error condition in the SERR register, do one of the following:

(1)   Generate SCSI RESET condition (X10 $\rightarrow$ SCMD).

(2)   Reset and disable (Bit 7 of SCTL register).

(3)   Control reset (Bit 6 of SCTL register).

(4)   Interrupt (SPC hardware error) reset ($X02 \rightarrow INTS$)
        Bits 7 and 6 (Data Error) of this register do not cause an interrupt, but can be
        reset by this setup.

PCTL
Address
#8

PCTL Register – Phase Control Register

OP	7 (MSb)	6	5	4	3	2	1	0 (LSb)	P
R / W	Bus Free Interrupt Enable			'0'		MSG Out	C/D Out	I/O Out	P

Register Function

The PCTL register is used to control the transfer phases; i.e., Data, Command, Status, and Message phases.

Bit 7:   Bus Free Interrupt Enable

With bit 7 set to 1, detection of the BUS FREE phase on the SCSI causes a disconnected interrupt to occur. To prevent an undesired interrupt from occurring, be sure to set bit 7 to 0 in the following cases:

(1)   When issuing the Select command.

(2)   When resetting a 'disconnected' interrupt.

Bit 2:   MSG Out

Bit 1:   C/D Out

Bit 0:   I/O Out

When the SPC serves as a TARGET, specify the information transfer phase to be executed in SCSI. These bit values are sent to SCSI as MSG, C/D, and I/O signals.

When the SPC acts as an INITIATOR, specify the pattern indicating the transfer phase to be executed. Before executing the transfer operation, the specified transfer phase pattern is compared with a bus phase actually requested by the TARGET. If they match, the transfer operation is initiated. Table 5–6 shows how to set a transfer command.

Also, use bit 0 (I/O OUT) to specify SELECT or RESELECT operation when the select command is issued to the SPC. See SELECT command for details.

Table 5–6. Transfer Phase Setting

Bit 2 MSG Out	Bit 1 C/D Out	Bit 0 I/O Out	SCSI Transfer Phase
0	0	0	Data Out
0	0	1	Data In
0	1	0	Command
0	1	1	Status
1	0	0	Unused
1	0	1	Unused
1	1	0	Message Out
1	1	1	Message In

MBC
Address
#9

MBC Register – Modified Byte Control Register

OP	7 (MSb)	6	5	4	3	2	1	0 (LSb)	P
R		'0'			Bit 3	MBC 2	1	0	P

Register Function

The MBC register controls the data count during transfer between the SPC internal data buffer register and the MPU (Program Transfer mode) or external buffer memory (DMA mode). When data are written into the TCL register, its four low-order bits are set as an initial value for the MBC register. In an output operation, data are prefetched into the SPC internal data buffer register. Each time one byte is prefetched, the MBC register is decreased by one.

Data prefetch stops when the transfer byte counter is decreased below 15 and the MBC register reaches 0. In an input operation, data received from SCSI is stored in the internal data buffer register. Each time data is sent to the MPU or external buffer memory, the MBC register is decreased. The difference between the transfer byte counter and the MBC register corresponds to the byte count of data remaining in the internal data buffer register.

> **Note:** *This register must not be read while the SPC is executing a DMA mode transfer operation.*

DREG
Address
#A

DREG Data Buffer Register

OP	7 (MSb)	6	5	4	3	2	1	0 (LSb)	P
R/W	Internal Data Register (8 Bytes FIFO)								
	7	6	5	4	3	2	1	0	P

Register Function

The SPC's internal data buffer register consists of eight bytes and operates on the FIFO principle. When executing the Transfer command in Program Transfer Mode, MPU transfers data using this register. Figure 5–15 shows the DREG access procedure used in Program Transfer Mode. It is recommended not to attempt the access procedure more than the number of times required.

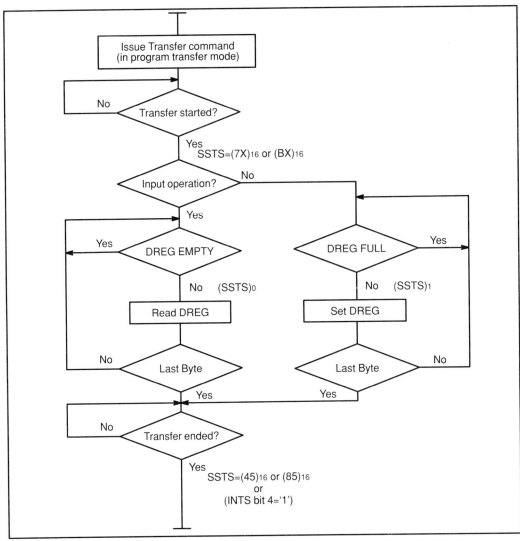

Figure 5–15. DREG Access Procedure In Program Transfer Mode

TEMP
Address
#B

TEMP REGISTER – Temporary Register

OP	7 (MSb)	6	5	4	3	2	1	0 (LSb)	P
R	7	6	Temporary Data (Input: From SCSI)				1	0	P
W	7	6	Temporary Data (Output: To SCSI)				1	0	P

For the R row: 7, 6, 5, 4, 3, 2, 1, 0, P
For the W row: 7, 6, 5, 4, 3, 2, 1, 0, P

Register Function

The TEMP register is used for controlling the SCSI data bus, except when hardware transfer is executed. It consists of two bytes, each of which is dedicated exclusively to receiving/sending data.

(1)   *Data receiving element (read only).*

a)   When a SELECTION/RESELECTION phase is detected in SCSI, the contents on the SCSI data bus are saved in the TEMP register. If a selected/reselected interrupt occurs, a bus device can be identified by the TEMP register contents. Read this register before resetting the selection or reselection interrupt status bit.

b)   For a manual transfer input operation, the contents of the SCSI data bus are saved in the timing sequence shown in Figure 5–16.

(2)   *Data sending element (write only).*

a)   Before issuing the Select command, set the contents to be sent to the SCSI data bus in the SELECTION/RESELECTION phase.

b)   For a manual transfer output operation, set the data to be sent out.

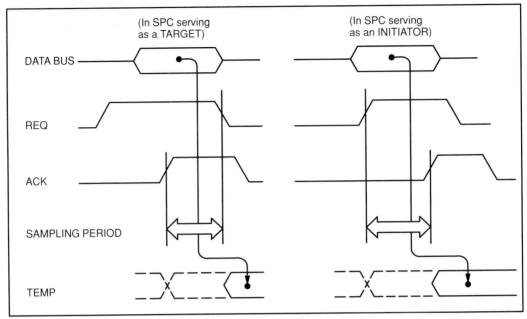

Figure 5–16.　Data Bus Save in Manual Transfer Input Operation

TCH, TCM, TCL

Address #C, D, E

(TCH, TCM, TCL) – Transfer Byte Counter, High, Middle, and Low

OP	7 (MSb)	6	5	4	3	2	1	0 (LSb)	P
R／W			TCH: Transfer Counter (MSB)						
	23	22	21	20	19	18	17	16	P
R／W			TCM: Transfer Counter (2nd Byte)						
	15	14	13	12	11	10	9	8	P
R／W			TCL: Transfer Counter (LSB)						
	7	6	5	4	3	2	1	0	P

Register Function

The transfer byte counter consists of three bytes and functions as a down counter. In execution of a hardware transfer operation, it is decreased by one each time one byte of data is transferred over SCSI. It indicates the remaining byte count of data to be transferred. In the Select command execution, this counter operates as a response waiting time supervisory timer and sequence control counter. See Select command and Transfer command for transfer byte counter initialization. While the transfer byte counter is operating, do not carry out a read/write.

> **Note:** *Do not read/write these registers while a transfer operation is occuring. If necessary, use the "TC = 0" bit in the SSTS register to determine when the transfer count has reached zero.*

EXBF
Address
#F

EXBF – External Buffer Register for Synchronous Controllers only

OP	7 (MSb)	6	5	4	3	2	1	0 (LSb)	P
R/W				External Buffer					P
	7	6	5	4	3	2	1	0	

Register Function

This register's address is reserved for access from the MPU data bus (D7 to D0, DP) to the DMA data bus (HDB7 to HDB0, HDBP). It does not not exist as an internal register in SPC but provides a pathway between buses. As shown in Figure 5–17, the MPU program can execute a write/read to/from the external buffer memory by using this virtual register.

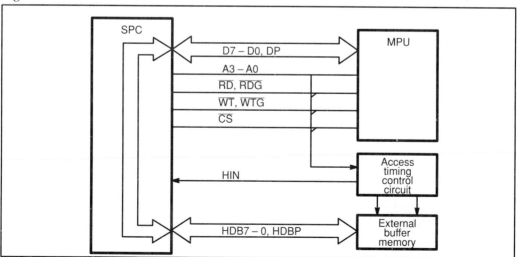

Figure 5–17.   Access from MPU to External Buffer Memory

Devices without a separate DMA data bus do not have this register. Examples of SPCs without this register are MB89351 and MB89352. This register is normally used by the MPU to load/unload an external memory buffer before/after (write to SCSI/read from SCSI) a DMA transfer.

Chapter 6

EXAMPLES OF EXTERNAL CIRCUIT CONNECTIONS

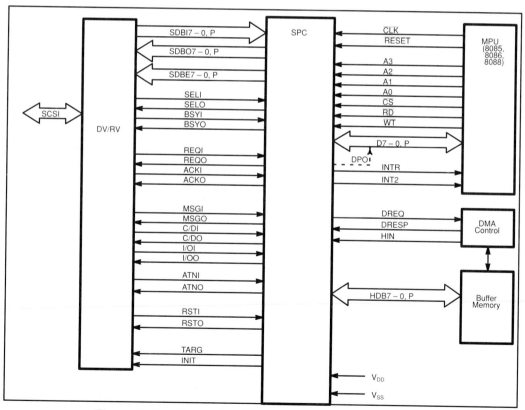

Figure 6–1.   Example of External Circuit Connections

External Circuit Blocks

The external circuit configuration depends on the application environment, intended purpose, and required performance. Examples of external circuit block applications that can be connected with MB87035/36 SPC are shown in Figures 6–2 and 6–3.

SCSI Driver/Receiver Circuits

Single-Ended Type

Table 6–1 lists the major components of a single-ended type SCSI driver/receiver circuit. Figure 6–2 shows a example of a connection of an SPC and the SCSI single-ended type driver/receiver circuits.

Table 6–1. Major Components of Single-Ended Type SCSI Driver/Receiver Circuit (Example)

Component	Part No.	Mfg.	Characteristics	Qty
REQ/ACK signal driver	MB412 [1]	Fujitsu	3-state buffer circuit 2 circuits, DIP 14	1
REQ/ACK signal receiver	MB413 [2] Resistor Resistor Capacitor	Fujitsu — — —	4 circuits, DIP 16 390 Ω ±2% 1/4 W 200 Ω ±2% 1/4 W 0.1 μF/50 V Ceramic	1 1 1 1
Other signal driver	MB463 [3]	Fujitsu	Open-collector buffer circuit 4 circuits, DIP 14	4
Other signal receiver	74LS240	Fujitsu TI	Schmitt trigger inverter 8 circuits, DIP 20	2
Terminator (Required only when the driver/receiver is located at either end of SCSI)	—	—	(Signal) +5 V 200 Ω 330 Ω	18 elements

Notes: [1] The MB412 is compatible with the SN7519.

[2] The MB413 is compatible with the Am26LS32.

[3] The MB463 is compatible with the SN7438.

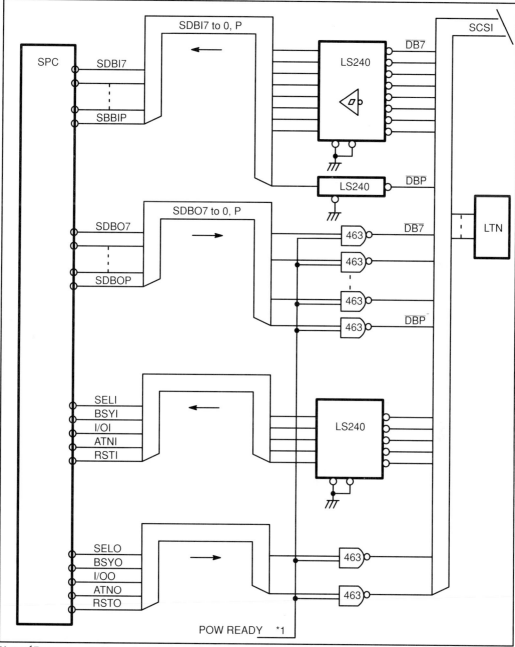

Note: [1]Recommended to protect against noise generated at power on/off.

Figure 6–2.   Example of Single-Ended Type SCSI Driver/Receiver Circuit

Continued on following page

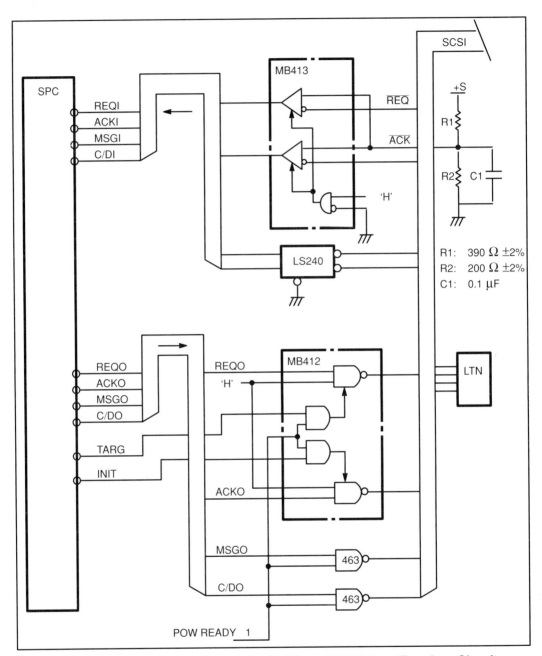

Figure 6–2. Example of Single-Ended Type SCSI Driver/Receiver Circuit

Note: [1]Recommended to protect against noise generated at power on/off.

Differential Type

Table 6–2 lists the major components of a differential type SCSI driver/receiver. Figure 6–3 shows an example of the connection of an SPC and the SCSI differential type driver/receiver circuit.

Table 6–2.   Major Components of Differential Type SCSI Driver/Receiver Circuit (*example*)

Component	Part No.	Mfr.	Characteristics	Qty
Driver/receiver (Common to all signals)	SN75176 MB561	TI Fujitsu	Differential transceiver 1DV +1RV/Dip 8	18
Terminator (Required only when the driver/receiver is located at either end of SCSI)	—	—	(Positive signal) (Negative signal) +5 330 Ω 150 Ω 330 Ω	18 element

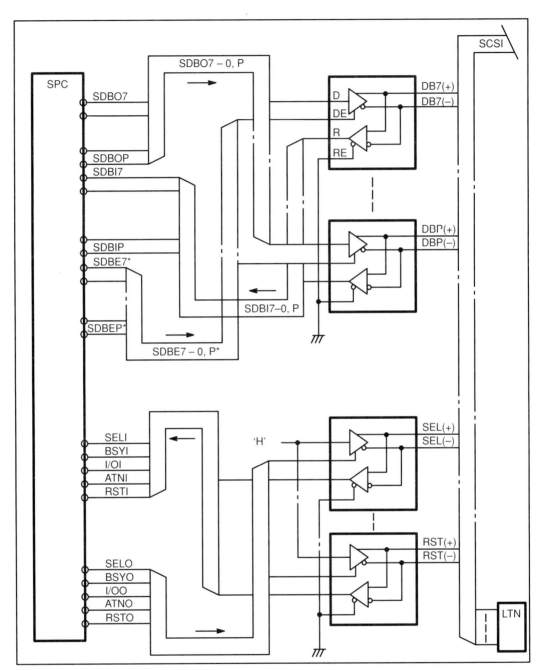

Figure 6–3.　Example of Differential Type SCSI Driver/Receiver Circuit

Note: *This signal is found only in the MB87035/36 SPCs.

Continued on following page

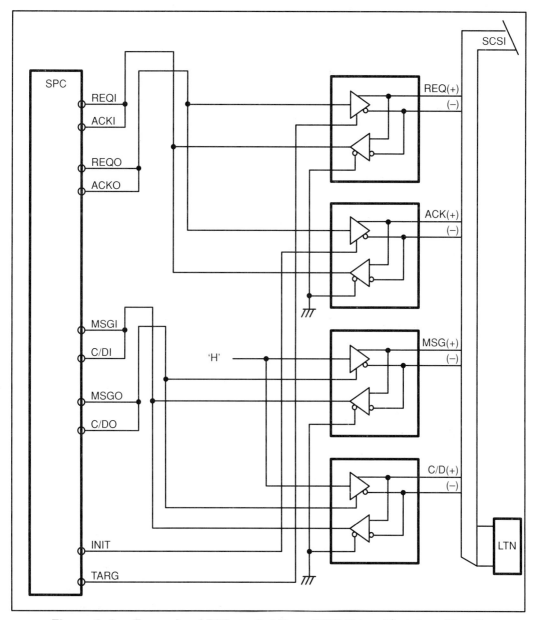

Figure 6–3.   Example of Differential Type SCSI Driver/Receiver Circuit

External Data Buffer

To provide a buffer area for high-speed data transfer or a temporary storage for data to be transferred, the external data buffer memory can be connected to the SPC as shown in Figure 6–1.

In this case, a buffer control circuit is required to control the timing of data transfer between the SPC and external buffer memory. To execute the transfer phase on SCSI, specify DMA Transfer Mode for the SPC. The SPC accesses the external buffer memory with the timing sequences shown in Figures 6–4 and 6–5. Data is transferred via the DMA data bus lines HDB7 to HDB0, HDBP. The transfer direction must be specified externally using the HIN signal. When requesting access to the external buffer memory, the SPC makes the DREQ signal active.

In an input operation, the DREQ signal is sent out when the SPC internal data buffer register holds data (8 bytes) received from SCSI. In an output operation, the DREQ signal is sent out when data corresponding to the byte count specified in the transfer byte counter is not all prefetched, and when the internal data buffer register has free byte locations available. The external buffer control circuit must return the DRESP signal in response to the DREQ signal on completion of transferring each byte. DRESP is a pulse signal whose trailing edge is used to indicate the end of transfer. The DREQ signal is held active as long as the above conditions exist in the SPC (this signal is not a transfer request signal for each byte). The access interface signals (DREQ, DRESP, HIN, HDB7 to HDB0, HDBP) to the external memory are asynchronous with an SPC clock signal supplied to the $\overline{\text{CLK}}$ pin.

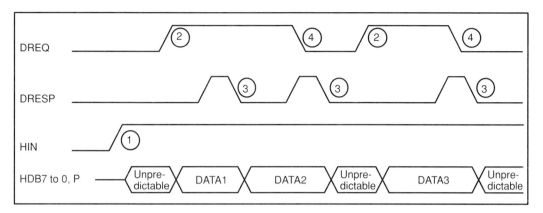

Figure 6–4.   Transfer with External Data Buffer (input operation)

Notes: 1 HIN signal puts the DMA data bus (HDB7 to 0, P) in an output mode. However, the
value on the DMA data bus is unpredictable until data is loaded into the SPC internal
data buffer register from SCSI

2 After receiving data from SCSI, the SPC issues the DREQ signal (transfer request) to the
external buffer memory. At this time, valid data is placed on the DMA data bus.

3 Data on the DMA data bus is held until the trailing edge of the DRESP signal.

4 After the DRESP signal is received, valid data is unloaded from the SPC internal data
buffer register. Then, the DREQ signal becomes inactive to stop transfer with the external
buffer memory until the next data becomes available.

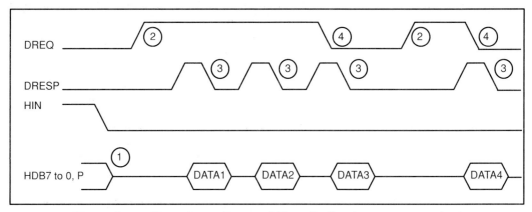

Figure 6–5.   Transfer to External Data Buffer (output operation)

Notes: 1 As long as the HIN signal is low, the DMA data bus (HDB7 to 0, P) is in an input mode.

2 A transfer request (DREQ) signal is issued when the SPC internal data buffer register has free byte locations available for prefetching data.

3 The external buffer control circuit puts data onto the DMA data bus and also sends the DRESP signal in response. On the trailing edge of the DRESP signal, the SPC loads data from the DMA bus into the internal data buffer register.

4 When no free location is available in the SPC internal data buffer register, the DREQ signal becomes inactive. Then, transfer from the external buffer memory is stopped until the next data prefetch becomes available. The data buffer register will be continuously accessed from the SCSI bus side until the REQ signal coming in is stopped.

Chapter 7

MB 87033B
PRODUCT PROFILE

MB87033B
SCSI Protocol Controller (SPC)
with On-Chip Drivers/Receivers

Edition 1.0
September 1989

GENERAL DESCRIPTION

The MB87033B SCSI Protocol Controller (SPC) is a CMOS LSI circuit specifically designed to control a Small Computer Systems Interface (SCSI). The MB87033B establishes the Fujitsu SPC family of protocol controllers by providing software enhancements and other functional features that will meet all facets of the SCSI specification (ANSI X 3.131-1986).

To achieve optimum performance and interface flexibility, the MB87033B provides an 8-byte First-In First-Out (FIFO) data buffer register and a 28-bit transfer byte counter which allows burst transfers of up to 256 megabytes. To improve programming requirements, "Attention Detect" and "Arbitration Fail" interrupts are provided and on-chip driver/receiver circuits simplify interface connections. Data transfers can be executed in either the asynchronous or synchronous mode with a maximum offset of 8 bytes.

SCSI Compatibility

- Supports all mandatory commands, many optional commands, and some extended commands of SCSI specification (ANSI X 3.131, 1986)
- Software compatible with MB8703X and MB8935X SPCs
- Serves as either INITIATOR or TARGET

Data Bus

- Independent buses for CPU and DMA controller

Transfer Modes

- Asynchronous
- Synchronous mode transfers with programmable offset of up to eight bytes (8 Byte FIFO)

Data Transfer Speed

- Up to a maximum of 5 megabytes/sec

Selectable Operating Modes

- DMA transfer
- Program transfer
- Manual transfer
- Diagnostic

Interface

- On-chip, single-ended Drivers/Receivers
- Guaranteed to sink 48mA regardless of the number of outputs simultaneously asserted.

Enhancements

- On-chip parity generation
- Attention condition detect interrupt
- Arbitration fail interrupt

Clock Requirements

- 10 MHz clock

Technology/Power Requirements

- Silicon-gate CMOS
- Single +5 V power supply

Available Packaging

- 84-pin plastic leadless chip carrier
- 80-pin plastic flat package

ABSOLUTE MAXIMUM RATINGS[1]

Rating	Symbol	Values		Unit
		Min.	Max.	
Supply Voltage	V_{DD}	$V_{SS}{}^{2} -0.3$	6.0	V
Input Voltage	V_I	$V_{SS}{}^{2} -0.3$	$V_{DD} + 0.3$	V
Output Voltage[2]	V_O	$V_{SS}{}^{2} -0.3$	$V_{DD} + 0.3$	V
Storage Temperature (Ceramic)	T_{STG}	-65	$+125$	$^{\circ}C$

Notes: 1 Permanent device damage may occur if the above **Absolute Maximum Ratings** are exceeded.
Functional operation should be restricted to the conditions as detailed in the operational sections of
this data sheet. Exposure to absolute maximum rating conditions for extended periods may affect
device reliability.

2 $V_{SS} = 0V$.

3 Not more than one output may be shorted at a time for a maximum duration of one second.

MB87033B BLOCK DIAGRAM

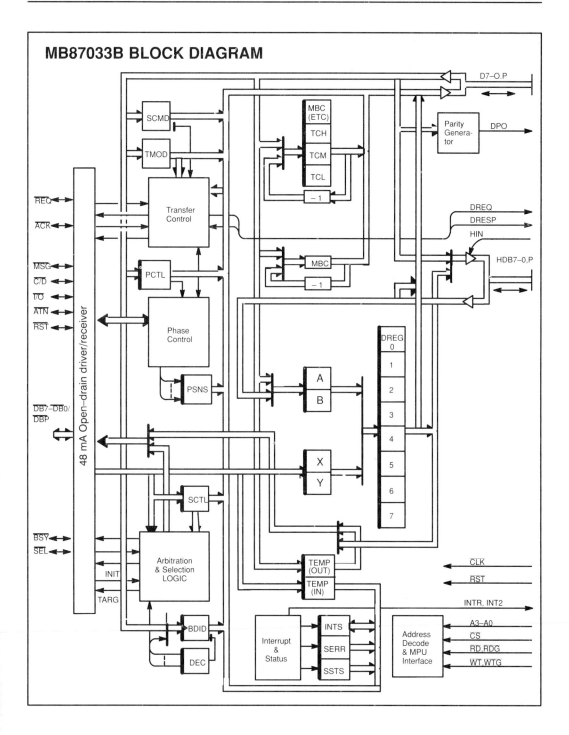

PIN ASSIGNMENTS

80-Pin Plastic Flat Package

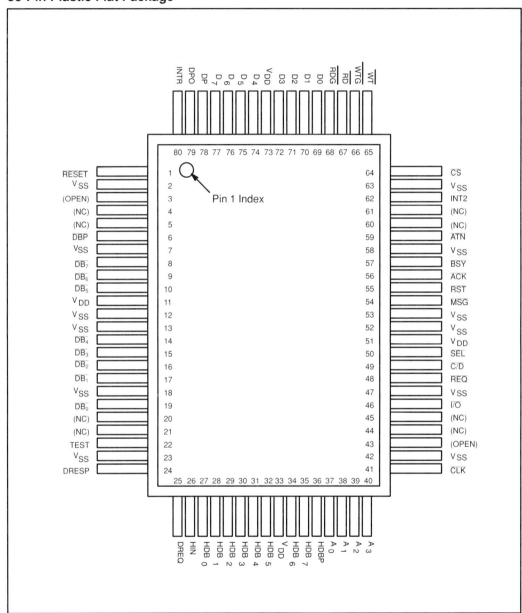

PIN ASSIGNMENTS

84-Pin Plastic Leadless Chip Carrier

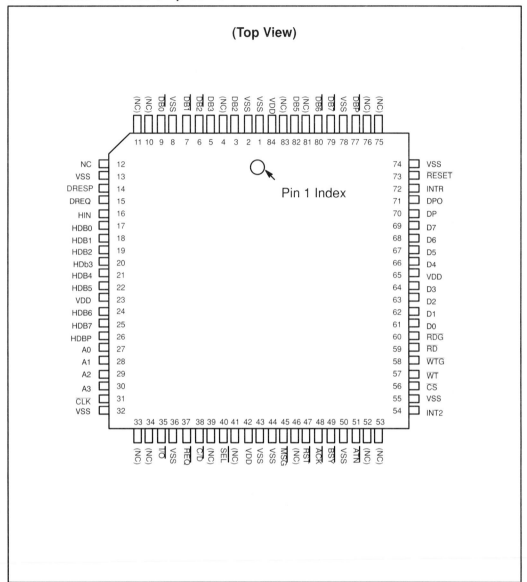

PIN DESCRIPTIONS

Pin Number		Designator	Function
FPT	**PLCC**		
1	73	RESET	When set to the active-low state, an asynchronous reset signal that clears all internal circuits of the SPC.
2,7, 12,13 18,23 42,47 52,53 58,63	1,2 8,13 32,36 43,44 50,55 74,78	V_{SS}	Power supply ground.
3,43	—	Open	Reserved. (Note: Do not make external connections to these pins.)
4,5 20,21 44,45 60,61	4,10 11,12 33,34 39,41 46,52 53,75 76,81,83	NC	No internal connection. (Note: These pins must be open connections at all times.)
8 9 10 14 15 16 17 19 6	79 80 82 3 5 6 7 9 77	DB7 DB6 DB5 DB4 DB3 DB2 DB1 DB0 DBP	Inputs/outputs for the SCSI data bus; these I/O pins connect directly to the SCSI connector. DB7 is the MSB; DB0 is the LSB. DBP is an odd parity bit.
11,33 51,73	23,42 65,84	VDD	+5V power supply.
22		TEST	Reserved for test functions. (Note. Do not make external connections to these pins.)
24	14	DRESP	DRESP is a response signal to the data transfer request signal DREQ. The DRESP pin must be refreshed with an applied pulse after each byte of data is transferred. In the DMA mode, DRESP is used as a timing signal for completion of a data-byte transfer.

Continued on following page

PIN DESCRIPTIONS

Pin Number		Designator	Function
FPT	**PLCC**		
25	15	DREQ	When executing a data transfer cycle in the DMA mode, DREQ is used to indicate a request for a data transfer between the SPC and external buffer memory. In the DMA mode, routing of data is as shown below. **Output Operation:** External buffer memory to SPC to SCSI bus. **Input Operation:** SCSI bus to SPC to external buffer memory. In an output operation, DREQ becomes active to request a data transfer to the external buffer memory when the FIFO contains valid data.
26	16	HIN	Indicates direction of transmission along data bus lines HDB0-HDB7 and HDBP in the DMA transfer mode. To be executed, direction of transmission must be properly coordinated with internal operation of the SPC. When HIN is low (inactive), the data bus lines are placed in the high-impedance state (input mode). When HIN is high (active) all bus lines are switched to the output mode.
35 34 32 31 30 29 28 27 36	25 24 22 21 20 19 18 17 26	HDB7 HDB6 HDB5 HDB4 HDB3 HDB2 HDB1 HDB0 HDBP	3-state bidirectional data bus for transferring data to or from the external buffer memory in the DMA mode. As shown below, the direction of data transmission depends on the HIN input signal. **HIN** **HDBn** **Operation** L Input Mode Output H Output Mode Input
37–40	27–30	A0–A3	Address input signals for selecting an internal register in the SPC. The MSB is A3; the LSB is A0. When $\overline{CS}$ is active low, read/write is enabled and an internal register is selected by these address inputs via data bus lines D0-D7 and DP.
41	31	$\overline{CLK}$	Input clock for controlling internal operations and data-transfer speeds of SPC.

Continued on following page

PIN DESCRIPTIONS

Pin Number		Designator	Function
FPT	PLCC		
57 50 48 56 54 49 46 59 55	49 40 37 48 45 38 35 51 47	$\overline{BSY}$ $\overline{SEL}$ $\overline{REQ}$ $\overline{ACK}$ $\overline{MSG}$ $\overline{C/D}$ $\overline{I/O}$ $\overline{ATN}$ $\overline{RST}$	Input/output control signals for SCSI bus.
62	54	INT2	A non-maskable interrupt request signal that indicates a reset condition on the SCSI bus.
64	56	$\overline{CS}$	Selection enable signal for accessing an internal register in the SPC. When CS is active low, the following signals are valid: $\overline{RD}$, $\overline{WT}$, A0–A3, D0–D7 and DP.
65	57	$\overline{WT}$	Input strobe used for writing data into an internal register of the SPC; this signal is asserted only if $\overline{CS}$ is active low. On the trailing edge of $\overline{WT}$, data placed on data bus lines D0-D7/DP is loaded into the internal register selected by address inputs A0-A3, except when all address lines are high (A0-A3 = H).
66	58	$\overline{WTG}$	While this signal is active low, data placed on data bus lines D0-D7/DP is output to HDB0-HDB7/HDBP, provided the following input conditions are satisfied: CS and HIN = H $\overline{A0}$–A3 = H
67 68	59 60	$\overline{RD}$ $\overline{RDG}$	Input strobes used for reading out contents of internal register; strobes are effective only when $\overline{CS}$ is active low. When $\overline{RDG}$ is active low, the contents of an internal register selected by address inputs A0–A3 are placed on data bus lines D0–D7/DP. For a data transfer cycle in the program transfer mode, the trailing edge of RD is used as a timing signal to indicate the end of data read.

Continued on following page

PIN DESCRIPTIONS

Pin Number		Designator	Function
FPT	**PLCC**		
69 70 71 72 74 75 76 77	61 62 63 64 66 67 68 69	D0 D1 D2 D3 D4 D5 D6 D7	Used for writing or reading data into or from an internal register of the SPC; these bus lines are 3-state and bidirectional. The MSB is D7; the LSB is D0. DP is an odd parity bit.
78	70	DP	When the $\overline{CS}$ and $\overline{RDG}$ inputs are active low, contents of the internal register are output to the data bus (read operation). In operations other than read, these bus lines are kept in a high-impedance state.
79	71	DPO	An odd parity output for data byte D7–D0. DPO represents an output when D7–D0/DP are placed in a high-impedance state; DPO is in a high-impedance state when D7–D0/DP serve as outputs. If a parity bit is not generated for external memory, DPO can be used as an input for DP.
80	72	INTR	When active high, requests an interrupt to indicate completion of an SPC internal operation or the occurrence of an error; the INTR interrupt request can be masked by user software. When an interrupt request is honored, INTR remains in the active state until cause of the interrupt is cleared.

ADDRESSING OF INTERNAL REGISTERS

The MB87033B SPC contains16 byte-wide registers that are externally accessible. These registers are used to control internal operations of the SPC and also to indicate processing/result status. A unique address, identified by address bits A3–A0, is assigned to each of the sixteen registers. These addresses are defined in Table 1.

Note: *The phase sense (PSNS) and SPC diagnostic (SDGC) registers have the same hexadecimal address. However, depending upon whether a read or write command is executed, the register provides two separate functions.*

Table 1. Internal Register Addressing

Register	Mnemonic	Operation	Chip Select ($\overline{CS}$)	Address Bits			
				A3	A2	A1	A0
Bus Device ID	BDID	R	0	0	0	0	0
		W					
SPC Control	SCTL	R	0	0	0	0	1
		W					
Command	SCMD	R	0	0	0	1	0
		W					
Transfer Mode	TMOD	R	0	0	0	1	1
		W					
Interrupt Sense	INTS	R	0	0	1	0	0
Reset Interrupt		W					
Phase Sense	PSNS	R	0	0	1	0	1
SPC Diagnostic Control	SDGC	W					
SPC Status	SSTS	R	0	0	1	1	0
SPC Error Status	SERR	R	0	0	1	1	1
Phase Control	PCTL	R	0	1	0	0	0
		W					
Modified Byte Counter	MBC	R	0	1	0	0	1
Extended Transfer Count		W					
Data Register	DREG	R	0	1	0	1	0
		W					

Continued on following page

Table 1. Internal Register Addressing

Register	Mnemonic	Operation	Chip Select (CS)	Address Bits			
				A3	A2	A1	A0
Temporary Register	TEMP	R	0	1	0	1	1
		W					
Transfer Counter (High)	TCH	R	0	1	1	0	0
		W					
Transfer Counter (Middle)	TCM	R	0	1	1	0	1
		W					
Transfer Counter (Low)	TCL	R	0	1	1	1	0
		W					
External Buffer	EXBF	R	0	1	1	1	1
		W					

BIT ASSIGNMENTS FOR INTERNAL REGISTERS

Table 2 lists the bit assignments for the sixteen internal registers defined in Table 1. In most cases, bit assignments for the MB87033B SPC are identical to those for the MB87030/31; however, in the MB87033B, some features are expanded and others are added to improve overall performance. These modifications and additions are summarized as follows:

MPU Bus Parity Generator

An odd parity bit is output from DPO (pin 79 in FPT, pin 71 in PLCC) for each data byte (D7-D0). DPO is a 3-state pin and is placed in a high-impedance state when data from D7-D0 is output to the MPU. If the MPU interface does not contain a parity generator, the output of DPO can be connected to the DP input pin of the SPC (pin 78 in FPT, pin 70 in PLCC).

Reset Condition Interrupt Request Signal

The INT2 output (pin 62 in FPT, pin 54 in PLCC) is a non-maskable interrupt request that, when driven High, notifies the MPU when a reset condition is detected on the SCSI bus. Bit 4 (Reset Condition Interrupt Mask Enable) of the Phase Control (PCTL) register does not affect the INT2 output pin.

When a bus reset condition is detected, the INTR output (pin 80 in FPT, pin 72 in PLCC) also is driven to the high state; however, the state of INTR can be masked by bit 4 of the PCTL register:

Bit 4 = 0:   INTR goes high when a reset condition is detected.

Bit 4 = 1:   INTR does not go high when a reset condition is detected.

Lost Arbitration Interrupt Request

If bit 6 (Lost Arbitration Interrupt Enable) of the phase control (PCTL) register is set to "1", a COMMAND COMPLETE interrupt is generated when the SPC (serving as initiator or target) loses in the ARBITRATION process. To determine the cause of a COMMAND COMPLETE interrupt (completion of SELECTION, RESELECTION, or lost ARBITRATION), refer to bits 6 (TARGET) and 7 (INITIATOR) of the SPC status (SSTS) register. If both bits are set to "0", the COMMAND COMPLETE interrupt is a result of lost arbitration.

Attention Condition Interrupt

If bit 5 (Attention Condition Interrupt Enable) of the phase control (PCTL) register is set to "1" and the SPC serves as a target, a service required interrupt occurs. To reset the service required interrupt, set bit 3 of the interrupt sense (INTS) register to "1" or revoke the current target role of the SPC.

Expansion of Transfer Byte Counter

If bit 0 of the transfer mode (TMOD) register is set to "1", the transfer byte counter is expanded to 28-bits. In the expanded mode, the high nibble (bits 24 through 27) are entered into the four most significant bit positions (7 bits through 4) of the modified byte count (MBC) register.

> **Note:** *When a hardware data transfer or execution of a SELECT command is in process, access to the TMOD register is forbidden.*

Bit 0 of the TMOD register =1

To access the highest four bits (bits 27 through 24) of the transfer byte counter, data reads or writes are addressed to the high nibble of the modified byte counter (MBC) register. When a TRANSFER or SELECT command is issued, the transfer byte count (or t_{WAIT}) should be placed in the high nibble of the MBC register rather than the TCH, TCM, and TCL registers.

Bit 0 of the TMOD register = 0

The transfer byte counter is not expanded to 28-bits; hence, reading the high nibble of MBC yields a "0" even though some particular value is written into the register. In this case, t_{WAIT} or the transfer byte count is based on a 24-bit transfer byte counter (identical to the MB87030/MB87031).

During read/write access of an internal register, the following rules are invoked:

(1) Internal registers include only those registers identified in Table 2.
(2) A write command to a read–only register is ignored.
(3) For write operations, all bit positions with a "—" (blank) designator can be written as "0" or as a "1".
(4) All bit positions with an assigned "0" are always read as a zero (0).

Table 2. Bit Assignments For Internal Registers

HEX Address	Register and Mnemonic	R/W Operation	7 (MSb)	6	5	4	3	2	1	0 (LSb)	Parity
0	Bus Device ID (BDID)	R	#7	#6	#5	#4	#3	#2	#1	#0	0
		W					SCSI Bus Device ID ID4 ID2 ID1				—
1	SPC Control (SCTL)	R	Reset & Disable	Control Reset	Diag Mode	ARBIT Enable	Parity Enable	Select Enable	Reselect Enable	INT Enable	P
		W									
2	Command (SCMD)	R	Command Code			RST Out	Intercept Xfer	Transfer PRG Xfer	Modifer 0	Term Mode	P
		W									
3	Transfer Mode (TMOD) Command	R	Sync. Xfer	Max. Transfer Offset 4 2 1			Min. Transfer Period 2 1		0	Xfer Counter Expand	P
		W									
4	Interrupt Sense (INTS)	R	Selected	Reselected	Disconnect	Command Complete	Service Required	Time Out	SPC Hard Error	Reset Condition	P
		W	Reset Interrupt								—
5	Phase Sense (PSNS)	R	REQ	ACK	ATN	SEL	BSY	MSG	C/D	I/O	P
	SPC Diag Control (SDGC)	W	Diag. REQ	Diag. ACK		—	Diag. BSY	Diag. MSG	Diag. C/D	Diag. I/O	—
6	SPC Status (SSTS)	R	Connected INIT TARG		SPC BSY	Xfer In Progress	SCSI RST	TC=0	DREG Status Full Empty		P
7	SPC Error Status (SERR)	R	Data Error SCSI SPC		0	0	TC Parity Error	Phase Error	Short Xfer Period	Offset Error	P

Continued on following page

Table 2. Bit Assignments For Internal Registers

HEX Address	Register and Mnemonic	R/W Operation	7 (MSb)	6	5	4	3	2	1	0 (LSb)	Parity
8	Phase Control (PCTL)	R	Bus Free Interrupt Enable	Arbitration Fail Interrupt Enable	Attention Condition Interrupt Enable	Reset Condition Interrupt Mask	0	Transfer Phase			P
		W						MSG Out	C/D Out	I/O Out	
9	Modified Byte Counter (MBC)	R	Extended Transfer Counter				Bit 3	Bit 2	Bit 1	Bit 0	
		W	Bit 27	Bit 26	Bit 25	Bit 24					P
A	Data Register (DREG)	R	Internal Data Register (8 Byte FIFO)								
		W	Bit 7	Bit 6	Bit 5	Bit 4	Bit 3	Bit 2	Bit 1	Bit 0	P
B	Temporary Register (TEMP)	R	Temporary Data (Input: From SCSI)								
			Bit 7	Bit 6	Bit 5	Bit 4	Bit 3	Bit 2	Bit 1	Bit 0	P
		W	Temporary Data (Output: To SCSI)								
			Bit 7	Bit 6	Bit 5	Bit 4	Bit 3	Bit 2	Bit 1	Bit 0	P
C	Transfer Counter High (TCH)	R	Transfer Counter High (MSB)								
		W	Bit 23	Bit 22	Bit 21	Bit 20	Bit 19	Bit 18	Bit 17	Bit 16	P
D	Transfer Counter Mid (TCM)	R	Transfer Counter Middle (2nd Byte)								
		W	Bit 15	Bit 14	Bit 13	Bit 12	Bit 11	Bit 10	Bit 9	Bit 8	P
E	Transfer Counter LOW (TCL)	R	Transfer Counter Low (LSB)								
		W	Bit 7	Bit 6	Bit 5	Bit 4	Bit 3	Bit 2	Bit 1	Bit 0	P
F	External Buffer (EXBF)	R	External Buffer								
		W	Bit 7	Bit 6	Bit 5	Bit 4	Bit 3	Bit 2	Bit 1	Bit 0	P

DC CHARACTERISTICS
(Recommended operating conditions unless otherwise specified)

SCSI Bus Pins

Parameter	Designator	Condition	Values			Unit
			Min.	Typ.	Max.	
Input Voltage	V_{IH}		2.0		5.25	V
	V_{IL}		0.0		0.8	V
Input Current	I_{IH}	V_{IH} = 5.25V			10	μA
	I_{IL}	V_{IL} = 0.0V			−10	μA
Output Voltage	V_{OL}	V_{DD} = 4.75V I_{OL} = 48 mA			0.5	V
Input Hysteresis Width	V_{HW}		0.2			V

Other than SCSI Bus Pins

Parameter	Designator	Condition	Values			Unit
			Min.	Typ.	Max.	
Input Voltage	V_{IH}		2.2		V_{DD} + 0.3	V
	V_{IL}		V_{SS}−0.3		0.8	V
Output Voltage	V_{OH}	I_{OH} = −0.4mA	4.2		V_{DD}	V
	V_{OL}	I_{OL} = 3.2mA	V_{SS}		0.4	
Input Leakage Current	I_{LIH}	V_{IH} = 5.25V			10	μA
	I_{LIL}	V_{IL} = 0.0V			−10	μA
Input/Output	I_{LIH}	V_{IH} = 5.25V			10	μA
Leakage Current	I_{LIL}	V_{IL} = 0.0V			−10	μA
Supply Current	I_{DD}	10 MHz Clock Outputs Open			30	mA

$TA = 0 - 70°C, V_{DD} + 5V \pm 5\%$

Continued on following page

DC CHARACTERISTICS
(Recommended operating conditions unless otherwise specified)

Capacitance

Parameter	Designator	Condition	Values			Unit
			Min.	Typ.	Max.	
Input pin capacitance	C_{IN}	$_TA = 25C$, $V_{DD}= V_I=OV$, $f - 1MHz$			9	pF
Output capacitance	C_{OUT}	$_TA = 25C$, $V_{DD}= V_I=OV$, $f - 1MHz$			9	pF
I/O pin capacitance[2]	$C_{I/O}$	$_TA = 25C$, $V_{DD}= V_I=OV$, $f - 1MHz$			11	pF
I/O pin capacitance[3]	$C_{I/O}$	$_TA = 25C$, $V_{DD}= V_I=OV$, $f - 1MHz$			30	pF

Notes: [1]SCSI bus Pins are $\overline{DB7}$–$\overline{DB0}$, $\overline{DBP}$, $\overline{RST}$, $\overline{SEL}$, $\overline{I/O}$, $\overline{C/D}$, $\overline{MSG}$, $\overline{ATN}$, $\overline{REQ}$, $\overline{ACK}$, and $\overline{BSY}$.
      [2]For all I/O pins except SCSI bus pins.
      [3]For SCSI bus pins only (see note 1).

AC CHARACTERISTICS

SCSI signal timing chart is described as follows:

Notes: 1 Output "L"
2 No device is outputting "L".
3 The other device is outputting "L".

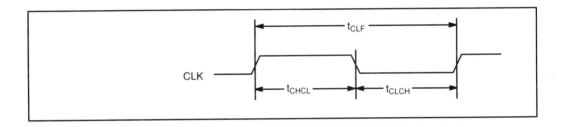

Clock

Parameter	Designator	Values			Unit
		Min.	Typ.	Max.	
Clock cycle time	t_{CLF}	100		200	ns
Clock "H" Pulse width	t_{CHCL}	50			ns
Clock "L" Pulse width	t_{CLCH}	40			ns

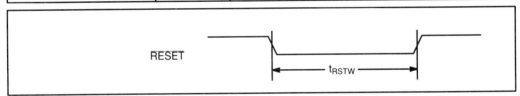

Hardware Reset

Parameter	Designator	Values			Unit
		Min.	Typ.	Max.	
Reset Pulse Width	t_{RSTW}	50			ns

AC CHARACTERISTICS (Continued)

Register Write (except EXBF)

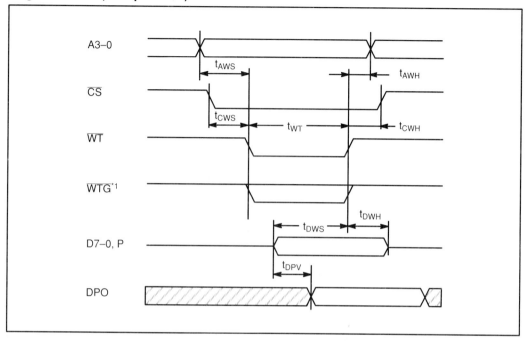

Register Write					
Parameter	Designator	Values			Unit
		Min.	Typ.	Max.	
Address set-up	t_{AWS}	35		.	ns
Address hold	t_{AWH}	5			ns
$\overline{CS}$ set-up	t_{CWS}	20			ns
$\overline{CS}$ hold	t_{CWH}	10			ns
Data bus set-up	t_{DWS}	25			ns
Data bus hold	t_{DWH}	20			ns
$\overline{WT}$ Pulse width	t_{WT}	50			ns
Data bus valid $\rightarrow$ DPO valid	t_{DPV}			55	ns

Note: 1 $\overline{WTG}$ is input at the same timing as $\overline{WT}$ or held to "H".

AC CHARACTERISTICS (Continued)

Register Write (EXBF)

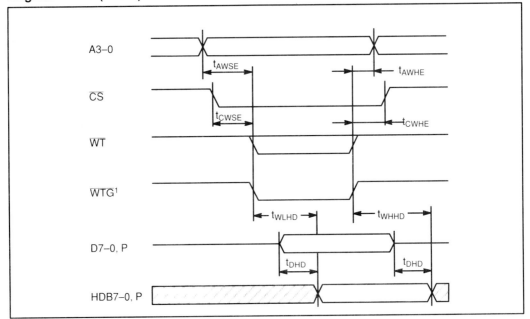

Register Write					
Parameter	Designator	Values			Unit
		Min.	Typ.	Max.	
Address set-up	t_{AWSE}	35			ns
Address hold	t_{AWHE}	5			ns
$\overline{CS}$ set-up	t_{CWSE}	20			ns
$\overline{CS}$ hold	t_{CWHE}	10			ns
$\overline{WTG}$[1] "L" → DMA pulse output valid	t_{WLHD}			55	ns
$\overline{WTG}$[1] "H" → DMA pulse output invalid	t_{WHHD}	10			ns
MPU data bus → DMA bus delay	t_{DHD}			50	ns

Note: 1 $\overline{WTG}$ is input at the same timing as $\overline{WT}$ or held to "H".

AC CHARACTERISTICS (Continued)

Register Read (except EXBF)

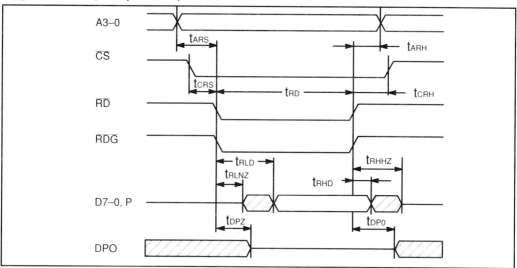

Register Read					
Parameter	Designator	Values			Unit
		Min.	Typ.	Max.	
Address set-up	t_{ARS}	35			ns
Address hold	t_{ARH}	5			ns
$\overline{CS}$ set-up	t_{CRS}	20			ns
$\overline{CS}$ hold	t_{CRH}	10			ns
$\overline{RDG}$ "L" " Data bus ourpur valid	t_{RLNZ}	10		40	ns
$\overline{RDG}$ "H" " Data bus output valid	t_{RHHZ}	10		40	ns
$\overline{RD}$ "L" " Data Valid D7–0	t_{RLD}			70	ns
DP				85	ns
$\overline{RD}$ "H" " Data Invalid	t_{RHD}	10			ns
$\overline{RD}$ Pulse width	t_{RD}	50			ns
*1 $\overline{RDG}$ "L" " Data High-Z	t_{DPZ}	10		40	ns
*1 $\overline{RDG}$ "H" " DPO	t_{DPO}	10		40	ns

Note: 1 = DPO goes to High-Z when both $\overline{RDG}$ and $\overline{CS}$ are "L".

AC CHARACTERISTICS (Continued)

Register Read (EXBF)

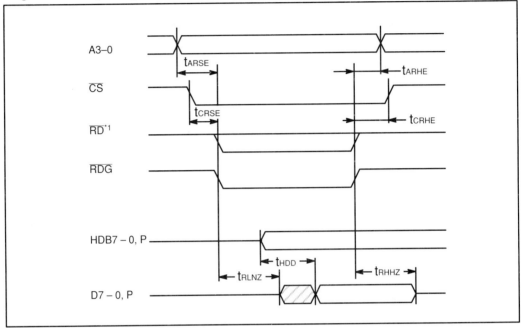

Note: 1 $\overline{RD}$ is input at the same timing as $\overline{RDG}$ or held to "H".

Register Read					
Parameter	**Designator**	**Values**			**Unit**
		Min.	**Typ.**	**Max.**	
Address set-up	t_{ARSE}	35			ns
Address hold	t_{ARHE}	5			ns
$\overline{CS}$ set-up	t_{CRSE}	20			ns
$\overline{CS}$ hold	t_{CRHE}	10			ns
$\overline{RDG}$ "L" → Data bus output	t_{RLNZ}	10		40	ns
$\overline{RDG}$ "H" → Data bus High-Z	t_{RHHZ}	10		40	ns
DMA bus → MPU data bus delay	t_{HDD}			50	ns

AC CHARACTERISTICS (continued)

DREG Access Cycle Time

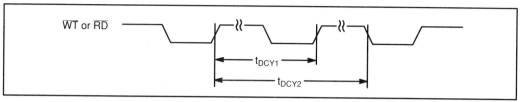

DREG		Values			Unit
Parameter	Designator	Min.	Typ.	Max.	
DREG access cycle time	t_{DCY1}	$2t_{CLF}$			ns
DREG access cycle time	t_{DCY2}	$3t_{CLF}$			ns

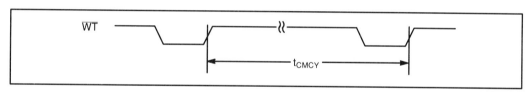

Command Issue Cycle Time		Values			Unit
Parameter	Designator	Min.	Typ..	Max	
SCMD register access cycle time	t_{CMCY}	$4t_{CLF}$			ns

AC CHARACTERISTICS (continued)

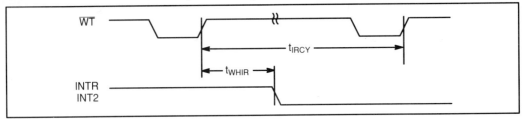

Interrupt Reset

Parameter	Designator	Values			Unit
		Min.	Typ.	Max.	
WT "H" " Interrupt output (INTR.INT2) "L"	t_{WHIR}	t_{CLF}		$3t_{CLF} + 80$	ns
INTS register access cycle time	t_{IRCY}	$4t_{CLF}$			ns

DMA Access Cycle Time

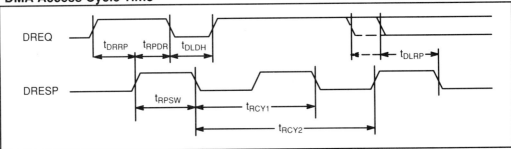

DMA Access Timing

Parameter	Designator	Values			Unit
		Min.	Typ.	Max.	
DREQ "H" $\rightarrow$ DRESP "H"	t_{DRRP}	t_{CLF}			ns
DRESP "H" $\rightarrow$ DREQ "L"	t_{RPDR}	5		70	ns
DREQ "L" $\rightarrow$ DREQ "H"	t_{DLDH}	0			ns
DRESP Pulse Width	t_{RPSW}	50			ns
DRESP Cycle time	t_{RCY1}	$2t_{CLF}$			ns
DRESP Cycle time	t_{RCY2}	$3t_{CLF}$			ns
DREQ "L" $\rightarrow$ DRESP "L"[1]	t_{DLRP}			$5t_{CLF}$	ns

Note: 1 This parameter is applicable when the data buffer hold function or the Transfer Pause   command is used and DREQ goes low asynchronously to DRESP. Under these conditions, data cannot be written to the data buffer until t_{DLRP} and t_{RPSW} are satisfied.

AC CHARACTERISTICS (continued)

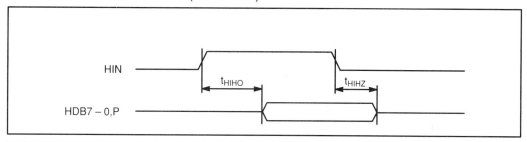

DMA Bus Output Control

Parameter	Designator	Values			Unit
		Min.	Typ.	Max.	
HIN "H" → DMA bus output	t_{HIHO}	5		40	ns
HIN "L" → DMA bus High-Z	t_{HIHZ}	5		40	ns

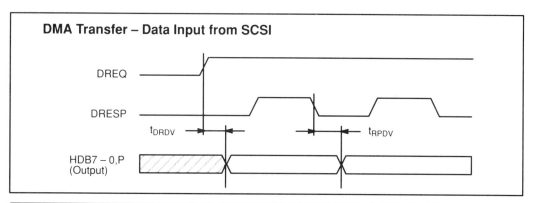

DMA Transfer – Data Input from SCSI

DMA Transfer (1) – Data Input from SCSI

Parameter	Designator	Values			Unit
		Min.	Typ.	Max.	
DREQ "H" → Output data[1] valid	t_{DRDV}			60	ns
DRESP "L" → Output data switch	t_{RPDV}	15		90	ns

Note: 1 This parameter is applied when the internal data buffer goes Not Empty from Empty.

AC CHARACTERISTICS (continued)

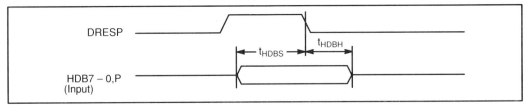

DMA Transfer – Data Output to SCSI

Parameter	Designator	Values			Unit
		Min.	Typ.	Max.	
Input data set up	t_{HDBS}	20			ns
Input data hold	t_{HDBH}	20			ns

Selection (1) Initiator (with Arbitration)

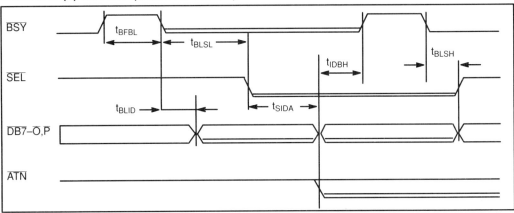

Selection (1) Initiator (with Arbitration)

Item	Symbol	Min.	Typ.	Max.	Unit
Bus free→ $\overline{BSY}$ 'L'[1]	t_{BFBL}	$(6+n)\, t_{CLF}$		$(7+n)\, t_{CLF}+80$	ns
$\overline{BSY}$ 'L' - sends its own ID bit	t_{BLID}	10		60	ns
$\overline{BSY}$ 'L' → $\overline{SEL}$ 'L'	t_{BLSL}	$32t_{CLF} - 40$		$32t_{CLF} + 30$	ns
$\overline{SEL}$ 'L' → ID, $\overline{ATN}$ send	t_{SIDA}	$11t_{CLF} - 30$		$11t_{CLF} + 60$	ns
ID send → $\overline{BSY}$ 'H'	t_{IDBH}	$2t_{CLF} - 60$		$2t_{CLF} + 30$	ns
$\overline{BSY}$ 'L' → $\overline{SEL}$ 'H' ID hold	t_{BLSH}	$2t_{CLF}$		$3t_{CLF} + 120$	ns

Note: 1 TCL register setting

Selection (2) Initiator (without Arbitration)

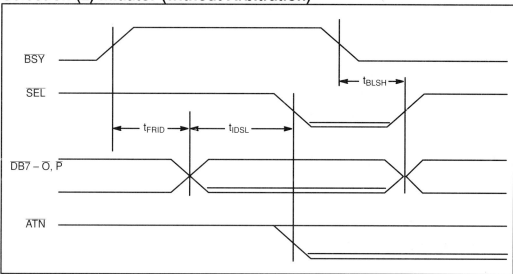

Selection (2) Initiator (without Arbitration)

Item	Symbol	Min.	Typ.	Max.	Unit
Bus free → ID send[1]	t_{FRID}	$(6+n)\, t_{CLF}$		$(7+n)\, t_{CLF} + 100$	ns
ID send → $\overline{SEL}$ 'L', $\overline{ATN}$ 'L'	t_{IDSL}	$11t_{CLF} - 60$		$11t_{CLF} + 40$	ns
$\overline{BSY}$ 'L'→ $\overline{SEL}$ 'H'. ID hold	t_{BLSH}	$2t_{CLF}$		$3t_{CLF} + 120$	ns

Note: 1 :n = TCL register setting

Selection (3) Target (with Arbitration)

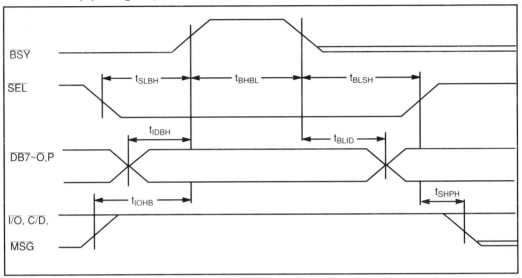

Selection (3) Target (with Arbitration)

Item	Symbol	Min.	Typ.	Max.	Unit
SEL 'L' → BSY 'H'	t_{SLBH}	0			ns
ID confirmation → BSY 'H'	t_{IDBH}	0			ns
I/O 'H' → BSY 'H'	t_{IOHB}	0			ns
BSY 'H' → BSY 'L'	t_{BHBL}	$4t_{CLF}$		$5t_{CLF} + 80$	ns
BSY 'L' → SEL 'H'	t_{BLSH}	0			ns
BSY 'L' → ID hold	t_{BLID}	30			ns
SEL 'H' phase signal output	t_{SHPH}	$3t_{CLF}$		$4t_{CLF} + 100$	ns

Selection (4) Target (without Arbitration)

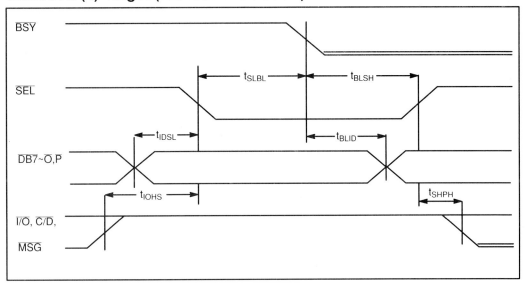

Selection (4) Target (without Arbitration)

Item	Symbol	Min.	Typ.	Max.	Unit
ID confirmation → SEL 'L'	t_{IDSL}	0			ns
I/O 'H' → SEL 'L'	t_{IOHS}	0			ns
SEL'L' → BSY'L'	t_{SLBL}	$2t_{CLF}$		$3t_{CLF} + 100$	ns
BSY 'L' → SEL 'H'	t_{BLSH}	0			ns
BSY 'L' → ID hold	t_{BLID}	30			ns
SEL 'H' → phase signal output	t_{SHPH}	$3t_{CLF}$		$4t_{CLF} + 100$	ns

Reselection (1) Target

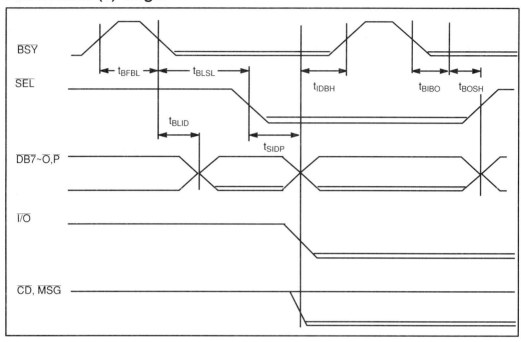

Reselection (1) Target

Item	Symbol	Min.	Typ.	Max.	Unit
Bus free → $\overline{\text{BSY}}$ 'L' [1]	t_{BFBL}	$(6+n)\,t_{CLF}$		$(7+n)\,t_{CLF} + 80$	ns
$\overline{\text{BSY}}$ 'L' – sends its own ID bit	t_{BLID}	-10		60	ns
$\overline{\text{BSY}}$ 'L' → $\overline{\text{SEL}}$ 'L'	t_{BLSL}	$32t_{CLF} - 40$		$32t_{CLF} + 30$	ns
$\overline{\text{SEL}}$ 'L' → ID, phase signal send	t_{SIDP}	$11t_{CLF} - 30$		$11t_{CLF} + 60$	ns
ID send → $\overline{\text{BSY}}$ 'H'	t_{IDBH}	$2t_{CLF} - 60$		$2t_{CLF} + 30$	ns
$\overline{\text{BSY}}$ 'L' → $\overline{\text{BSY}}$ 'L' send	t_{BIBO}	$2t_{CLF}$		$3t_{CLF} + 90$	ns
$\overline{\text{BSY}}$ 'L' send → SEL ID hold	t_{BOSH}	$t_{CLF} - 20$		$t_{CLF} + 60$	ns

Note: 1 n = TCL register setting

Reselection (2) Initiator

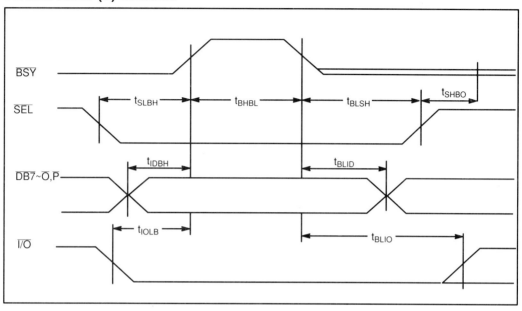

Reselection (2) Initiator

Item	Symbol	Min.	Typ.	Max.	Unit
$\overline{SEL}$ 'L' $\longrightarrow$ $\overline{BSY}$ 'H'	t_{SLBH}	0			ns
ID confirmation $\longrightarrow$ $\overline{BSY}$ 'H'	t_{IDBH}	0			ns
I/O 'L' $\longrightarrow$ $\overline{BSY}$ 'H'	t_{IOLB}	0			ns
$\overline{BSY}$ 'H' $\longrightarrow$ $\overline{BSY}$ 'L'	t_{BHBL}	$4t_{CLF}$		$5t_{CLF} + 80$	ns
$\overline{BSY}$ 'L' $\longrightarrow$ SEL 'H'	t_{BLSH}	0			ns
$\overline{BSY}$ 'L' $\longrightarrow$ $\overline{ID}$ hold	t_{BLID}	30			ns
$\overline{BSY}$ 'L' $\longrightarrow$ I/O signal hold	t_{BLIO}	20			ns
$\overline{SEL}$ 'H' $\longrightarrow$ $\overline{BSY}$ 'L' send stop	t_{SHBO}	$2t_{CLF}$		$3t_{CLF} + 100$	ns

Asynchronous Transfer Initiator (1) REQ-ACK Timing

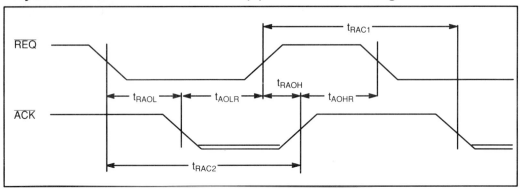

Asynchronous Transfer Initiator (1) REQ-ACK Timing

Item	Symbol	Min.	Typ.	Max.	Unit
REQ 'L' $\rightarrow$ ACK 'L'[3]	t_{RAOL}	15		90	ns
ACK 'L' $\rightarrow$ REQ 'H'	t_{AOLR}	0			ns
REQ 'H' $\rightarrow$ ACK 'H'[3]	t_{RAOH}	15		100	ns
ACK 'H' $\rightarrow$ REQ 'L'	t_{AOHR}	10			ns
REQ 'H' $\rightarrow$ ACK 'L'[1,3]	t_{RAC1}	$2t_{CLF}$		$3t_{CLF} + 120$	ns
REQ 'L' $\rightarrow$ ACK 'H'[2,3]	t_{RAC2}	$2t_{CLF}$		$3t_{CLF} + 130$	ns

Notes: [1]The time for REQ 'H' $\rightarrow$ ACK 'L' is determined by the longer of ($t_{RAOH} + t_{AOHR} + t_{RAOL}$) and t_{RAC1}.

[2]Apply for input operations. The time of REQ 'L' $\rightarrow$ ACK 'H' is determined by the longer of ($t_{RAOL} + t_{AOLR} + t_{RAOH}$) and t_{RAC1}.

[3]The times assigned in this section do not apply in the following cases:

    (1) For output operations, if the data buffer is empty.

    (2) For input operations, if the data buffer is full.

    (3) During transfer of the first or last byte.

    (4) During input operations, when the SPC automatically sends the $\overline{ATN}$ signal.

Asynchronous Transfer Initiator (2) Output Operation

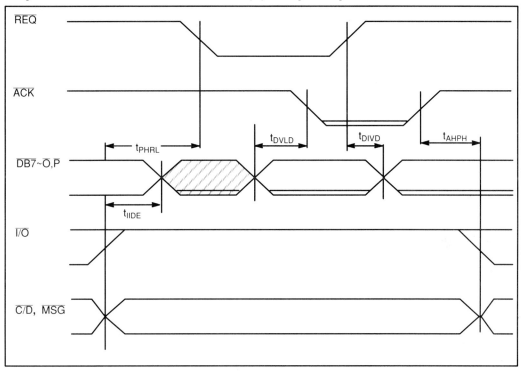

Asynchronous Transfer Initiator (2) Output Operation

Item	Symbol	Min.	Typ.	Max.	Unit
$\overline{I/O}$ 'H' → data bus output	t_{IIDE}	10		110	ns
Phase designation → $\overline{REQ}$ 'L'	t_{PHRL}	100			ns
Data bus output confirmation → $\overline{ACK}$ 'L'	t_{DVLD}	$2t_{CLF}-80$			ns
$\overline{REQ}$ 'H' → data bus hold	t_{DIVD}	15			ns
$\overline{ACK}$ 'H' → phase change	t_{AHPH}	10			ns

Asynchronous Transfer Initiator (3) Input Operation

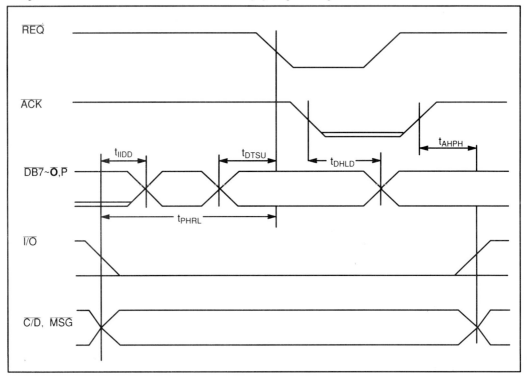

Asynchronous Transfer Initiator (3) Input Operation					
Item	Symbol	Min.	Typ.	Max.	Unit
$\overline{I/O}$ 'L' → data bus output stop	t_{IIDD}			110	ns
Phase designation → $\overline{REQ}$ 'L'	t_{PHRL}	100			ns
Data bus confirmation → $\overline{REQ}$ 'L'	t_{DTSU}	10			ns
$\overline{ACK}$ 'L' → data bus hold	t_{DHLD}	15			ns
ACK 'H' → phase change	t_{AHPH}	10			ns

Asynchronous Transfer Target (1) REQ-ACK Timing

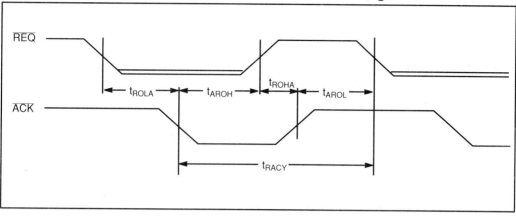

Asynchronous Transfer Target (1) REQ-ACK Timing					
Item	Symbol	Min.	Typ.	Max.	Unit
REQ 'L' — ACK 'L'	t_{ROLA}	0			ns
ACK 'L' → REQ 'H'	t_{AROH}	10		90	ns
REQ 'H' → ACK 'H'	t_{ROHA}	0			ns
ACK 'H' → REQ 'L' *2	t_{AROL}	10		70	ns
ACK 'H' → REQ 'L' *1, *2	t_{RACY}	$2t_{CLF}$		$3t_{CLF} + 110$	ns

Notes: 1 The time for ACK'L' → REQ'L' is determined by the longer of ($t_{AROH} + t_{ROHA} + t_{AROL}$) and t_{RACY}.
2 The times assigned in this section do not apply to the following:
(1) For output operations, if the data buffer is empty.
(2) For input operations, if the data buffer is full.

Asynchronous Transfer (2) Output Operation

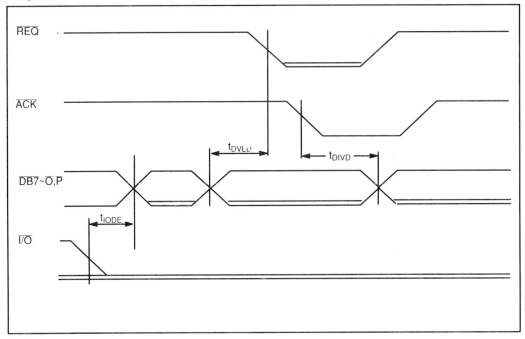

Asynchronous Transfer (2) Output Operation

Item	Symbol	Min.	Typ.	Max.	Unit
I/O 'L' → data bus output	t_{IODE}	$7t_{CLF}$		$8t_{CLF} + 110$	ns
Data bus output confirmation → REQ 'L'	t_{DVLD}	$2t_{CLF} - 80$			ns
ACK 'L' → data bus hold	t_{DIVD}	15			ns

Asynchronous Transfer Target (3) Input Operation

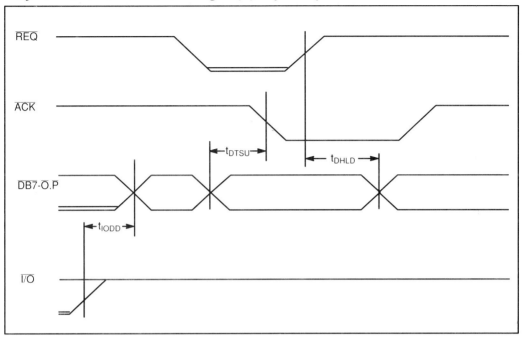

Asynchronous Transfer Target (3) Input Operation					
Item	Symbol	Min.	Typ.	Max.	Unit
I/O 'H' → data bus output stop	t_{IODD}			60	ns
Data bus confirmation → ACK 'L'	t_{DTSU}	10			ns
REQ 'H' → data hold	t_{DHLD}	15			ns

Synchronous Transfer Initiator (1) REQ/ACK Cycle

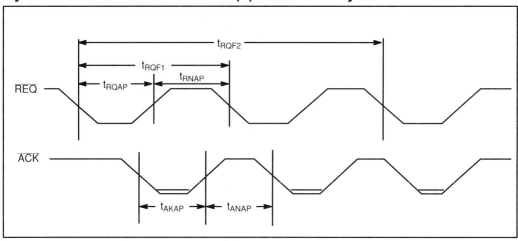

Synchronous Transfer Initiator (1) REQ/ACK Cycle

Item	Symbol	Min.	Typ.	Max.	Unit
$\overline{REQ}$ Assertion Period	t_{RQAP}	50			ns
$\overline{REQ}$ Nonassertion Period	t_{RNAP}	50			ns
$\overline{REQ}$ cycle time	t_{RQF1}	t_{CLF}			ns
$\overline{REQ}$ cycle time	t_{RQF2}	$3t_{CLF}$			ns
$\overline{ACK}$ Assertion Period	t_{AKAP}	t_{CLF} - 10			ns
ACK Nonassertion Period[1]	t_{ANAP}	$n.t_{CLF}$ - 30			ns

Note: 1 n depends on the TMOD register setting.

TMOD Register		
Bit 3	Bit 2	n
0	0	1
0	1	2
1	0	3
1	1	4

Synchronous Transfer Initiator (2) REQ/ACK Timing

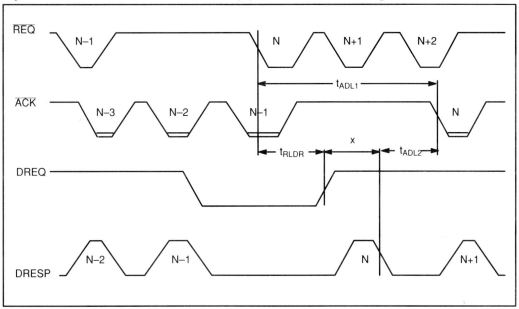

Synchronous Transfer Initiator (2) REQ/ACK Timing					
Item	Symbol	Min.	Typ.	Max.	Unit
$\overline{ACK}$ Assertion delay time[1]	t_{ADL1}	$3t_{CLF}$		$4t_{CLF} + 100$	ns
$\overline{REQ}$ 'L' " DREQ 'H'[2]	t_{RLDR}	$t_{CLF} + 50$		$3t_{CLF} + 60$	ns
$\overline{ACK}$ Assertion delay time [2,3]	t_{ADL2}	$3t_{CLF}$		$4t_{CLF} + 120$	ns

Notes: [1]Apply to output operations and to input operations when the maximum offset value is 4 or less.
[2]Apply to input operations.
[3]Apply to input operations when the maximum offset value is 5.8.

This is the minimum time after receiving the DRESP of byte N, until the ACK of byte N is transferred. In this case, the minimum time required from receiving the REQ of byte N until transferring the ACK of byte N is t_{RLDR} + (DRESP assertion time x) + t_{ALD2} .

Synchronous Transfer Initiator (3) Output Operation

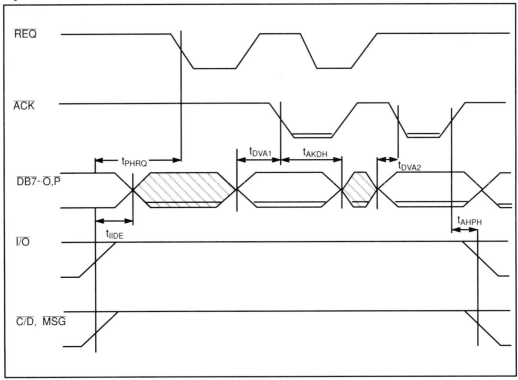

Synchronous Transfer Initiator (3) Output Operation (Continued)

Item	Symbol	Min.	Typ.	Max.	Unit
$\overline{I/O}$ 'H' → data bus output	t_{IIDE}	10		110	ns
Phase designation → $\overline{REQ}$'L'	t_{PHRQ}	100			ns
Data bus output[1]	t_{DVA1}	$2t_{CLF}$ - 70			ns
confirmation → $\overline{ACK}$'L'[2]	t_{DVA2}	$n.t_{CLF}$ - 60			
$\overline{ACK}$ 'L' → data bus hold	t_{AKDH}	t_{CLF} - 20			ns
$\overline{ACK}$ 'H' → phase change	t_{AHPH}	10			ns

Notes: 1 n depends on the TMOD register setting.
2 The time from data bus output confirmation to $\overline{ACK}$ 'L' is set by the shorter of t_{DVA1} and t_{DVA2}.

TMOD Register		
Bit 3	Bit 2	n
0	0	1
0	1	2
1	0	3
1	1	4

Synchronous Transfer Initiator (4) Input Operation

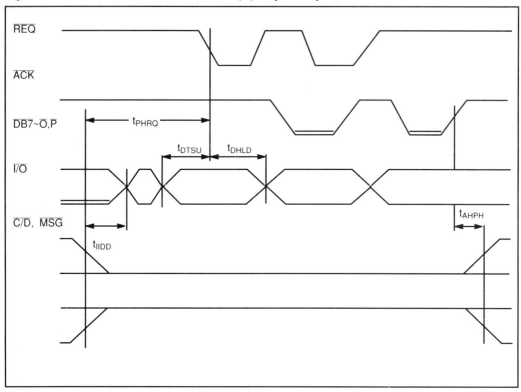

Synchronous Transfer Initiator (4) Input Operation

Item	Symbol	Min.	Typ.	Max.	Unit
I/O 'H' → data bus output stop	t_{IIDD}			110	ns
Phase designation → REQ'L'	t_{PHRQ}	100			ns
Data bus confirmation → REQ'L'	t_{DTSU}	10			ns
ACK 'L' → data bus hold	t_{DHLD}	40			ns
ACK 'H' → phase change	t_{AHPH}	10			ns

Synchronous Transmission Target (1) REQ/ACK Synchronization

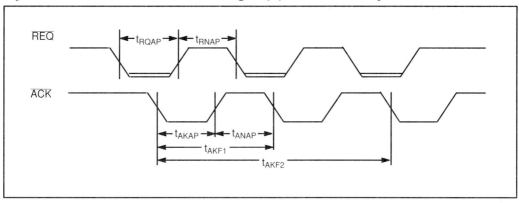

Synchronous Transmission Target (1) REQ/ACK Synchronization					
Item	Symbol	Min.	Typ.	Max.	Unit
REQ Assertion Period	t_{RQAP}	$t_{CLF} - 10$			
REQ Non Assertion Period	t_{RNAP}	$nt_{CLF} - 30$			
ACK Assertion Period	t_{AKAP}	50			
ACK Non Assertion Period	t_{ANAP}	50			ns
ACK Cycle Time (1)	t_{AKF1}	t_{CLF}			
ACK Cycle Time (2)	t_{AKF2}	$3t_{CLF}$			

n is set by the TMOD register.

TMOD Register		
Bit 3	Bit 2	n
0	0	1
0	1	2
1	0	3
1	1	4

Synchronous Transmission Target (2) REQ/ACK Timing

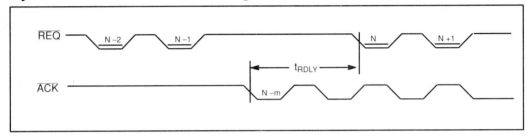

Synchronous Transmission Target (2) REQ/ACK Timing

Item	Symbol	Min.	Typ.	Max.	Unit
REQ Propagation delay time (skew)[1]	t_{RDLY}	$3t_{CLF}$		$4t_{CLF}+100$	ns

Note: [1] Minimum time required when the maximum offset value is set to m(m = 1 to 8) from receiving ACK signal for byte N–m to transmitting the REQ signal for byte N. The above timing diagram shows the case where the result of sending REQ for byte N–1 and the offset amount, namely the number of the preceding REQ transmitted, continues up to the maximum offset value of m after which REQ is deasserted.

Synchronous Transmission Target (3) Output Operation

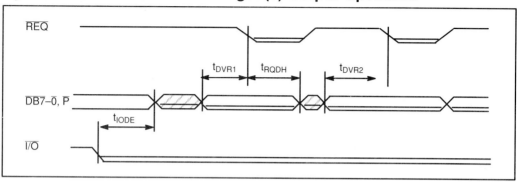

Synchronous Transmission Target (3) Output Operation

Item	Symbol	Min.	Typ.	Max.	Unit
I/O "L" → data bus output	t_{IODE}	$7t_{CLF}$		$8t_{CLF}+110$	
Data bus output settles	t_{DVR1}	$2t_{CLF}-70$		—	
→ REQ "L"[1,2]	t_{DVR2}	$nt_{CLF}-60$		—	ns
I/O "L" → data bus hold	t_{RQDH}	$t_{CLF}-20$		—	

Notes: [1] n is set by the TMOD register.

[2] The time from data bus output setting to ACK going 'L' is the shorter of the time t_{DVA1} and t_{DVA2}.

TMOD Register

Bit 3	Bit 2	n
0	0	1
0	1	2
1	0	3
1	1	4

Synchronous Transmission Target (4) Input Operation

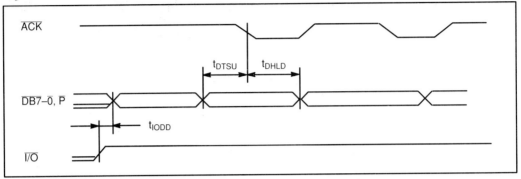

Synchronous Transmission Target (4) Input Operation					
Item	**Symbol**	**Min.**	**Typ.**	**Max.**	**Unit**
I/O "H" → data bus output disabled	t_{IODD}	—		60	
Data bus output settles → ACK "L"	t_{DTSU}	10		—	ns
ACK "L" → data bus hold	t_{DHLD}	40		—	

Bus Free (1) Arbitration Failure

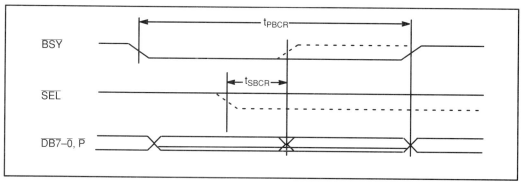

Bus Free (1) Arbitration Failure

Item	Symbol	Min.	Typ.	Max.	Unit
Arbitration start $\rightarrow$ $\overline{BSY}$ "H" and ID bit transmission stops[1]	t_{PBCR}	$32t_{CLF}-30$		$32t_{CLF}+60$	ns
$\overline{SEL}$ "L" by other bus devices $\rightarrow$ $\overline{BSY}$ "H" and ID bit transmission stops[1]	t_{SBCR}	$2t_{CLF}$		$32t_{CLF}+130$	

Bus Free (2) Selection/Reselection Timeout

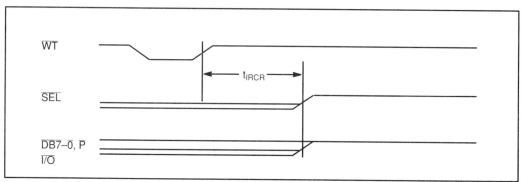

Bus Free (2) Selection/Reselection Timeout

Item	Symbol	Min.	Typ.	Max.	Unit
Timeout Interrupt set $\rightarrow$ $\overline{SEL}$ "H" and bus cleared	t_{IRCR}	—	$3t_{CLF}+130$		ns

Bus Free (3) Enable

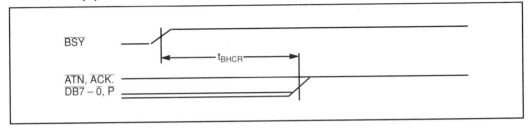

Bus Free (3) Enable

Item	Symbol	Min.	Typ.	Max.	Unit
$\overline{BSY}$ "H" → bus cleared	t_{BHCR}	—		$5t_{CLF}+120$	ns

Bus Free (4) Target

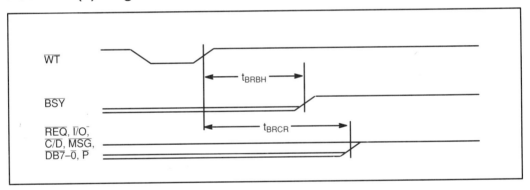

Bus Free (4) Target

Item	Symbol	Min.	Typ.	Max.	Unit
Bus release command Issued → $\overline{BSY}$ "H"	t_{BRBH}	—	$3t_{CLF}+100$		ns
Bus release command Issued → bus cleared	t_{BRCR}		$3t_{CLF}+130$		

AC Characteristics

T_A = 0 to 70°C, V_{DD} = +5 V ±5%, V_{SS} = 0 V

Non-SCSI Pins

Pin Name	C_L	Unit
INTR, INT2, DREQ	60	
DPO	65	pF
D7 – D0, DP, HDB7 – O, HDBP	85	

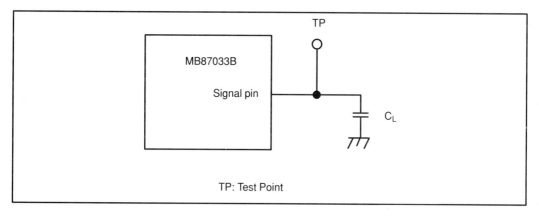

TP: Test Point

SCSI Pins

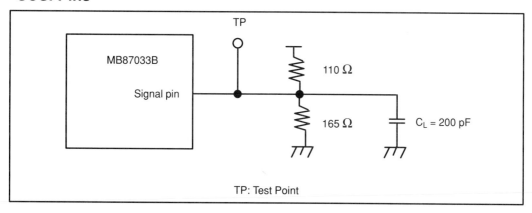

TP: Test Point

PACKAGE DIMENSIONS

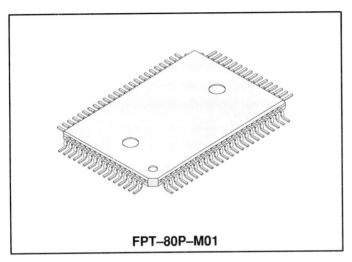

FPT–80P–M01

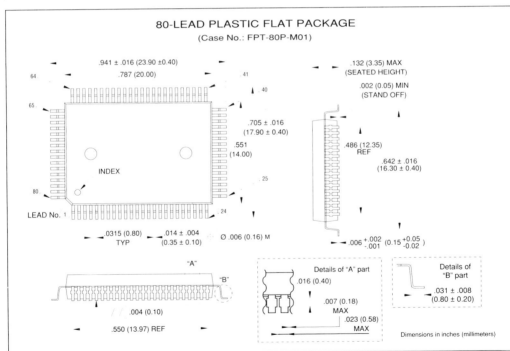

80-LEAD PLASTIC FLAT PACKAGE
(Case No.: FPT-80P-M01)

.941 ± .016 (23.90 ±0.40)

.787 (20.00)

.132 (3.35) MAX
(SEATED HEIGHT)

.002 (0.05) MIN
(STAND OFF)

.705 ± .016
(17.90 ± 0.40)

.551
(14.00)

.486 (12.35)
REF

.642 ± .016
(16.30 ± 0.40)

INDEX

LEAD No. 1

.0315 (0.80)
TYP

.014 ± .004
(0.35 ± 0.10)

Ø .006 (0.16) M

.006 $^{+.002}_{-.001}$ (0.15 $^{+0.05}_{-0.02}$)

"A"

"B"

.004 (0.10)

.550 (13.97) REF

Details of "A" part

.016 (0.40)

.007 (0.18)
MAX

.023 (0.58)
MAX

Details of
"B" part

.031 ± .008
(0.80 ± 0.20)

Dimensions in inches (millimeters)

PACKAGE DIMENSIONS

84–Lead Plastic Leaded Chip Carrier

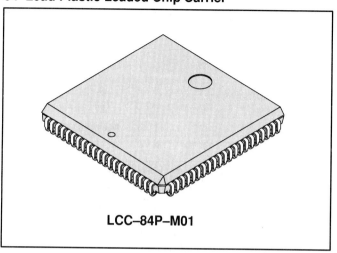

LCC–84P–M01

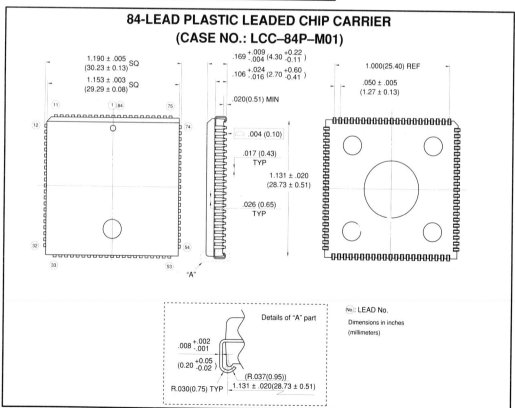

**84-LEAD PLASTIC LEADED CHIP CARRIER
(CASE NO.: LCC–84P–M01)**

Details of "A" part

No.: LEAD No.

Dimensions in inches
(millimeters)

Chapter 8

MB 87035/36
PRODUCT PROFILE

MB87035/36
SCSI Protocol Controller (SPC)
for use with Differential or Single-end Drivers

Edition 1.0
September 1989

GENERAL DESCRIPTION

The MB87035/36 SCSI Protocol Controller (SPC) is a CMOS LSI circuit specifically designed to control a Small Computer Systems Interface (SCSI). The MB87035/36 is an enhanced version of Fujitsu's MB87030 SCSI protocol controller and is pin for pin and register compatible with the MB87030, making it upward software and hardware compatible.

To achieve optimum performance and interface flexibility, the MB87035/36 provides an 8-byte First-In First-Out (FIFO) data buffer register and a 28-bit transfer byte counter which allows burst transfers of up to 256 megabytes. To improve programming requirements, "Attention Detect" and "Arbitration Fail" interrupts are provided. Data transfers can be executed in either the asynchronous or synchronous mode with a maximum offset of 8 bytes. Separate SCSI IN and SCSI OUT ports simplify the interface to differential drivers.

SCSI Compatibility

- Supports all mandatory commands, many optional commands, and some extended commands of SCSI specification (ANSI X 3.131-1986)
- Software and pin for pin compatible with MB87030
- Serves as either INITIATOR or TARGET

Data Bus

- Independent buses for CPU and DMA controller
- Independant SCSI IN and SCSI OUT buses

Data Transfer Modes/Speed

- Asynchronous mode transfers up to 3 megabytes/sec
- Synchronous mode transfers with programmable offset of eight bytes (8-Byte FIFO) up to a maximum of 5 megabytes/sec

Selectable Operating Modes

- DMA transfer
- Program transfer
- Manual transfer
- Diagnostic

Interface

- Usable with single-ended drivers/receivers (off-chip)
- Optimized for differential drivers (off-chip)

Clock Requirements

- 10 MHz clock

Technology/Power Requirements

- Silicon-gate CMOS
- Single +5 V power supply

Enhancements (features not available with MB87030)

- Select with ATN command support
- Maximum 10 MHz operating clock
  5.0 Megabyte/Second transfer rate
- Package and pinout compatible with
  MB87030
  Exception: (See attachment)
- Upward software compatible with MB87030
  and MB87031

- 28-bit transfer byte counter
- Data bus parity generator
- Attention condition detect interrupt
- Arbitration fail interrupt

Available Packaging

- 88-pin plastic PGA
- 100-pin Plastic Flatpack (PQFP)

ELECTRICAL CHARACTERISTICS

Permanent device damage may occur if the above absolute maximum ratings are exceeded. Functional operation should be restricted to the conditions as detailed in the operations sections of this data sheet. Exposure to absolute maximum rating conditions for extended periods may affect device reliability.

ABSOLUTE MAXIMUM RATINGS

Rating	Designator	Values		Unit
Supply Voltage[1]	V_{DD}	V_{SS} = 0.5 to +7.0		V
Input Voltage[1]	V_I	V_{SS} −0.5 to V_{DD} +0.5		V
Output Voltage[1]	V_O	V_{SS} −0.5 to V_{DD} +0.5		V
Operating Temperature	T_{OP}	−25 to +85		°C
Storage Temperature	T_{STG}	−40 to +125		°C
Output Current[2]	I_O	V_{DD} = MAX	$V_O = V_{DD}$ +70	mA
			$V_O = 0V$ −40	

Notes: [1]V_{SS} = 0V
[2]In the case of pin 1, 1 second.

RECOMMENDED OPERATING CONDITIONS

Recommended operating conditions are specified to guarantee the function of the device. Therefore, as long as the device is used within the specified limits, device reliability is guaranteed.

Rating	Designator	Values	Unit
Supply Voltage	V_{DD}	+5.0 ± 5%	V
Operating Ambient Temperature	T_a	0 to +70	°C
H Level Output Current	I_{OH}	Maximum −0.4	mA
L Level Output Current	I_{OL}	Maximum 3.2	mA

MB87035/36 BLOCK DIAGRAM

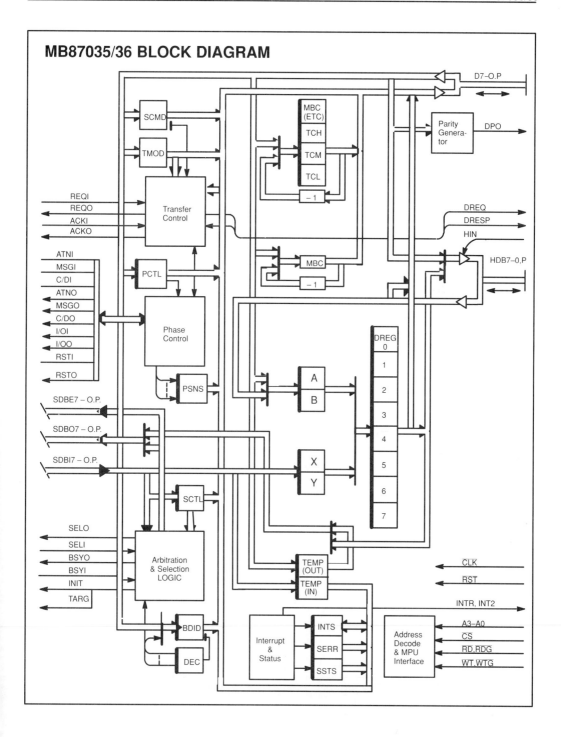

PIN ASSIGNMENTS
PGA–88P–M01

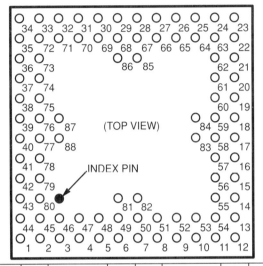

(TOP VIEW)

INDEX PIN

Pin No.	I/O	Designator	Pin No.	I/O	Designator	Pin No.	I/O	Designator	Pin No.	I/O	Designator
1	I	HIN	23	O	SDBOP	45	I	A1	67	O	SDBE5
2	I/O	HDBO0	24	O	SDBE7	46	I	A2	68	O	SDBE4
3	I/O	HDBO1	25	I	SDBI7	47	I	A3	69	I	SDBI4
4	I/O	HDBO2	26	O	SDBE6	48	I/O	D4	70	O	SDBO3
5	I/O	HDBO3	27	O	SDBO5	49	I/O	D5	71	I	SDBI2
6	I/O	HDBO4	28	I	SDBI5	50	I/O	D6	72	O	SDBO1
7	I/O	HDBO5	29	O	SDBO4	51	I/O	D7	73	O	SDBE0
8	I/O	HDBO6	30	O	SDBE3	52	I/O	DP	74	I	SDBI0
9	I/O	HDBO7	31	I	SDBI3	53	O	INTR	75	I	$\overline{RST}$
10	I/O	HDBOP	32	O	SDBO2	54	I	I/OI	76	O	DREQ
11	O	INIT	33	O	SDBE2	55	I	C/DI	77	I	$\overline{WT}$
12	O	TARG	34	I	SDBI1	56	I	SELI	78	O	DPO
13	O	I/OO	35	O	SDBE1	57	I	MSG1	79	I/O	D2
14	O	C/DO	36	O	SDBO0	58	I	REQI	80	I/O	D3
15	O	SELO	37	I	$\overline{CS}$	59	I	RSTI	81	Power Supply	V_{SS}
16	O	MSGO	38	I	$\overline{CLK}$	60	I	ACKI	82	Power Supply	V_{DD}
17	O	REQO	39	I	$\overline{RD}$	61	I	BSYI	83	Power Supply	V_{DD}
18	O	RSTO	40	O	INT2	62	I	ANTI	84	Power Supply	V_{SS}
19	O	ACKO	41	I	DRESP	63	I	SDBIP	85	Power Supply	V_{SS}
20	O	BSYO	42	I/O	D0	64	O	SDBO7	86	Power Supply	V_{DD}
21	O	ATNO	43	I/O	D1	65	O	SDBO6	87	Power Supply	V_{DD}
22	O	SDBEP	44	I	A0	66	I	SDBI6	88	Power Supply	V_{SS}

PIN ASSIGNMENTS
100-Pin Plastic Quad Flatpack (PQFP)

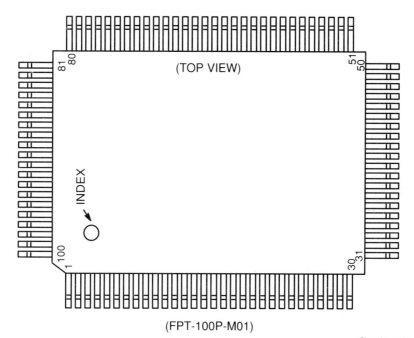

(FPT-100P-M01)

Continued on next page

PIN ASSIGNMENTS
100-Pin Plastic Quad Flatpack (PQFP)

Pin No.	I/O	Designator	Pin No.	I/O	Designator	Pin No.	I/O	Designator	Pin No.	I/O	Designator	Pin No.	I/O	Designator
1	I	DRESP	26	I/O	D2	51	O	TARG	76	O	SDBE5			
2	O	DREQ	27	I/O	D3	52	O	INIT	77	O	SDBO5			
3	Power Supply	V_{DD}	28	Power Supply	V_{DD}	53	Power Supply	V_{DD}	78	Power Supply	V_{DD}			
4	Power Supply	V_{SS}	29	Power Supply	V_{SS}	54	Power Supply	V_{SS}	79	Power Supply	V_{SS}			
5	I	HIN	30	I/O	D4	55	I	ACKI	80	—	NC			
6	I/O	HDB0	31	I/O	D5	56	O	ACKO	81	I	SDBI4			
7	I/O	HDB1	32	I/O	D6	57	—	NC	82	O	SDBE4			
8	I/O	HDB2	33	I/O	D7	58	—	NC	83	O	SDBO4			
9	I/O	HDB3	34	I/O	DP	59	I	BSYI	84	I	SDBI3			
10	I/O	HDB4	35	I	A0	60	O	BSYO	85	O	SDBE3			
11	I/O	HDB5	36	I	A1	61	I	ATNI	86	O	SDBO3			
12	I/O	HDB6	37	I	A2	62	O	ATNO	87	I	SDBI2			
13	I/O	HDB7	38	I	A3	63	I	RSTI	88	O	SDBE2			
14	I/O	HDBP	39	I	$\overline{RST}$	64	O	RSTO	89	O	SDBO2			
15	Power Supply	V_{SS}	40	Power Supply	V_{SS}	65	Power Supply	V_{SS}	90	Power Supply	V_{SS}			
16	I	$\overline{CLK}$	41	I	REQI	66	I	SDBIP	91	I	SDBI1			
17	I	$\overline{CS}$	42	O	REQO	67	O	SDBEP	92	O	SDBE1			
18	I	$\overline{WT}$	43	I	I/OI	68	O	SDBOP	93	O	SDBO1			
19	O	DPO	44	O	I/OO	69	I	SDBI7	94	I	SDBI0			
20	I	$\overline{RD}$	45	I	C/DI	70	O	SDBE7	95	O	SDBE0			
21	O	INT2	46	O	C/DO	71	O	SDBO7	96	O	SDBO0			
22	O	INTR	47	I	SELI	72	I	SDBI6	97	—	NC			
23	—	NC	48	O	SELO	73	O	SDBE6	98	—	NC			
24	I/O	D0	49	I	MSGI	74	O	SDBO6	99	—	NC			
25	I/O	D1	50	O	MSGO	75	I	SDBI5	100	—	NC			

PIN DESCRIPTIONS

Pin No. MB87035 PGA	Pin No. MB87036 QFP	Designator	Function
1	5	HIN	Indicates direction of transmission along data bus lines HDB0–HDB7 and HDBP in the DMA transfer mode. For transmission to be executed, direction of transmission must be properly coordinated with internal operation of the SPC. When HIN is low, the data bus lines are placed in the high-impedance state (input mode). When HIN is high, all bus lines are switched to the output mode.
2–9 10	6–13 14	HDB0–HDB7 HDBP	3-state bidirectional data bus for transferring data to or from the external buffer memory in the DMA mode. As shown below, the direction of data transmission dlepends on the HIN input signal. **HIN HDBn Operation** L Input Mode Output H Output Mode Input
11 12	52 51	INIT TARG	These two signals indicate operating state of SPC; they are also available as control signals for the SCSI driver/receiver circuits. **Initiator Target Status** L L SPC is not connected to SCSI. L H SPC is executing RESELECTION phase or is operating as a TARGET. H L SPC is executing SELECTION phase or is operating as an INITIATOR.
13 14 15 16 17 18 19 20 21	44 46 48 50 42 64 56 60 62	I/OO C/DO SELO MSGO REQO RSTO ACKO BSYO ATNO	Used to output SCSI control signals. REQO, MSGO, C/DO, and I/OO are active high only when the SPC serves as a TARGET. ACKO and ATNO are active high only when the SPC serves as an INITIATOR.
22 24 26 67 68 30 33 35 73	67 70 73 76 82 85 88 92 95	SDBEP SDBE7 SDBE6 SDBE5 SDBE4 SDBE3 SDBE2 SDBE1 SDBE0	Drive enable signals (corresponding to respective bit positions) when a 3-state buffer is used for the SCSI data bus. SDBE7-SDBE0 and SDBEP correspond to SDBO7–SDBO0 and SDBOP, respectively. Relationships with respect to the SCSI bus are shown below.

SCSI BUS STATUS	SDBOn		SDBEn	
	ID[1]	ĪD	ID	ĪD
Bus Free	L	L	L	L
Arbitration	H	L	H	L
Selection/Reselection	D[2]	D[2]	H	H
Information Transfer				
SPC ″ SCSI	D[2]	D[2]	H	H
SCSI u SPC	L	L	L	L

Notes: [1]D indicates bit positions corresponding to the SCSI bus device ID; ĪD indicates the other bit position.

[2]D indicates transfer of valid information.

Continued on next page

PIN DESCRIPTIONS

Pin No. MB87035 PGA	Pin No. MB87036 QFP	Designator	Function
25 66 28 69 31 71 34 74 63	69 72 75 81 84 91 94 66	SDBI7 SDBI6 SDBI5 SDBI4 SDBI3 SDBI2 SDBI1 SDBI0 SDBIP	Inputs for the SCSI data bus; most significant bit (MSB) is SDBI7; least significant bit (LSB) is SDBI0. SDBIP is an odd parity bit; parity checking for the SCSI data bus is programmable.
64 65 27 29 70 32 72 36 23	71 74 77 83 86 89 93 96 68	SDBO7 SDBO6 SDBO5 SDBO4 SDBO3 SDBO2 SDBO1 SDBO0 SDBOP	Outputs for the SCSI data bus; most significant bit (MSB) is SDBO7; least significant bit (LSB) is SDBO0. SDBOP is an odd parity bit. If the bus driver is an open collector device, these signals should be applied directly to the driver circuit. If the bus driver is a 3-state device, these signals are used as data and SDBO7–SDBO0 and SDBOP are used as drive-enable signals.
37	17	$\overline{\text{CS}}$	Selection enable signal for accessing an internal register in SPC. When $\overline{\text{CS}}$ is active, input/output signals $\overline{\text{RD}}$, $\overline{\text{WT}}$, A0–A3, D0–D7, and DP are active.
38	16	$\overline{\text{CLK}}$	Input clock for controlling internal operation and data transfer speed of SPC.
39	20	$\overline{\text{RD}}$	Input strobes used for reading out contents of internal register; strobes are effective only when $\overline{\text{CS}}$ is active low. For a data transfer cycle in the program transfer mode, the trailing edge of $\overline{\text{RD}}$ is used as a timing signal to indicate the end of data read.
41	1	DRESP	During a data transfer cycle in the DMA mode, DRESP is a response signal to the data transfer request signal DREQ. The DRESP pin must be refreshed with an applied pulse after each byte of data is transferred. In output operations, the falling edge of DRESP is used for sampling data on HDB0-HDB7 and HDBP bus lines; in input operations, the SPC holds data to be transferred onto HDB0-HDB7 and HDBP until the falling edge of DRESP occurs.
51 50 49 48 80 79 43 42 52	33 32 31 30 27 26 25 24 34	D7 D6 D5 D4 D3 D2 D1 D0 DP	Used for writing or reading data from or to an internal register in SPC; these bus lines are 3-state and bidirectional. The most significant bit (MSB) is D7; the least significant bit (LSB) is D0. DP is an odd parity bit. When the $\overline{\text{CS}}$ and $\overline{\text{RD}}$ inputs are active Low, contents of the internal register are output to the data bus (read operation). In operations other than read, these bus lines are kept in a hgh-impedance state.

Continued on next page

PIN DESCRIPTIONS

Pin No. MB87035 PGA	Pin No. MB87036 QFP	Designator	Function
44–47	35–38	A0–A3	Address input signals for selecting an internal register in the SPC. The MSB is A3; the LSB is A0. When $\overline{CS}$ is active low, read/write is enabled and an internal register is selected by these address inputs via data bus lines D0-D7 and DP.
53	22	INTR	Requests an interrupt to indicate completion of an SPC internal operation or the occurrence of an error. Interrupt masking is allowed except for an interrupt caused by the RSTI input (reset condition of SCSI). When an interrupt is permitted, the INTR signal remains active until the interrupt is cleared.
56 61 58 60 57 55 54 62 59	47 59 41 55 49 45 43 61 63	SELI BSYI REQI ACKI MSGI C/DI I/OI ATNI RSTI	Used for receiving SCSI control signals; outputs of the SCSI receiver can be directly connected. (Waveform distortion or any other disturbance should not occur in the REQI and ACKI signals which are used as timing control signals for sequencing data transfers.)

76	2	DREQ	When executing a data transfer cycle in the DMA mode, DREQ is used to indicate a request for data transfer between the SPC and external buffer memory. In the DMA mode, routing of data is as shown below.
			
			Output Operations:
			  From external buffer memory to HDB0-HDB7/HDBP to SPC internal data buffer register (8 Bytes) to SDBO0-SDBO7/SDBOP to SCSI.
			
			Input Operations:
			  From SCSI to SDBI9-SDBI7/SDBIP to SPC internal data buffer register (8 bytes) to HDB0-HDB7/HDBP to external buffer memory.
			
			In an output operation, DREQ becomes active to request a data transfer from the external buffer memory when the SPC internal data buffer register has free space available. In an input operation. DREQ becomes active to request a data transfer to the external buffer memory when the SPC internal buffer memory contains valid data.

Continued on next page

PIN DESCRIPTIONS

Pin No. MB87035	Pin No. MB87036	Designator	Function
PGA	QFP		
77	18	$\overline{WT}$	Input strobe used for writing data into an SPC internal register; this signal is asserted only when $\overline{CS}$ is active low. On the trailing edge of $\overline{WT}$, data placed on data bus lines D0-D7/DP is loaded into the internal register selected by address inputs A0-A3, except when all address lines are high (A0-A3 = H). For a data transfer cycle in the program transfer mode, the trailing edge of $\overline{WT}$ is used as a timing signal to indicate a data-ready state.
78	19	DPO	An odd parity output for data byte D7-D0, DPO represents an output when D7-D0/DP are placed in a high-impendance state; DPO is in a high-impedance state when D7-D0/DP serve as outputs. If a parity bit is not genetrated for external memory, DPO can be used as an input for DP.
81, 84 85, 88	4, 29, 54, 79 15, 40 65, 90	V_{SS}	Power supply ground, (0 V).
82. 83 86, 87	3, 28, 53, 78	V_{DD}	+5 V Power Supply.
40	21	INT2	The INT2 output is a non-maskable interrupt request that, when driven High, notifies the SPC when a reset condition is detected on the SCSI bus.
—	23, 57 58, 80 97, 98 99, 100	NC	No connects.

ADDRESSING OF INTERNAL REGISTERS

The MB87035/36 contains 16 byte-wide registers that are externally accessible. These registers are used to control internal operations of the SPC and also to indicate processing/result status. A unique address, identified by address bits A3-A0, is assigned to each of the sixteen registers. These addresses are defined in Table 1. (Note: The phase sense (PSNS) and SPC diagnostic (SDGC) registers have the same hexadecimal address; however, depending upon whether a read or write command is executed, the registers provide two separate functions.)

Table 1. Internal Register Addressing

Register	Mnemonic	Operation	Chip Select ($\overline{CS}$)	A3	A2	A1	A0
Bus Device ID	BDID	R	0	0	0	0	0
		W					
SPC Control	SCTL	R	0	0	0	0	1
		W					
Command	SCMD	R	0	0	0	1	0
		W					
Transfer Mode	TMOD	R	0	0	0	1	1
		W					
Interrupt Sense	INTS	R	0	0	1	0	0
Reset Interrupt		W					
Phase Sense	PSNS	R	0	0	1	0	1
SPC Diagnostic Control	SDGC	W					
SPC Status	SSTS	R	0	0	1	1	0
—		W					
SPC Error Status	SERR	R	0	0	1	1	1
—		W					
Phase Control	PCTL	R	0	1	0	0	0
		W					
Modified Byte Counter	MBC	R	0	1	0	0	1
Extended Transfer Count		W					

Continued on next page

Table 1. Internal Register Addressing

Register	Mnemonic	Operation	Chip Select ($\overline{CS}$)	Address Bits			
				A3	A2	A1	A0
Data Register	DREG	R	0	1	0	1	0
		W					
Temporary Register	TEMP	R	0	1	0	1	1
		W					
Transfer Counter High	TCH	R	0	1	1	0	0
		W					
Transfer Counter Middle	TCM	R	0	1	1	0	1
		W					
Transfer Counter Low	TCL	R	0	1	1	1	0
		W					
External Buffer	EXBF	R	0	1	1	1	1
		W					

BIT ASSIGNMENTS FOR INTERNAL REGISTERS

Table 2 lists the bit assignments for the sixteen internal registers defined in Table 1. In most cases, bit assignments for the MB87035/36 SPCs are identical to those for the MB87030; however, in the MB87035/36, some features are expanded and others are added to improve overall performance. These modifications and additions are summarized as follows:

Table 2. Bit Assignments For Internal Registers

HEX Address	Register and Mnemonic	R/W Oper- ation	7 (MSb)	6	5	4	3	2	1	0 (LSb)	Parity
0	Bus Device ID (BDID)	R	#7	#6	#5	#4	#3	#2	#1	#0	0
		W						SCSI Bus Device ID ID4	ID2	ID1	—
1	SPC Control (SCTL)	R	Reset & Dis- able	Con- trol Reset	Diag Mode	ARBIT Enable	Parity Enable	Select Enable	Re- select Enable	INT Enable	P
		W									
2	Command (SCMD)	R	Command Code			RST Out	Inter- cept Xfer	Transfer Modifer PRG Xfer	0	Term Mode	P
		W									
3	Transfer Mode (TMOD)	R	Sync	Max. Transfer Offset			Min. Transfer Offset			Xfer Count- er Expand	P
		W	Xfer								
				4	2	1	2	1	0		
4	Interrupt Sense (INTS)	R	Selec- ted	Resel- ected	Discon- nect	Com- mand Com- plete	Service Re- quired	Time Out	SPC Hard Error	Reset Condi- tion	P
		W	Reset Interrupt								—
5	Phase Sense (PSNS)	R	REQ	ACK	ATN	SEL	BSY	MSG	C/D	I/O	P
	SPC Diag Control (SDGC)	W	Diag. REQ	Diag. ACK	—	—	Diag. BSY	Diag. MSG	Diag. C/D	Diag. I/O	—
6	SPC Status (SSTS)	R	Connected INIT	TARG	SPC BSY	Xfer In Pro- gress	SCSI RST	TC=0	DREG Status Full	Empty	P
7	SPC Error Status (SERR)	R	Data Error SCSI	SPC	0	0	TC Parity Error	Phase Error	Short Xfer Period	Offset Error	P

Continued on next page

Table 2. Bit Assignments For Internal Registers

HEX Address	Register and Mnemonic	R/W Oper-ation	7 (MSb)	6	5	4	3	2	1	0 (LSb)	Parity
8	Phase Control (PCTL)	R	Bus Free Inter-rupt Enable	Arbit-ration Fail Inter-rupt Enable	Atten-tion Condi-tion Inter-rupt Enable	Reset Condi-tion Inter-rupt mask	0	Transfer Phase			P
		W						MSG Out	C/D Out	I/O Out	
9	Modified Byte Counter (MBC)	R	Extended Transfer Counter				MBC				P
			Bit 27	Bit 26	Bit 25	Bit 24	Bit 3	Bit 2	Bit 1	Bit 0	
A	Data Register (DREG)	R	Internal Data Register (8 Byte FIFO)								
		W	Bit 7	Bit 6	Bit 5	Bit 4	Bit 3	Bit 2	Bit 1	Bit 0	P
B	Temporary Register (TEMP)	R	Temporary Data (Input: From SCSI)								P
			Bit 7	Bit 6	Bit 5	Bit 4	Bit 3	Bit 2	Bit 1	Bit 0	
		W	Temporary Data (Output: To SCSI)								P
			Bit 7	Bit 6	Bit 5		Bit 3	Bit 2	Bit 1	Bit 0	
C	Transfer Counter High (TCH)	R	Transfer Counter High (MSB)								
		W	Bit 23	Bit 22	Bit 21	Bit 20	Bit 19	Bit 18	Bit 17	Bit 16	P
D	Transfer Counter Middle (TCM)	R	Transfer Counter Middle (2nd Byte)								
		W	Bit 15	Bit 14	Bit 13	Bit 12	Bit 11	Bit 10	Bit 9	Bit 8	P
E	Transfer Counter LOW (TCL)	R	Transfer Counter Low (LSB)								
		W	Bit 7	Bit 6	Bit 5	Bit 4	Bit 3	Bit 2	Bit 1	Bit 0	P
E	External Buffer (EXBF)	R	External Buffer								
		W	Bit 7	Bit 6	Bit 5	Bit 4	Bit 3	Bit 2	Bit 1	Bit 0	P

MPU Bus Parity Generator

An odd parity bit is output from DPO for each data byte (D7-D0). DPO is a 3-state pin and is placed in a high-impedance state when data from D7-D0 is output to the MPU. If the MPU interface does not contain a parity generator, the output of DPO can be connected to the DP input pin of the SPC.

Reset Condition Interrupt Request Signal

The INT2 output is a non-maskable interrupt request that, when driven High, notifies the SPC when a reset condition is detected on the SCSI bus. Bit 4 (Reset Condition Interrupt Mask Enable) of the Phase Control (PCTL) register does not affect the INT2 output pin.

When a bus reset condition is detected, the INTR output also is driven to the high state; however, the state of INTR can be masked by bit 4 of the PCTL register:

Bit 4 = 0:   INTR goes high when a reset condition is detected.

Bit 4 = 1:   INTR does not go high when a reset condition is detected.

Lost Arbitration Interrupt Request

If bit 6 (Lost Arbitration Interrupt Enable) of the phase control (PCTL) register is set to "1", a COMMAND COMPLETE interrupt is generated when the SPC (serving as initiator or target) loses in the ARBITRATION process. To determine the cause of a COMMAND COMPLETE interrupt (completion of SELECTION, RESELECTION, or lost ARBITRATION), refer to bits 6 (TARGET) and 7 (INITIATOR) of the SPC status (SSTS) register. If both bits are set to "0", the COMMAND COMPLETE interrupt is a result of lost arbitration.

Attention Condition Interrupt

If bit 5 (Attention Condition Interrupt Enable) of the phase control (PCTL) register is set to "1" and the SPC serves as a target, a service required interrupt occurs. To reset the service required interrupt, set bit 3 of the interrupt sense (INTS) register to "1" or revoke the current target role of the SPC.

Expansion of Transfer Byte Counter

If bit 0 of the transfer mode (TMOD) register is set to "1", the transfer byte counter is expanded to 28 bits. In the expanded mode, the high nibble (bits 24 through 27) are entered into the four most significant bit positions (7 bits through 4) of the modified byte count (MBC) register.

> **Note:** *When a hardware data transfer or execution of a SELECT command is in process, access to the TMOD register is forbidden.*

Bit 0 of the TMOD register =1

To access the highest four bits (bits 24 through 27) of the transfer byte counter, data reads or writes are addressed to the high nibble of the modified byte counter (MBC) register. When a TRANSFER or SELECT command is issued, the transfer byte count (or t_{WAIT}) should be placed in the high nibble of the MBC register rather than the TCH, TCM, and TCL registers.

Bit 0 of the TMOD register = 0

The transfer byte counter is not expanded to 28 bits; hence, reading the high nibble of MBC yields a "0" even though some particular value is written into the register. In this case, t_{WAIT} or the transfer byte count is based on a 24-bit transfer byte counter (identical to the MB87030).

During read/write access of an internal register, the following rules are invoked:

(1)　Internal registers include only those registers identified in Table 2.
(2)　A write command to a read–only register is ignored.
(3)　For write operations, all bit positions with a "—" (blank) designator can be written as "0" or as a "1".
(4)　All bit positions with an assigned "0" are always read as a zero (0).

Select with ATN Command

- *Initiation:*
  Writing 21H to the SCMD register with the PCTL register's bit 0 (I/O Out) = "0". (When the PCTL register's Bit 0 = "1", the Select command is initiated.)

- *Ignore:*
  The Select with ATN command is ignored (no operation) when MB87035/36 has already been connected with the SCSI bus or when the MB87035/36 is executing the connecting sequence.

- *Cancellation:*
  The Select with ATN command is cancelled in the following cases:
  1. When terminating the selection by time-out.

  2. When failing in arbitration.

  3. When Bus Release command is issued.

  4. When selected by another device.

> **Note:** *A combination of the Set ATN command and the Select command can also be used.*

DC CHARACTERISTICS

DC characteristics of input and output buffers are guaranteed to the worst case value over the recommended range of operating conditions.

V_{DD} = 5 V ± 5%. V_{SS} = 0 V. T_a = 0 to 70°C

Parameter	Designator	Conditions	Values			Unit
			Minimum	Typical	Maximum	
Supply Voltage	I_{DDS}	Static	—	—	0.1	mA
Output High Voltage	V_{OH}	I_{OH} = −0.4 mA	4.2	—	V_{DD}	V
Output Low Voltage	V_{OL}	I_{OL} = 3.2 mA	V_{SS}	—	0.4	V
Input High Voltage	V_{IH}	TTL Level	2.2	—	V_{DD} +0.5	V
		CMOS Level	V_{DD} x 0.7	—	—	V
Input Low Voltage	V_{IL}	TTL Level	—	—	0.8	V
		CMOS Level	—	—	V_{DD} x 0.3	V
Input Leakage current (during tristate pin input)	I_{LI}	V_I = 0V to V_{DD}	−10	—	10	mA
	I_{LZ}		−10	—	10	mA

INPUT/OUTPUT PIN CAPACITANCE

Parameter	Designator	Values	Unit
Input Pin	C_{IN}	9	pF
Output Pin	C_{OUT}	9	pF
Input/Output Pin	$C_{I/O}$	11	pF

Measurement conditions: T_a = 25°C V_{DD} = V_I = 0 V, f = 1 MHz

AC CHARACTERISTICS

Clock Timing

Parameter	Designator	Values		Unit
		Min.	Max.	
Clock Cycle	t_{CLF}	125	200	ns
Clock High Time	t_{CHCL}	50	—	ns
Clock Low Time	t_{CLCH}	40	—	ns

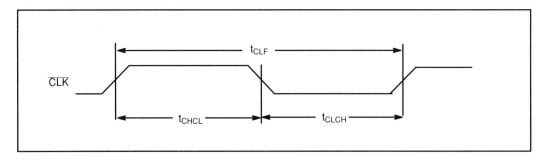

Hardware Reset

Parameter	Designator	Values		Unit
		Min.	Max.	
Reset Pulse Width	t_{RSTW}	50	—	ns

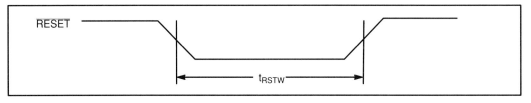

AC CHARACTERISTICS

Register Write (excluding EXBF register)				
Parameter	Designator	Values		Unit
		Min.	Max.	
Address Setup	t_{AWS}	35	—	ns
Address Hold	t_{AWH}	5	—	ns
CS Setup	t_{CWS}	20	—	ns
CS Hold	t_{CWH}	10	—	ns
Data Bus Setup	t_{DWS}	25	—	ns
Data Bus Hold	t_{DWH}	15	—	ns
Write Pulse Width	t_{WT}	50	—	ns
Data Bus Valid to DPO Valid	t_{DPV}	—	55	ns

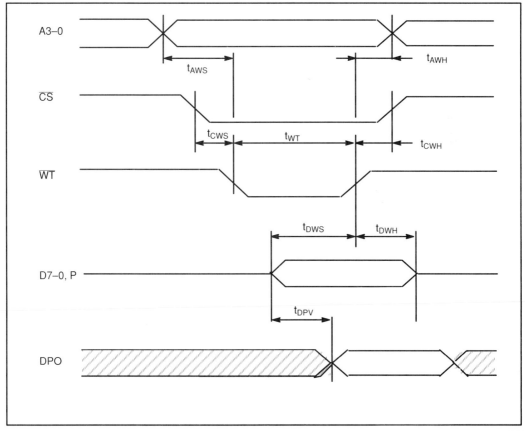

AC CHARACTERISTICS

EXBF Register Write				
Parameter	Designator	Values		Unit
		Min.	Max.	
Address Setup	t_{AWSE}	35	—	ns
Address Hold	t_{AWHE}	5	—	ns
$\overline{CS}$ Setup	t_{CWSE}	20	—	ns
$\overline{CS}$ Hold	t_{CWHE}	10	—	ns
$\overline{WT}$ "L" to DMA bus output valid	t_{WLHD}	—	55	ns
$\overline{WT}$ "H" to DMA bus output valid	t_{WHHD}	10	—	ns
MPU data bus to DMA bus delay	t_{DHD}	—	50	ns

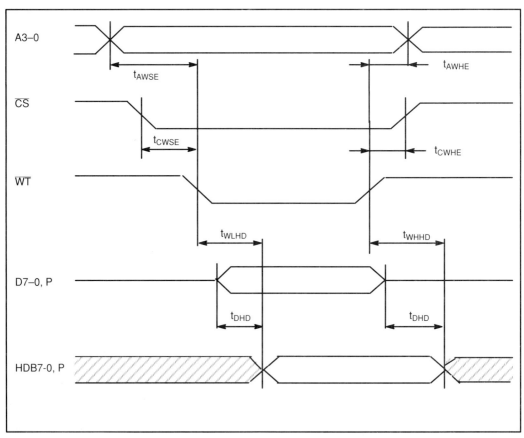

AC CHARACTERISTICS

Register Read (excluding EXBF register)				
Parameter	**Designator**	**Values**		**Unit**
		Min.	**Max.**	
Address Setup	t_{ARS}	35	—	ns
Address Hold	t_{ARH}	5	—	ns
$\overline{CS}$ Setup	t_{CRS}	20	—	ns
$\overline{CS}$ Hold	t_{CRH}	10	—	ns
$\overline{RD}$ "L" to data bus output	t_{RLNZ}	10	40	ns
$\overline{RD}$ "H" to data bus high Z	t_{RHHZ}	10	40	ns
$\overline{RD}$ "L" to data valid — D7 to D0	t_{RLD}	—	70	ns
$\overline{RD}$ "L" to data valid — DP	t_{RLD}	—	85	ns
$\overline{RD}$ "H" to data invalid	t_{RHD}	10	—	ns
$\overline{RD}$ pulse width	t_{RD}	50	—	ns
$\overline{RD}$ "L" to DPO high Z*	t_{DPZ}	10	40	ns
$\overline{RD}$ "H" to DPO output	t_{DPO}	10	40	ns

*DPO becomes High Z when both $\overline{RD}$ and $\overline{CS}$ are "L"

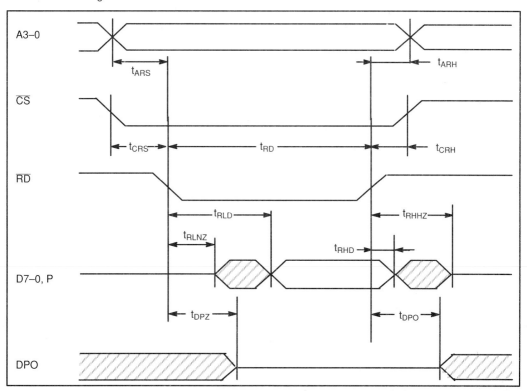

AC CHARACTERISTICS

EXBF Register Read

Parameter	Designator	Values		Unit
		Min.	Max.	
Address Setup	t_{ARSE}	35	—	ns
Address Hold	t_{ARHE}	5	—	ns
$\overline{CS}$ Setup	t_{CRSE}	20	—	ns
$\overline{CS}$ Hold	t_{CRHE}	10	—	ns
$\overline{RD}$ "L" to data bus output	t_{RLNZ}	10	40	ns
$\overline{RD}$ "H" to data bus high Z	t_{RHHZ}	10	40	ns
DMA bus to MPU data bus delay	t_{HDD}	—	50	ns

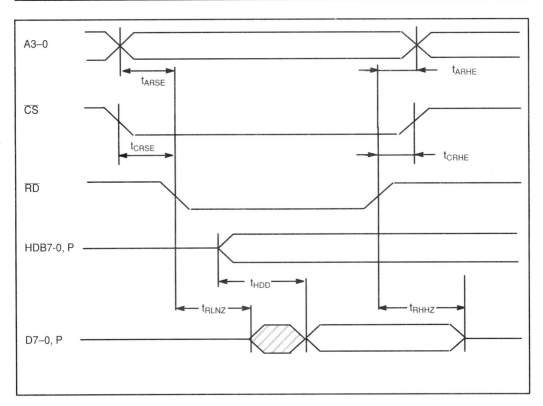

AC CHARACTERISTICS

DREG Access Cycle Time

Parameter	Designator	Values		Unit
		Min.	Max.	
DREG access cycle time 1	t_{DCY1}	$2t_{CLF}$	—	ns
DREG access cycle time 2	t_{DCY2}	$3t_{CLF}$	—	ns

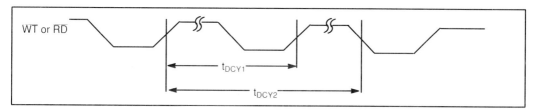

Command Issue Cycle Time

Parameter	Designator	Values		Unit
		Min.	Max.	
SCMD register write cycle	t_{CMCY}	$4t_{CLF}$	—	ns

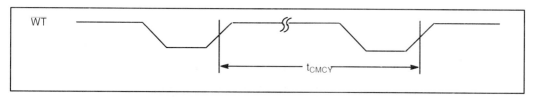

Interrupt REset

Parameter	Designator	Values		Unit
		Min.	Max.	
$\overline{WT}$ "H" to interrupt signal "L"	t_{WHIR}	t_{CLF}	$3t_{CLF}$ +80	ns
INTS register write cycle	t_{IRCY}	$4t_{CLF}$	—	ns

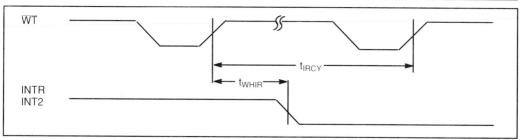

AC CHARACTERISTICS

DMA Access Timing

Parameter	Designator	Values		Unit
		Min.	Max.	
DREQ "H" to DRESP "H"	t_{DRRP}	t_{CLF}	—	ns
DRESP "H" to DREQ "L"	t_{RPDR}	5	70	ns
DREQ "L" to DREQ "H"	t_{DLDH}	0	—	ns
DRESP pulse width	t_{RPSW}	50	—	ns
DRESP cycle time 1	t_{RCY1}	$2t_{CLF}$	—	ns
DRESP cycle time 2	t_{RCY2}	$3t_{CLF}$	—	ns
DREQ "L" to DRESP "L"	t_{DLRP}	—	$5t_{CLF}$	ns

Notes: Utilized when using data buffer storage function and/or using transfer pause command. In these cases, if DREQ and DRESP do not become "L" simultaneously, the response to DREQ is undetermined. Also, write to data buffer will not be performed correctly unless t_{DLRP} and t_{RPSW} are complete.

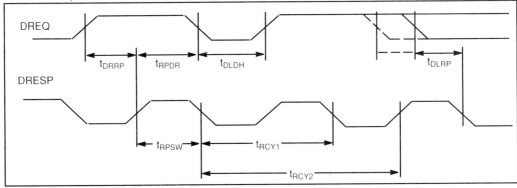

DMA Bus Output Control

Parameter	Designator	Values		Unit
		Min.	Max.	
HIN "H" to DMA bus output	t_{HIHO}	5	40	ns
HIN "L" to DMA bus high Z	t_{HIHZ}	5	40	ns

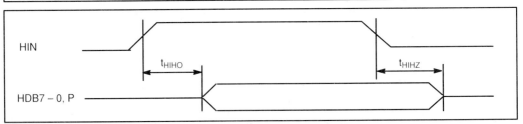

AC CHARACTERISTICS

DMA Transfer: Data Received from SCSI

Parameter	Designator	Values		Unit
		Min.	Max.	
DREQ "H" to data output valid*	t_{DRDV}	—	60	ns
DRESP "L" to data switch	t_{RPDV}	15	90	ns

*Utilized when internal data buffer is changed from Not Empty to Empty.

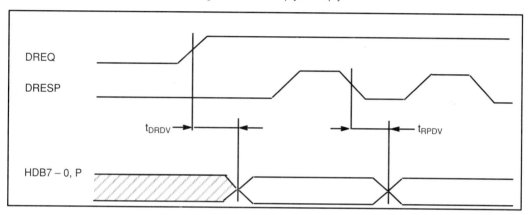

DMA Transfer: Sending Data to SCSI

Parameter	Designator	Values		Unit
		Min.	Max.	
Input data setup	t_{HDRS}	20	—	ns
Input data hold	t_{HDRH}	15	—	ns

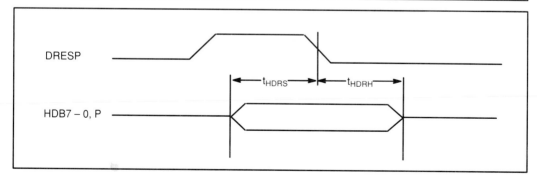

AC CHARACTERISTICS

Selection: Initiator (including arbitration)

Parameter	Designator	Values Min.	Values Max.	Unit
Bus free to BYSO "H"	t_{BFBO}	$(6 + n)\, t_{CLF}{}^*$	$(7 + n)\, t_{CLF} + 70^*$	ns
BSYO "H" to to sending its own ID bit	t_{BHID}	0	60	ns
BSYO "H" to SELO "H"	t_{BHSO}	$32 t_{CLF} - 40$	$32 t_{CLF} + 30$	ns
SELO "H" to to sending ID	t_{SOID}	$11 t_{CLF} - 30$	$11 t_{CLF} + 50$	ns
SELO "H" to INIT "H"	t_{SOIT}	$11 t_{CLF} - 30$	$11 t_{CLF} + 50$	ns
INIT "H" to ATNO "H"	t_{ITAT}	-10	30	ns
Sending ID to BSYO "L"	t_{IDBL}	$2 t_{CLF} - 50$	$2 t_{CLF} + 30$	ns
BSYI "H" to SEYO "L", ID hold	t_{BISL}	$2 t_{CLF}$	$3 t_{CLF} + 120$	ns
SELO "L" to INTR "H"	t_{SCIR}	—	40	ns

*n = TCL register setting value

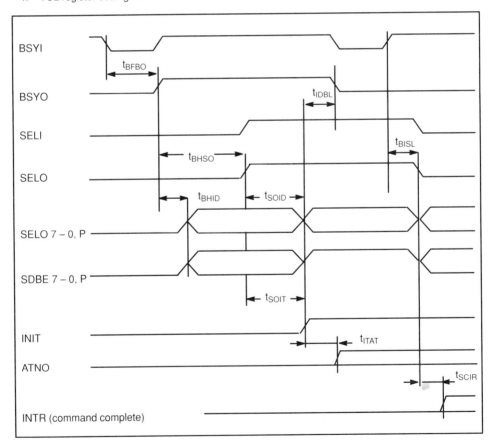

AC CHARACTERISTICS

Selection: Initiator (no arbitration)

Parameter	Designator	Values Min.	Values Max.	Unit
Bus free to sending ID	t_{FRID}	$(6 + n) \, t_{CLF}{}^{*}$	$(7 + n) \, t_{CLF} + 90^{*}$	ns
Sending ID to SELO "H"	t_{IDSO}	$11 t_{CLF} - 50$	$11 t_{CLF} + 30$	ns
Sending ID to INIT "H"	t_{IDIT}	$11 t_{CLF} - 50$	$11 t_{CLF} + 40$	ns
INIT "H" to ATNO "H"	t_{ITAT}	-10	30	ns
BSYI "H" to SELO "L", ID hold	t_{BISL}	$2 t_{CLF}$	$3 t_{CLF} + 120$	ns
SELO "L" to INTR "H"	t_{SCIR}	—	40	ns

*n = TCL register setting value

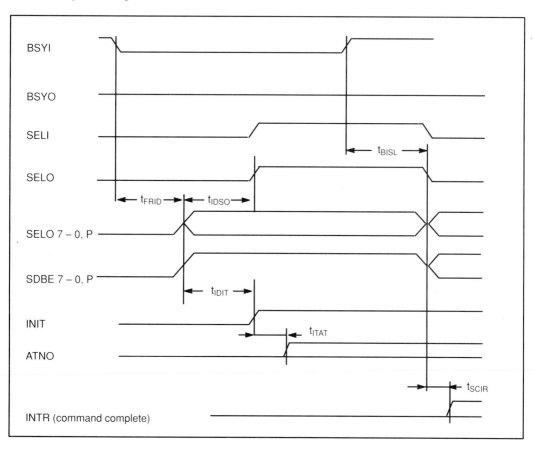

Selection: Target (including arbitration)

Parameter	Designator	Values Min.	Values Max.	Unit
SELI "H" to BSYI "L"	t_{SIBI}	0	—	ns
ID valid to BSYI "L"	t_{IDBI}	0	—	ns
I/OI "L" to BSYI "L"	t_{IIBI}	0	—	ns
BSYI "L" to BSYO "H"	t_{BLBO}	$4t_{CLF}$	$5t_{CLF} + 60$	ns
BSYO "H" ID hold	t_{BOID}	20	—	ns
BSYO "H" to SELI "L"	t_{BOSI}	0	—	ns
SELI "L" to TARG "H"	t_{SLTG}	$3t_{CLF}$	$4t_{CLF} + 70$	ns
TARG "H" to Phase signal output	t_{TGPH}	−10	30	ns
SELI "L" to INTR "H"	t_{SLIR}	—	$3t_{CLF} + 70$	ns

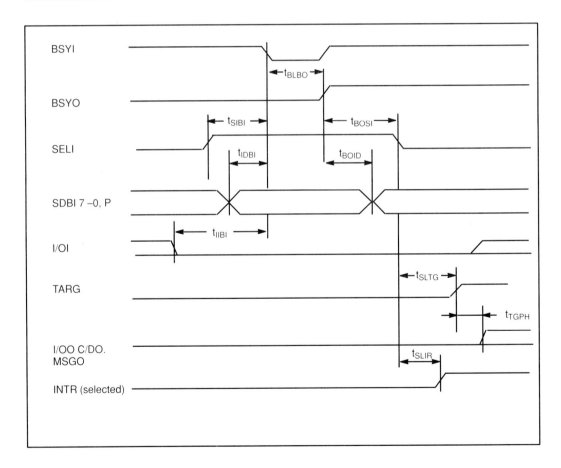

AC CHARACTERISTICS

Selection: Target (no arbitration)

Parameter	Designator	Values Min.	Values Max.	Unit
ID valid to SELI "H"	t_{IDSI}	0	—	ns
I/OI "L" to SELI "H"	t_{IISI}	0	—	ns
SELI "H" to BSYO "H"	t_{SLBO}	$4t_{CLF}$	$5t_{CLF} +100$	ns
BSYO "H" to ID hold	t_{BOID}	20	—	ns
BSYO "H" to SELI "L"	t_{BOSI}	0	—	ns
SELI "L" to TARG "H"	t_{SLTG}	$3t_{CLF}$	$4t_{CLF} +70$	ns
TARG "H" to Phase signal output	t_{TGPH}	−10	30	ns
SELI "L" to INTR "H"	t_{SLIR}	—	$3t_{CLF} +70$	ns

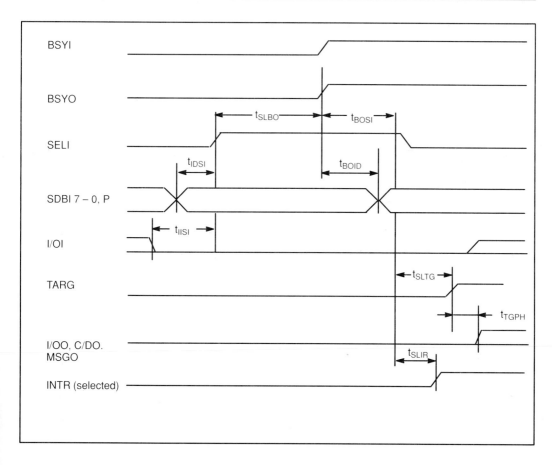

AC CHARACTERISTICS

Reselection: Target				
Parameter	Designator	Values		Unit
		Min.	Max.	
Bus free to BYSO "H"	t_{BFBO}	$(6 + n) t_{CLF}*$	$(7 + n) t_{CLF} + 70*$	ns
BSYO "H" to sending its own ID bit	t_{BHID}	0	60	ns
BSYO "H" to SELO "H"	t_{BHSO}	$32t_{CLF} -40$	$32t_{CLF} +30$	ns
SELO "H" to sending ID	t_{SOID}	$11t_{CLF} -30$	$11t_{CLF} +50$	ns
SELO "H" to TARG "H"	t_{SOTG}	$11t_{CLF} -30$	$11t_{CLF} +50$	ns
TARG "H" to sending phase signal	t_{TGPH}	-10	30	ns
Sending ID to BSYO "L"	t_{IDBL}	$2t_{CLF} -50$	$2t_{CLF} +30$	ns
BSYI "H" to BSYO "H"	t_{BIBO}	$2 t_{CLF}$	$3t_{CLF} +90$	ns
BSYO "H" to SELO "L", ID hold	t_{BOSL}	$t_{CLF} -20$	$t_{CLF} +60$	ns
SELO "L" to INTR "H"	t_{SCIR}	—	40	ns

*n = TCL register setting value

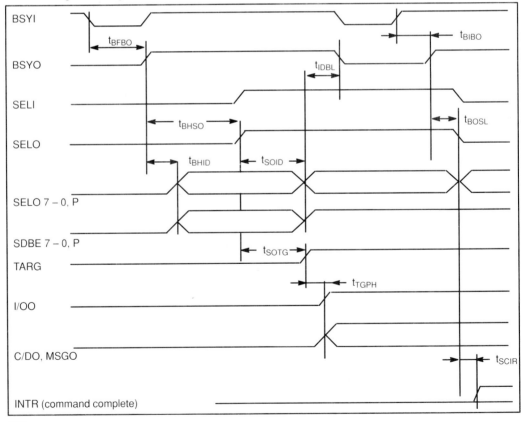

AC CHARACTERISTICS

Reselection: Initiator

Parameter	Designator	Values Min.	Values Max.	Unit
SELI "H" to BSYI "L"	t_{SIBI}	0	—	ns
ID valid to BSYI "L"	t_{IDBI}	0	—	ns
I/OI "H" to BSYI "L"	t_{IIBI}	0	—	ns
BSYI "L" to BSYO "H"	t_{BLBO}	$4t_{CLF}$	$5t_{CLF} +60$	ns
BSYO "H" to ID hold	t_{BOID}	20	—	ns
BSYO "H" to SELI "L"	t_{BOSI}	0	—	ns
BSYO "H" to I/$\overline{D}$ hold	t_{BOII}	20	—	ns
SELI "L" to INIT "H"	t_{SLIT}	$3t_{CLF}$	$4t_{CLF} +70$	ns
SELI "L" to BSYO "L"	t_{SIBO}	$2t_{CLF}$	$3t_{CLF} +60$	ns
SELI "L" to INTR "H"	t_{SLIR}	—	$3t_{CLF} +70$	ns

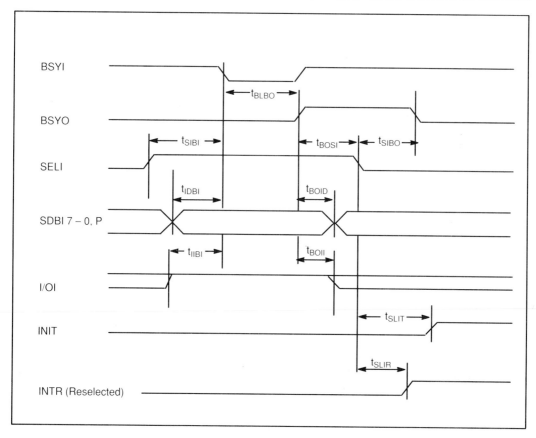

AC CHARACTERISTICS

Asynchronous Transfer: Initiator REQ-ACK Timing

Parameter	Designator	Values		Unit
		Min.	Max.	
REQI "H" to ACKO "H"	t_{RAOH}	10	75 [3]	ns
ACKO "H" to REQI "L"	t_{AOHR}	0	—	ns
REQI "L" to ACKO "L"	t_{RAOL}	10	75 [3]	ns
ACKO "L" to REQI "H"	t_{AOLR}	10	—	ns
REQI "L" to ACKO "H"[1]	t_{RAC1}	$2t_{CLF}$	$3t_{CLF}+110$ [3]	ns
REQI "H" to ACKO "L"[2]	t_{RAC2}	$2t_{CLF}$	$3t_{CLF}+110$ [3]	ns

Notes: [1]The time from REQI "L" to ACK "H" is set by the longer one of either ($t_{RAOL} + t_{AOLR} + t_{RAOH}$) or t_{RAC1}.

[2]Used during input. The time from REQ1 "H" to ACKO "L" is set by the longer one of either ($t_{RAOH} + t_{AOHR} + t_{RAOL}$) or t_{RAC2}.

[3]The time value of this table is not valid under the following conditions:
    1. Data buffer is empty during output.
    2. Data buffer is full during input.
    3. During the transfer of the first bit or the last bit.
    4. When SPC automatically sends ATNO signals during input.

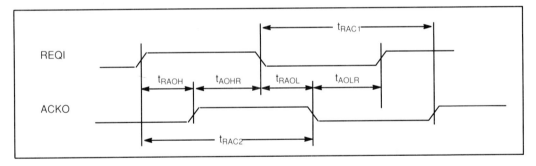

AC CHARACTERISTICS

Asynchronous Transfer: Initiator Output

Parameter	Designator	Values		Unit
		Min.	Max.	
I/O "L" to Data bus output	t_{IIDE}	10	100	ns
Set Phase to REQI "H"	t_{PHRQ}	100	—	ns
Data bus output invalid to ACKO "H"	t_{DVLD}	$2t_{CLF}-80$	—	ns
REQI "L" to Data bus hold	t_{DIVD}	15	—	ns
ACKO "L" to Phase change	t_{ALPH}	10	—	ns

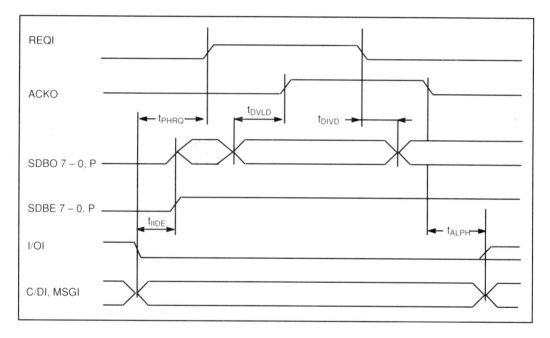

AC CHARACTERISTICS

Asynchronous Transfer: Initiator Input

Parameter	Designator	Values		Unit
		Min.	Max.	
I/OI "H" to Data bus output terminate	t_{IIDD}	—	100	ns
Set Phase to REQI "H"	t_{PHRQ}	100	—	ns
Data bus valid to REQI "H"	t_{TDSU}	10	—	ns
ACKO "H" to Data bus hold	t_{DHLD}	15	—	ns
ACKO "L" to Phase change	t_{ALPH}	10	—	ns

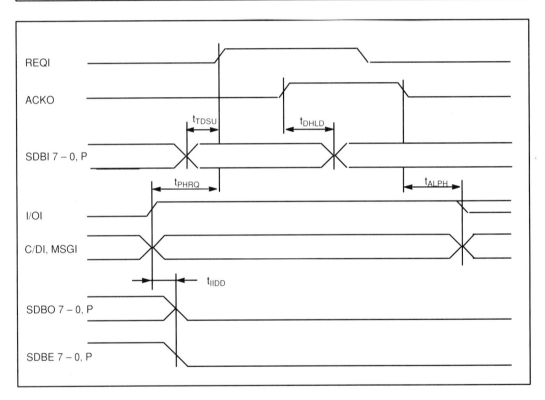

AC CHARACTERISTICS

Asynchronous Transfer: Target, REQ-ACK Timing

Parameter	Designator	Values		Unit
		Min.	Max.	
REQO "H" to ACKI "H"	t_{ROHA}	20	—	ns
ACKI "H" to REQO "L"	t_{AROL}	10	60	ns
REQO "L" to ACKI "L"	t_{ROLA}	0	—	ns
ACKI "L" to REQO "H"	t_{AROH}	10	70 [2]	ns
ACKI "H" to REQO "H"[1]	t_{RACY}	$2t_{CLF}$	$3t_{CLF} + 110$ [2]	ns

Notes: [1]The time for ACKI "H" to REQO "H" is set by the longer one of either ($t_{AROL} + t_{ROLA} + t_{AROH}$) or t_{RACY}.

[2]The time value of this table is not valid under the following conditions:
  a. When data buffer is empty during output.
  b. When data buffer is full during input.

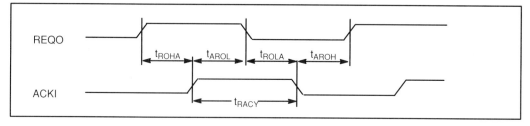

AC CHARACTERISTICS

Asynchronous Transfer: Target, Output

Parameter	Designator	Values		Unit
		Min.	**Max.**	
I/O "H" to Data bus output	t_{IODE}	$7t_{CLF}$	$8t_{CLF} + 110$	ns
Data bus output valid to REQO "H"	t_{DVLD}	$2t_{CLF} - 80$	—	ns
ACKI "H" to Data bus hold	t_{DIVD}	15	—	ns

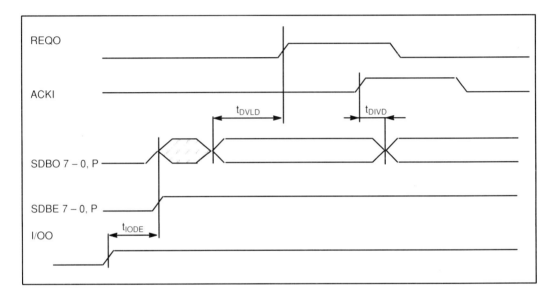

AC CHARACTERISTICS

Asynchronous Transfer: Target, Input				
Parameter	Designator	Values		Unit
		Min.	Max.	
I/O "L" to Data bus output terminate	t_{IODD}	—	60	ns
Data bus output valid to ACKI "H"	t_{DTSU}	10	—	ns
REQO "L" to Data bus hold	t_{DHLD}	15	—	ns

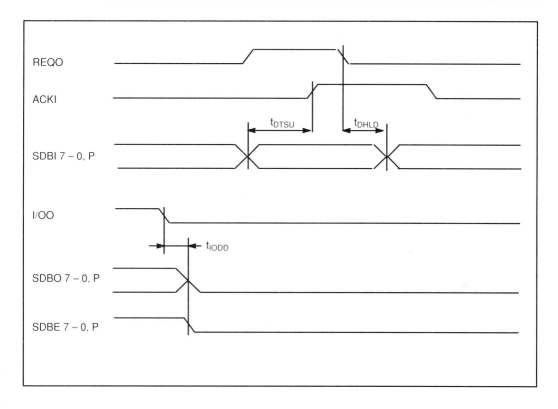

AC CHARACTERISTICS

Synchronous Transfer: Initiator, REQ-ACK Cycle

Parameter	Designator	Values		Unit
		Min.	Max.	
REQI Assertion Period	t_{RIAP}	50	—	ns
REQI Nonassertion Period	t_{RINP}	50	—	ns
REQI Cycle time1	t_{RQF1}	t_{CLF}	—	ns
REQI Cycle time2	t_{RQF2}	$3t_{CLF}$	—	ns
ACKO Assertion Period	t_{AKAP}	$t_{CLF} - 10$	—	ns
ACKO Nonassertion Period	t_{ANAP}	$nt_{CLF} - 10^*$	—	ns

Notes: *n is set by TMOD register.

TMOD Register		n
Bit3	Bit2	
0	0	1
0	1	2
1	0	3
1	1	4

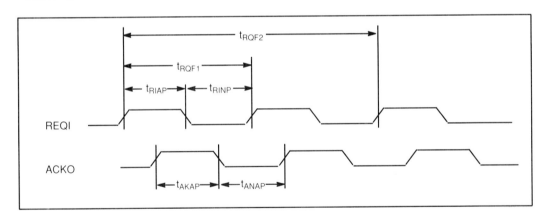

AC CHARACTERISTICS

Synchronous Transfer: Initiator, REQ-ACK Timing

Parameter	Designator	Values		Unit
		Min.	Max.	
ACKO Answer delay time1[1]	t_{ADL1}	$3t_{CLF}$	$4t_{CLF} +100$	ns
REQI "H" to DREQ "H"[2]	t_{RHDR}	$t_{CLF} +40$	$3t_{CLF} +60$	ns
ACKO Answer delay time2[3]	t_{ADL2}	$3t_{CLF}$	$4t_{CLF} +120$	ns

Notes: [1]For the case when maximum input offset value is less than 4 or during output. The minimum time between receiving bit N of REQI and sending bit N of ACKO. (Not applicable when data buffer is empty during output.)

[2]During input

[3]Applicable when maximum input offset value is between 5 and 8. This is the minimum time between receiving bit N of DRESP and sending bit N of ACKO. In this case, the minimum time between receiving bit N of REQI and sending bit N of ACKO is (t_{RHDR} +(DRESP answer time X) + t_{ADL2})

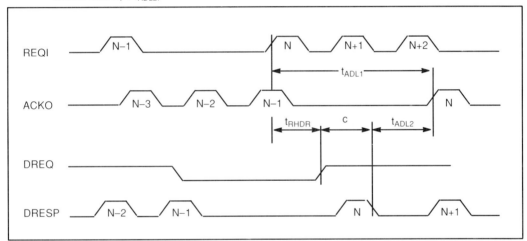

AC CHARACTERISTICS

Synchronous Transfer: Initiator, Output

Parameter	Designator	Values		Unit
		Min.	Max.	
I/OI "L" to Data bus output	t_{IIDE}	10	100	ns
Set Phase to REQI "H"	t_{PHRQ}	100	—	ns
Data bus output valid to ACKO "H"[1]	t_{DVA1}	$2t_{CLF} - 70$	—	ns
	t_{DVA2}	$nt_{CLF} - 60$ [2]	—	ns
ACKO "H" to Data bus hold	t_{AKDH}	$t_{CLF} - 20$	—	ns
ACKO "L" to Phase change	t_{ALPH}	10	—	ns

Notes: [1] The time from data bus output valid to ACKO "H" is set by the shorter one of t_{DVA1} or t_{DVA2}.
[2] n is set by TMOD register.

TMOD Register		n
Bit3	Bit2	
0	0	1
0	1	2
1	0	3
1	1	4

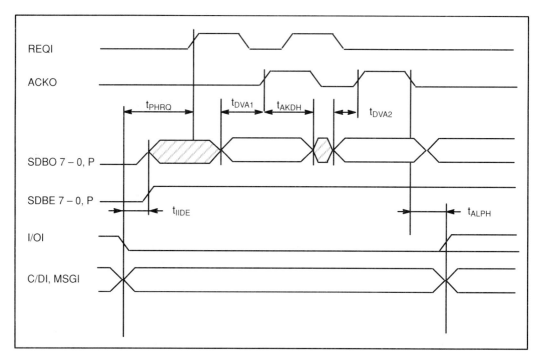

AC CHARACTERISTICS

Synchronous Transfer: Initiator, Input

Parameter	Designator	Values		Unit
		Min.	**Max.**	
I/OI "H" to Data bus output terminate	t_{IIDD}	—	100	ns
Set Phase to REQI "H"	t_{PHRQ}	100	—	ns
Data bus valid to REQI "H"	t_{DTSU}	10	—	ns
REQI "H" to Data bus hold	t_{DTHD}	40	—	ns
ACKO "L" to Phase change	t_{ALPH}	10	—	ns

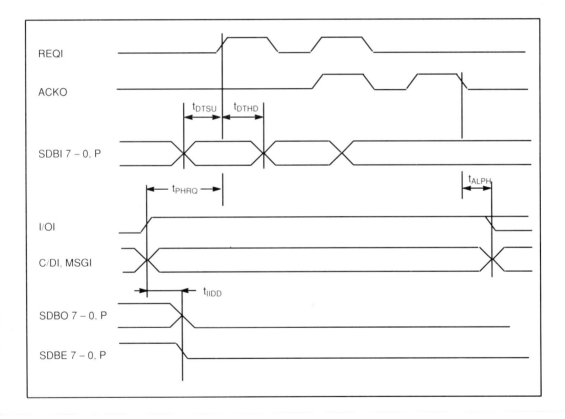

AC CHARACTERISTICS

Synchronous Transfer: Target, REQ-ACK Cycle

Parameter	Designator	Values		Unit
		Min.	Max.	
REQO Assertion Period	t_{RQAP}	$t_{CLF} - 10$	—	ns
REQO Nonassertion Period	t_{RNAP}	$nt_{CLF} - 10^*$	—	ns
ACKI Assertion Period	t_{AIAP}	50	—	ns
ACKI Nonassertion Period	t_{AINP}	50	—	ns
ACKI Cycle time1	t_{AKF1}	t_{CLF}	—	ns
ACKI Cycle time2	t_{AKF2}	$3t_{CLF}$	—	ns

Notes: *n is set by TMOD register.

TMOD Register		n
Bit3	Bit2	
0	0	1
0	1	2
1	0	3
1	1	4

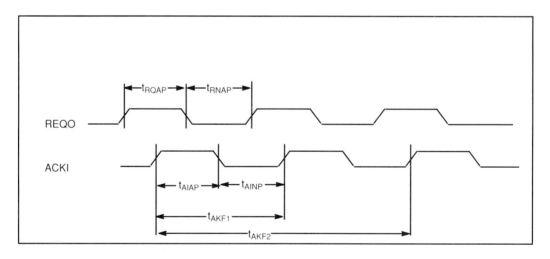

AC CHARACTERISTICS

Synchronous Transfer: Target, REQ-ACK Timing

Parameter	Designator	Values		Unit
		Min.	Max.	
REQO Send delay time[1]	t_{RDLY}	$3t_{CLF}$	$4t_{CLF} + 100$	ns

Notes: [1]The time between receiving bit $(N - m)$ of ACKI and sending bit N of REQO during maximum offset value is set at m (m = 1 to 8).

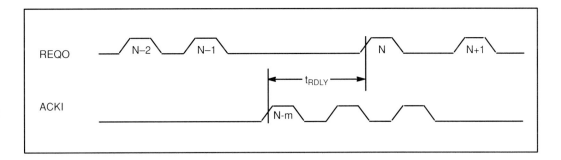

AC CHARACTERISTICS

Synchronous Transfer: Target, Output

Parameter	Designator	Values		Unit
		Min.	Max.	
I/OO "H" to Data bus output	t_{IODE}	$7t_{CLF}$	$8t_{CLF} +110$	ns
Data bus output valid to REQO "H"[2]	t_{DVR1}	$2t_{CLF} -70$	—	ns
	t_{DVR2}	$nt_{CLF} -60$ [1]	—	ns
REQO "H" to Data bus hold	t_{RQDH}	$t_{CLF} -20$	—	ns

Notes: [1] is set by TMOD register.
[2] The time between data bus output valid and REQO "H" is set by the shorter one of t_{DVR1} or t_{DVR2}.

TMOD Register		n
Bit3	Bit2	
0	0	1
0	1	2
1	0	3
1	1	4

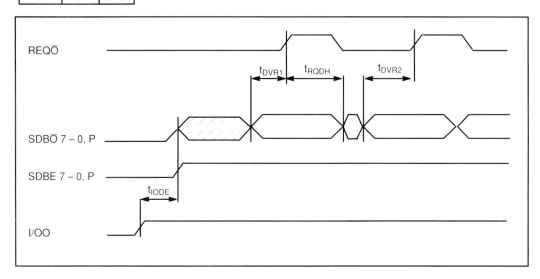

AC CHARACTERISTICS

Synchronous Transfer: Target, Input

Parameter	Designator	Values		Unit
		Min.	Max.	
I/OO "L" to Data bus output	t_{IODD}	—	60	ns
Data bus output valid to ACKI "H"	t_{DTSU}	10	—	ns
ACKI "H" to Data bus hold	t_{DTHD}	40	—	ns

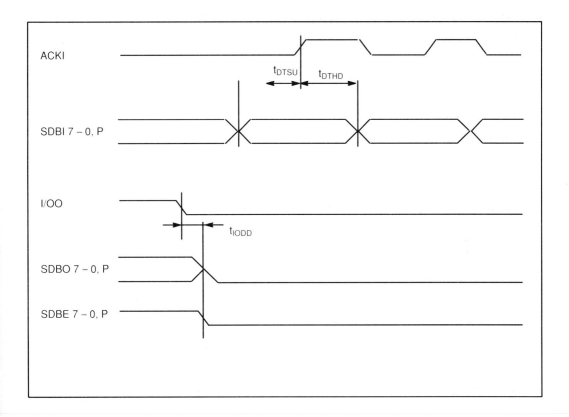

AC CHARACTERISTICS

Bus Free: Arbitration Failure

Parameter	Designator	Values		Unit
		Min.	Max.	
Begin arbitration to BSYO "L", ID bit send terminate[1]	t_{PBCR}	$32t_{CLF} -40$	$32t_{CLF} +60$	ns
SELI "H" to BSYO "L", ID bit send terminate[2]	t_{SBCR}	$2t_{CLF}$	$3t_{CLF} +120$	ns

Notes: [1]When choosing ID bit which has a higher priority number than itself.
[2]When other bus device asserts SEL signals.

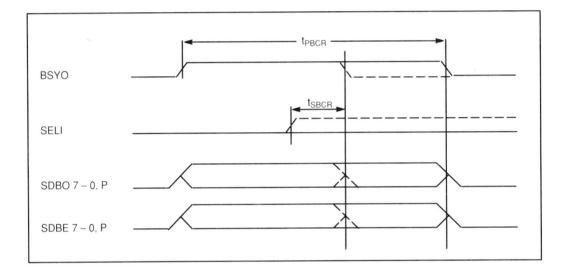

AC CHARACTERISTICS

Bus Free: Selection, Reselection Timeout

Parameter	Designator	Values		Unit
		Min.	Max.	
Timeout interrupt reset to SELO "L", bus clear, INIT or TARG "L"	t_{IRCR}	—	$3t_{CLF} + 110$	ns

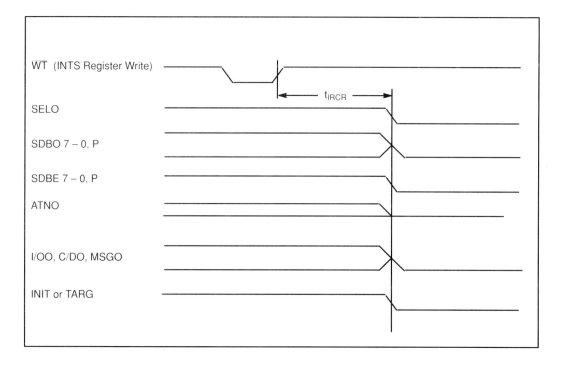

AC CHARACTERISTICS

Bus Free: Initiator (Disconnected)				
Parameter	Designator	Values		Unit
		Min.	Max.	
BSYI "L" to INIT "L" bus clear	t_{BLCR}	—	$5t_{CLF} + 120$	ns
BSYI "L" to INTR "H"	t_{BLIR}	—	$6t_{CLF} + 80$	ns

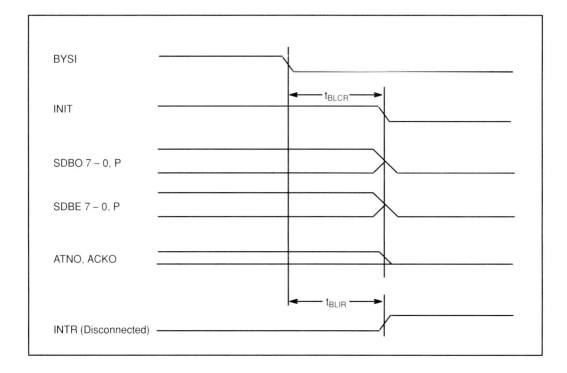

AC CHARACTERISTICS

Bus Free: Target (Bus Release Command)

Parameter	Designator	Values		Unit
		Min.	Max.	
Issue Bus Release Command to BSYO "L"	t_{BRBL}	—	$3t_{CLF} + 80$	ns
Issue Bus Release Command to TARG "L", bus clear	t_{BRCR}	—	$3t_{CLF} + 130$	ns

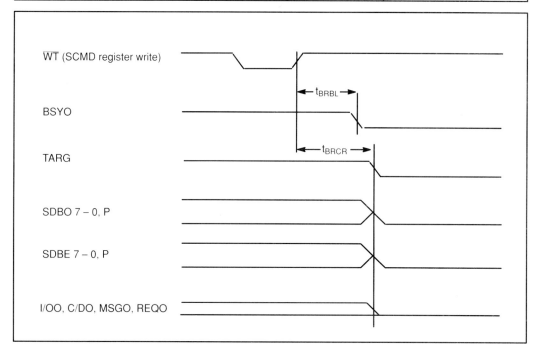

AC CHARACTERISTICS

Reset Condition: Send RST Signal				
Parameter	Designator	Values		Unit
		Min.	Max.	
Write "1" to SCMD register bit 4 to RSTO "H"	t_{RSTO}	—	60	ns
RSTO "H" to send signal terminate	t_{RSOD}	—	80	ns

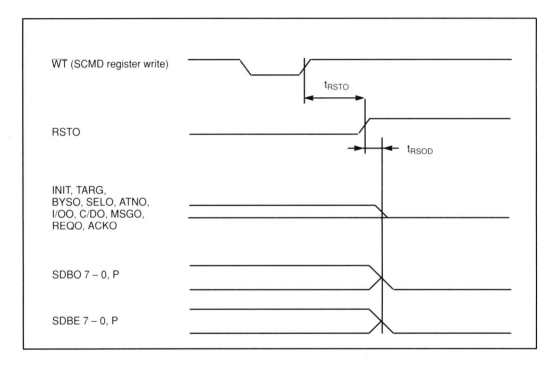

AC CHARACTERISTICS

Reset Condition: RST Signal Detection

Parameter	Designator	Values		Unit
		Min.	**Max.**	
Reset condition detection time	t_{SRIW}	$3t_{CLF}$	—	ns
RSTI "H" to signal send terminate	t_{RSID}	—	$4t_{CLF} +120$	ns

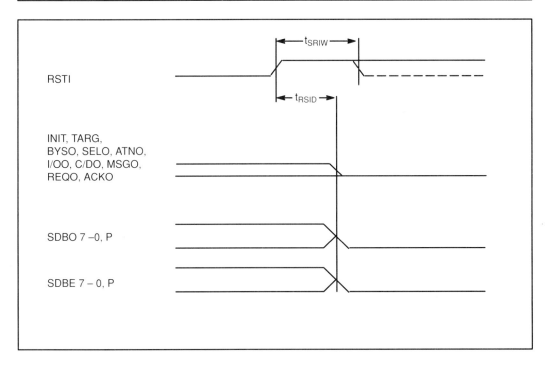

AC CHARACTERISTICS

AC Characteristics Measurement Condition

Pin Name	C_L	Unit
D7 – D0, DP, HDB7 – HDB0, HDBP	85	pF
DPO	65	pF
Other than above output pins	60	pF

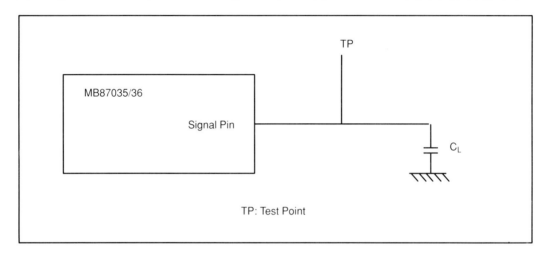

TP: Test Point

PIN GRID ARRAY (MB87035)

88-Lead Plastic Pin Grid Array

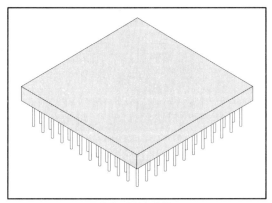

PGA–88P–M01

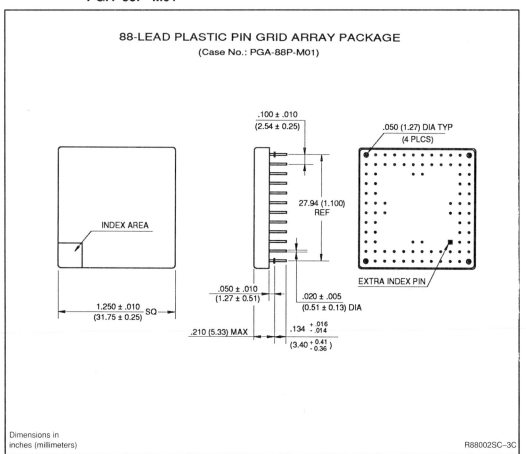

88-LEAD PLASTIC PIN GRID ARRAY PACKAGE
(Case No.: PGA-88P-M01)

.100 ± .010
(2.54 ± 0.25)

.050 (1.27) DIA TYP
(4 PLCS)

27.94 (1.100)
REF

INDEX AREA

EXTRA INDEX PIN

1.250 ± .010 SQ
(31.75 ± 0.25)

.050 ± .010
(1.27 ± 0.51)

.020 ± .005
(0.51 ± 0.13) DIA

.210 (5.33) MAX

$.134 ^{+.016}_{-.014}$

$(3.40 ^{+0.41}_{-0.36})$

Dimensions in
inches (millimeters)

R88002SC–3C

FLAT PACKAGE (MB87036)

100-Lead Plastic Pin Grid Array

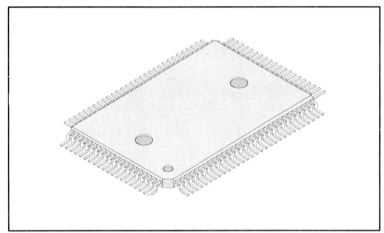

FPT–100P–M01

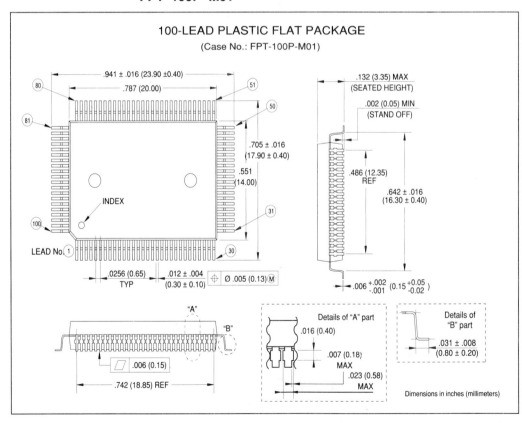

100-LEAD PLASTIC FLAT PACKAGE
(Case No.: FPT-100P-M01)

.941 ± .016 (23.90 ±0.40)
.787 (20.00)

80
51
50
81
.705 ± .016
(17.90 ± 0.40)
.551
(14.00)
INDEX
31
100
LEAD No. 1
30

.0256 (0.65) TYP   .012 ± .004 (0.30 ± 0.10)   ⌖ Ø .005 (0.13) Ⓜ

.132 (3.35) MAX
(SEATED HEIGHT)
.002 (0.05) MIN
(STAND OFF)
.486 (12.35) REF
.642 ± .016
(16.30 ± 0.40)

.006 +.002 -.001 (0.15 +0.05 -0.02)

"A"
"B"

▱ .006 (0.15)
.742 (18.85) REF

Details of "A" part
.016 (0.40)
.007 (0.18) MAX
.023 (0.58) MAX

Details of "B" part
.031 ± .008
(0.80 ± 0.20)

Dimensions in inches (millimeters)

Additional Notes About Input Clock Frequency

MB87035/36 guarantees performance up to input clock frequency of 10 MHz. However, if the input clock frequency exceeds 8 MHz, SCSI timing requirments may not be satisfied.

- If used with systems which must meet SCSI timing requirements, input clock frequency may be between 5 and 8 MHz.

- If used with systems which do not have to meet SCSI requirements, input clock frequency may be between 5 and 10 MHz.

Timing Requirement Conditions if Input Clock Frequency >8MHz

Item	Action Condition	Appli-cation INIT	Appli-cation TARG	Timing Parameter	Time Condition (Minimum Value) SCSI Specification	Time Condition (Minimum Value) MB87035/36 AC Characteristics[1]
1	Selection Phase	O		The time between asserting SEL after arbitration and sending ID to data bus	1.2 ms	$11 t_{CLF} - 30$ ns
	Reselection Phase		O			
2	Reselection Phase		O	The time between the target asserting BSY after acknowledging BSY from the initiator and negating SEL.	90 ns	$t_{CLF} - 20$ ns
3	Information Transfer Phase		O	The time between activating I/O to True and activating of data bus	800 ns	$7 t_{CLF}$ ns
4	Synchronous Transfer Output	O	O	Data bus hold time after asserting ACK or REQ	100 ns	$t_{CLF} - 20$ ns
5	Asynchronous Transfer Output[3]	O	O	The time between acknowledging data bus output and asserting ACK or REQ	55 ns	$2 t_{CLF} - 80$ ns
6	Synchronous Transfer Output[3]	O	O	The time between acknowledging data bus output and asserting ACK or REQ	55 ns	$2 t_{CLF} - 70$ ns also $n \bullet t_{CLF} - 60$ ns[2]
7	Synchronous Transfer	O	O	ACK, REQ negation period	90 ns	$n \bullet t_{CLF} - 10$ ns[2]

Notes: [1] t_{CLF} is clock cycle (ns)

[2] n is set by TMOD register (n = 1-4)

[3] Items 5 – 7 can violate SCSI specifications depending on the setting of TMOD register and/or the transmission characteristics of the interface. Items 6 and 7 can violate SCSI specifications if the appropriate value is not set for the TMOD register even if clock input is below 8 MHz.

Chapter 9

**MB 89351
PRODUCT PROFILE**

MB89351
SCSI Protocol Controller

Edition 1.0
June 1990

AC CHARACTERISTICS

The Fujitsu MB89351 is a Small Computer System Interface (SCSI) Protocol Controller (SPC) specifically designed to implement a SCSI-bus to CPU/DMAC interface. Except for SCSI synchronous mode transfers, the MB89351 can handle virtually all interface control procedures of the SCSI bus laid down by SCSI-I specification (ANSI X3.131-1986) and is adaptable to either an 8-bit or a 16-bit CPU. To optimize efficiency and reduce CPU overhead, the MB89351 uses an 8-byte FIFO data buffer register and a 24-bit transfer byte counter. The SPC can serve in a wide range of applications acting as an INITIATOR or TARGET device for the SCSI. Thus, the device can be used as an I/O controller or as a host adapter.

The MB89351 SPC is fabricated in silicon-gate CMOS and housed in a 64-pin plastic shrink DIP or a 64-pin plastic flat package.

SCSI Compatibility
- Serves as either an INITIATOR or a TARGET
- DMA interface and parity check

Data Transfer Rate/Byte Counter
- Up to 3.0 Megabytes per second
- 8-byte FIFO Data Buffer
- 24-Bit transfer byte counter

Drive Options
- Single-ended
- Differential

Selectable Transfer Mode
- DMA transfer
- Program transfer
- Manual transfer

Clock Requirements
- 8 MHz clock with 33%-to-66% duty   cycle

Technology/Power Requirements
- Silicon-Gate CMOS
- Single +5 V power supply

Available Packaging
- 64-pin plastic shrink DIP (suffix -PSH)
- 64-pin plastic flat package (suffix -PF)

ABSOLUTE MAXIMUM RATINGS[1]

Rating	Designator	Values		Unit
		Min.	Max.	
Supply Voltage	V_{CC}	$V_{SS} - .05$	$V_{SS} + 7.0$	V
Input Voltage[2]	V_{IN}	$V_{SS} - .05$	$V_{SS} + 7.0$	V
Output Voltage[2]	V_{OUT}	$V_{SS} - 0.3$	$V_{SS} + 7.0$	V
Operating Ambient Temperature	T_A	0	+70	°C
Storage Temperature	T_{STG}	−55	+150	°C

Notes: 1 Permanent device damage may occur if the above absolute maximum ratings are exceeded. Functional operation should be restricted to the conditions as detailed in the operational sections of this data sheet. Exposure to absolute maximum rating conditions for extended periods may affect device reliability.

2 Should not exceed $V_{CC} + 0.5V$.

RECOMMENDED OPERATING CONDITIONS

Parameter	Designator	Values			Unit	Remarks
		Min.	Typ.	Max.		
Supply Voltage	V_{CC}	4.50	5.0	5.50	V	
	V_{SS}		0		V	
Operating Ambient Temperature	T_A	0		+70	°C	

MB89351 BLOCK DIAGRAM

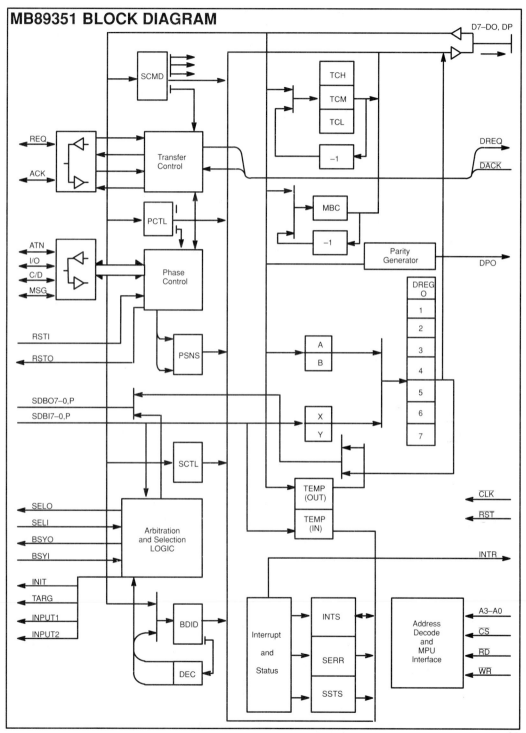

PIN ASSIGNMENTS AND INTERFACE DIAGRAM

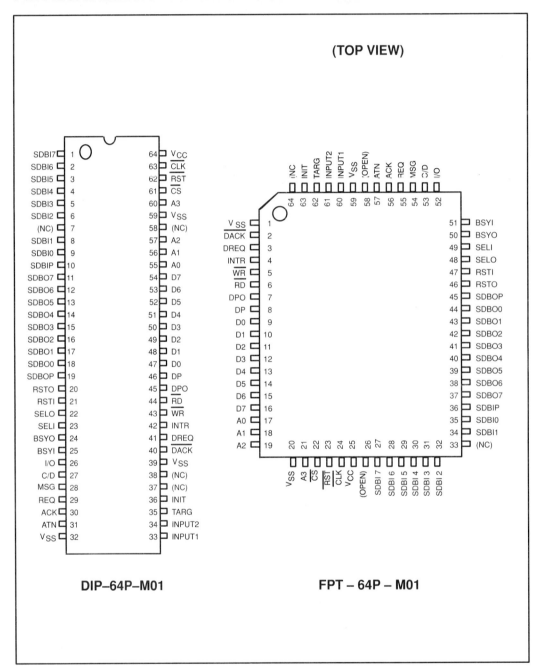

DIP–64P–M01

FPT – 64P – M01

PIN ASSIGNMENTS AND INTERFACE DIAGRAM

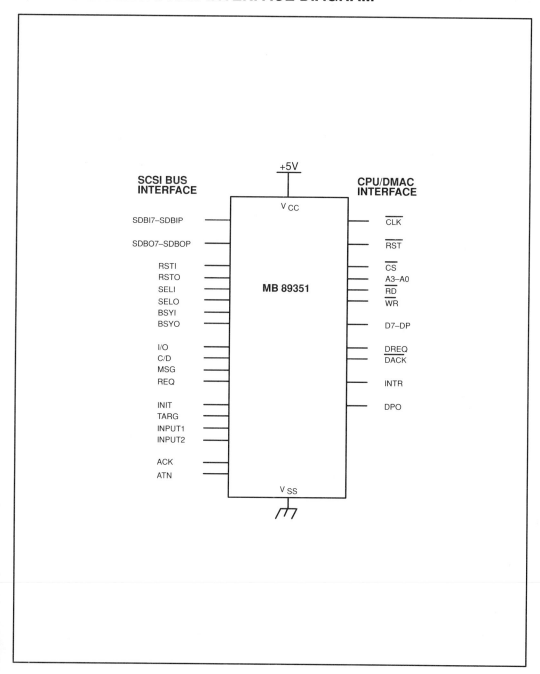

PIN DESCRIPTIONS

Designator	Pin No.		Function
	DIP	**FPT**	
V_{CC}	64	25	+5V power supply.
V_{SS}	32,39,59	1,20,59	Circuit ground.
$\overline{\text{CLK}}$	63	24	Clock input for controlling internal operation and data transfer speed of the SPC.
$\overline{\text{RST}}$	62	23	Asynchronous reset signal used to clear all internal circuits of the SPC.
$\overline{\text{CS}}$	61	22	Input selection enable signal for accessing an internal register. When active low, the following input/output signals are valid: RD, WR, A0–A3, DP0–DP7 and DP.
A3 A2 A1 A0	60 57 56 55	21 19 18 17	Address input signals for selecting an internal register in SPC. MSB is A3; LSB is A0. When $\overline{\text{CS}}$ is active low, read/ write is enabled for an internal register selected by these address inputs via data bus lines D0–D7 and DP.
$\overline{\text{RD}}$	44	6	The read strobe ($\overline{\text{RD}}$) input is used to readout the contents of an internal SPC register and is asserted only if $\overline{\text{CS}}$ is active low. The register to be read is specified by A0–A3; the input address data is input via D0–D7 and DP. In the program transfer mode, the falling edge of $\overline{\text{RD}}$ terminates the data read cycle.
$\overline{\text{WR}}$	43	5	The write strobe ($\overline{\text{WR}}$) input is used to write into an internal SPC register and is asserted only if $\overline{\text{CS}}$ is active low. On the falling edge of $\overline{\text{WR}}$, the data present on D0–D7 and DP is loaded into the internal register specified by A0–A3 (except when A0 = A1 = A2 = A3 = H). In the program transfer mode, the falling edge of $\overline{\text{WR}}$ indicates a data–ready condition to the MPU.

Continued on following page

PIN DESCRIPTIONS

Designator	Pin No.		Function
	DIP	**FPT**	
D7 – DP	54 – 46	16 – 8	Used to write/read data to/from an internal register in the SPC. The data bus is 3–state and bidirectional. The MSB is D7 and the LSB is D0; DP is an odd parity bit. When both $\overline{CS}$ and RDG inputs are active low (read operation), the contents of a selected internal register are output to the data bus. In operations other than read, the data bus is kept at a high–impedance level.
DPO	45	7	Outputs an odd parity for D0–D7. If parity bit is not generated for external memory, DPO can be used as an input parity bit for DP.
INTR	42	4	The INTR output signal is issued by the SPC and requests an interrupt to indicate completion of an internal operation or the occurrence of an error. Except for an interrupt caused by the RSTI input (reset condition in SCSI), interrupt masking is allowed. When an interrupt request is granted, the INTR signal remains active until the interrupt is cleared. In the program transfer mode, the INTR signal can be used as a data request signal instead of reading internal registers of the SPC; the data–request function is enabled by proper settings of the appropriate registers. The INTR signal is automatically disabled when interrupt conditions are not present.
DREQ	41	3	When the MB89351 is operating in the DMA mode and the data request (DREQ) output signal is active high, data is transferred between external memory and the SPC or vice–versa. During output operations, DREQ is active when the data buffers in the SPC are not full. During input operations, DREQ is active when valid data is present in the buffers. In either case, DMA transfers can occur and DREQ is asserted.
$\overline{DACK}$	40	2	An active low response signal to the DREQ which request data transfer between SPC and the external memory in the DMA mode. This signal, in DMA mode, functions similarly to the signal combination of $\overline{CS}$=low, A3=high, A2=low, A1=high, and A0=low (selection of DREG) in the program transfer mode. Since the DREG is selected by this $\overline{DACK}$ signal in the DMA mode instead of the address input from A3–A0, data transfer between DREG of SPC and external memory is possible.

Continued on following page

PIN DESCRIPTIONS

Designator	Pin No.		Function
	DIP	FPT	
SDBI7,SDBI6 SDBI5,SDBI4 SDBI3,SDBI2 SDBI1,SDBI0 SDBIP	1,2 3,4 5,6 8,9 10	27,28 29,30 31,32 34,35 36	Inputs from the SCSI data bus. The MSB is SDBI7; the LSB is SDBI0. SDBIP is an odd parity bit. Parity checking for the SCSI data bus is programmable.
SDBO7 SDBO6 SDBO5 SDBO4 SDBO3 SDBO2 SDBO1 SDBO0 SDBOP	11 12 13 14 15 16 17 18 19	37 38 39 40 41 42 43 44 45	Outputs to the SCSI data bus. The MSB is SDBO7; the LSB is SDBO0. SDBOP is an odd parity bit. An open-collector bus driver is used to connect the SCSI bus. **(Note: For the SDBI and SDBO pin groupings, only one pin is used for output and the other pins are used for input during arbitration. During selection, reselection, and normal data transfers, all pins are used for outputs. Typical system connections are shown in the Pin Assignments and Interface Diagram).**
RSTO,RSTI	20,21	46,47	RSTI is a reset input from other SCSI devices; RSTO is a reset output to other SCSI devices. Both signals are active high and can be masked.
SELO,SELI	22,23	48,49	SELO is an output that corresponds to the INITIATOR or TARGET device; SELI inputs the response to the SPC during the selection or reselection phase. Both signals are active high.
BSYO,BSYI	24,25	50,51	BSYO indicates the SCSI bus is in the output mode of operation, whereas, BSYI indicates the bus is operating in the input mode. One or the other of these signals is active high during arbitration and in the "connected status" mode of operation.
I/O	26	52	During the data transfer phase, the I/O signal indicates the transfer direction. When I/O is high, data is transferred from the TARGET to the INITIATOR. When I/O is low, data is transferred from the INITIATOR to the TARGET.
C/D	27	53	During the data transfer phase, the C/D signal is set high during the command-, status-, and message-phases of operation.
MSG	28	54	In the data transfer phase, the MSG signal is set high only during the message phase.

Continued on following page

PIN DESCRIPTIONS

Designator	Pin No.		Function
	DIP	FPT	
REQ	29	55	In the data transfer phase, the REQ signal is used to notify the INITIATOR that the TARGET is ready to receive or send data. The REQ input is used as a timing control signal in the data transfer sequence.
INiT,TARG	36,35	63,62	These two output signals indicate the operational status of the SPC. The INIT and TARG outputs can also be used as SLCSI driver circuit control signals. **INIT** **TARG** **SPC Status** L L Logically disconnected from the SCSI. L H Executing the reselection phase or operating as a TARGET. H L Executing the selection phase or operating as an INITIATOR.
INPUT1,INPUT2	33,34	60,61	These two outputs are directly related to the preceding INIT and TARG signals. INPUT1 corresponds to INIT and INPUT2 corresponds to TARG. However, unlike INIT and TARG, INPUT1 and INPUT2 are set High when the SPC is not logically connected to the SCSI.
ACK	30	56	In the data transfer phase, the acknowledge signal is in response to a transfer request (REQ) signal from the TARGET. In the same way as REQ, an ACK input is used as a timing signal in the data transfer sequence.
ATN	31	57	Except during arbitration and during the bus free phase, the ATN signal is used to notify the TARGET that the INITIATOR has a prepared message.
NC	7,37, 38,58	33,64	No connection.
Open	—	26,58	Reserved (do not make external connections to these pins).

AC CHARACTERISTICS (Continued)

SPC has internal registers consisting of 17 bytes that are accessible from an external circuit. These internal registers are used for controlling SPC internal operation and indicating SPC processing status/result status. A unique address is assigned to each internal register, and a particular register is identified by address bits A3 to A0. The following table shows internal register addressing:

Table 1. Internal Register Addressing

Register	Mnemonic	Operation	Chip Select ($\overline{CS}$)	A3	A2	A1	A0
Bus Device ID	BDID	R	0	0	0	0	0
		W					
SPC Control	SCTL	R	0	0	0	0	1
		W					
Command	SCMD	R	0	0	0	1	0
		W					
Open	—	—	0	0	0	1	1
Interrupt Sense	INTS	R	0	0	1	0	0
Reset Interrupt		W					
Phase Sense	PSNS	R	0	0	1	0	1
SPC Diagnostic Control	SDGC	W					
SPC Status	SSTS	R	0	0	1	1	0
—		W					
SPC Error Status	SERR	R	0	0	1	1	1
—		W					
Phase Control	PCTL	R	0	1	0	0	0
		W					
Modified Byte Counter	MBC	R	0	1	0	0	1
—		W					

Continued on following page

Table 1.   Internal Register Addressing

Register	Mnemonic	Operation	Chip Select (CS̄)	Address Bits			
				A3	A2	A1	A0
Data Register	DREG	R	0	1	0	1	0
		W					
Temporary Register	TEMP	R	0	1	0	1	1
		W					
Transfer Counter High	TCH	R	0	1	1	0	0
		W					
Transfer Counter Middle	TCM	R	0	1	1	0	1
		W					
Transfer Counter Low	TCL	R	0	1	1	1	0
		W					

BIT ASSIGNMENTS

The following table shows the bit assignments to each internal register. When accessing an internal register (in read/write), remember the following:

(1)   The internal register block includes the read-only/write-only register and those having different meanings in read and write operations.

(2)   A write command to a read-only register is ignored.

(3)   If the write-only register is read out, the data and parity bit are undefined.

(4)   At bit positions indicating "_" for a write in Table 3.2.2, either 1 of 0, or may be written.

Table 2.   Bit Assignments for Internal Registers

HEX Address	Register and Mnemonic	R/W Oper- ation	7 (MSb)	6	5	4	3	2	1	0 (LSb)	Parity
0	Bus Device ID (BDID)	R	#7	#6	#5	#4	#3	#2	#1	#0	0
0	Bus Device ID (BDID)	W						SCSI Bus Device ID ID4	ID2	ID1	—
1	SPC Control (SCTL)	R	Reset & Disable	Control Reset	Diag Mode	ARBIT Enable	Parity Enable	Select Enable	Reselect Enable	INT Enable	P
1	SPC Control (SCTL)	W	Reset & Disable	Control Reset	Diag Mode	ARBIT Enable	Parity Enable	Select Enable	Reselect Enable	INT Enable	P
2	Command (SCMD)	R	Command Code			RST Out	Intercept Xfer	Transfer Modifer PRG Xfer	0	Term Mode	P
2	Command (SCMD)	W	Command Code			RST Out	Intercept Xfer	PRG Xfer	0	Term Mode	P
4	Interrupt Sense (INTS)	R	Selected	Reselected	Disconnect	Command Complete	Service Required	Time Out	SPC Hard Error	Reset Condition	P
4	Interrupt Sense (INTS)	W	Reset Interrupt								—
5	Phase Sense (PSNS)	R	REQ	ACK	ATN	SEL	BSY	MSG	C/D	I/O	P
5	SPC Diag Control (SDGC)	W	Diag. REQ	Diag. ACK	XFER Enable		Diag. BSY	Diag. MSG	Diag. C/D	Diag. I/O	—
6	SPC Status (SSTS)	R	Connected INIT	TARG	SPC BSY	XFER In Progress	SCSI RST	TC=0	DREG Status Full	Empty	P
6	SPC Status (SSTS)	W	—								—

Continued on following page

Table 2. Bit Assignments For Internal Registers

HEX Address	Register and Mnemonic	R/W Oper-ation	7 (MSb)	6	5	4	3	2	1	0 (LSb)	Parity
7	SPC Error Status (SERR)	R	Data Error SCSI	Data Error SPC	XFER Out	0	TC Parity Error	0	Short XFER Period	0	P
		W	—								—
8	Phase Control (PCTL)	R	Bus Free Inter-rupt Enable	0				Transfer Phase			P
		W						MSG Out	C/D Out	I/O Out	
9	Modified Byte Counter (MBC)	R			0		Bit 3	Bit 2 (MBC)	Bit 1	Bit 0	P
		W	—							—	P
A	Data Register (DREG)	R	Internal Data Register (8 Byte FIFO)								
		W	Bit 7	Bit 6	Bit 5	Bit 4	Bit 3	Bit 2	Bit 1	Bit 0	P
B	Temporary Register (TEMP)	R	Temporary Data (Input: From SCSI)								
			Bit 7	Bit 6	Bit 5	Bit 4	Bit 3	Bit 2	Bit 1	Bit 0	P
		W	Temporary Data (Output: To SCSI)								
			Bit 7	Bit 6	Bit 5	Bit 4	Bit 3	Bit 2	Bit 1	Bit 0	P
C	Transfer Counter High (TCH)	R	Transfer Counter High (MSB)								
		W	Bit 23	Bit 22	Bit 21	Bit 20	Bit 19	Bit 18	Bit 17	Bit 16	P
D	Transfer Counter Mid (TCM)	R	Transfer Counter Middle (2nd Byte)								
		W	Bit 15	Bit 14	Bit 13	Bit 12	Bit 11	Bit 10	Bit 9	Bit 8	P
E	Transfer Counter LOW (TCL)	R	Transfer Counter Low (LSB)								
		W	Bit 7	Bit 6	Bit 5	Bit 4	Bit 3	Bit 2	Bit 1	Bit 0	P

DC CHARACTERISTICS

(Recommended operating conditions unless otherwise specified)

Parameter	Designator	Conditions	Values			Unit
			Min.	Typ.	Max.	
Input High Voltage	V_{IH}		2.2			V
Input Low Voltage	V_{IL}				0.8	V
Output High Voltage	V_{OH}	I_{OH}= −0.4 mA	4.0			V
Output Low Voltage	V_{OL}	I_{OL} = +3.2 mA			0.4	V
Input Leakage Current	I_{IL}	V_{IN} = 0 V to 5.25 V	−10		20	μA
Output Leakage Current	I_{IZ}	V_{IN} = 0 V to 5.25 V	−40		40	μA
Active Supply Current	I_{CC}	fc = 8MHz, All outputs open			10	mA
Standby Supply Current	I_{CS}	fc = 8 MHz, All outputs open, inputs fixed, RST active			40	μA

AC CHARACTERISTICS
(Recommended operating conditions unless otherwise noted)

CPU/DMAC Interface

$(V_{CC} = 5\ V \pm 10\%,\ V_{SS} = 0\ V,\ T_A = 0\ to\ 70°C)$

CLK Input					
Parameter	Designator	Values			Unit
		Min.	Typ.	Max.	
$\overline{CLK}$ Cycle Time	t_{CLF}	125		200	ns
$\overline{CLK}$ High Time	t_{CHCL}	44			ns
$\overline{CLK}$ Low Time	t_{CLCH}	44			ns
$\overline{CLK}$ Rise Time	t_r			10	ns
$\overline{CLK}$ Fall Time	t_f			10	ns

$\overline{CLK}$ Input Timing

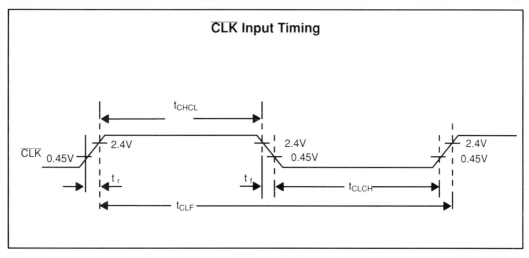

AC CHARACTERISTICS (Continued)

RST Input

Parameter	Designator	Values			Unit
		Min.	Typ.	Max.	
$\overline{\text{RST}}$ Pulse Width	t_{RSTW}	100			ns

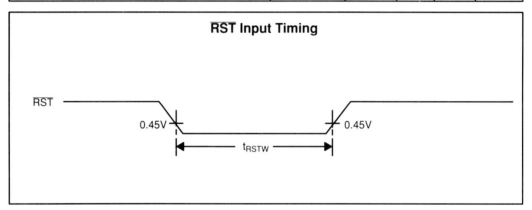

$\overline{\text{RST}}$ Input Timing

AC CHARACTERISTICS (Continued)

Register Read						
Parameter	**Designator**	**Test Conditions**	**Values**			**Unit**
			Min.	**Typ.**	**Max.**	
Address Setup Time	t_{ARS}		40			ns
Address Hold Time	t_{ARH}		10			ns
$\overline{CS}$ Setup Time	t_{CRS}		25			ns
$\overline{CS}$ Hold Time	t_{CRH}		10			ns
Data Valid Time (from $\overline{RD}$ Low)	t_{RLD}	CL = 80 pF			90	ns
Data Hold Time (from $\overline{RD}$ High)	t_{RHD}	CL = 20 pF	10		60	ns
$\overline{RD}$ Pulse Width	t_{RD}		120			ns

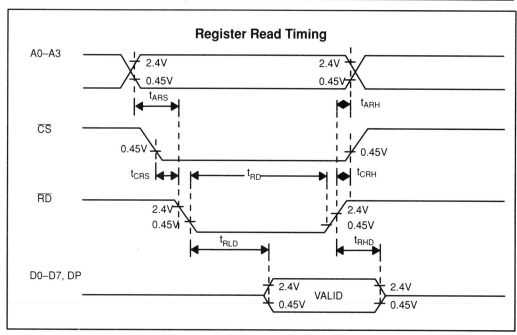

Register Read Timing

AC CHARACTERISTICS (Continued)

Register Write						
Parameter	Designator	Test Conditions	Values			Unit
			Min.	Typ.	Max.	
Address Setup Time	t_{AWS}		40			ns
Address Hold Time	t_{AWH}		10			ns
$\overline{CS}$ Setup Time	t_{CWS}		25			ns
$\overline{CS}$ Hold Time	t_{CWH}		10			ns
Data Valid Time (from $\overline{WR}$ Low)	t_{DWS}		30			ns
Data Hold Time (from $\overline{WR}$ High)	t_{DWH}		20			ns
$\overline{WR}$ Pulse Width	t_{WR}		100			ns

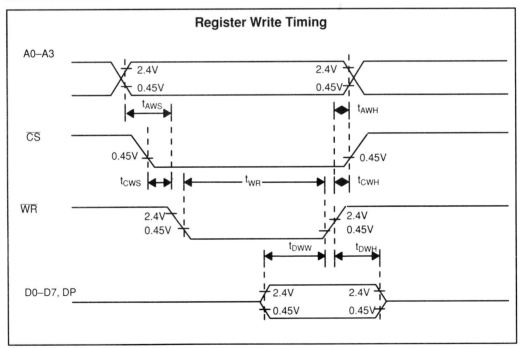

Register Write Timing

AC CHARACTERISTICS (Continued)

DPO (Data Parity Output)

Parameter	Designator	Test Conditions	Values			Unit
			Min.	Typ.	Max.	
DPO Valid Time (from D7–D0 to DPO (Valid)	t_{DPVD}	CL = 30 pF			60	ns

DPO Output Timing

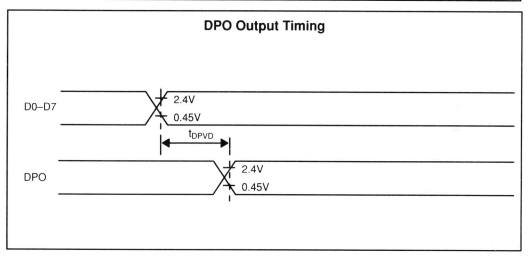

AC CHARACTERISTICS (Continued)

INTR (Interrupt Request) Output						
Parameter	Designator	Test Conditions	Values			Unit
			Min.	Typ.	Max.	
$\overline{\text{WR}}$ Service Time (from INTR High to $\overline{\text{WR}}$ High)	t_{IRWL}		0			ns
INTR Release Time (from $\overline{\text{WR}}$ High to INTER Low)	t_{WHIR}	CL = 10pf	t_{CLF}		$2t_{CLF}+100$	ns
INTR Reset Cycle Time[1]	t_{WRCY}		$4t_{CLF}$			ns

Note: 1 Applicable only when interrupt reset is executed.

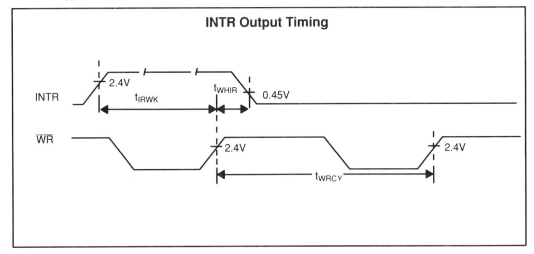

INTR Output Timing

AC CHARACTERISTICS (Continued)

DMA Access

Parameter	Designator	Test Conditions	Values			Unit
			Min.	Typ.	Max.	
DACK Service Time (from DREQ High to $\overline{DACK}$ Low)	t_{DHAL}		0			ns
$\overline{WR}^1$ and $\overline{RD}$ Service Time (from $\overline{DACK}$ Low to $\overline{WR}$ or $\overline{RD}$ Low)	t_{ARWL}		40			ns
DREQ Release Time (from $\overline{WR}^1$ or $\overline{RD}$ Low to DREQ Low)	t_{RWDL}	CL = 30 pF	35		150	ns
$\overline{DACK}$ Hold Time (from $\overline{WR}^1$ or $\overline{RD}$ High to $\overline{DACK}$ High)	t_{RWAH}		10			ns
DREQ Interval (from DREQ Low to DREQ High)	t_{DLDH}		0			ns
DREG Access Cycle Time (1)	t_{RWCY}		$2t_{CLF}$			ns
DREG Access Cycle Time (2)	t_{DMCY}		$3t_{CLF}$			ns

Note: 1 The $\overline{WR}$ parameter is applicable when data buffer register will be full; the $\overline{RD}$ parameter is applicable when the data buffer register will be empty.

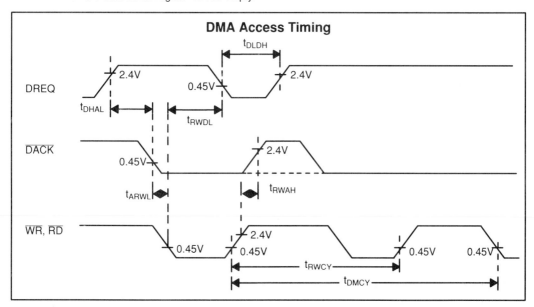

DMA Access Timing

AC CHARACTERISTICS (Continued)

DREG Access – Program Transfer with INTR (Input Operation)						
Parameter	Designator	Test Conditions	Values			Unit
			Min.	Typ.	Max.	
RD Service Time (From INTR High to RD Low)	t_{IHRL}		0			ns
INTR Release Time (From RD High to INTR Low)	t_{RHIL}	CL = 20pF	35		150	ns
INTR Recovery Time (From INTR Low to INTR High)	t_{ILIH}		0			ns
RD Recovery Time (From RD High to RD Low)	t_{RHRL}		50			ns

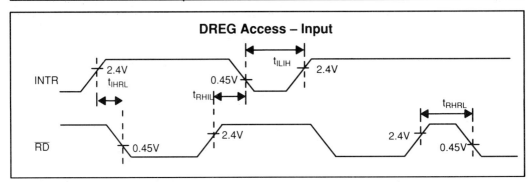

DREG Access – Input

AC CHARACTERISTICS (Continued)

DREG Access – Program Transfer with INTR (Output Operation)						
Parameter	Designator	Test Conditions	Values			Unit
			Min.	Typ.	Max.	
$\overline{WR}$ Service Time (from INTR High to $\overline{WR}$ Low)	t_{IHWL}		0			ns
INTR Release Time (from $\overline{WR}$ Low to INTR Low)	t_{WLIL}	CL = 20pF	35		150	ns
INTR Recovery Time (from INTR Low to INTR High)	t_{ILIH}		0			ns
$\overline{WR}$ Cycle Time	t_{WRCY}		$2t_{CLF}$			ns

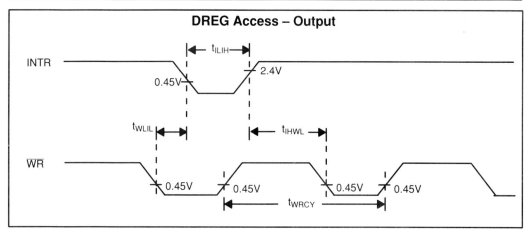

DREG Access – Output

AC CHARACTERISTICS (Continued)

INIT/TARG and INPUT1/INPUT2 Output						
Parameter	**Designator**	**Test Conditions**	**Values**			**Unit**
			Min.	**Typ.**	**Max.**	
INPUT2 Valid Time (From INIT High to INPUT2 Low)	t_{IH2L}	CL = 30pF	0		20	ns
INPUT2 Invalid Time (From INIT Low to INPUT2 High)	t_{IL2H}	CL = 30pF	−20		20	ns
INPUT1 Valid Time (From TARG High to INPUT1 Low)	t_{TH1L}	CL = 40pF	0		20	ns
INPUT1 Invalid Time (From TARG Low to INPU12 High)	t_{TL1H}	CL = 40pF	−20		20	ns

AC CHARACTERISTICS (Continued)

INIT/TARG and INPUT1/INPUT2 Output Timing

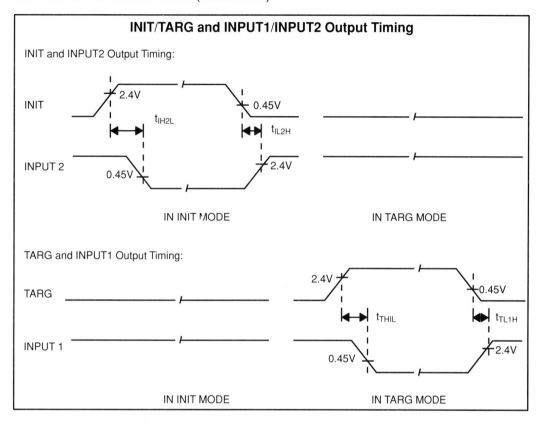

AC CHARACTERISTICS (Continued)

SCSI Bus Interface – Selection Phase Timing

Initiator with Arbitration						
Parameter	**Designator**	**Test Conditions**	**Values**			**Unit**
			Min.	**Typ.**	**Max.**	
Bus Free Time[2]	t_{BFR}		$4t_{CLF}+50$			ns
From BSYI Low to BSYO High	t_{BFBO}	CL = 10pF	$(6 + n)$ $\times t_{CLF}$[1]		$(7 + n)$ $\times t_{CLF}+60$	ns
From BSYO High to Device ID Out	t_{BHID}	CL = 30pF	0		60	ns
From BSYO High to Prioritize	t_{ARB}		$32t_{CLF}-60$			ns
From Data Bus Valid to Prioritize	t_{AIDV}		100			ns
From Bus Usage Permission Granted SELO High	t_{AWSO}	CL = 10pF	0		50	ns
From SELO High to SELECT ID Output	t_{SOID}	CL = 30pF	$11t_{CLF}-30$			ns
From SELO High to INIT High	t_{SOIT}	CL = 10pF	$11t_{CLF}$			ns
From INIT High to ANT High	t_{ITAT}	CL = 10pF	0		60	ns
From SELECT ID Output to BSYO Low	t_{IDBL}	CL = 10pF	$2t_{CLF}-80$			ns
From BSYO Low to BSYI Low	t_{BOBI}	CL = 10pF	0			ns
From BSYI High to BSYO Low	t_{BISO}	CL = 10pF	$2t_{CLF}$		$3t_{CLF}+60$	ns
From BSYI High to $\overline{\text{SELO}}$ Low	t_{BIDH}	CL = 10pF	$2t_{CLF}$			ns
From SELO Low to INTR High	t_{SCIR}	CL = 30pF			60	ns
From SELI High to BSYO Low, ID Bit Low	t_{SBCR}	CL = 30pF (BSYO) CL = 30pF (SDBO0–SDBO7, SDBOP)			$3t_{CLF}+100$	ns
From Priority Judge to BSYO and ID Bit Low	t_{PBCR}	CL = 30pF (BSYO) CL = 30pF (SDBO0–SDBO7, SDBOP)			80	ns

Notes: 1 n = value of TCL register.
2 The bus free time is the minimum time interval until the booked select command is executed.

AC CHARACTERISTICS (Continued)

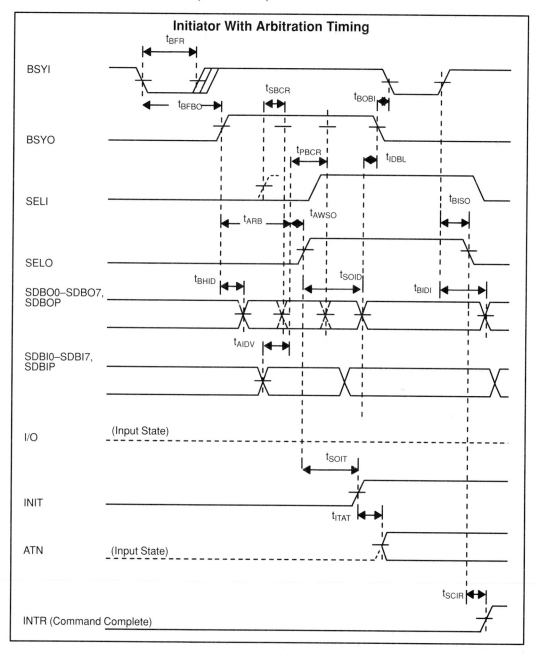

AC CHARACTERISTICS (Continued)

Initiator Without Arbitration						
Parameter	**Designator**	**Test Conditions**	**Values (Note)**			**Unit**
			Min.	**Typ.**	**Max.**	
From BSYI Low to SELECT ID Output	t_{FRID}	CL = 30pF	$(6 + n)^1$ x t_{CLF}		$(7 + n)$ x $t_{CLF}+60$	ns
From ID Output to SELO High	t_{IDSO}	CL = 10pF	$11t_{CLF}-80$			ns
From ID Output to INIT High	t_{IDIT}	CL = 10pF	$11t_{CLF}-80$			ns
From INIT High to ATN High	t_{ITAA}	CL = 10pF	0		60	ns
From BSYI High to SELO Low	t_{BISO}	CL = 10pF	$2t_{CLF}$			ns
From BSYI High to SELECT ID Hold	t_{BIDh}		$2t_{CLF}$			ns
From SELO Low to INTR High	t_{SCIR}	CL = 30pF			60	ns

Note: 1 n = value of TCL register.

AC CHARACTERISTICS (Continued)

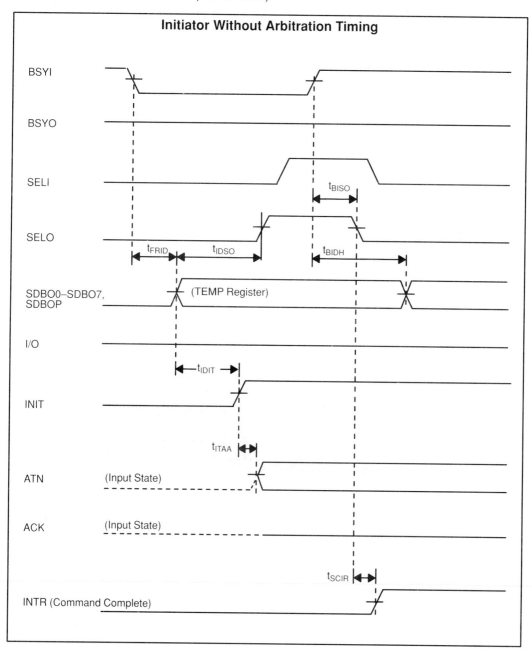

Initiator Without Arbitration Timing

AC CHARACTERISTICS (Continued)

Target With Arbitration

Parameter	Designator	Test Conditions	Values Min.	Values Typ.	Values Max.	Unit
From SELI High to BSYI Low	t_{SIBI}		0			ns
From Data Bus (ID) Valid to BSYI Low	t_{IDBI}		0			ns
From I/O Low to BSYI Low	t_{IIBI}		0			ns
From BSYI to BSYO High	t_{BIBO}	CL = 30pF	$4t_{CLF}$		$5t_{CLF}+60$	ns
From BSYO High to ID Hold	t_{BOID}		60			ns
From BSYO High to SELI Low	t_{BOSI}		0			ns
From SELI Low to TARG High	t_{SLTG}	CL = 30pF	$3t_{CLF}$		$4t_{CLF}+80$	ns
From TARG High to Phase Signal Output	t_{TGPH}	CL = 10pF	0		50	ns
From I/O High to Data Bus Enable	t_{IODE}	CL = 10pF	$7t_{CLF}$			ns
From SELI Low to INTR High	t_{SLIR}	CL = 30pF			$3t_{CLF}+80$	ns

AC CHARACTERISTICS (Continued)

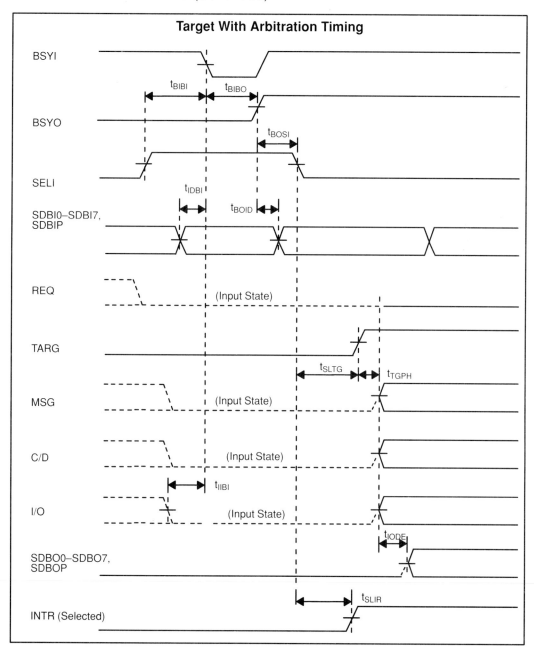

AC CHARACTERISTICS (Continued)

Target Without Arbitration						
Parameter	Designator	Test Conditions	Values			Unit
			Min.	Typ.	Max.	
From Data Bus (ID) Valid to SELI High	t_{IDSI}		0			ns
From I/O Low to SELI High	t_{IISI}		0			ns
From SELI High to BSYO High	t_{SLBO}	CL = 30pF	$2t_{CLF}$		$3t_{CLF}+50$	ns
From BSYO High to ID Hold	t_{BOID}		60			ns
From BSYO High to SELI Low	t_{BOSI}		0			ns
From SELI Low to TARG High	t_{SLTG}	CL = 30pF	$3t_{CLF}$		$4t_{CLF}+80$	ns
From TARG High to Phase Signal Output	t_{TGPH}	CL = 10pF	0		50	ns
From I/O High to Data Bus Enable	t_{IODE}	CL = 10pF	$7t_{CLF}$			ns
From SELI Low to INTR High	t_{SLIR}	CL = 30pF			$3t_{CLF}+80$	ns

AC CHARACTERISTICS (Continued)

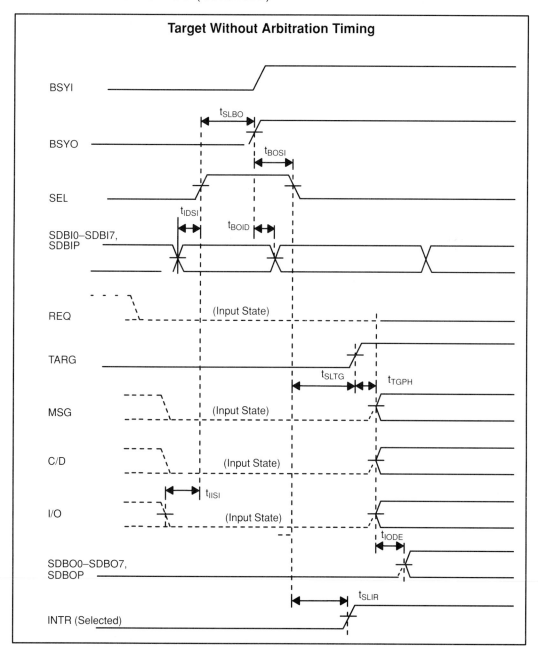

AC CHARACTERISTICS (Continued)

SCSI Bus Interface – Reselection Phase Timing

Target							
Parameter	**Designator**	**Test Conditions**	**Values**			**Unit**
			Min.	**Typ.**	**Max.**	
Bus Free time[2]	t_{BFR}					ns
From BSYI Low to BSYO High	t_{BFBO}	CL = 10pF	$(6+n)^1$ x t_{CLF}		$(7+n)$ x $t_{CLF}+60$	ns
From BSYO High to Device ID Out	t_{BHID}	CL = 30pF	0		60	ns
From BSYO High to Prioritize	t_{ARB}		$32t_{CLF}-60$			ns
From Data Bus Valid to Prioritize	t_{AIDV}		100			ns
From Bus Usage Permission Granted to SELO High	t_{AWSO}	CL = 10pF	0		50	ns
From SELO High to RESELECT ID Output	t_{SOID}	CL = 30pF	$11t_{CLF}-30$			ns
From SELO High to TARG High	t_{SOTG}	CL = 10pF	$11t_{CLF}-50$			ns
From TARG High to Phase Signal Output	t_{TGPH}	CL = 30pF	0		50	ns
From I/O High to BSYO Low	t_{IOBL}	CL = 10pF	$2t_{CLF}-80$			ns
From RESELECT ID Output to BSYO Low	t_{IDBL}	CL = 10pF	$2t_{CLF}-80$			ns
From BSYO Low to BSYI Low	t_{BOBI}	CL = 10pF	0		t_{CLF}	ns
From BSYI High to SELO Low	t_{BISO}	CL = 10pF	$3t_{CLF}$			ns
From BSYI High to RESELECT ID Hold	t_{BIDh}	CL = 10pF	$2t_{CLF}$			ns
From SELO Low to INTR High	t_{SCIR}	CL = 30pF			80	ns
From SELI High to BSYO and ID Bit Low	t_{SBCR}	CL = 30pF (BSYO) CL = 30pF (SDBO0–SDBO7 SDBOP)			$3t_{CLF}+80$	ns
From Prioritize to BSYO and ID Bit Low	t_{PBCR}	CL = 30pF (BSYO) CL = 30pF (SDBO0–SDBO7, SDBOP)			60	ns
From BSYI High to BSYI High	t_{BIBO}	CL = 10pF	$2t_{CLF}+20$		$3t_{CLF}+60$	ns

Notes: [1]n = value of TCL register.

[2]The bus free time is the minimum time interval until the booked select command is executed.

AC CHARACTERISTICS (Continued)

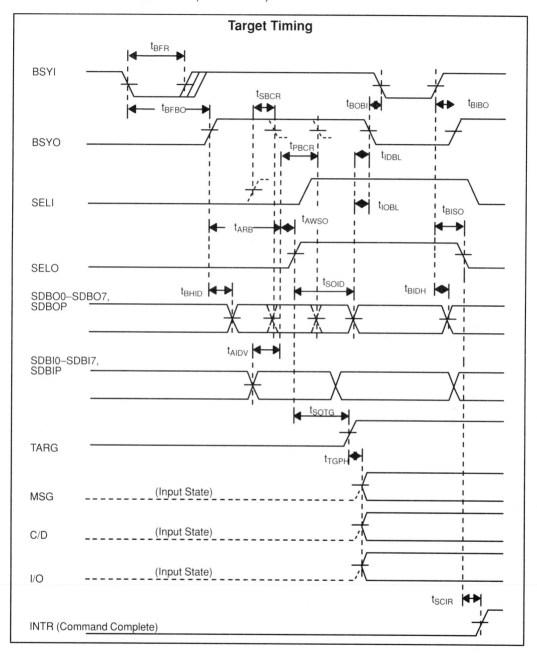

AC CHARACTERISTICS (Continued)

Initiator						
Parameter	**Designator**	**Test Conditions**	**Values**			**Unit**
			Min.	**Typ.**	**Max.**	
From SELI High to BSYI Low	t_{SIBI}		0			ns
From Data Bus (ID) Valid to BSYI Low	t_{IDBI}		0			ns
From I/O High to BSYI Low	t_{IIBI}		0			ns
From BSYI Low to BSYO High	t_{SLBO}	CL = 30pF	$4t_{CLF}$		$5t_{CLF+60}$	ns
From BSYO High to ID Hold	t_{BOID}		60			ns
From BSYO High to SELI Low	t_{BOSI}		0			ns
From SELI Low to BSYO Low	t_{SIBO}	CL = 30pF	$2t_{CLF}$		$3t_{CLF+60}$	ns
From SELI Low to I/O Hold	t_{SIIH}		100			ns
From SELI Low to INTR High	t_{SLIR}	CL = 30pF			$3t_{CLF+80}$	ns
From SELI Low to INIT High	t_{SLIT}	CL = 30pF	$3t_{CLF}+30$		$4t_{CLF+80}$	ns
From INIT High to Data Bus Enable when I/O is Low	t_{ITDE}	CL = 10pF			50	ns

AC CHARACTERISTICS (Continued)

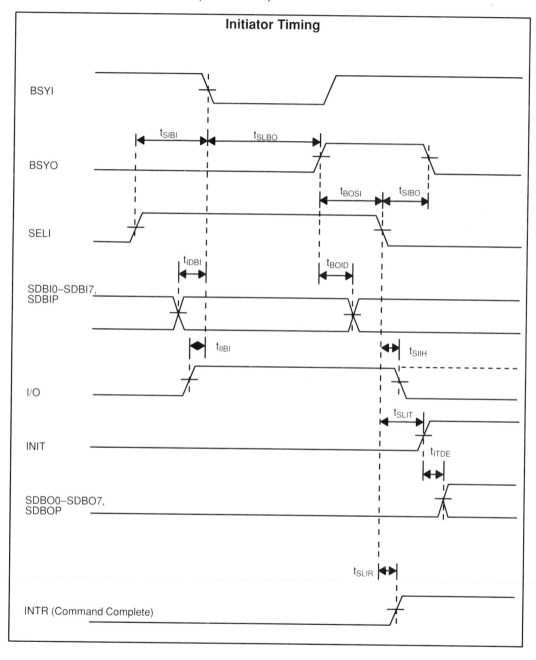

AC CHARACTERISTICS (Continued)

SCSI Bus Interface – Transfer Phase Timing

Asynchronous Transfer Output (Initiator)						
Parameter	Designator	Test Conditions	Values			Unit
			Min.	Typ.	Max.	
From I/O Low to Data Bus Enable	t_{IIDE}	CL = 10pF	10			ns
From Phase Specify to REQ High	t_{PHRQ}		100			ns
From ACK Low to Phase Change	t_{ALPH}[1]	CL = 10pF	10			ns
From REQ High to ATN Low	t_{RATL}[2]	CL = 10pF	$2t_{CLF}$			ns
From ATN Low to ACK High	t_{ATLA}[2]	CL = 10pF	$t_{CLF}-20$			ns
From Data Bus Valid to ACK High	t_{DVAK}	CL = 10pF	$2t_{CLF}-80$			ns
From REQ Low to Data Bus Hold	t_{RLDV}	CL = 10pF	15			ns
From REQ High to ACK High	t_{RHAH}	CL = 10pF	20			ns
From ACK High to REQ Low	t_{AHRL}		0			ns
From REQ Low to ACK Low	t_{RLAI}	CL = 10pF	10			ns
From ACK Low to REQ High	t_{ALRH}		10			ns
From REQ Low to ACK High	t_{RLNA}	CL = 10pF	$2t_{CLF}$			ns
From REQ High to Phase Change	t_{RHPH}[1]		$3t_{CLF}$			ns

Notes: 1 Phase change must satisfy both t_{ALPH} and t_{RHPH} specifications.
         2 This specification is applicable only when the last byte of the message transfer phase is transferred using the hardware transfer mode.

AC CHARACTERISTICS (Continued)

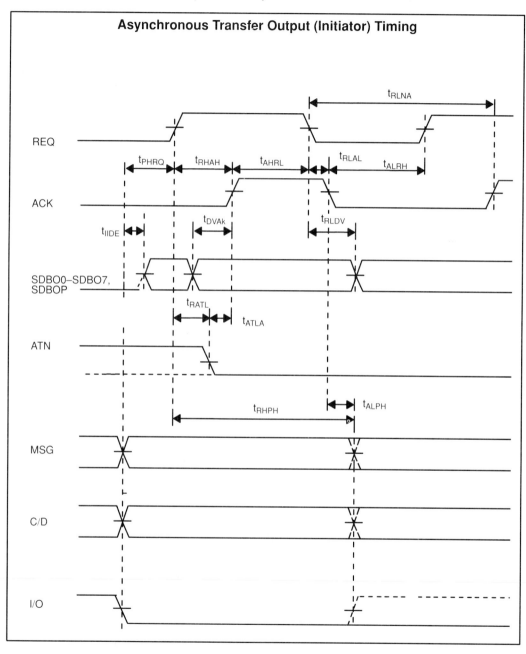

Asynchronous Transfer Output (Initiator) Timing

AC CHARACTERISTICS (Continued)

Asynchronous Transfer Output (Target)						
Parameter	Designator	Test Conditions	Values			Unit
			Min.	Typ.	Max.	
From I/O High to Data Bus Enable	t_{IODE}	CL = 10pF	$7t_{CLF}$			ns
From Data Bus Valid to REQ High	t_{DVPQ}	CL = 10pF	$2t_{CLF}-80$			ns
From ACK High to Data Bus Hold	t_{AKDV}	CL = 10pF	15			ns
From REQ High to ACK High	t_{RHAH}		20			ns
From ACK High to REQ Low	t_{AHRL}	CL = 30pF	10		100	ns
From REQ Low to ACK Low	t_{RLAL}		0			ns
From ACK Low to REQ High	t_{ALRH}	CL = 10pF	10			ns
From ACK High to REQ High	t_{AHRH}	CL = 10pF	$2t_{CLF}$			ns

AC CHARACTERISTICS (Continued)

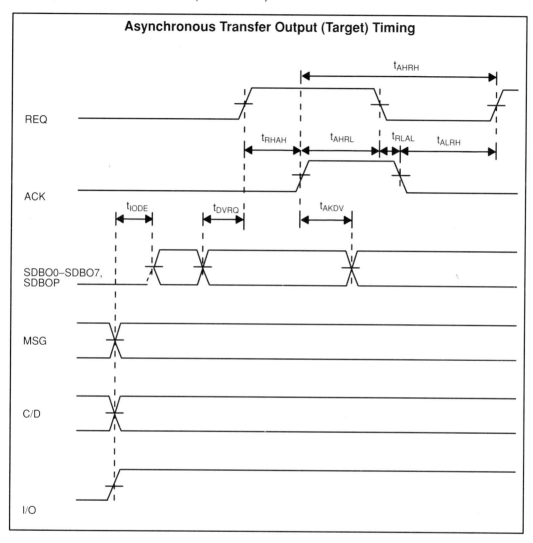

Asynchronous Transfer Output (Target) Timing

AC CHARACTERISTICS (Continued)

Asynchronous Transfer Input (Initiator)

Parameter	Designator	Test Conditions	Min.	Typ.	Max.	Unit
From I/O High to Data Bus Disable	t_{IIDD}	CL = 30pF			60	ns
From Phase Specify to REQ High	t_{PHRQ}		100			ns
From ACK Low to Phase Change	t_{ALPH}[1]		10			ns
From Data Bus Valid to REQ High	t_{DVRQ}		10			ns
From ACK High to Data Bus Hold	t_{AKDV}		15			ns
From REQ High to ACK High	t_{RHAH}	CL = 10pF	20			ns
From ACK High to REQ Low	t_{AHRL}		0			ns
From REQ Low to ACK Low	t_{RLAL}	CL = 10pF	20			ns
From ACK Low to REQ High	t_{ALRH}		10			ns
From REQ Low to ACK High	t_{RLNA}	CL = 10pF	t_{CLF}			ns
From ATN High to ACK Low	t_{ATAL}[2]	CL = 10pF	t_{CLF}−20			ns
From REQ High to Phase Change	t_{RHPH}[1]		$3t_{CLF}$			ns

Notes: 1 Phase change must satisfy both t_{ALPH} and t_{RHPH} specifications.
2 Based on this timing parameter, the ATN signal is transferred only when parity check function is enabled and a parity error is detected on the input data.

AC CHARACTERISTICS (Continued)

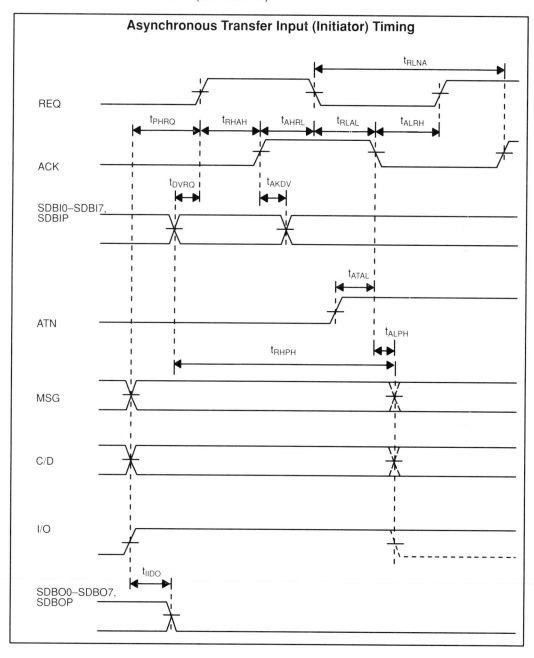

Asynchronous Transfer Input (Initiator) Timing

AC CHARACTERISTICS (Continued)

Asynchronous Transfer Input (Target)						
Parameter	Designator	Test Conditions	Values			Unit
			Min.	Typ.	Max.	
From I/O Low to Data Bus Disable	t_{IODD}	CL = 30pF			30	ns
From Data Bus Valid to ACK High	t_{DVAK}		10			ns
From REQ Low to Data Bus Hold	t_{RLDV}	CL = 10pF	15			ns
From REQ High to ACK High	t_{RHAH}		20			ns
From ACK High to REQ Low	t_{AHRL}	CL = 30pF	10		100	ns
From REQ Low to ACK Low	t_{RLAL}		0			ns
From ACK Low to REQ High	t_{ALRH}	CL = 10pF	10			ns
From ACK High to REQ High	t_{AHRH}	CL = 10pF	$2t_{CLF}$			ns

AC CHARACTERISTICS (Continued)

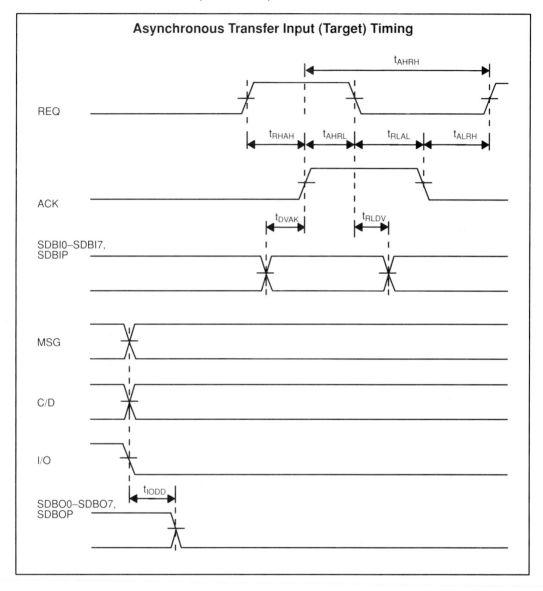

Asynchronous Transfer Input (Target) Timing

AC CHARACTERISTICS (Continued)

Parameter	Designator	Test Conditions	Values			Unit
Transfer Phase Change (Target)						
			Min.	Typ.	Max.	
From WR High to MSG, C/D, I/O	t_{PHCH}	CL = 30pF	10		100	ns

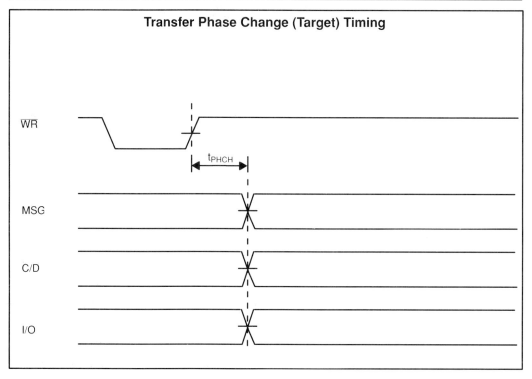

Transfer Phase Change (Target) Timing

AC CHARACTERISTICS (Continued)

Manual Transfer (Note)[1]						
Parameter	Designator	Test Conditions	Values			Unit
			Min.	Typ.	Max.	
From $\overline{\text{WR}}$ High to Data Bus Valid for TEMP Register	t_{WTDV}	CL = 30pF			100	ns
From $\overline{\text{WR}}$ High to REQ High, ACK High for SET ACK/REQ Command	t_{STRA}	CL = 30pF	$2t_{CLF}$		$3t_{CLF}+60$	ns
From $\overline{\text{WR}}$ High to REQ Low, ACK Low for RESET ACK/REQ Command	t_{RTRA}	CL = 30pF	$2t_{CLF}$		$3t_{CLF}+60$	ns

Note: 1 Timing sequences not shown are the same as those for asynchronous transfers.

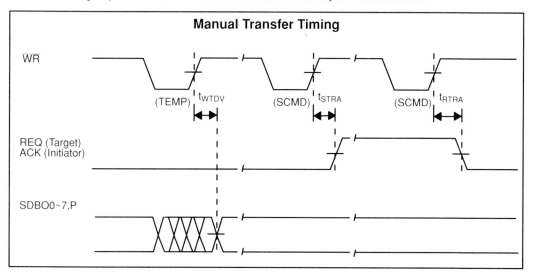

Manual Transfer Timing

AC CHARACTERISTICS (Continued)

SCSI Bus Interface – Attention Condition

Initiator						
Parameter	Designator	Test Conditions	Values			Unit
			Min.	Typ.	Max.	
From $\overline{WR}$ high to ATN High, ATN Low for SET/RESET ATN Command	t_{ATNO}	CL = 30pF	$2t_{CLF}$		$3t_{CLF}+60$	ns

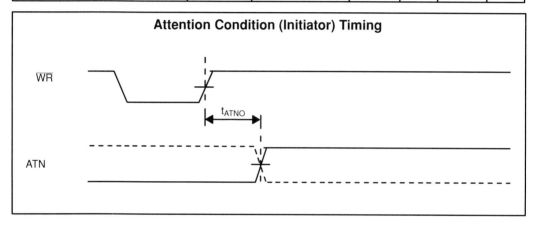

Attention Condition (Initiator) Timing

AC CHARACTERISTICS (Continued)

SCSI Bus Interface – Bus Free

Initiator (Disconnected)

Parameter	Designator	Test Conditions	Values			Unit
			Min.	Typ.	Max.	
From BSYI Low to INIT Low	t_{BLIT}	CL = 30pF			$5t_{CLF}+60$	ns
From INIT Low to Bus Clear	t_{ITCR}	CL = 30pF			80	ns
From BSYI Low to INTR High	t_{BLIR}	CL = 30pF			$6t_{CLF}+80$	ns

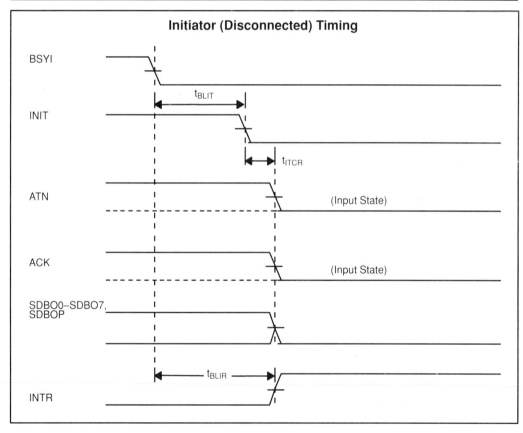

Initiator (Disconnected) Timing

AC CHARACTERISTICS (Continued)

Target (Bus Release Command)

Parameter	Designator	Test Conditions	Values			Unit
			Min.	Typ.	Max.	
From $\overline{\text{WR}}$ High (SCMD Register) to BSYO Low	t_{WRLS}	CL = 30pF			$3t_{CLF}+60$	ns
From $\overline{\text{WR}}$ High (SCMD Register) to TARG Low	t_{WRGL}	CL = 40pF			$3t_{CLF}+60$	ns
From TARG Low to Bus Clear	t_{TGCR}	CL = 30pF			80	ns

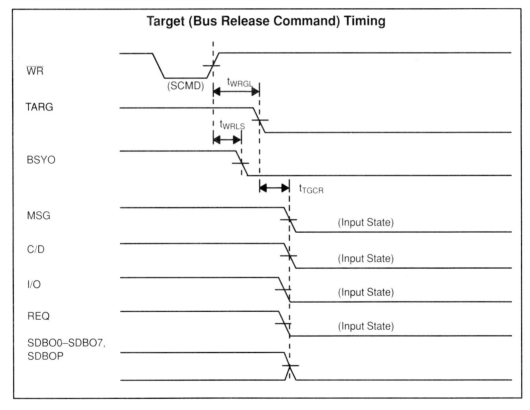

Target (Bus Release Command) Timing

AC CHARACTERISTICS (Continued)

Termination (Time Out) – Selection and Reselection Phases

Parameter	Designator	Test Conditions	Values			Unit
			Min.	Typ.	Max.	
From $\overline{WR}$ High (INTS Register) to SELO low	t_{WSL}	CL = 30pF			$3t_{CLF}+60$	ns
From $\overline{WR}$ High (INTS Register) to Data Bus Disable	t_{WDBL}	CL = 30pF			$3t_{CLF}+100$	ns
From $\overline{WR}$ High (INTS Register) to TARG Low or INIT Low	t_{WTIL}	CL = 40pF			$3t_{CLF}+60$	ns
From TARG Low to I/O High-Z	t_{TGIO}	CL = 30pF			50	ns
From $\overline{WR}$ High (INTS Register) to Data Bus Disable	t_{WIRL}	CL = 30pF			$3t_{CLF}+60$	ns

Termination (Time Out) Selection and Reselection Phases Timing

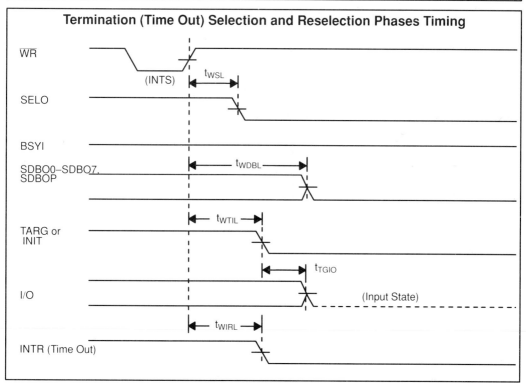

AC CHARACTERISTICS (Continued)

SCSI Bus Interface – Reset Condition

RST INPUT						
Parameter	**Designator**	**Test Conditions**	**Values**			**Unit**
			Min.	**Typ.**	**Max.**	
RSTI Pulse Width	t_{SRIN}		$3t_{CLF}$			ns
Reset Delay	t_{RSID}	CL = 30pF			$4t_{CLF}+110$	ns

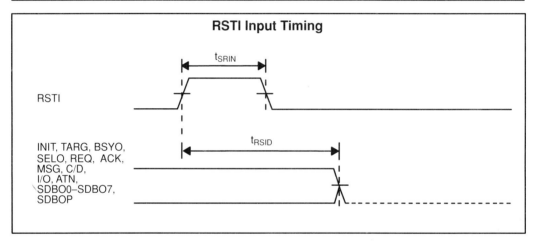

RSTI Input Timing

AC CHARACTERISTICS (Continued)

RST Output

Parameter	Designator	Test Conditions	Values			Unit
			Min.	Typ.	Max.	
From $\overline{\text{WR}}$ High (SCMD Register's Bit 4) to RSTO High	t_{RSTO}	CL = 30pF	10		80	ns
Reset Delay	t_{RSOD}	CL = 30pF			110	ns

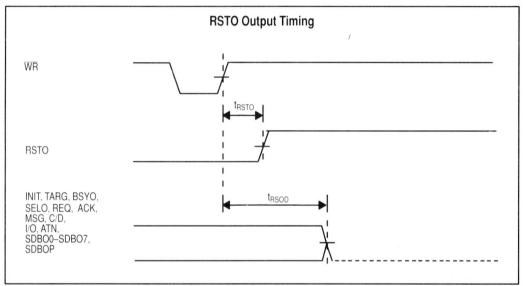

RSTO Output Timing

AC CHARACTERISTICS (Continued)

AC Test Conditions (Input)

Timing Reference Levels for CPU/DMAC Interface

Logical 1 = 2.4 V_{DC}
Logical 0 = 0.45 V_{DC}

AC Test Conditions (Output)

Timing Reference Levels for SCSI Bus Interface

Logical 1 = 2.4 V_{DC}
Logical 0 = 0.45 V_{DC}

Capacitive Output Loading

Input/Output Pins	Values			Unit
	Min.	Typ.	Max.	
D0 – D7, DP		—	80	pF
DPO		10	30	pF
INTR		10	30	pF
DREQ		10	30	pF
TARG, INPUT1		20	40	pF
INIT, INPUT2		10	30	pF
SDBO0 – SDBO7, SDBOP		10	30	pF
RSTO, SELO, BSYO		10	30	pF
MSG, C/D, I/O		10	30	pF
REQ, ACK, ANT		10	30	pF

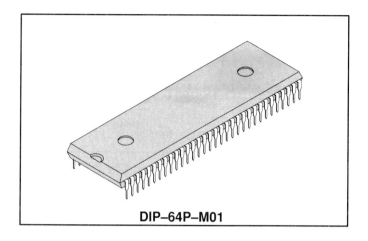

DIP–64P–M01

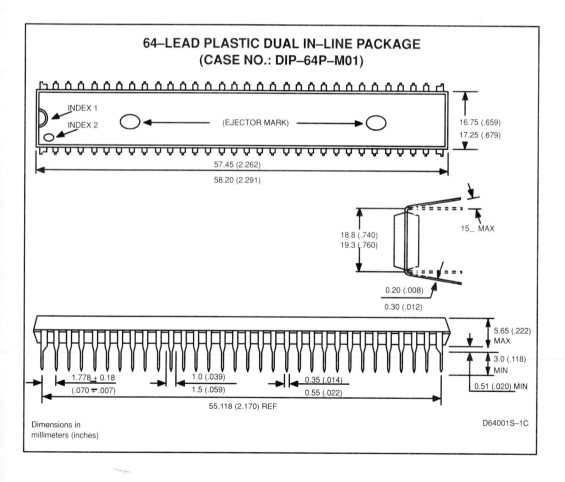

64–LEAD PLASTIC DUAL IN–LINE PACKAGE
(CASE NO.: DIP–64P–M01)

INDEX 1

INDEX 2

(EJECTOR MARK)

16.75 (.659)
17.25 (.679)

57.45 (2.262)
58.20 (2.291)

18.8 (.740)
19.3 (.760)

15_ MAX

0.20 (.008)
0.30 (.012)

5.65 (.222) MAX

3.0 (.118) MIN

0.51 (.020) MIN

1.778 + 0.18
(.070 ∓ .007)

1.0 (.039)
1.5 (.059)

0.35 (.014)
0.55 (.022)

55.118 (2.170) REF

Dimensions in
millimeters (inches)

D64001S–1C

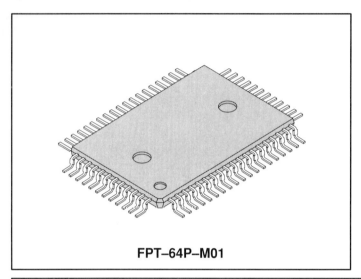

FPT–64P–M01

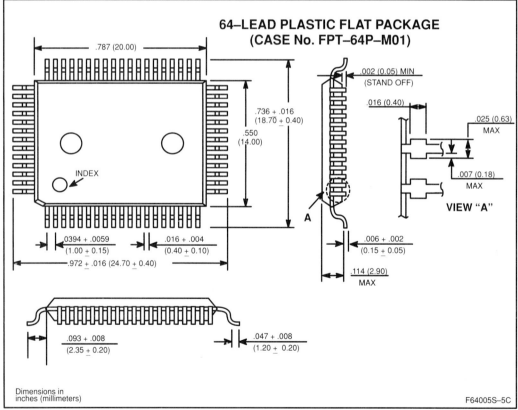

64–LEAD PLASTIC FLAT PACKAGE
(CASE No. FPT–64P–M01)

.787 (20.00)

.736 + .016
(18.70 + 0.40)

.550
(14.00)

INDEX

.0394 + .0059
(1.00 + 0.15)

.016 + .004
(0.40 + 0.10)

.972 + .016 (24.70 + 0.40)

.002 (0.05) MIN
(STAND OFF)

.016 (0.40)

.025 (0.63)
MAX

.007 (0.18)
MAX

A

.006 + .002
(0.15 + 0.05)

.114 (2.90)
MAX

VIEW "A"

.093 + .008
(2.35 + 0.20)

.047 + .008
(1.20 + 0.20)

Dimensions in
inches (millimeters)

F64005S–5C

Chapter 10

MB 89352
PRODUCT PROFILE

MB89352
SCSI Protocol Controller (SPC)
with On-Chip Drivers/Receivers

Edition 1.0
September 1989

GENERAL DESCRIPTION

The MB89352 CMOS LSI SPC (SCSI Protocol Controller) is a circuit designed for easy control of the small computer system interface (SCSI).

The MB89352 can be used as a peripheral LSI circuit for an 8- or 16-bit MPU to realize high-level SCSI control. The SPC can control all the SCSI interface signals and handle almost all the interface control procedures. The on-chip driver/receivers allow for direct connection to the SCSI BUS.

This LSI circuit has an 8-byte FIFO data buffer register and a transfer byte counter that is 24 bits long. Furthermore, the MB89352 can serve as either an INITIATOR or a TARGET device for the SCSI, and can therefore be used for either an I/O controller or a host adapter.

SCSI Compatibility

- Full support for SCSI control (ANSI X3.1311986 Specification) except for synchronized transfer mode
- Serves as either INITIATOR or TARGET

Data Transfer Rate/Byte Counter

- 8-byte FIFO data timing control
- 24-bit transfer byte counter

Drive Options (on-chip driver/receiver)

- Single-ended

Selectable Transfer Modes

- DMA Transfer
- Program Transfer
- Manual Transfer

Clock Requirements

- 8 MHz clock

Technology/Power Requirements

- Silicon-gate CMOS
- Single +5 V power supply

Available Packaging

- 48-pin DIP or FLAT plastic packages

ABSOLUTE MAXIMUM RATINGS[1]

Rating	Designator	Values		Unit
		Min.	Max.	
Supply Voltage	V_{CC}	$V_{SS} -0.3$	7.0	V
Input Voltage	V_I	$V_{SS} -0.3$	7.3	V
Output Voltage[2]	V_O	$V_{SS} -0.3$	7.3	V
Storage Temperature	T_{STG}	−55	150	°C

Notes: 1 Permanent device damage may occur if the above absolute maximum ratings are exceeded. Functional operation should be restricted to the conditions as detailed in the operational sections of this data sheet. Exposure to absolute maximum rating conditions for extended periods may affect device reliability.

2 Should not exceed V_{CC} + 0.5V.

RECOMMENDED OPERATING CONDITIONS

Parameter	Designator	Values			Unit
		Min.	Typ.	Max.	
Supply Voltage	V_{CC}	4.75	5.0	5.25	V
Operating Ambient Temperature	T_A	0		+ 70	°C

MB89352 BLOCK DIAGRAM

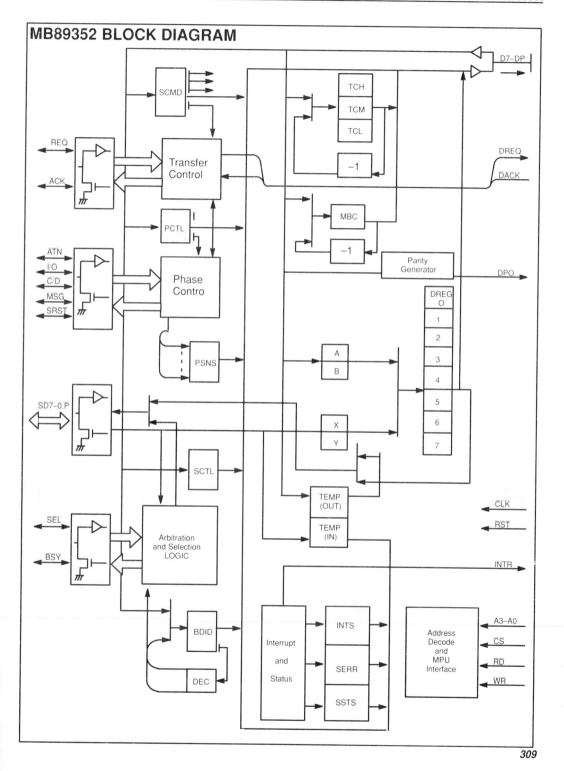

PIN ASSIGNMENTS

48-Pin Plastic DIP

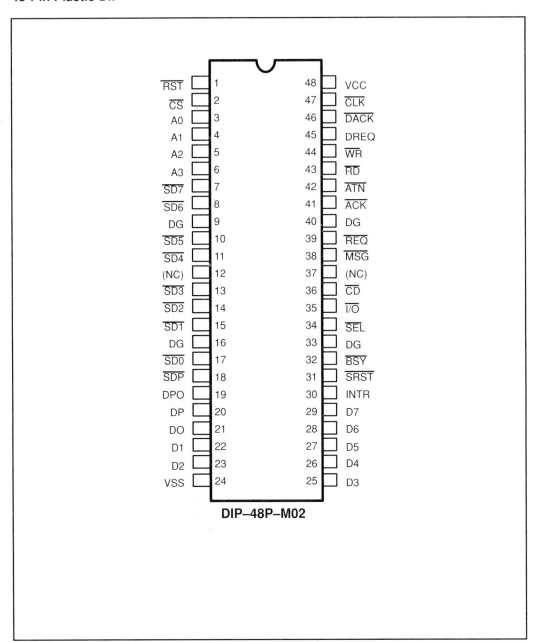

$\overline{RST}$	1	48	VCC
$\overline{CS}$	2	47	$\overline{CLK}$
A0	3	46	$\overline{DACK}$
A1	4	45	DREQ
A2	5	44	$\overline{WR}$
A3	6	43	$\overline{RD}$
$\overline{SD7}$	7	42	$\overline{ATN}$
$\overline{SD6}$	8	41	$\overline{ACK}$
DG	9	40	DG
$\overline{SD5}$	10	39	$\overline{REQ}$
$\overline{SD4}$	11	38	$\overline{MSG}$
(NC)	12	37	(NC)
$\overline{SD3}$	13	36	$\overline{CD}$
$\overline{SD2}$	14	35	$\overline{I/O}$
$\overline{SD1}$	15	34	$\overline{SEL}$
DG	16	33	DG
$\overline{SD0}$	17	32	$\overline{BSY}$
$\overline{SDP}$	18	31	$\overline{SRST}$
DPO	19	30	INTR
DP	20	29	D7
DO	21	28	D6
D1	22	27	D5
D2	23	26	D4
VSS	24	25	D3

DIP–48P–M02

PIN ASSIGNMENTS (Continued)

48-Pin Plastic Flat Package

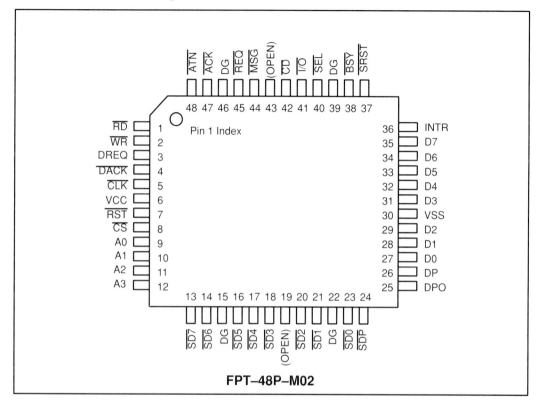

FPT-48P-M02

PIN DESCRIPTIONS

Designator	Pin No.		I/O	Function
	DIP	FPT		
V_{CC}	48	6	—	+5V power supply.
V_{SS}	24	30	—	Circuit ground.
DG	9 16 33 40	15 22 39 46	—	Ground (OV) for internal drivers. The SCSI bus drivers can sink up to 48-mA each. Up to 16 drivers can be active at once. We recommend a good solid ground plane.
$\overline{CLK}$	47	5	I	Clock input for controlling internal operation and data transfer speed of the SPC.
$\overline{RST}$	1	7	I	Asynchronous reset signal used to clear all internal circuits of the SPC.
$\overline{CS}$	2	8	I	Input selection enable signal for accessing an internal register. When active low, the following input/output signals are valid: RD, WR, A3-A0, DP7-DP0 and DP.
A0 A1 A2 A3	3 4 5 6	9 10 11 12	I	Address input signals for selecting an internal register in SPC. MSB is A3; LSB is A0. When $\overline{CS}$ is active, read/ write is enabled for an internal register selected by these address inputs via data bus lines D0-D7 and DP.
$\overline{RD}$	43	1	I	This strobe input is used for reading out the contents of the SPC internal register, and is effective only when $\overline{CS}$ input is active. While $\overline{RD}$ is active, the contents of an internal register selected by A0 to A3 inputs are placed on data bus lines D7 to D0, DP. For a data transfer cycle in the program transfer mode, the rising edge of $\overline{RD}$ is used as a timing signal indicating the end of data read.
$\overline{WR}$	44	2	I	The strobe input is used for writing data into an SPC internal register, and is effective only when $\overline{CS}$ input is active. On the rising edge of this signal, data placed on data bus lines D0 to D7, DP are loaded into an internal register selected by A0 to A3 inputs. For a data transfer cycle in the program transfer mode, the rising edge of this signal is used as a timing signal indicating data ready status.
DP D0 D1 D2 D3 D4 D5 D6 D7	20 21 22 23 25 26 27 28 29	26 27 28 29 31 32 33 34 35	I/O	Used to write/read data to/from an internal register in the SPC. The data bus is 3-state and bidirectional. The MSB is D7 and the LSB is D0; DP is an odd parity bit. When both $\overline{CS}$ and RD inputs are active, the contents of a selected internal register are output to the data bus. In operations other than read/write, the data bus is kept at a high-Z level.

Continued on following page

PIN DESCRIPTIONS

Designator	Pin No.		I/O	Function
	DIP	FPT		
DPO	19	25	O	Outputs an odd parity of D0–D7. If parity bit is not generated for external memory, DPO can be used as an input parity bit for DP.
INTR	30	36	O	The INTR output signal is issued by the SPC and requests an interrupt to indicate completion of an internal operation or the occurrence of an error. Except for an interrupt caused by the RSTI input (reset condition in SCSI). When an interrupt request is granted, the INTR signal remains active until the interrupt is cleared.
DREQ	45	3	O	For a data transfer cycle in DMA mode, this signal isused to indicate a request for data transfer between the SPC and the external buffer memory. In an output operation, this signal becomes active to request a data transfer from the external buffer memory when the SPC internal data buffer register has free space available. In an input operation, it becomes active to request data transfer to the external buffer memory when the SPC internal data buffer resgister contains valid data.
$\overline{\text{DACK}}$	46	4	I	An active low response signal to the DREQ which request data transfer in between SPC and the external memory in the DMA mode. This signal in DMA mode functions similarly to the signal combination of $\overline{\text{CS}}$=low, A3=high, A2=low, A1–high, and A0=low (selection of DREG) in the program transfer mode. Since the DREG is selected by this $\overline{\text{DACK}}$ signal in the DMA mode instead of the address input from A3–A0, data transfer in between DREG of SPC and external memory is possible.
SD0 SD1 SD2 SD3 SD4 SD5 SD6 SD7 SDP	17 15 14 13 11 10 8 7 18	23 21 20 18 17 16 14 13 24	I/O	Active low bi–directional SCSI data bus. MSB : $\overline{\text{SD7}}$, LSB : $\overline{\text{SD0}}$ Odd parity bit : $\overline{\text{SDP}}$ Parity check for the SCSI data bus is programmable.
$\overline{\text{SEL}}$	34	40	I/O	A signal to issue or detect selection or reselection phase. In selection phase, an initiater asserts this signal, and in reselection phase the signal is asserted by the target.
$\overline{\text{BSY}}$	32	38	I/O	This signal indicates the SCSI bus use condition.This signal goes "L" when SPC is in arbitration phase or working as a target. Also, this signal is used to detect bus free phase with $\overline{\text{SEL}}$ signal.

Continued on following page

PIN DESCRIPTIONS

Designator	Pin No.		I/O	Function
	DIP	FPT		
I/O C/D MSG	36 36 38	41 42 44	 I/O	Signals to indicate actual phase of information transfer phase as follows: **MSG** **C/D** **I/O** **Phase Name** 0 0 0 Data Out Phase 0 0 1 Data In Phase 0 1 0 Command Phase 0 1 1 Status Phase 1 0 0 Reserved 1 0 1 Reserved 1 1 0 Message Out Phase 1 1 1 Message In Phase These signals are output from the target and initiator receives them always.
$\overline{\text{REQ}}$	39	45	I/O	In the data transfer phase, the REQ signal is used to notify the INITIATOR that the TARGET is ready to receive or send data. The REQ input is used as a timing control signal in the data transfer sequence.
$\overline{\text{ACK}}$	41	47	I/O	In the data transfer phase, the acknowledge signal is in response to a transfer request (REQ) signal from the TARGET. In the same way as REQ, an ACK input is used as a timing signal in the data transfer sequence.
$\overline{\text{ATN}}$	42	48	I/O	A signal to indicate attention condition. This signal is only output from an initiator.
$\overline{\text{SRST}}$	31	37	I/O	SCSI reset signal to be enabled by register setting. SCSI input from other SCSI devices is non-maskable.
NC	12, 37		—	Not connected
OPEN	—	19, 43		Reserved. (Do not make external connections to these pins)

ADDRESSING OF INTERNAL REGISTERS

SPC has internal registers, consisting of 15 bytes, that are accessible from an external circuit. These internal registers are used for controlling SPC internal operation and indicating SPC processing status/result status. A unique address is assigned to each internal register, and a particular register is identified by address bits A3 to A0. The following table shows internal register addressing:

Table 1.   Internal Register Addressing

Register	Mnemonic	Operation	Chip Select ($\overline{CS}$)	Address Bits			
				A3	A2	A1	A0
Bus Device ID	BDID	R	0	0	0	0	0
		W					
SPC Control	SCTL	R	0	0	0	0	1
		W					
Command	SCMD	R	0	0	0	1	0
		W					
Open	—	—	0	0	0	1	1
Interrupt Sense	INTS	R	0	0	1	0	0
Reset Interrupt		W					
Phase Sense	PSNS	R	0	0	1	0	1
SPC Diagnostic Control	SDGC	W					
SPC Status	SSTS	R	0	0	1	1	0
—		W					
SPC Error Status	SERR	R	0	0	1	1	1
—		W					
Phase Control	PCTL	R	0	1	0	0	0
		W					
Modified Byte Counter	MBC	R	0	1	0	0	1
—		W					

Continued on following page

Table 1.   Internal Register Addressing

Register	Mnemonic	Operation	Chip Select (CS)	Address Bits			
				A3	A2	A1	A0
Data Register	DREG	R	0	1	0	1	0
		W					
Temporary Register	TEMP	R	0	1	0	1	1
		W					
Transfer Counter High	TCH	R	0	1	1	0	0
		W					
Transfer Counter Middle	TCM	R	0	1	1	0	1
		W					
Transfer Counter Low	TCL	R	0	1	1	1	0
		W					

BIT ASSIGNMENTS

The following table shows the bit assignments to each internal register. When accessing an internal register (in read/write), remember the following:

1. The internal register block includes the read–only/write–only register and those having different meanings in read and write operations.

2. A write command to a read–only register is ignored.

3. If the write–only register is read out, the data and parity bit are undefined.

4. At bit positions indicating "_" for a write in either 1 or 0 may be written.

Table 2. Bit Assignments for Internal Registers

HEX Address	Register and Mnemonic	R/W Operation	7 (MSb)	6	5	4	3	2	1	0 (LSb)	Parity
0	Bus Device ID (BDID)	R	#7	#6	#5	#4	#3	#2	#1	#0	0
		W		— —				ID4	ID2	ID1	—
1	SPC Control (SCTL)	R/W	Reset & Disable	Control Reset	Diag Mode	ARBIT Enable	Parity Enable	Select Enable	Reselect Enable	INT Enable	P
2	Command (SCMD)	R	Command Code	Command Code	Command Code	RST Out	Intercept Xfer	Transfer Modifer — PRG Xfer	0	Term Mode	P
		W	Command Code	Command Code	Command Code			PRG Xfer	0	Term Mode	
3		R									
		W									
4	Interrupt Sense (SERR)	R	Selected	Reselected	Disconnect	Command Complete	Service Required	Time Out	SPC Hard Error	Reset Condition	P
		W			Reset Interrupt						—
5	Phase Sense (PSNS)	R	REQ	ACK	ATN	SEL	BSY	MSG	C/D	I/O	P
	SPC Diag. Control (SDGC)	W	Diag. REQ	Diag ACK	Xfer Enable		Diag. BSY	Diag. MSG	Diag. C/D	Diag. I/O	—
6	SPC Status (SSTS)	R	Connected INIT	TARG	SPC BSY	XFER In Progress	SCSI RST	TC=0	DREG Status Full	Empty	P
		W			—						—

Continued on following page

Bit Assignments For Internal Registers

HEX Address	Register and Mnemonic	R/W Oper-ation	7 (MSb)	6	5	4	3	2	1	0 (LSb)	Parity
8	Phase Control (PCTL)	R	Bus Free Inter-rupt Enable	0			Transfer Phase				P
		W	Bus Free Inter-rupt Enable	0				MSG Out	C/D Out	I/O Out	
9	Modified Byte Counter (MBC)	R	0				Bit 3	MBC Bit 2	Bit 1	Bit 0	P
		W	—							—	P
A	Data Register (DREG)	R	Internal Data Register (8 Byte FIFO)								
		W	Bit 7	Bit 6	Bit 5	Bit 4	Bit 3	Bit 2	Bit 1	Bit 0	P
B	Temporary Register (TEMP)	R	Temporary Data (Input: From SCSI)								
			Bit 7	Bit 6	Bit 5	Bit 4	Bit 3	Bit 2	Bit 1	Bit 0	P
		W	Temporary Data (Output: To SCSI)								
			Bit 7	Bit 6	Bit 5	Bit 4	Bit 3	Bit 2	Bit 1	Bit 0	P
C	Transfer Counter High (TCH)	R	Transfer Counter High (MSB)								
		W	Bit 23	Bit 22	Bit 21	Bit 20	Bit 19	Bit 18	Bit 17	Bit 16	P
D	Transfer Counter Mid (TCM)	R	Transfer Counter Middle (2nd Byte)								
		W	Bit 15	Bit 14	Bit 13	Bit 12	Bit 11	Bit 10	Bit 9	Bit 8	P
E	Transfer Counter LOW (TCL)	R	Transfer Counter Low (LSB)								
		W	Bit 7	Bit 6	Bit 5	Bit 4	Bit 3	Bit 2	Bit 1	Bit 0	P

These bit assignments for the MB89352 internal registers are identical to those in the MB87030, MB87031, and MB89351. Therfore, SPC replacement from one to another is very easy and does not require any new software design.

DC CHARACTERISTICS (T_A=0–70°C, V_{CC}=5V $\pm$5%)
(Recommended operating conditions unless otherwise specified)

SCSI Bus Signal Pins

Parameter	Designator	Conditions	Values			Unit
			Min.	Typ.	Max.	
Input High Voltage	V_{IH}		2.0	—	5.25	V
Input Low Voltage	V_{IL}		0	—	0.8	V
Input High Current	I_{IH}	V_{IH} + 5.25V	—	100	400	μA
Input Low Current	I_{IL}	V_{IL} + OV	—	−100	−400	μA
Output Low Voltage	V_{OL}	V_{CC} = 4.75V I_{OL} + 48mA	—	—	0.5	V
Input Hysteresis Width	V_{HM}	—	0.2	0.4	—	V

DC CHARACTERISTICS (Continued)

MPU Bus Signal Pins

Parameter	Designator	Conditions	Values			Unit
			Min.	Typ.	Max.	
Input High Voltage	V_{IH}		2.2	—	V_{CC} + 0.3	V
Input Low Voltage	V_{IL}		V_{SS} −0.3	—	0.8	V
Output High Voltage	V_{OH}	I_{OH} + 0.4 mA	4.0		V_{CC}	V
Output Low Voltage	V_{OL}	I_{OL} + 3.2 mA	V_{SS}		0.4	V
Input Leakage Current	I_{LIH}	V_{IH} + 5.25			20	μA
	I_{LIL}	V_{IL} + 0.0			−10	μA
Input/Output Leakage Current	I_{LZH}	V_{IH} + 5.25			40	μA
	I_{LZL}	V_{IL} + 0.0			−40	μA
Power Supply Current	I_{CC}	Input Clock = 8 MHz All Output Pins Open			10	mA

AC CHARACTERISTICS (Continued)

(Recommended operating conditions unless otherwise noted)

Clock Signal

CLK Input					
Parameter	Designator	Values			Unit
		Min.	Typ.	Max.	
$\overline{CLK}$ Cycle Time	t_{CLF}	125		200	ns
$\overline{CLK}$ High Time	t_{CHCL}	44			ns
$\overline{CLK}$ Pulse Width	t_{CLCH}	44			ns
$\overline{CLK}$ Rising Skew Time	t_r			10	ns
$\overline{CLK}$ Falling Skew Time	t_f			10	ns

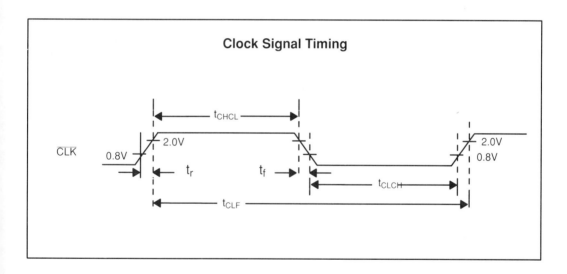

Clock Signal Timing

AC CHARACTERISTICS (Continued)

RST Input					
Parameter	**Designator**	**Values**			**Unit**
		Min.	**Typ.**	**Max.**	
RST Pulse Width	t_{RSTW}	100			ns

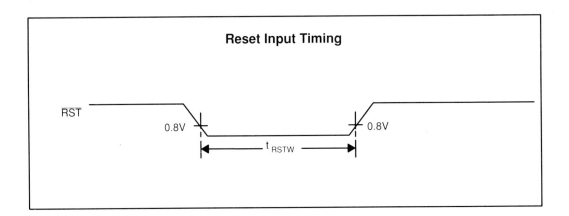

Reset Input Timing

AC CHARACTERISTICS (Continued)

Register Read

Parameter	Designator	Values			Unit
		Min.	Typ.	Max.	
Address Setup Time	t_{ARS}	40			ns
Address Hold Time	t_{ARH}	10			ns
$\overline{CS}$ Setup Time	t_{CRS}	25			ns
$\overline{CS}$ Hold Time	t_{CRH}	10			ns
Data Valid Time (from $\overline{RD}$ Low) (C_L = 80pF)	t_{RLD}			90	ns
Data Valid Time (from $\overline{RD}$ Hi gh) (C_L = 20pF)	t_{RHD}	10		60	ns
$\overline{RD}$ Pulse Width	t_{RD}	120			ns

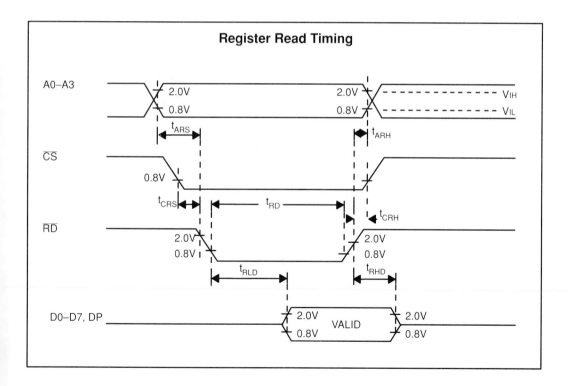

Register Read Timing

AC CHARACTERISTICS (Continued)

Register Write

Parameter	Designator	Values			Unit
		Min.	Typ.	Max.	
Address Setup Time	t_{AWS}	40			ns
Address Hold Line	t_{AWH}	10			ns
$\overline{CS}$ Setup Time	t_{CWS}	25			ns
$\overline{CS}$ Hold Time	t_{CWH}	10			ns
Data Bus Setup Time	t_{DWS}	30			ns
Data Bus Hold Time	t_{DWH}	20			ns
WR Pulse Width	t_{WR}	100			ns

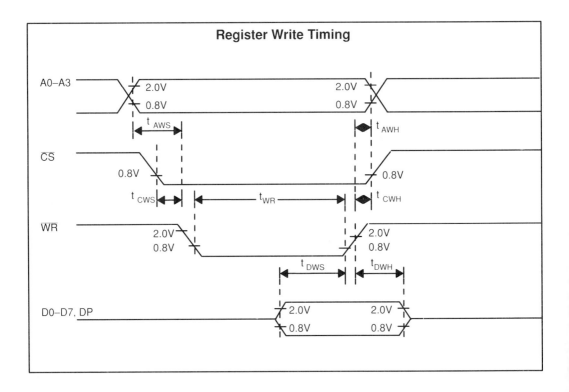

Register Write Timing

AC CHARACTERISTICS (Continued)

DPO (Data Parity Output)						
Parameter	**Designator**	**Test Conditions**	**Values**			**Unit**
			Min.	**Typ.**	**Max.**	
Data Bus (D0 – D7) Valid to DPO Valid	t_{DPVD}	CL = 30pF			60	ns

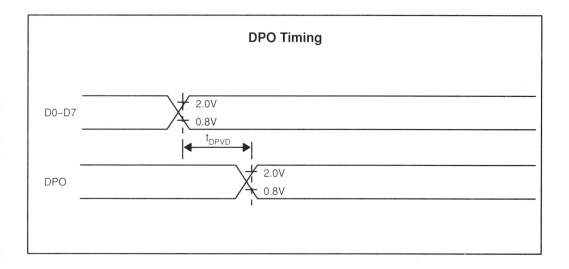

DPO Timing

AC CHARACTERISTICS (Continued)

INTR (Interrupt Request) Output						
Parameter	Designator	Test Conditions	Values			Unit
			Min.	Typ.	Max.	
$\overline{WR}$ High to INTR Low (Interrupt reset)	t_{WHIR}	CL = 10pf	t_{CLF}		$2t_{CLF} + 100$	ns
INTR High to $\overline{WR}$ High	t_{IRWL}		0			ns
INTR Reset Cycle Time[1]	t_{WRCY}		$4t_{CLF}$			ns

Note: [1]Applicable only when interrupt reset is executed.

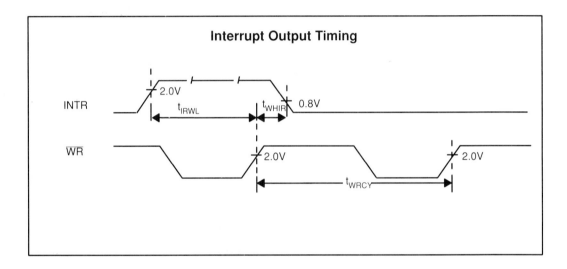

Interrupt Output Timing

AC CHARACTERISTICS (Continued)

DMA Access

Parameter	Designator	Test Conditions	Min.	Typ.	Max.	Unit
			Values			
			Min.	Typ.	Max.	Unit
DREQ High to $\overline{\text{DACK}}$ Low	t_{DHAL}		0			ns
$\overline{\text{WR}}$ and $\overline{\text{RD}}$ Service Time (From $\overline{\text{DACK}}$ Low to $\overline{\text{WR}}$ or $\overline{\text{RD}}$ Low)	t_{ARWL}		40			ns
DREQ Release Time (From $\overline{\text{WR}}$ or $\overline{\text{RD}}$ Low to DREQ Low)[1]	t_{RWDL}	CL = 30 pF	35		150	ns
DACK Hold Time (From $\overline{\text{WR}}$ or $\overline{\text{RD}}$ High to $\overline{\text{DACK}}$ Low)	t_{RWAH}		10			ns
DREG Interval (From DREQ Low to DREQ High)	t_{DLDH}		0			ns
DREG Access Cycle Time (1)	t_{RWCY}		$2t_{CLF}$			ns
DREG Access Cycle Time (2)	t_{DMCY}		$3t_{CLF}$			ns

Note: 1 The $\overline{\text{WR}}$ parameter is applicable when the data buffer register is full; the $\overline{\text{RD}}$ parameter is applicable when the data buffer register is empty.

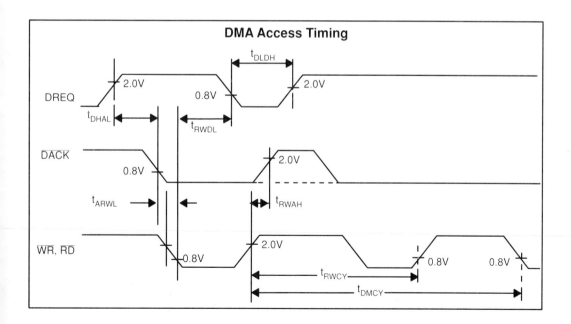

DMA Access Timing

AC CHARACTERISTICS (Continued)

Parameter	Designator	Test Conditions	Values			Unit
			Min.	Typ.	Max.	
$\overline{RD}$ Service Time (From INTR High to $\overline{RD}$ Low)	t_{IHRL}		0			ns
INTR Release Time (From $\overline{RD}$ High to INTR Low) (Note)	t_{RHIL}	CL = 20 pF	35		150	ns
INTR Recovery Time (From INTR Low to INTR High)	t_{ILIH}		0			ns
$\overline{RD}$ Recovery Time (From $\overline{RD}$ High to $\overline{RD}$ Low)	t_{RHRL}		50			ns

DREG Access – Program Transfer with INTR (Input Operation)

Note: This parameter is applicable when the data buffer register is full in the output operation and empty in the input operation.

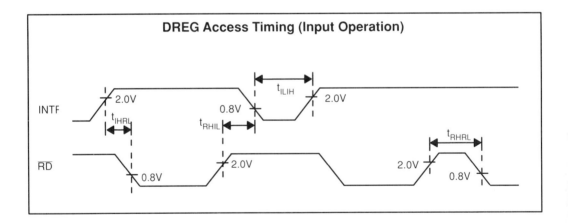

DREG Access Timing (Input Operation)

AC CHARACTERISTICS (Continued)

DREG Access – Program Transfer with INTR (Output Operation)						
Parameter	Designator	Test Conditions	Values			Unit
			Min.	Typ.	Max.	
WR Service Time (From INTR High to WR Low)	t_{IHWL}		0			ns
INTR Release Time (From WR High to INTR Low) (Note)	t_{WLIL}	CL = 20 pF	35		150	ns
INTR Recovery Time (From WR Low to INTR High)	t_{ILIH}		0			ns
WR Cycle Time	t_{WRCY}		$2t_{CLF}$			ns

Note: This parameter is applicable when the data buffer register is full in the output operation and empty in the input operation.

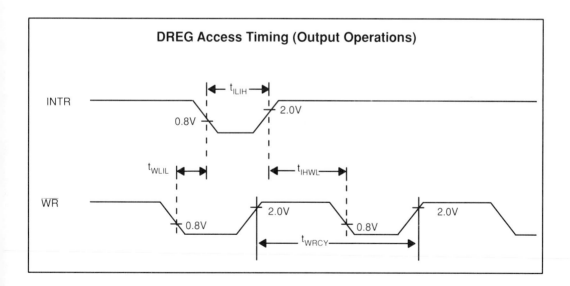

DREG Access Timing (Output Operations)

AC CHARACTERISTICS (Continued)

SCSI Bus Interface Selection Phase Timing

INITIATOR — Selection With Arbitration

Parameter	Designator	Values			Unit
		Min.	Typ.	Max.	
Bus Free Time[*]	t_{BFR}	$4t_{CLF}+50$			ns
Start of Arbitration	t_{BFBL}	$(6+n)^{**} \times t_{CLF}$		$(7+n) \times t_{CLF}+60$	ns
$\overline{BSY}$ Low to Self ID# Output	t_{BLID}	0		60	ns
$\overline{BSY}$ Low to Prioritize	t_{ARB}	$32t_{CLF}-60$			ns
Data Bus Valid to Prioritize	t_{AIDV}	200			ns
Bus Usage Permission Granted to $\overline{SEL}$ Low	t_{AWSL}	0		80	ns
$\overline{SEL}$ Low to Data Bus ID Output, $\overline{ATN}$ Low	t_{SIDA}	$11t_{CLF}-30$			ns
Select ID# Output to $\overline{BSY}$ High	t_{IDBH}	$2t_{CLF}-80$			ns
$\overline{BSY}$ Low to $\overline{SEL}$ High	t_{BLSH}	$2t_{CLF}$			ns
$\overline{BSY}$ Low to Select ID# Hold	t_{BIDH}	$2t_{CLF}$			ns
$\overline{SEL}$ High to INTR High	t_{SHIR}			60	ns
$\overline{SEL}$ Low to $\overline{BSY}$ High, ID Bit High	t_{SBCR}			$3t_{CLF}+180$	ns
Prioritize to $\overline{BSY}$ High, ID Bit High	t_{PBCR}			110	ns

Notes: [*]Bus Free Time : The minimum time period until the booked select command is executed.
        [**]TCL register value.

All SCSI Timing Signals

Note: All SCSI timing signals are defined according to the following rules:

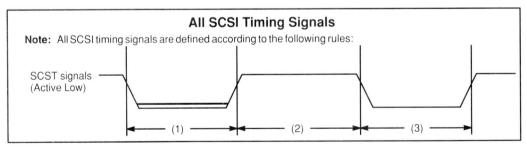

SCST signals (Active Low)

(1)   (2)   (3)

Notes: (1) The SPC outputs low level signal to the bus.
           (2) All devices hooked up to the bus do not output low level signals.
           (3) Other devices hooked up to the bus output low level signals.

AC CHARACTERISTICS (Continued)

SCSI Bus Interface Selection Phase Timing

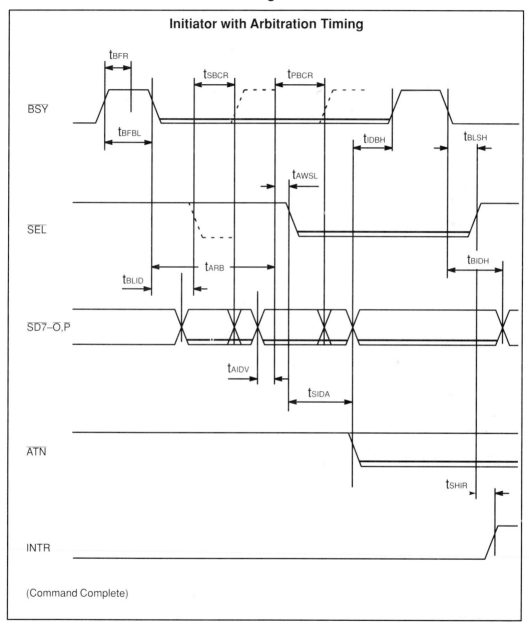

Initiator with Arbitration Timing

(Command Complete)

AC CHARACTERISTICS (Continued)

INITIATOR — Selection Without Arbitration

Parameter	Designator	Values			Unit
		Min.	Typ.	Max.	
$\overline{BSY}$ High to Select ID# Output	t_{FRID}	$(6+n) \times t_{CLF}$		$(7+n) \times t_{CLF}+140$	ns
ID# Output to $\overline{SEL}$ Low	t_{IDSL}	$11t_{CLF}-80$			ns
$\overline{SEL}$ Low to $\overline{ATN}$ Low	t_{SLAT}	$11t_{CLF}-80$			ns
$\overline{BSY}$ Low to $\overline{SEL}$ High	t_{BLSH}	$2t_{CLF}$			ns
$\overline{BSY}$ Low to ID# Hold	t_{BIDH}	$2t_{CLF}$			ns
$\overline{SEL}$ High to INTR High	t_{SHIR}			60	ns

Note: n=TCL register set value.

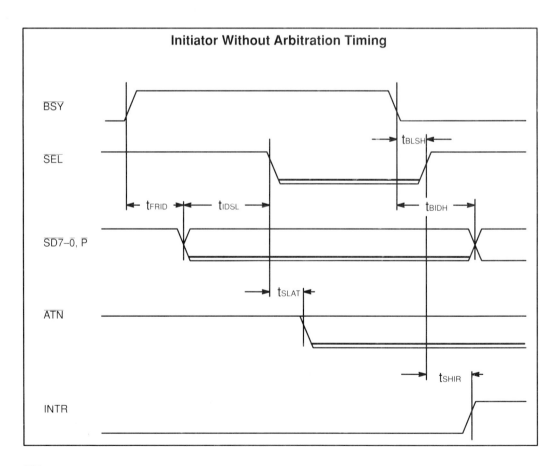

Initiator Without Arbitration Timing

AC CHARACTERISTICS (Continued)

TARGET — Selection With Arbitration

Parameter	Designator	Min.	Typ.	Max.	Unit
S̅E̅L̅ Low to B̅S̅Y̅ High	t$_{SLBH}$	0			ns
Data Bus Valid (ID#) to B̅S̅Y̅ High	t$_{IDBH}$	0			ns
I̅/̅O̅ High to B̅S̅Y̅ High	t$_{IOHB}$	0			ns
B̅S̅Y̅ High to B̅S̅Y̅ Low	t$_{BHBL}$	4t$_{CLF}$		5t$_{CLF}$+140	ns
B̅S̅Y̅ Low to ID# Hold	t$_{BLID}$	60			ns
B̅S̅Y̅ Low to S̅E̅L̅ High	t$_{BLSH}$	0			ns
S̅E̅L̅ High to Phase Signal Output	t$_{SHPH}$	3t$_{CLF}$		4t$_{CLF}$+160	ns
I̅/̅O̅ Low to Data Bus Output	t$_{IODE}$	7t$_{CLF}$			ns
S̅E̅L̅ High to INTR High	t$_{SHIR}$			3t$_{CLF}$+130	ns

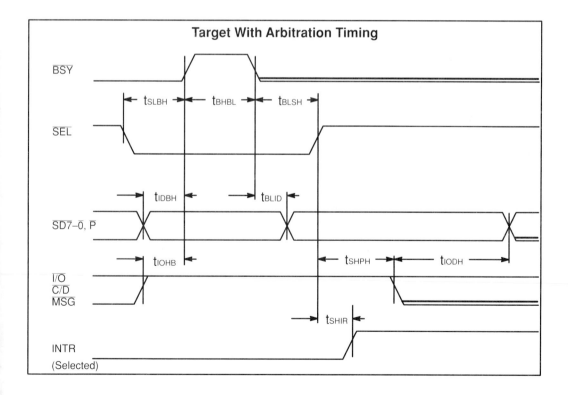

Target With Arbitration Timing

AC CHARACTERISTICS (Continued)

TARGET — Selection Without Arbitration					
Parameter	Designator	Values			Unit
		Min.	Typ.	Max.	
Data Bus Valid (ID#) to $\overline{SEL}$ Low	t_{IDSL}	0			ns
$\overline{I/O}$ High to $\overline{SEL}$ Low	t_{IOHS}	0			ns
$\overline{SEL}$ Low to $\overline{BSY}$ Low	t_{SLBL}	$2t_{CLF}$		$3t_{CLF}+130$	ns
$\overline{BSY}$ Low to ID# Hold	t_{BLID}	60			ns
$\overline{BSY}$ Low to $\overline{SEL}$ High	t_{BLSH}	0			ns
$\overline{SEL}$ High to Phase Signal Output	t_{SHPH}	$3t_{CLF}$		$4t_{CLF}+160$	ns
I/O Low to Data Bus Output	t_{IODE}	$7t_{CLF}$			ns
$\overline{SEL}$ High to INTR High	t_{SHIR}			$3t_{CLF}+130$	ns

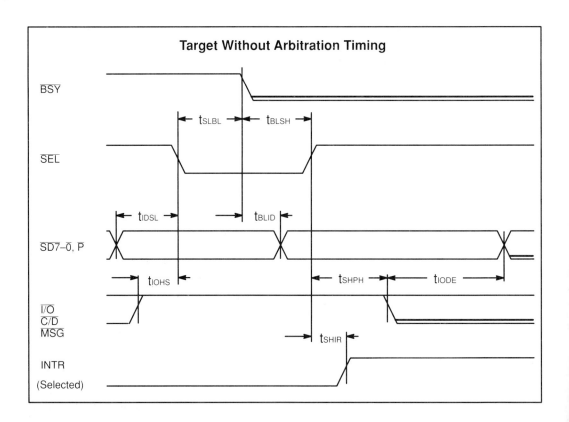

Target Without Arbitration Timing

AC CHARACTERISTICS (Continued)

SCSI BUS INTERFACE – RESELECTION PHASE TIMING

TARGET — Reselection Phase Timing					
Parameter	**Designator**	**Values**			**Unit**
		Min.	**Typ.**	**Max.**	
Bus Free Time*	t_{BFR}	$4t_{CLF}+50$			ns
Start of Arbitration	t_{BFBL}	$(6+n)^{**} \times t_{CLF}$		$(7+n) \times t_{CLF}+140$	ns
$\overline{BSY}$ Low to Self ID# Output	t_{BLID}	0		60	ns
$\overline{BSY}$ Low to Prioritize	t_{ARB}	$32t_{CLF}-60$			ns
Data Bus Valid to Prioritize	t_{AIDV}	200			ns
Bus Usage Permission Granted to $\overline{SEL}$ Low t_{AWSL}	t_{AWSL}	0		80	ns
$\overline{SEL}$ Low to Data Bus ID Output, Phase Signal Output	t_{SIDP}	$11t_{CLF}-50$			ns
Select ID# Output to $\overline{BSY}$ High	t_{IDBH}	$2t_{CLF}-80$			ns
$\overline{BSY}$ Low to $\overline{BSY}$ Low Output	t_{BIBO}	$2t_{CLF}+20$		$3t_{CLF}+140$	ns
$\overline{BSY}$ Low to $\overline{SEL}$ High	t_{BLSH}	$2t_{CLF}$			ns
$\overline{BSY}$ Low to Select ID# Hold	t_{BIDH}	$2t_{CLF}$			ns
$\overline{SEL}$ High to INTR High	t_{SHIR}			60	ns
$\overline{SEL}$ Low to $\overline{BSY}$ High, ID Bit High	t_{SBCR}			$3t_{CLF}+180$	ns
Prioritize to $\overline{BSY}$ High, ID Bit High	t_{PBCR}			110	ns

Notes: *Bus Free Time:=The minimum time period till the booked select command is executed.
           **n=TCL register value

AC CHARACTERISTICS (Continued)

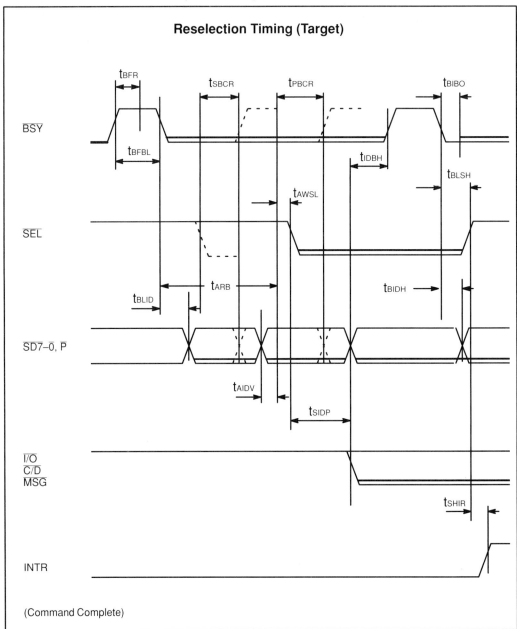

Reselection Timing (Target)

(Command Complete)

AC CHARACTERISTICS (Continued)

INITIATOR — Reselection Phase Timing

Parameter	Designator	Values			Unit
		Min.	Typ.	Max.	
$\overline{\text{SEL}}$ Low to $\overline{\text{BSY}}$ High	t_{SLBH}	0			ns
Data Bus Valid (ID#) to $\overline{\text{BSY}}$ High	t_{IDBH}	0			ns
$\overline{\text{I/O}}$ Low to $\overline{\text{BSY}}$ High	t_{IOLB}	0			ns
$\overline{\text{BSY}}$ High to $\overline{\text{BSY}}$ Low	t_{BHBL}	$4t_{CLF}$		$5t_{CLF}+140$	ns
$\overline{\text{BSY}}$ Low to ID# Hold	t_{BLID}	60			ns
$\overline{\text{BSY}}$ Low to $\overline{\text{SEL}}$ High	t_{BLSH}	0			ns
$\overline{\text{SEL}}$ High to $\overline{\text{BSY}}$ Low Output	t_{SHBO}	$2t_{CLF}$		$3t_{CLF}+140$	ns
$\overline{\text{SEL}}$ High to Data Bus Valid (When $\overline{\text{I/O}}$ is High)	t_{SHDE}	$3t_{CLF}+30$		$4t_{CLF}+160$	ns
$\overline{\text{SEL}}$ High to $\overline{\text{I/O}}$ High	t_{SHIO}	200			ns
$\overline{\text{SEL}}$ High to INTR High	t_{SHIR}			$3t_{CLF}+130$	ns

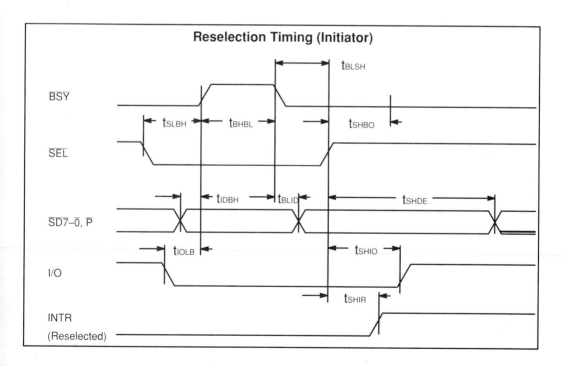

Reselection Timing (Initiator)

AC CHARACTERISTICS (Continued)

SCSI BUS INTERFACE – INFORMATION TRANSFER PHASE TIMING

INITIATOR —Asynchronous Transfer Output

Parameter	Designator	Values			Unit
		Min.	Typ.	Max.	
$\overline{I/O}$ High to Data Bus Output	t_{IIDE}	10			ns
Phase Set to $\overline{REQ}$ Low	t_{PHRL}	100			ns
$\overline{REQ}$ Low to $\overline{ACK}$ Low	t_{RAOL}	20			ns
Data Bus Valid to ACK Low	t_{DVLD}	$2t_{CLF}-80$			ns
$\overline{ACK}$ Low to $\overline{REQ}$ High	t_{AOLR}	0			ns
$\overline{REQ}$ High to $\overline{ACK}$ High	t_{RAOH}	10			ns
$\overline{ACK}$ High to $\overline{REQ}$ Low	t_{AOHR}	0			ns
$\overline{REQ}$ High to $\overline{ACK}$ Low	t_{RACY}	$2t_{CLF}$			ns
$\overline{REQ}$ High to Data Bus Hold	t_{DIVD}	15			ns
$\overline{REQ}$ Low to $\overline{ATN}$ High[1]	t_{RATH}	$2t_{CLF}$			ns
$\overline{ATN}$ High to $\overline{ACK}$ Low[1]	t_{ATHA}	$t_{CLF}-20$			ns
$\overline{REQ}$ Low to Phase Change[2]	t_{RLPH}	$3t_{CLF}$			ns
$\overline{ACK}$ High to Phase Change[2]	t_{AHPH}	10			ns

Notes: 1 This spec is applicable to the last byte transfer of message out phase in hardware transfer mode.
        2 When the transfer phase is changed, both t_{RLPH} and t_{ALPH} should be specified.

AC CHARACTERISTICS (Continued)

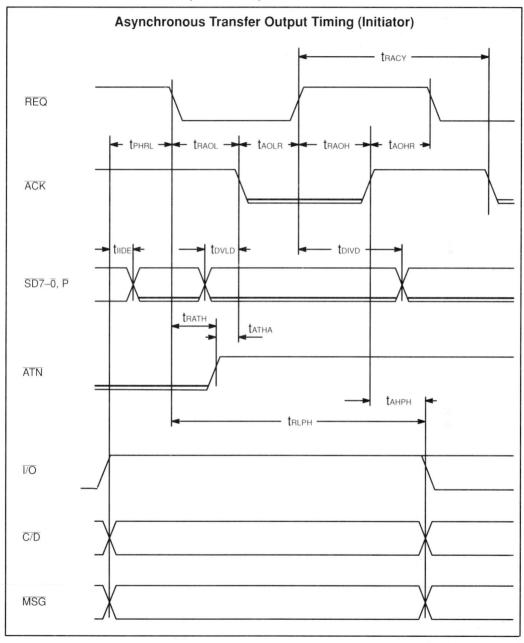

Asynchronous Transfer Output Timing (Initiator)

AC CHARACTERISTICS (Continued)

Parameter	Designator	Values			Unit
		Min.	Typ.	Max.	
$\overline{I/O}$ Low to Data Bus Output	t_{IODE}	$7t_{CLF}$			ns
Data Bus Valid to $\overline{REQ}$ Low	t_{DVLD}	$2t_{CLF}-80$			ns
$\overline{ACK}$ Low to Data Bus Hold	t_{DIVD}	15			ns
$\overline{REQ}$ Low to $\overline{ACK}$ Low	t_{ROLA}	0			ns
$\overline{ACK}$ Low to $\overline{REQ}$ High	t_{AROH}	10		180	ns
$\overline{REQ}$ High to $\overline{ACK}$ High	t_{ROHA}	0			ns
$\overline{ACK}$ High to $\overline{REQ}$ Low	t_{AROL}	10			ns
$\overline{ACK}$ Low to $\overline{REQ}$ Low	t_{RACY}	$2t_{CLF}$			ns

TARGET —Asynchronous Transfer Output

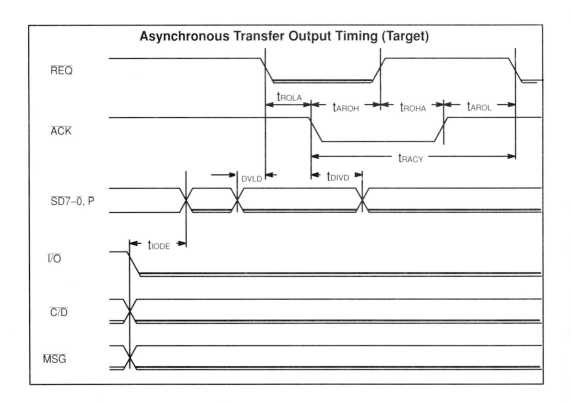

Asynchronous Transfer Output Timing (Target)

AC CHARACTERISTICS (Continued)

Parameter	Designator	Values			Unit
		Min.	**Typ.**	**Max.**	
$\overline{I/O}$ Low to Data Bus Output Terminate	t_{IIDD}			140	ns
Phase Set to $\overline{REQ}$ Low	t_{PHRL}	100			ns
Data Bus Valid to $\overline{REQ}$ Low	t_{DSTU}	10			ns
$\overline{REQ}$ Low to $\overline{ACK}$ Low	t_{RAOL}	20			ns
$\overline{ACK}$ Low to $\overline{REQ}$ High	t_{AOLR}	0			ns
$\overline{ACK}$ Low to Data Bus Hold	t_{DHLD}	15			ns
$\overline{REQ}$ High to $\overline{ACK}$ High	t_{RAOH}	10			ns
$\overline{ACK}$ High to $\overline{REQ}$ Low	t_{AOHR}	0			ns
$\overline{REQ}$ High to $\overline{ACK}$ Low	t_{RACY}	$2t_{CLF}$			ns
$\overline{ATN}$ Low to $\overline{ACK}$ High[1]	t_{ATAH}	$t_{CLF}-20$			ns
$\overline{REQ}$ Low to Phase Change[2]	t_{RLPH}	$3t_{CLF}$			ns
$\overline{ACK}$ High to Phase Change[2]	t_{AHPH}	10			ns

INITIATOR —Asynchronous Transfer Input

Notes: 1 Applicable to the last byte transfer of message out phase in hardware transfer mode.
2 When the transfer phase is changed, both t_{RLPH} and t_{AHPH} should be specified.

AC CHARACTERISTICS (Continued)

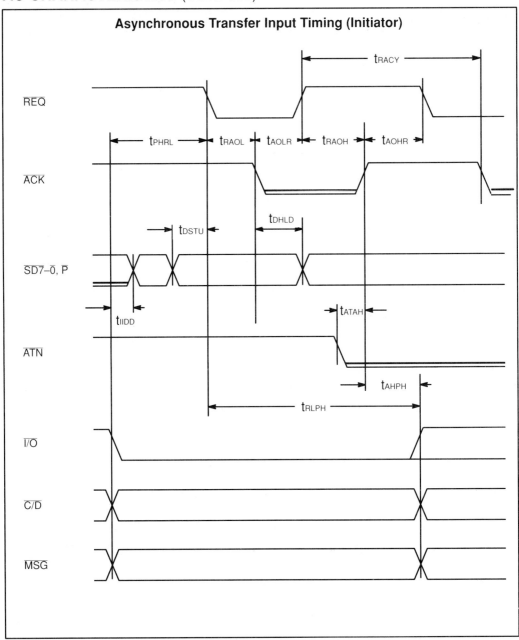

Asynchronous Transfer Input Timing (Initiator)

AC CHARACTERISTICS (Continued)

TARGET —Asynchronous Transfer Input

Parameter	Designator	Min.	Typ.	Max.	Unit
I/O High to Data Bus Output Terminate	t_{IODD}			30	ns
Data Bus Valid to ACK Low	t_{DSTU}	10			ns
REQ High to Data Bus Hold	t_{DHLD}	15			ns
REQ Low to ACK Low	t_{ROLA}	0			ns
ACK Low to REQ High	t_{AROH}	10		180	ns
REQ High to ACK High	t_{ROHA}	0			ns
ACK High to REQ Low	t_{AROL}	10			ns
ACK Low to REQ Low	t_{RACY}	$2t_{CLF}$			ns

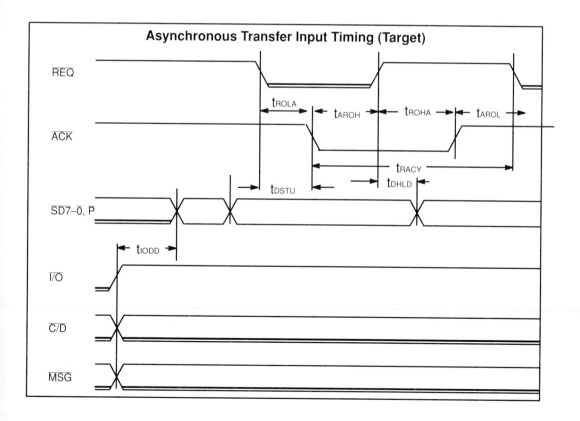

Asynchronous Transfer Input Timing (Target)

AC CHARACTERISTICS (Continued)

Transfer Phase Change (Target)					
Parameter	Designator	Values			Unit
		Min.	Typ.	Max.	
From $\overline{WR}$ High to $\overline{MSG}$, $\overline{C/D}$, $\overline{I/O}$ change	t_{PHCH}	10		130	ns

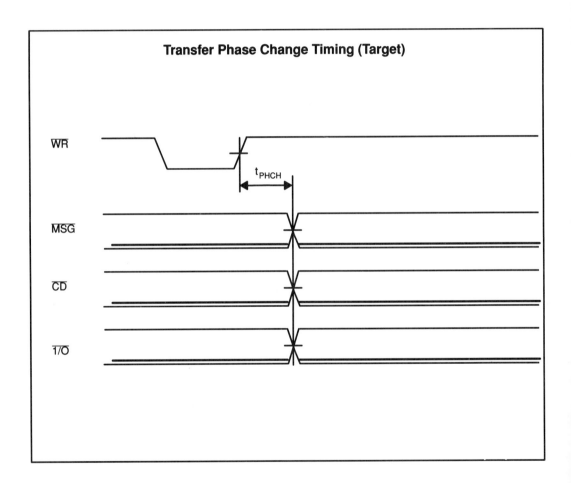

Transfer Phase Change Timing (Target)

AC CHARACTERISTICS (Continued)

Manual Transfer

Parameter	Designator	Values			Unit
		Min.	Typ.	Max.	
From $\overline{WR}$ High to Data Bus Valid forTEMP Register	t_{WRDV}			130	ns
From $\overline{WR}$ High to REQ Low, ACK Low for SET ACK/REQ Command	t_{STRA}	$2t_{CLF}$		$3t_{CLF} + 90$	ns
From $\overline{WR}$ High to REQ High, ACK High for RESET ACK/REQ Command	t_{RTRA}	$2t_{CLF}$		$3t_{CLF} + 90$	ns

Note: Timing relationships not shown are the same as those for asynchronous transfers.

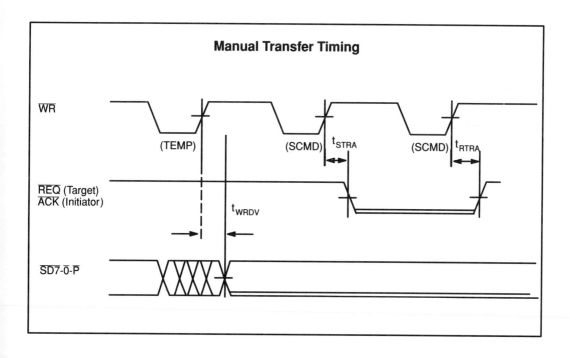

Manual Transfer Timing

AC CHARACTERISTICS (Continued)

SCSI BUS INTERFACE – ATTENTION CONDITION

INITIATOR - Attention Condition					
Parameter	Designator	Values			Unit
		Min.	Typ.	Max.	
From $\overline{WR}$ High to $\overline{ATN}$ Change (SET/RESET ATN Command)	t_{WATN}	$2t_{CLF}$		$3t_{CLF}+90$	ns

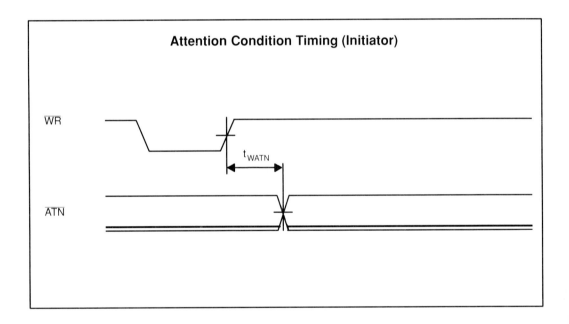

Attention Condition Timing (Initiator)

AC CHARACTERISTICS (Continued)

SCSI BUS INTERFACE – BUS FREE

INITIATOR — Bus Free (Disconnection)						
Parameter	Designator	Values				Unit
		Min.	Typ.	Max.		
$\overline{\text{BSY}}$ High to Bus Clear	t_{BHCR}			$5t_{CLF}+140$		ns
$\overline{\text{BSY}}$ High to INTR High	t_{BHIR}			$6t_{CLF}+80$		ns

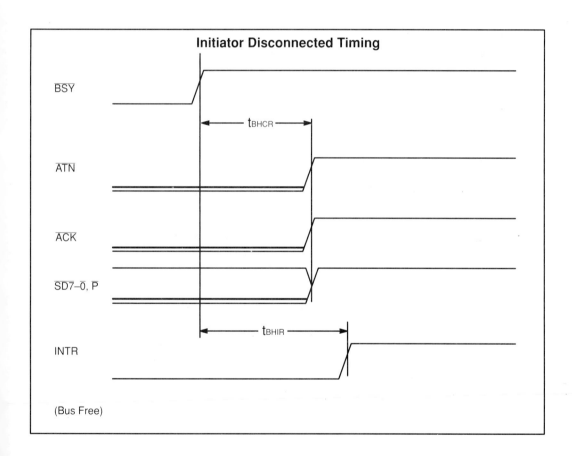

Initiator Disconnected Timing

(Bus Free)

AC CHARACTERISTICS (Continued)

TARGET (Bus Release Command)					
Parameter	Designator	Values			Unit
		Min.	Typ.	Max.	
$\overline{WR}$ High to Bus Clear (Bus Release Command)	t_{BRCR}			$3t_{CLF}+100$	ns

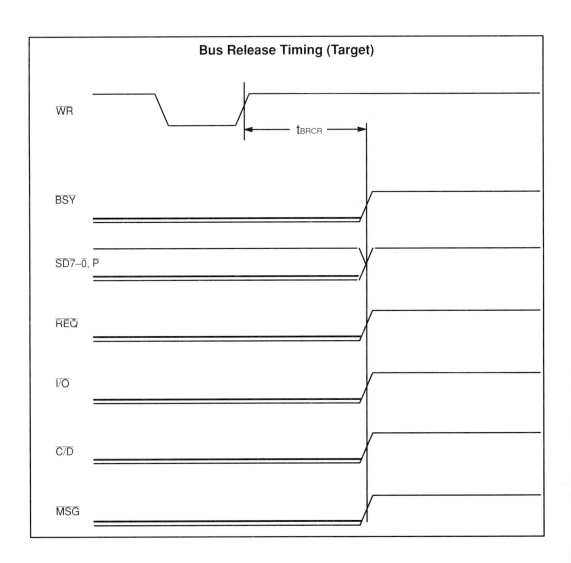

Bus Release Timing (Target)

AC CHARACTERISTICS (Continued)

TERMINATION (Time Out) – Selection and Reselection Phases

Parameter	Designator	Values			Unit
		Min.	Typ.	Max.	
$\overline{WR}$ High to $\overline{SEL}$, $\overline{SD7-0}$, P, $\overline{I/O}$ High (Reset Time Out Interruption)	t_{BRCR}			$3t_{CLF}+100$	ns ns
$\overline{WR}$ High to INTR Low	t_{WRIR}			$3t_{CLF}+60$	ns

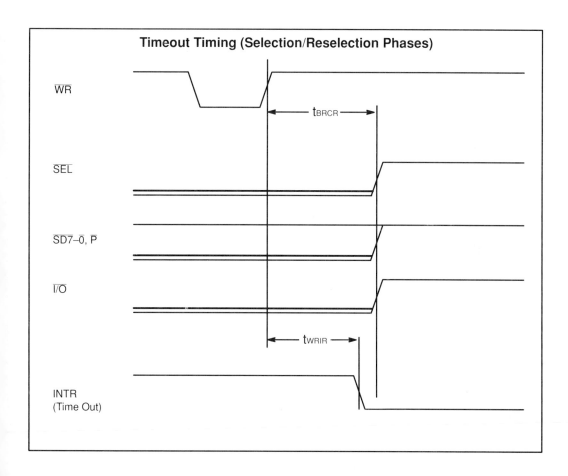

Timeout Timing (Selection/Reselection Phases)

AC CHARACTERISTICS (Continued)

SCSI BUS INTERFACE – RESET CONDITION

SRST – Reset Condition (Output)

Parameter	Designator	Values			Unit
		Min.	Typ.	Max.	
$\overline{WR}$ High to $\overline{SRST}$ Low (Write "I" to SCMD Bit-4)	t_{WRST}	10		110	ns
Reset Delay	t_{RTSD}			140	ns

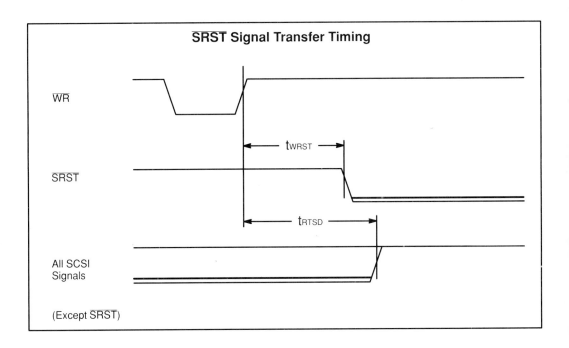

$\overline{SRST}$ Signal Transfer Timing

$\overline{WR}$

t_{WRST}

$\overline{SRST}$

t_{RTSD}

All SCSI
Signals

(Except $\overline{SRST}$)

AC CHARACTERISTICS (Continued)

SCSI BUS INTERFACE – RESET CONDITION

SRST – Reset Condition (Input)					
Parameter	Designator	Values			Unit
		Min.	Typ.	Max.	
SRST Pulse Width	t_{RSTW}	$3t_{CLF}$			ns
Reset Delay	t_{RTID}			$4t_{CLF}+200$	ns

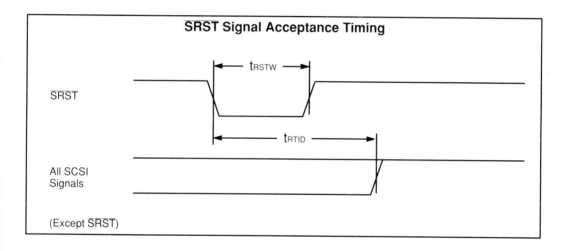

SRST Signal Acceptance Timing

SRST

All SCSI
Signals

(Except SRST)

AC CHARACTERISTICS (Continued)

Capacitance			
Parameter	**Values**		**Unit**
	Typ.	**Max.**	
D7 – D0, DP	—	80	pF
DPO, INTR, DREQ	10	30	pF
$\overline{SD7}$ - $\overline{SD0}$, $\overline{SDP}$	—	300	pF
$\overline{SRST}$, $\overline{SEL}$, $\overline{BSY}$, $\overline{I/O}$, $\overline{C/D}$, $\overline{MSG}$, $\overline{REQ}$, $\overline{ACK}$, $\overline{ATN}$	—	300	pF

The AC characteristics of all SCSI bus signal pins are measured on the following test circuit.

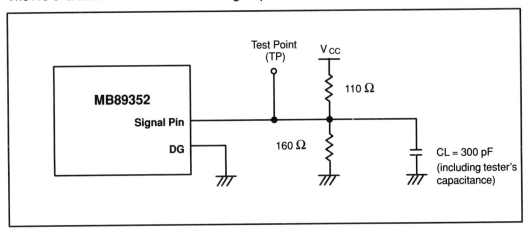

PACKAGE DIMENSIONS

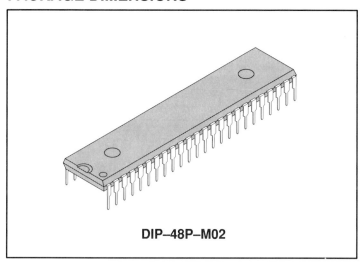

DIP–48P–M02

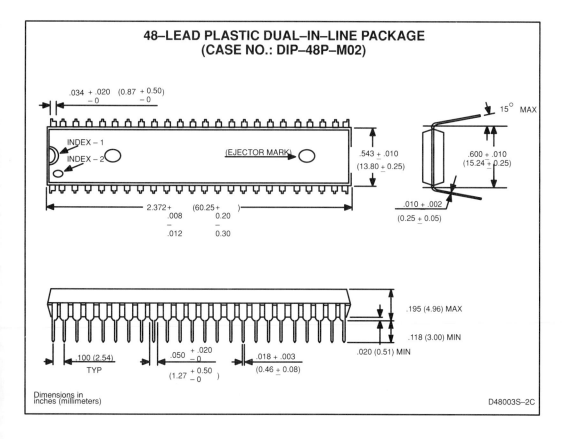

48–LEAD PLASTIC DUAL–IN–LINE PACKAGE
(CASE NO.: DIP–48P–M02)

Dimensions in
inches (millimeters)

D48003S–2C

PACKAGE DIMENSIONS

48–Lead Plastic Flat Package

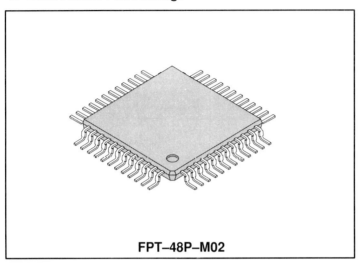

FPT–48P–M02

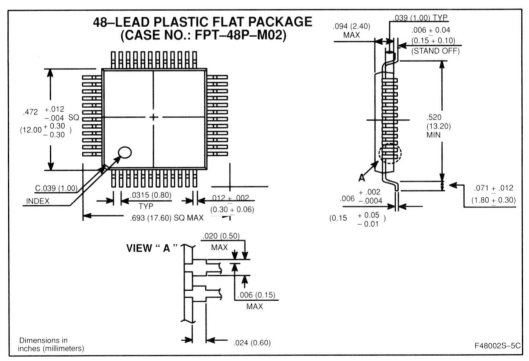

48–LEAD PLASTIC FLAT PACKAGE
(CASE NO.: FPT–48P–M02)

.472 +.012 −.004 SQ
(12.00 +0.30 −0.30)

C.039 (1.00)

INDEX

.0315 (0.80)
TYP

.012 + .002
(0.30 + 0.06)

.693 (17.60) SQ MAX

.094 (2.40) MAX

.039 (1.00) TYP

.006 + 0.04
(0.15 + 0.10)
(STAND OFF)

.520
(13.20)
MIN

A

.006 + .002 −.0004
(0.15 + 0.05 −0.01)

.071 + .012
(1.80 + 0.30)

VIEW " A "

.020 (0.50)
MAX

.006 (0.15)
MAX

.024 (0.60)

Dimensions in
inches (millimeters)

F48002S–5C

Chapter 11

FUJITSU'S SCSI CONNECTORS

Fujitsu SCSI Connectors

A complete SCSI configuration is achieved by daisy-chaining SCSI devices on a common cable (SCSI bus). In this arrangement, all signals are common among the devices connected on the SCSI bus. The connectors and cables, both shielded and non-shielded, specified in the ANSI Standard for SCSI (ANSI X3.131.86) are discussed in Chapter One.

The data sheets in this chapter provide specific information about the ANSI–standard SCSI connectors/terminators offered by Fujitsu. Designed for SCSI interface connections with personal computers, Fujitsu's FCN Series connectors include the following models:

FCN–230 Half Pitch Series Connectors

FCN–230 Half Pitch Series Terminators

FCN–680 Series Connectors

FCN–780 Series Terminators

FCN-230 Half Pitch Series Connectors

Edition 1.0
July 1990

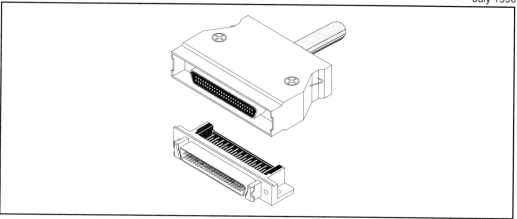

GENERAL DESCRIPTION

The FCN-230 series are designed as connections for SCSI interfaces for personal computers.

FEATURES

- 1.27 mm (0.05 in.) contact pitch arrangement in two rows allows high density mounting
- Terminals are spaced in a four-row zigzag array (1.27 mm (0.05 in.) x 1.905 mm (0.075 in.) for easy PC board design
- IDC or solder termination for discrete wiring available

- Metal cover for EMI protection
- Insulation material recognized by UL (94 V-0)
- Each of the contacts on the female connector of the mold type are alternately inset to facilitate two-step coupling, significantly reducing insertion force

MATERIALS

Material	Copper Alloy
Insulator	Polyester, UL94V-0
Plating	Gold over Palladium over Nickel (PAGOS)

SPECIFICATIONS

Temperature Range	−55°C to +105°C					
Maximum Rated Current	1ADC (PCB to cable) 2ADC (PCB to PCB)					
Maximum Rated Voltage	240 V AC					
Contact Resistance	30 mΩ max. (6 V DC, 0, 1A)					
Insulation Resistance	1000 MΩ min. (500 V DC)					
Dielectric Withstand Voltage	750 V AC for 1 minute					

Insertion Force (kg)	PCB to PCB No. of Contacts			34	48	68	96
	Force			3.0	4.0	5.5	7.0
	PCB to Cable No. of Contacts	20	26	28	36	50	68
	Force	5.5	5.8	6.0	6.5	8.0	9.0

Withdrawal Force (kg)	PCB to PCB No. of Contacts			34	48	68	96
	Force			0.68	0.96	1.36	1.92
	PCB to Cable No. of Contacts	20	26	28	36	50	68
	Force	0.8	1.0	1.12	1.44	2.0	2.3

Applicable PC Board	0.8 to 1.6 mm (0.031 to 0.063 in.) thick
Applicable Wire	IDC Type: AWG #28 or #30 (wire diameter): φ0.5 to φ0.65 (φ0.020 to φ0.024) or φ0.8 to φ0.88 (φ0.031 to φ0.035) Solder Type: AWG #26 max.

FCN-230 SERIES, METAL SHELL TYPE SOCKET (SCSI II TYPE)

Dimensions
Unit: mm (Inch)

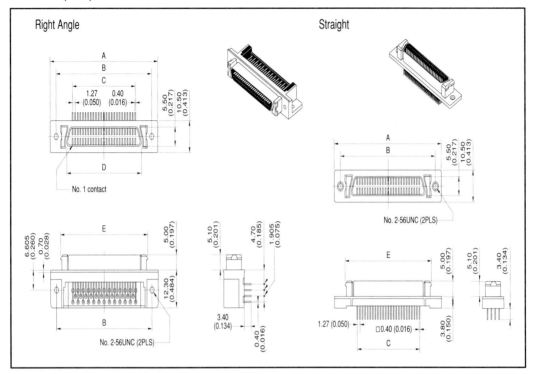

Part Numbers for Metal Shell Type Socket

No. of Contacts	Part Number		Dimensions				
	Right Angle	Straight	A	B	C	D	E
20	FCN-235D020-G/E, H	FCN-234D020-G/E, H	33.40 (1.315)	27.43 (1.080)	11.43 (0.450)	15.60 (0.614)	23.24 (0.915)
26	FCN-235D026-G/E, H	FCN-234D026-G/E, H	37.21 (1.465)	31.24 (1.230)	15.24 (0.600)	19.41 (0.764)	27.05 (1.065)
28	FCN-235D028-G/E	FCN-234D028-G/E	38.48 (1.515)	32.51 (1.280)	16.51 (0.650)	20.68 (0.814)	28.32 (1.115)
50	FCN-235D050-G/E	FCN-234D050-G/E	52.45 (2.065)	46.48 (1.830)	30.48 (1.200)	34.65 (1.364)	42.29 (1.665)
68	FCN-235D068-G/E	FCN-234D068-G/E	63.88 (2.515)	57.91 (2.280)	41.91 (1.650)	46.08 (1.814)	53.72 (2.115)

FCN-230 SERIES, METAL SHELL TYPE IDC PLUG (SCSI II TYPE)

Dimensions

Unit: mm (Inch)

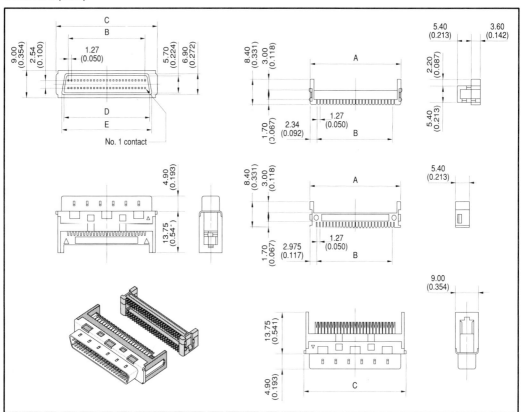

Part Numbers for Metal Shell Type IDC Plug

No. of Contacts	External Diameter of Applied Wire	Part Number	Diameter				
			A	B	C	D	E
50	φ0.8 to 0.88 mm (0.031 to 0.035)	FCN-237R050-G/F	35.80 (1.409)	30.48 (1.200)	40.30 (1.587)	34.85 (1.372)	36.05 (1.419)
	φ0.5 to 0.65 mm (0.020 to 0.026)	FCN-237R050-G/E					
68	φ0.8 to 0.88 mm (0.031 to 0.035)	FCN-237R068-G/F	47.23 (1.859)	41.91 (1.650)	51.73 (2.037)	46.28 (1.822)	47.48 (1.869)
	φ0.5 to 0.65 mm (0.020 to 0.026)	FCN-237R068-G/E					

FCN-230 SERIES METAL COVER

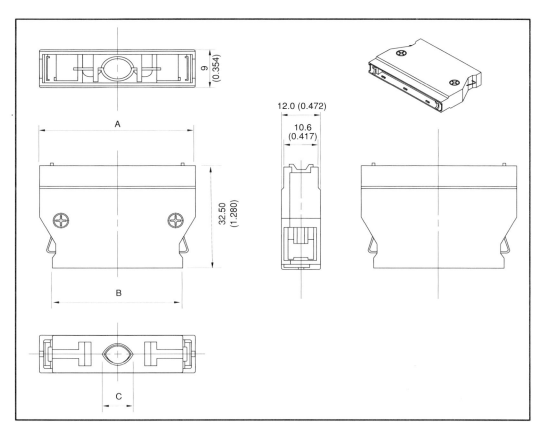

Part Numbers for Metal Cover

Standard Cable Hole Type

No. of Contacts	Part Number	Dimensions		
		A	**B**	**C**
50	FCN-230C050-A/E	48.00 (1.890)	40.20 (1.583)	8.5 x 7.0 (0.335 x 0.276)
68	FCN-230C068-A/E	59.43 (2.340)	51.63 (2.033)	9.0 x 8.0 (0.354 x 0.315)

Wide Cable Hole Type

No. of Contacts	Part Number	Dimensions		
		A	**B**	**C**
50	FCN-230C050-C/E	48.00 (1.890)	40.20 (1.583)	9 x 10 (0.354 x 0.394)
68	FCN-230C068-C/E	59.43 (2.340)	51.63 (2.033)	9 x 10 (0.354 x 0.394)

FCN-230 SERIES, METAL COVER WITH POLARIZATION

Dimensions

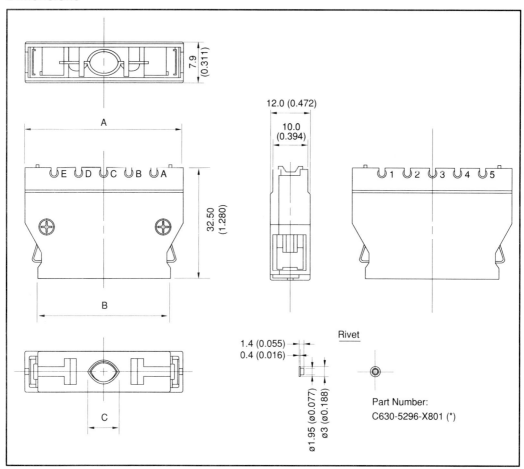

Part Numbers for Metal Cover with Polarization

Standard Cable Hole Type

No. of Contacts	Part Number	Dimensions		
		A	B	C
50	FCN-230C050-B/E	48.00 (1.890)	40.20 (1.583)	8.5 x 7.0 (0.335 x 0.276)
68	FCN-230C068-B/E	59.43 (2.340)	51.63 (2.033)	9.0 x 8.0 (0.354 x 0.315)

Part Numbers for Metal Cover with Polarization (Continued)

Wide Cable Hole Type

No. of Contacts	Part Number	Dimensions		
		A	B	C
50	FCN-230C050-D/E	48.00 (1.890)	40.20 (1.583)	14.7 x 10.4 (0.579 x 0.409)
68	FCN-230C068-D/E	59.43 (2.340)	51.63 (2.033)	14.7 x 10.4 (0.579 x 0.409

Part Numbering System

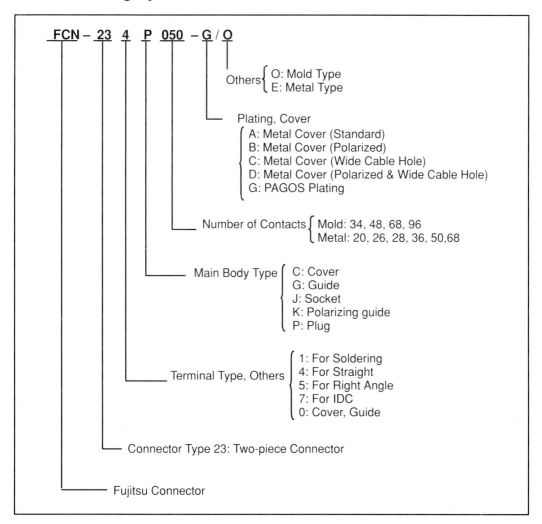

FCN – 23 4 P 050 – G / O

Others { O: Mold Type
         E: Metal Type

Plating, Cover
{ A: Metal Cover (Standard)
  B: Metal Cover (Polarized)
  C: Metal Cover (Wide Cable Hole)
  D: Metal Cover (Polarized & Wide Cable Hole)
  G: PAGOS Plating

Number of Contacts { Mold: 34, 48, 68, 96
                     Metal: 20, 26, 28, 36, 50, 68

Main Body Type { C: Cover
                 G: Guide
                 J: Socket
                 K: Polarizing guide
                 P: Plug

Terminal Type, Others { 1: For Soldering
                        4: For Straight
                        5: For Right Angle
                        7: For IDC
                        0: Cover, Guide

Connector Type 23: Two-piece Connector

Fujitsu Connector

FCN-230 Half Pitch Series
Terminators

Edition 1.0
August 1990

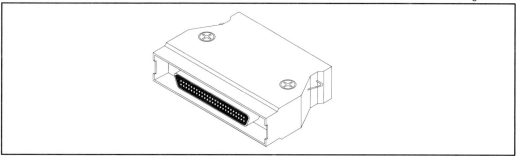

GENERAL DESCRIPTION

The FCN-230 series with terminating resistor is designed as a terminal resistance unit for SCSI interfaces for personal computers.

FEATURES

- Compact and economical through the use of miniature hybrid ICs
- Easy to connect/disconnect by hand
- EMI shielded

MATERIALS

Insulator	PPS
Shell	Steel (Nickel Plating)
Cover	ABS (Nickel Plating)
Contact	Copper Alloy (Gold Plating)

SPECIFICATIONS

Temperature Range	−40 °C to +80 °C
Rated Current (Connector)	3 A DC
Rated Voltage (Connector)	250 V AC
Contact Resistance (Connector)	15 mΩ maximum
Insulation Resistance (Connector)	1,000 MΩ or more (between FG and signal)
Dielectric Strength (Connector)	300 V AC for 1 minute (between FG and signal)

CIRCUIT DIAGRAM – ALTERNATE 1 TERMINATOR

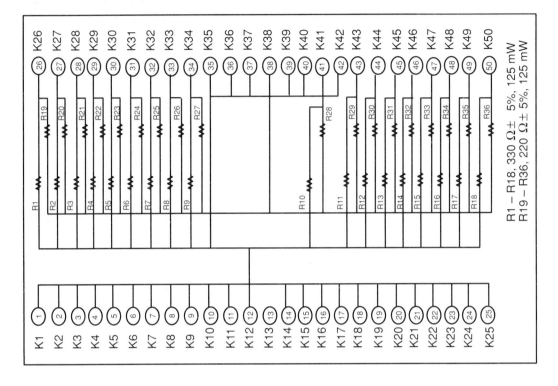

DIMENSIONS – ALTERNATE 1 TERMINATOR

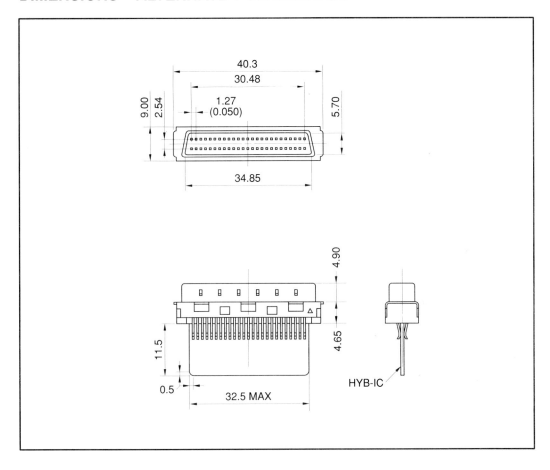

CIRCUIT DIAGRAM – ALTERNATE 2 TERMINATOR

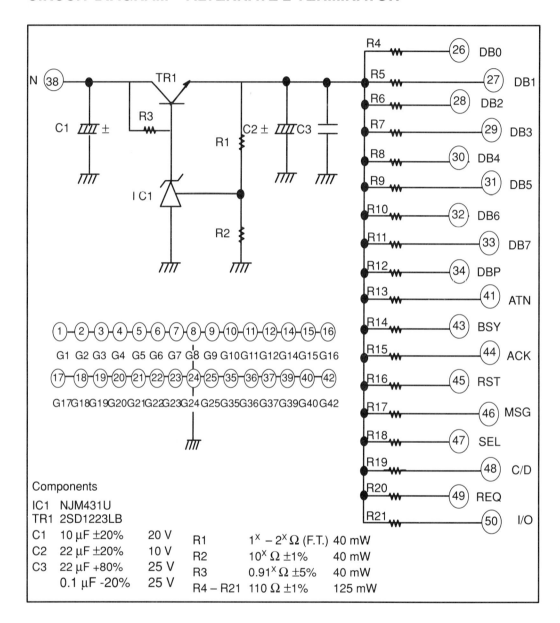

Components

IC1 NJM431U
TR1 2SD1223LB

C1	10 μF ±20%	20 V	R1	$1^X - 2^X\,\Omega$ (F.T.)	40 mW
C2	22 μF ±20%	10 V	R2	$10^X\,\Omega$ ±1%	40 mW
C3	22 μF +80%	25 V	R3	$0.91^X\,\Omega$ ±5%	40 mW
	0.1 μF -20%	25 V	R4 – R21	110 Ω ±1%	125 mW

DIMENSIONS – ALTERNATE 2 TERMINATOR

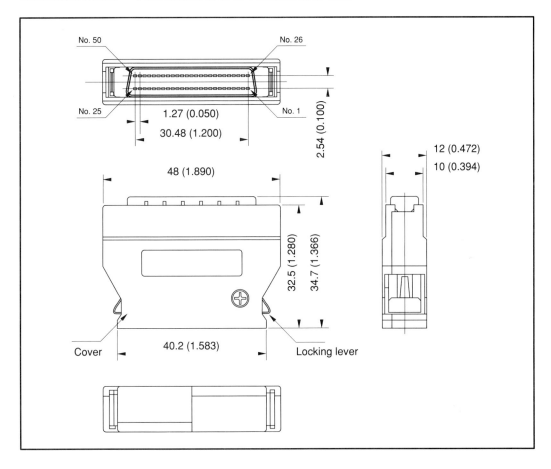

FCN-680 Series Connectors

Edition 1.0
August 1990

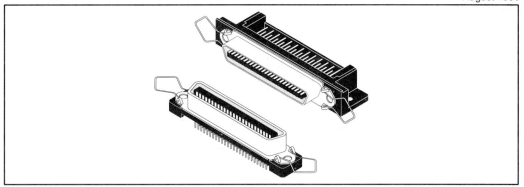

GENERAL DESCRIPTION

The FCN–680 series connectors are designed for interfacing with Centronics and GPIB configurations as well as SCSI.

FEATURES

- FCN–680 series connectors can be mated with other microribbon connectors

- FCN-680 series connectors can be cleaned with flux such as chlorothene

- FCN-680 series connectors are designed for Centronics and GPIB Interface, as well as SCSI

- FCN-680 series connectors are protected from EMI by the structure of the metal shell

MATERIALS

Insulator	Polyester (UL94V-0)
Contact	Copper Alloy
Contact Plating	Gold
Shell	Copper, (Nickel Plating)

SPECIFICATIONS

Operating Temperature	−55 °C to +105 °C
Current Rating	3 A DC
Voltage Rating	250 V AC
Control Resistance	30 mΩ min. (6 V AC, 0,3 A)
Insulation Resistance	100 MΩ min. (500 V AC)
Dielectric Strength	500 V AC for 1 minute

APPLICATIONS EXAMPLE

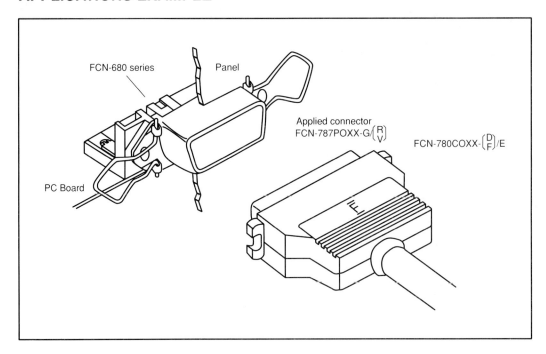

STRAIGHT SOCKET, METAL TYPE
Dimensions

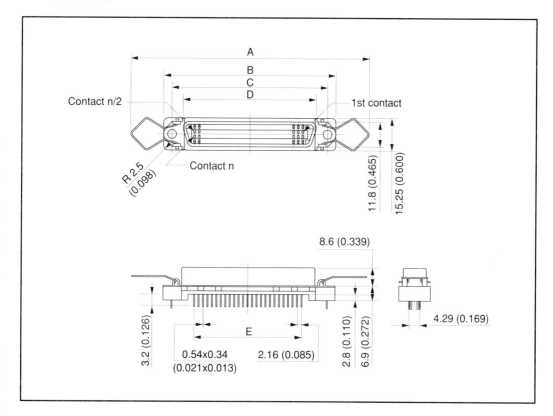

Part Number

No. of Contacts	Part Number	A	B	C	D	E
50	FCN-684-J050-L/Y#A	114.86 (4.522)	82.80 (3.260)	74.86 (2.947)	64.12 (2.524)	51.84 (2.041)

RIGHT-ANGLE SOCKET, METAL TYPE

Dimensions

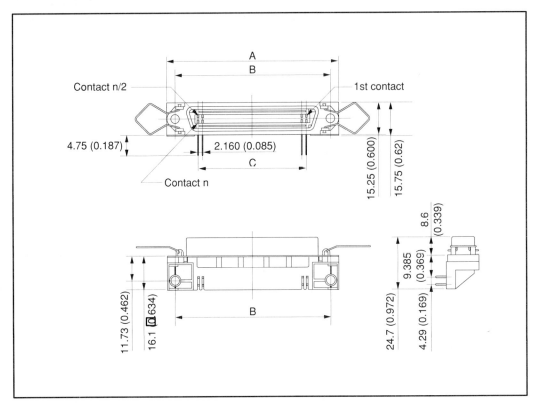

Part Number

No. of Contacts	Part Number	A	B	C
50	FCN–685–J050–L/ ☐	82.80 (3.260)	74.86 (2.947)	51.84 (2.041)

Meaning of ☐   U: None

Y: With forked spring

Z: With L shape accessory (Panel side M4, PC board side M3)

X: With L shape accessory (Panel side M3, PC board side φ3)

FCN-780 Series
SCSI I and II Terminators

Edition 1.0
August 1990

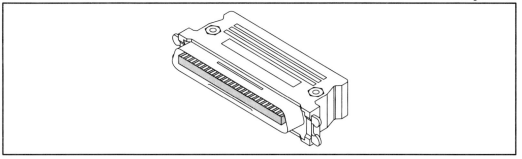

GENERAL DESCRIPTION

The FCN-780 series with terminating resistor is designed as a terminal resistance unit for SCSI interfaces for personal computers.

FEATURES

- Compact and economical through the use of miniature hybrid ICs
- Easy to connect/disconnect by hand
- EMI shielded

MATERIALS

Insulator	PPS
Shell	Steel (Nickel Plating)
Cover	ABS (Nickel Plating)
Contact	Copper Alloy (Gold Plating)

SPECIFICATIONS

Temperature Range	−40 °C to +80 °C
Rated Current (Connector)	3 A DC
Rated Voltage (Connector)	250 V AC
Contact Resistance (Connector)	15 mΩ maximum
Insulation Resistance (Connector)	1,000 MΩ or more (between FG and signal)
Dielectric Strength (Connector)	300 V AC for 1 minute (between FG and signal)

CIRCUIT DIAGRAM – ALTERNATE 1 TERMINATOR

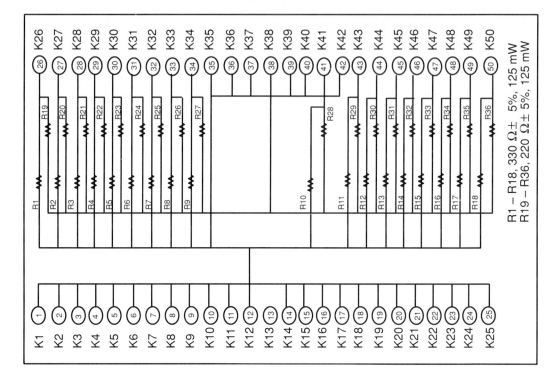

R1 – R18, 330 Ω± 5%, 125 mW
R19 – R36, 220 Ω± 5%, 125 mW

DIMENSIONS – ALTERNATE I SINGLE ENDED TERMINATOR

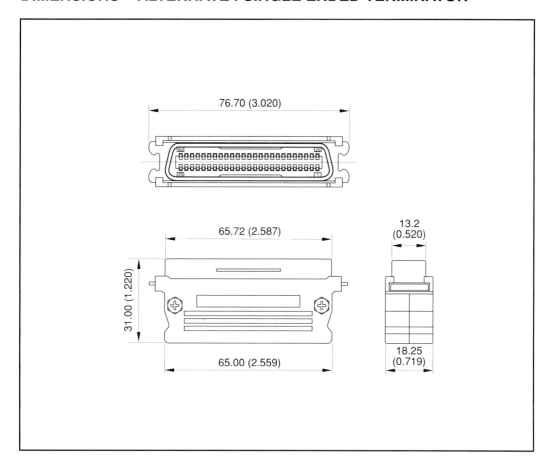

CIRCUIT DIAGRAM – ALTERNATE 2 TERMINATOR

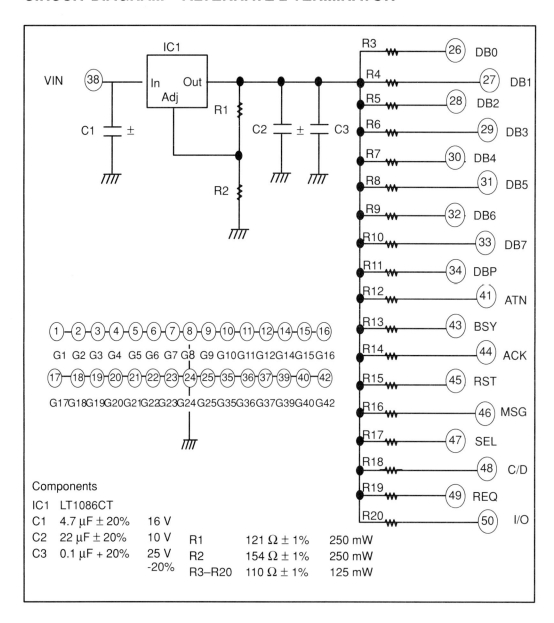

DIMENSIONS – ALTERNATE 2 SINGLE ENDED TERMINATOR

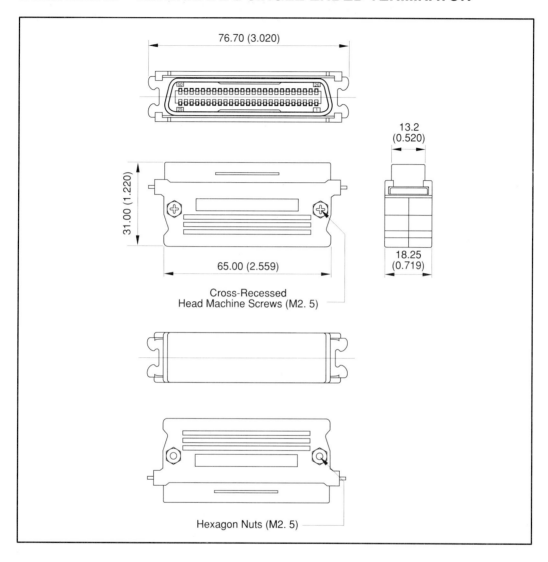

76.70 (3.020)

13.2 (0.520)

31.00 (1.220)

65.00 (2.559)

18.25 (0.719)

Cross-Recessed
Head Machine Screws (M2. 5)

Hexagon Nuts (M2. 5)

Appendix A

**American National Standard
X3.131–1986**

4.7   SCSI Bus Timing

Unless otherwise indicated, the delay-time measurements for each SCSI device, shown in 4.7.1 through 4.7.14, shall be calculated from signal conditions existing at that SCSI device's own SCSI bus connection. Thus, these measurements (except cable skew delay) can be made without considering delays in the cable.

4.7.1   Arbitration Delay (2.2 microseconds).

The minimum time an SCSI device shall wait from asserting BSY for arbitration until the DATA BUS can be examined to see if arbitration has been won. There is no maximum time.

4.7.2   Assertion Period (90 nanoseconds).

The minimum time that a target shall assert REQ while using synchronous data transfers. Also, the minimum time that an initiator shall assert ACK while using synchronous data transfers.

4.7.3   Bus Clear Delay (800 nanoseconds).

The maximum time for an SCSI device to stop driving all bus signals after:

> (1) The BUS FREE phase is detected (BSY and SEL both false for a bus settle delay)

> (2) SEL is received from another SCSI device during the ARBITRATION phase

> (3) The transition of RST to true.

Note: For the first condition above, the maximum time for an SCSI device to clear the bus is 1200 nanoseconds from BSY and SEL first becoming both false. If an SCSI device requires more than a bus settle delay to detect BUS FREE phase, it shall clear the bus within a bus clear delay minus the excess time.

4.7.4   Bus Free Delay (800 nanoseconds).

The minimum time that an SCSI device shall wait from its detection of the BUS FREE (BSY and SEL both false for a bus settle delay) until its assertion of BSY when going to the ARBITRATION phase.

4.7.5   Bus Set Delay (1.8 microseconds).

The maximum time for an SCSI device to assert BSY and its SCSI ID bit on the DATA BUS after it detects BUS FREE phase (BSY and SEL both false for a bus settle delay) for the purpose of entering the ARBITRATION phase.

4.7.6   Bus Settle Delay (400 nanoseconds).

The time to wait for the bus to settle after changing certain control signals as called out in the protocol definitions.

4.7.7   Cable Skew Delay (10 nanoseconds).

The maximum difference in propagation time allowed between any two SCSI bus signals when measured between any two SCSI devices.

4.7.8   Data Release Delay (400 nanoseconds).

The maximum time for an initiator to release the DATA BUS signals following the transition of the I/O signal from false to true.

4.7.9   Deskew Delay (45 nanoseconds).

The minimum time required for deskew of certain signals.

4.7.10   Hold Time (45 nanoseconds).

The minimum time added between the assertion of REQ or ACK and the changing of the data lines to provide hold time in the initiator or target, respectively, while using synchronous data transfers.

4.7.11   Negation Period (90 nanoseconds).

The minimum time that a target shall negate REQ while using synchronous data transfers. Also, the minimum time that an initiator shall negate ACK while using synchronous data transfers.

4.7.12   Reset Hold Time (25 microseconds).

The minimum time for which RST is asserted. There is no maximum time.

4.7.13   Selection Abort Time (200 microseconds).

The maximum time that a target (or initiator) shall take from its most recent detection of being selected (or reselected) until asserting a BSY response. This timeout is required to ensure that a target (or initiator) does not assert BSY after a SELECTION (or RESELECTION) phase has been aborted. This is not the selection timeout period; see 5.1.3.5 and 5.1.4.2 for a complete description.

4.7.14   Selection Timeout Delay (250 milliseconds, recommended).

The minimum time that an initiator (or target) should wait for a BSY response during the SELECTION (or RESELECTION) phase before starting the timeout procedure. Note that this is only a recommended time period. The specifications for the peripheral devices shall be consulted for the actual timing requirements.

4.7.15   Transfer Period (set during a MESSAGE phase).

The Transfer Period specifies the minimum time allowed between the leading edges of successive REQ pulses and of successive ACK pulses while using synchronous data transfers. (See 5.1.5.2 and 5.5.5.)

Appendix B

INSTALLATION GUIDE AND PROGRAMMERS REFERENCE FOR SE352 PC HOST ADAPTER

SCSI Host Adapter Evaluation Board for the PC, XT, or AT

- 3.0 Megabyte/Second Asynchronous Transfer Rate*

- Supports up to Eight Arbitrating SCSI Devices and 64 LUNs.

The Fujitsu PC to SCSI host adapter board (SE352) is a complete solution to connecting the PC, XT, or AT to the SCSI bus. The board supports ARBITRATION and RESELECTION. An optional ROM includes software to control the on-board Fujitsu SCSI Protocol Controller (SPC). The board and ROM are all you need to thoroughly evaluate the operation of the Fujitsu SPC and it can be used as a tool for debugging your own SCSI driver by replacing the socketed ROM with a static RAM. Your code can then be down-loaded directly from the PC to the RAM. The ROM or RAM may be located on any 16 K boundary within the PC's one megabyte address range via a DIP switch provided on the board. The PC will look between addresses C8000 and E0000 for the extended BIOS, so the board memory should be located somewhere in this range

The 16 SPC registers are memory mapped for speed and flexibility. Memory mapping the registers eliminates I/O port contention and allows the controller to coexist with the standard disk controller.

The DMA channel is selected via a jumper and can be located on channel 1, 2, or 3 (normally the disk controller uses channel 3). The interrupt level is also selectable via a jumper and can be set at levels 5, 6, or 7 (normally the disk controller uses level 5).

*Actual data transfer rate will be limited by the PC I/O or DMA bandwidth

Hardware Features

- Half card for IBM PC, XT, AT, and compatibles

- Selectable SCSI ID: 0 to 7

- Selectable PC wait state generator for PC data bus: 0 to 3 wait states

- Programmable memory map decode and socket for 8K or 16K EPROM, EEPROM, ROM, and RAM

- 32 selectable PC memory maps in 8K or 16K increments

- External and internal SCSI connectors to interface with external or internally mounted SCSI peripherals

- Odd parity generation for PC bus to SPC

- PC DMA channel interface support

- SPC interrupt mask register

Software Features

- On-board 8086 code to drive a SCSI mass storage device which in turn can boot the PC at power-up

- Common Command Set accessed as either an independent PC DOS device driver or as a memory resident program via software interrupts

- Direct disk I/O function available through standard MS-DOS interrupt 25H and 26H function calls

- Contains all logic to interface to standard PC or AT bus DMA control

Software Layers

User Interface Layer   Gives the computer "User" (programmer) a pseudo high-level support mechanism for supporting SCSI I/O functions. It executes commands via the 8086's software interrupt instructions in much the same way as PC-DOS operating system calls do. The SCSI instructions can be accessed from this layer using common 8086 languages such as an assembler, Pascal, and C.

Machine Interface Layer   Interface between PC/XT/AT machine and layers one and two. DMA, Synchronous and Asynchronous I/O are

	supported in this layer. Also, device driver and/or memory resident program support.
SCSI Layer	Supports the Common Command Set and extended commands.
Hardware I/O Layer	Supports the low level primitive I/O control between the computer and the SPC.

Feature List for the SE352 SCSI Host Adapter

General

Interface	PC/XT/AT
MS/PC DOS	DOS Driver for DOS 2.0 to 4.0 Partitioning software User application interface
BIOS ROM	Available
CD-ROM	Initiator or target One internal standard 50-pin dual row SCSI connector One external standard 50-pin D-shell SCSI connector Supports DMA or programmed I/O transfers Supports hardware or polled interrupts Memory mapped I/O for increased performance Low power CMOS controller Half-size card 8-bit bus interface 8K ROM socket EEPROM configuration memory available Address selectable on any 8K boundary Jumperable DMA channel, 1.3 Jumperable interrupt request level, 2.7 Removable termination resistors Jumperable termination power Fused termination power
Diagnostics	On-chip
Form Factor	5.75 x 4.4 x .7

Protocol

Version	ANSI SCSI-I and SCSI-II
SCSI Message Support:	All non-extended messages
Version	Common Command Set CCS 4B
Mode	Hardware – INITIATOR or TARGET

Physical

Bus	Supports Arbitration/Disconnect/Reselect
Parity Checking	Yes
Transfer type	Asynchronous
Handshake	Hardware controlled
Electrical	Single-ended
Bus Chip	Fujitsu MB89352
Burst Rate	0.3 to 3 MB/s (dependent on PC speed/DMA controller)
Connector	Standard SCSI 50 pin D-shell external Standard SCSI 50 pin dual row internal
Terminators	Removable
Termination Power	Selectable

Logical

Firmware	DOS driver or ROM or both
Initial Configuration	Automatic (single INITIATOR – single TARGET)
Reset	Hard or soft

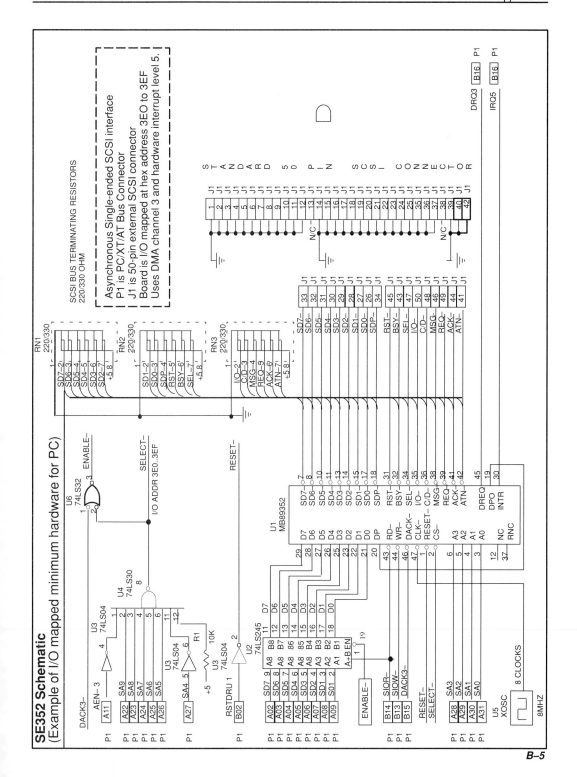

SE352 Schematic
(Example of I/O mapped minimum hardware for PC)

Contact your nearest Fujitsu Sales Office for information on demonstrations and loan agreements for the SCSI board. (See Fujitsu Sales Information)

SE352 SCSI Host Adapter Installation Procedure

The SE352 is an 8-bit half-card SCSI Host Adapter Board that can be placed in any 8-, 16- or 32-bit slot of an IBM compatible PC/XT/AT computer. Before inserting the card into the computer, you must select the board address, the data transfer option (DMA or programmed I/O), and the zero-wait state enable/disable option (ROM BIOS option only).

If the board has an external SCSI connector installed, make sure the lower bail clip is flush against the connector, pointing outwards, then remove the upper bail clip before inserting the board; squeeze the sides of the clip together to remove it. After the board is in place, you can replace the upper bail clip. Connect the SCSI peripherals to the internal, external, or both SCSI bus connectors, turn on the SCSI devices, then turn on the computer. The machine should now be ready to access the SCSI peripherals.

All user selectable options are set by using the six-section DIP switch (SW1) and the jumper strip (W1 through W13). Both these items are labeled and are located toward the bottom of the board near the edge connector.

In AT class machines, the non-volatile CMOS configuration memory must be modified for proper operation with SCSI disk drives. If the machine will be operated with only SCSI disk drives, then the Drive Type 1 and 2 parameters for both drives must be set to zero. If the machine will use a standard ST-506 or ESDI drive and a SCSI drive, then the Drive Type 1 parameter must be set to whatever the correct type is for the ST-506 or ESDI drive and the Drive Type 2 parameter must be set to zero for the SCSI devices. Failure to correctly set the drive type values may prevent the machine from booting.

Board Address Selection

Switch SW1 is used to select the memory address of the board. The board occupies 16K bytes in the memory space of the computer. The board can be positioned at the 32 memory address locations described in Table B–1 below. If the ROM BIOS option is installed (U6) then the board must be positioned at location C0000H through EC000H.

Switch positions S1 through S5 are used for address selection: position S6 is not used. A "1" corresponds to the switch being in the OFF or OPEN position, a "0" corresponds to the ON or CLOSED position. The board is shipped with the memory address set at location CC00H, which corresponds to DIP switch sections S1 through S5 set at OFF, ON, ON, OFF, OFF. Switch position 1 corresponds to the PC bus address line SA18, position 2 to SA17, etc., as shown in Table B–1 below.

Table B–1 is a list of all possible memory addresses for the SE352 board. The description on the right of each address indicates items mapped at that address in a standard PC. The board must be positioned at an address that does not conflict with items at the same address in a standard PC/XT/AT. It is recommended that an address between `C800:0000H` and `EC00:0000H` be used, since this area is not used by anything in a standard PC/XT/AT.

Table B–1. Switch Settings for Board Address Selection

S1	S2	S3	S4	S5	S6	Hex Address	PC Use
ON	ON	ON	ON	ON	OFF	8000:0000	640K RAM AREA
ON	ON	ON	ON	OFF	OFF	8400:0000	640K RAM AREA
ON	ON	ON	OFF	ON	OFF	8800:0000	640K RAM AREA
ON	ON	ON	OFF	OFF	OFF	8C00:0000	640K RAM AREA
ON	ON	OFF	ON	ON	OFF	9000:0000	640K RAM AREA
ON	ON	OFF	ON	OFF	OFF	9400:0000	640K RAM AREA
ON	ON	OFF	OFF	ON	OFF	9800:0000	640K RAM AREA
ON	ON	OFF	OFF	OFF	OFF	9C00:0000	640K RAM AREA
ON	OFF	ON	ON	ON	OFF	A000:0000	EGA/VGA
ON	OFF	ON	ON	OFF	OFF	A400:0000	EGA/VGA
ON	OFF	ON	OFF	ON	OFF	A800:0000	EGA/VGA
ON	OFF	ON	OFF	OFF	OFF	AC00:0000	EGA/VGA
ON	OFF	OFF	ON	ON	OFF	B000:0000	MONO SCREEN
ON	OFF	OFF	ON	OFF	OFF	B400:0000	MONO SCREEN
ON	OFF	OFF	OFF	ON	OFF	B800:0000	COLOR SCREEN
ON	OFF	OFF	OFF	OFF	OFF	BC00:0000	COLOR SCREEN
OFF	ON	ON	ON	ON	OFF	C000:0000	CGA ROM AREA
OFF	ON	ON	ON	OFF	OFF	C400:0000	AVAILABLE
OFF	ON	ON	OFF	ON	OFF	C800:0000	AVAILABLE
OFF	ON	ON	OFF	OFF	OFF	CC00:0000	AVAILABLE - AS SHIPPED

Continued on following page

Table B–1. Switch Settings for Board Address Selection (Continued)

S1	S2	S3	S4	S5	S6	Hex Address	PC Use
OFF	ON	OFF	ON	ON	OFF	D000:0000	AVAILABLE
OFF	ON	OFF	ON	OFF	OFF	D400:0000	AVAILABLE
OFF	ON	OFF	OFF	ON	OFF	D800:0000	AVAILABLE
OFF	ON	OFF	OFF	OFF	OFF	DC00:0000	AVAILABLE
OFF	OFF	ON	ON	ON	OFF	E000:0000	AVAILABLE PC/XT ONLY
OFF	OFF	ON	ON	OFF	OFF	E400:0000	AVAILABLE PC/XT ONLY
OFF	OFF	ON	OFF	ON	OFF	F800:0000	AVAILABLE PC/XT ONLY
OFF	OFF	ON	OFF	OFF	OFF	EC00:0000	AVAILABLE PC/XT ONLY
OFF	OFF	OFF	ON	ON	OFF	F000:0000	PC/XT/AT ROM SPACE
OFF	OFF	OFF	ON	OFF	OFF	F400:0000	PC/XT/AT ROM SPACE
OFF	OFF	OFF	OFF	ON	OFF	F800:0000	PC/XT/AT ROM SPACE
OFF	OFF	OFF	OFF	OFF	OFF	FC00:0000	PC/XT/AT ROM SPACE

Data Transfer Option

The SE352 can transfer data using DMA (hardware transfer) or PIO (programmed I/O, software transfer) mode of operation. DMA operation is recommended if there is an available DMA channel in the machine, since this usually gives the best performance. If other devices in the system are occupying the DMA channels then the board can be operated using PIO mode. PIO operation is usually slower than DMA, although in some high speed machines (20 to 33 MHz 80386) there is almost no difference.

To enable DMA operation on channels 1 through 3, place a jumper block in the corresponding DRQ and DACK position for the desired channel (see Table B–2, Transfer Mode Selection). For example, to use DMA channel 1, place a jumper in position W1 and W4. *It is important that two and only two jumpers be installed, as the computer will not operate properly otherwise.* Use either DMA channel 1 or 3, because channel 2 is used for the floppy disk controller in most machines.

To enable the PIO mode of operation, remove all jumper blocks in positions W1 through W6.

Table B–2. Transfer Mode Selection (Jumper Strip W1 through W6)

W1	W2	W3	W4	W5	W6	Jumper Name
DACK1	DACK2	DACK3	DRQ5	DRQ6	DRQ7	Bus Signal
IN	–	–	IN	–	–	DMA TRANSFER CHANNEL 1
–	IN	–	–	IN	–	DMA TRANSFER CHANNEL 2
–	–	IN	–	–	IN	DMA TRANSFER CHANNEL 3
–	–	–	–	–	–	PROGRAMMED I/O TRANSFER

Hardware Interrupt Request Selection

Jumper positions W7 through W12 correspond to the PC's hardware interrupt signals IRQ2 through IRQ7. (The hardware interrupt signal is not used with the standard DOS drivers or SCSI ROM BIOS from Galbo and Associates) *Unless a custom software package has been purchased that uses hardware interrupt, NO jumper should be installed in these locations.* See Table B–3, Hardware Interrupt Request Selection.

Table B–3. Hardware Interrupt Request Selection (Jumper Strip W7 through W12)

W7	W8	W9	W10	W11	W12	Jumper Name
IRQ2	IRQ3	IRQ4	IRQ5	IRQ6	IRQ7	Bus Signal
IN	–	–	–	–	–	INTERRUPT REQUEST 2
–	IN	–	–	–	–	INTERRUPT REQUEST 3
–	–	IN	–	–	–	INTERRUPT REQUEST 4
–	–	–	IN	–	–	INTERRUPT REQUEST 5
–	–	–	–	IN	–	INTERRUPT REQUEST 6
–	–	–	–	–	IN	INTERRUPT REQUEST 7

Because the SE352 SCSI ROM BIOS code does not require the use of a hardware interrupt when running under MS-DOS, all jumpers from W7 through W12 should be removed. Future versions of drivers for OS/2 and UNIX may require the use of a hardware interrupt.

Zero Wait State Operation

If the board contains the SCSI ROM BIOS option (U6 installed), inserting a jumper in position W13 will allow the ROM BIOS code to run with zero wait state. This option can offer a significant performance increase on some machines (usually AT class) when the SE352 is using the PIO mode of operation. The SE352 has an average access time under 200 nanoseconds and can usually run on most machines with this option enabled.

If the board was purchased without the ROM BIOS option, this jumper will not have any effect. See Table B–4, Zero Wait State Selection.

Table B–4. Zero Wait State Selection (Jumper Strip W13)

Jumper Name	W13
Bus Signal	OWS

Jumper Installed	Zero-Wait State Bus Access
Jumper Removed	Normal Bus Access

SCSI Bus Termination Resistors

Sockets U7 and U8 hold the removable SCSI termination resistors. If the SE352 is the last device on the end of the SCSI bus then the termination resistors shipped with the board should be installed in these sockets. The device on the other end of the SCSI bus cable should also have its terminators installed. If the SE352 is not on the end of the SCSI bus, then these resistors should be removed. There must be two and only two devices on the SCSI bus that have terminating resistors installed.

Any more than two devices will electrically overload the bus and will prevent correct operation. Also, if none of the devices have terminators installed, the bus will not operate. The board is delivered with the resistors installed in sockets U7 and U8.

Connectors

Connector J2 is used for connection to SCSI devices installed internally in the PC via a 150-pin ribbon cable. Pin 1 is located toward the top of the board, near the rear of the PC.

Optical connector J1 is a standard 50-pin external SCSI connector; the cable is self-locating. This connector is used to connect external SCSI devices such as CD-ROMs, scanners, and additional disk drives.

It is possible to run the board with SCSI devices connected to both the internal and external SCSI connectors. In this case, the SE352 is not electrically at the end of the SCSI bus so the terminating resistors in U6 and U7 should be removed. The devices at each end of both the external and internal connector cable should have their terminating resistor installed.

Multiple SCSI Devices

All SCSI devices are addressed using a SCSI bus address that is a numeric value in the range of zero to seven. Most devices have a means of allowing the user to select the bus address, usually through the insertion or removal of jumper blocks or setting of a DIP switch. *Each device connected to the SCSI bus must have a unique SCSI address.*

Violating this requirement will cause bus contention resulting in the failure or erratic operation of the SCSI I/O system.

Booting

An SE352 with the SCSI ROM BIOS option installed will boot up in one of two possible ways, depending upon the configuration of the PC described below.

Standard PC Drives and SCSI Drives

In a machine with a standard PC drive (ST-506 or ESDI) installed, the SE352 will install the SCSI drive(s) as the next physical drive(s) of the machine, after the standard PC drive. The machine will boot from the ST-506 drive. For example, in a machine that has an internal ST-506 drive and one SCSI disk drive (installed internally or externally), the ST-506 drive will be brought up as the primary drive and the SCSI drive will be the secondary drive. *Booting from the SCSI drive is not possible when a standard PC drive is installed.*

SCSI Drives Only

The SE352 will boot the machine from the highest addressed SCSI drive and the other (if any) lower addressed SCSI drive(s) will be installed as the next device(s) in sequence. For example, a machine that has two SCSI hard drives attached as SCSI address #6 and #3 will boot from the #6 drive and will install the #3 drive as the next device in sequence.

Loading Uninitialized Drives

When the machine is first turned on or restarted from the keyboard, the SCSI ROM BIOS will attempt to load the SCSI drives as explained above. If the SCSI drives are removed or off-line, the SCSI ROM BIOS will keep attempting to locate a SCSI drive for up to two minutes. This search delay can be avoided by pressing the ESC key during the boot process. When the ESC key is pressed, the message SCSI LOAD ABORTED will appear and the boot process will continue normally. Even though the SCSI drives will not be loaded as DOS devices, the BIOS will allow SCSI drives to be low-level formatted through the use of a built-in utility.

SE352 SCSI ROM BIOS Built-in Utilities

Low-level SCSI Format Utility

The SCSI ROM BIOS option contains a low-level format utility for SCSI direct access devices. A SCSI device, such as a hard disk, must be formatted before it can be used by DOS. To invoke the utility, enter the DOS debugger and start execution at address ss00:0005, where ss is the board's base memory segment address. For example, if the board address is at CC00H (as shipped) then type the following, ending each line typed with the ENTER or RETURN key. The * symbol represents the ENTER or RETURN key.

$$\textbf{DEBUG *} \qquad \text{(enter DOS debugger)}$$

$$\textbf{G = CC00:5 *} \qquad \text{(start program execution)}$$

When the SCSI format utility is running, it will prompt for the SCSI device address, logical unit number (LUN) of the device, and the interleave factor. Enter the appropriate number for each prompt, ending each line with and ENTER or RETURN key. Typing only the RETURN key in response to a prompt will have the same effect as entering a 0 value.

If the SCSI device does not support LUNs, then enter 0 at the LUN prompt. (Most disk drives sold in the PC market do not support LUNs).

If the SCSI device does not support interleave, type 0 at the prompt. Tape drives and some SCSI disks do not support the interleave factor.

If interleave is supported, finding the optimum factor for a disk depends upon many things, such as CPU speed, CPU wait-states, CPU bus speed, CPU type (8086/80286/80386), and whether DMA operation is used or not. Some experimentation may be required to achieve the highest possible transfer rates. In general, if the SE352 is operating using DMA, then an interleave factor of 0 will probably give the best performance.

After all parameters are entered, the utility will prompt to proceed. Entering a Y (yes) at this point will begin the SCSI format operation and *all data on the device will be erased*. Pressing any other key will cancel the format operation. Formatting time varies with the device capacity; some large disk drives take up to 30 minutes to format.

An error message will appear if any of the entered parameters are invalid. Invoke the utility again to correct the values and retry the operation.

The format utility will return to DOS after it completes the operation.

Appendix C

SPC DRIVER EXAMPLES IN C LANGUAGE

The following code is a group of routines that demonstrate the essential elements necessary for the implementation of a SCSI driver using Fujitsu's family of controllers. These routines make certain assumptions about the hardware interface, but are software compatible with all the Fujitsu SCSI controllers.

For this example the controller is memory mapped somewhere in the address space of the host CPU. This example assumes that the controller will be used in a polled environment (not interrupt driven) using programmed I/O (no DMA). Using the device in this mode requires much more code than in an interrupt-driven/DMA environment, but the code will be less dependent on system hardware. At the end of this example is a re-write of the data transfer routine using DMA transfer instead of a programmed I/O; the code is considerably smaller and simpler.

This code shows the programming and operation of the major functions of the Fujitsu family of SCSI controllers. It is not intended to be a tutorial for SCSI protocol or to show the construction of a driver for an SCSI host adapter.

This code was tested for syntax errors under the following compiler: Borland Turbo 'C' 2.0

For detailed information on the SCSI protocol see the ANSI documentation mentioned in this book's Acknowledgements section.

```
/*************************************************************/
/*          For information on Fujistu's SCSI controllers, SPCs
            */
/*          contact:                                        */
/*                                                          */
/*          Fujitsu Microelectronics, Inc.                  */
/*          3545 North First Street                         */
/*          San Jose, CA.95134-1804                         */
/*          (408) 922-9000                                  */
/*                                                          */
/*          or your local Fujitsu representative.           */
/*                                                          */
/************************************************************ */
/*                                                          */
/*          Copyright (C) 1990 Fujitsu Microelectronics Inc.  */
/*          Copyright (C) 1990 Galbo and Associates, Inc.   */
/*                                                          */
/*************************************************************/
```

```
/***********************************************************************/
/*      Constants                                                      */
/***********************************************************************/

#define TRUE    (1 == 1)
#define FALSE   (! TRUE)


/*      selection time-out delays */

#define SELECTION_TIMEOUT    4400L     /* 275 msec @ 8 MHz */
#define BUS_DELAY            4         /* 1200 nsec @ 8 MHz */


/*      data transfer direction */

#define READ                 0         /* read from SCSI bus */
#define WRITE                1         /* write to SCSI bus */


/*      selection return values */

#define SELECTED             100       /* target successfully selected */
#define LOST_ARBITRATION     -100      /* selection failed */
#define TIMEOUT              -101      /* selection failed */
#define ERROR_INTR           -102      /* unexpected interrupt occurred */


/*      data transfer return values */

#define OK                   200       /* transfer complete */
#define OKPAD                201       /* transfer complete with padding */
#define SERVICE_REQUIRED     -200      /* early phase change */
#define PARITY_ERROR         -201      /* read parity error */


/*      phase decoder return values */

#define NO_PHASE_REQUESTED   0
#define ILLEGAL_PHASE        -300      /* illegal SCSI phase requested */


#define DEFAULT_SPC_ADDR     0xd0001ff0L;

/***********************************************************************/
/*      All Fujitsu SCSI controllers contain the following 16         */
/*      8-bit registers.  This structure assumes the compiler that can */
/*      pack bytes within structures.                                  */
/***********************************************************************/

struct  SPCREGPACK
{
  unsigned char _BDID,          /* bus device ID */
                _SCTL,          /* SPC control */
                _SCMD,          /* SPC command */
                _TMOD,          /* transfer mode */
                _INTS,          /* interrupt sense */
                _PSNS,          /* phase sense */
                _SSTS,          /* SPC status */
                _SERR,          /* SPC error status */
                _PCTL,          /* phase control */
```

```
                    _MBC,          /* modified byte counter */
                    _DREG,         /* FIFO data register */
                    _TEMP,         /* temporary register */
                    _TCH,          /* transfer counter high */
                    _TCM,          /* transfer counter mid */
                    _TCL,          /* transfer counter low */
                    _EXBF;         /* external buffer */
} far *spc = (struct SPCREGPACK far *) DEFAULT_SPC_ADDR;

/**********************************************************************/
/*     Assume the Fujitsu SCSI Protocol Controller is accessed via    */
/*     memory mapped addressing, the following constants are used      */
/*     to read and write to the registers.                            */
/**********************************************************************/

#define BDID              ( spc->_BDID )
#define SCTL              ( spc->_SCTL )
#define SCMD              ( spc->_SCMD )
#define TMOD              ( spc->_TMOD )
#define INTS              ( spc->_INTS )
#define PSNS              ( spc->_PSNS )
#define SSTS              ( spc->_SSTS )
#define SERR              ( spc->_SERR )
#define PCTL              ( spc->_PCTL )
#define MBC               ( spc->_MBC  )
#define DREG              ( spc->_DREG )
#define TEMP              ( spc->_TEMP )
#define TCH               ( spc->_TCH  )
#define TCM               ( spc->_TCM  )
#define TCL               ( spc->_TCL  )
#define EXBF              ( spc->_EXBF )
#define SDGC              ( spc->_PSNS )            /* the SDGC reg has the */
                                                   /* ... same addr as PSNS */
/**********************************************************************/
/*     Array to convert SCSI addresses to SCSI ID's (for arbitration)  */
/**********************************************************************/

unsigned char   Addr2ID[] = { 0x01, 0x02, 0x04, 0x08,
                              0x10, 0x20, 0x40, 0x80 };

/**********************************************************************/
/*     Variables needed for this example.                             */
/**********************************************************************/

unsigned char   msgin, msgout, status;
int             cmdlength, datalength;
unsigned char   *cmdptr, *dataptr;

extern void     setup_dma();

/**********************************************************************/
/*     INITIALIZE SPC                                                 */
/*     Initialize SCSI controller.                                    */
/*                                                                    */
/*     Entry: init_addr - SCSI address of initiator,  0..7            */
/**********************************************************************/
```

```
void    init_SPC(init_addr)
int     init_addr;      /* this initiator's SCSI address, 0..7 */
{
  SCTL = 0xc0;          /* reset controller */
  BDID = init_addr;
  TMOD = 0x00;
/*                                                                       */
/*      Release reset with arbitration on, parity checking on,           */
/*      reselection on (INITIATOR), hardware interrupts disabled.        */
/*                                                                       */
  SCTL = 0x1a;
  SDGC = 0x00;          /* no xfer intr for 89352                 */
}


/***********************************************************************/
/*      SELECT TARGET                                                  */
/*      Arbitrate for the SCSI bus and select a target device.         */
/*                                                                     */
/*      Entry: targ_addr - Target's SCSI bus address, 0..7             */
/*             targ_lun - Target's LUN (logical unit number)           */
/*      Exit:  > 0 if successful selection                             */
/*             < 0 if unsuccessful                                     */
/***********************************************************************/

int     select(targ_addr, targ_lun)
int     targ_addr;      /* the selected target's SCSI address, 0..7 */
int     targ_lun;       /* the selected target's logical unit number */
{
  PCTL = 0x00;          /* phase control reg indicates selection phase */
/*                                                                       */
/*      Set the TEMP register to the target's SCSI ID (not address)      */
/*      OR'ed with the initiator's ID (in the BDID register). This       */
/*      is done so that the target knows the ID of the initiator for     */
/*      reselection purposes.                                            */
/*                                                                       */
  TEMP = BDID | Addr2ID[targ_addr];
/*                                                                       */
/*      The transfer counter registers double as selection time-out      */
/*      registers during arb/selection.  Set these registers to the      */
/*      desired value.  The time-out values are dependent upon the       */
/*      SPC's clock speed.                                                */
/*                                                                       */
  TCH = SELECTION_TIMEOUT >> 8;        /* high byte of selection time-out */
  TCM = SELECTION_TIMEOUT & 0xff;      /* low byte of selection time-out  */
  TCL = BUS_DELAY;              /* bus settle and bus free delay */
/*                                                                       */
/*      Assert the SCSI attention signal during the selection phase,      */
/*      this will notify the target that the initiator wants to send      */
/*      an IDENTIFY message after successful selection.  The ATN signal   */
/*      will not be activated until AFTER the selection phase has         */
/*      successfully completed.                                           */
/*                                                                       */
  SCMD = 0x60;          /* assert ATN signal */
/*                                                                       */
/*      Start the arbitration and selection sequence.                    */
```

```
/*                                                             */
  SCMD = 0x10;            /* send select command */
/*                                                             */
/*      Wait for the interrupt register to signal the end of the    */
/*      selection phase or check if the SPC lost the bus arbitration */
/*      phase.                                                  */
/*                                                             */
  while (! INTS)                 /* wait for interrupt indicated */
  {                              /* ... if no interrupt, check for lost arb    */
    if (! (SSTS & 0x20))         /* ... test if arb/selection still in progress */
    {                            /* ... arb/selection finished, no intr pending */
      return (LOST_ARBITRATION);/* indicate unsuccessful selection          */
    }
  }
/*                                                             */
/*      An interrupt occurred, check if it's the command complete   */
/*      interrupt, indicating successful arb/selection.             */
/*                                                             */
  if (INTS & 0x10)               /* command complete intr bit set ? */
  {
/*                                                             */
/*      Command complete interrupt indicated.                   */
/*      Arb/Selection was successful, check if target is requesting  */
/*      a message out, if so, send the IDENTIFY message with the     */
/*      disconnection and reselection supported bits set and an      */
/*      initiator LUN of 0.                                     */
/*                                                             */
    if ((PSNS & 0x87) == (0x86))        /* if target requesting msg out */
    {                                   /* ... phase after selection */
      msgout = 0xc0 | targ_lun; /* support disconnect/reselect */
      messsage_out(&msgout);    /* send message */
    }                           /* ... and select the target LUN */
  }
  else                          /* no command complete intr */
  {
/*                                                             */
/*      An interrupt occurred but it was not command complete,       */
/*      indicating that the arb/selection was not successful.        */
/*                                                             */
    if (INTS & 0x04)            /* time-out interrupt ? */
    {
      return (TIMEOUT);         /* indicate time-out */
    }
    else                        /* not time-out intr */
    {
      return (ERROR_INTR);      /* must be a bus reset, disconnect or   */
    }                           /* ... or SPC error intr                */
  }
  return (SELECTED);            /* indicate successful arb/selection */
}                               /* ... we are connected to the target */


/***********************************************************************/
/*      TRANSFER DATA TO SCSI                                   */
/*      Read or write a stream of bytes to the SCSI bus and        */
/*      check for the following conditions:                     */
/*      1) # of bytes transferred == # of bytes requested - normal  */
```

```
/*      2) # of bytes transferred > # of bytes requested - pad      */
/*      3) # of bytes transferred < # of bytes requested - phase change */
/*                                                                  */
/*      Entry:  dp - pointer to list of bytes                       */
/*              length - number of bytes in list                    */
/*              type - READ or WRITE                                */
/*      Exit:   > 0 - transferred all bytes in list                 */
/*              < 0 - transfer terminated early                     */
/*******************************************************************/

int     transfer_data(dp, length, io)
unsigned char   *dp;
unsigned long   length;
int             io;             /* transfer type READ or WRITE */
{
  TCH = length >> 16;           /* high byte of transfer count  */
  TCM = (length >> 8) & 0xff;   /* middle byte                  */
  TCL = length & 0xff;          /* low byte                     */
/*                                                              */
/*      Start SCSI programmed I/O transfer                      */
/*                                                              */
  SCMD = 0x84;
/*                                                              */
/*      Wait for SPC to start processing the command            */
/*                                                              */
  while ((SSTS & 0xf0) != 0xb0) ;
/*                                                              */
/*      Wait for an available location in the output FIFO, then */
/*      send byte.                                              */
/*                                                              */
  while (length)                /* while not finished sending */
  {
    if (! INTS)                 /* send while no interrupts pending */
    {
/*                                                              */
/*      Read or write a byte to the SPC's FIFO                  */
/*                                                              */
      if (io == WRITE)
      {
/*                                                              */
/*      Write a byte to the FIFO if the FIFO is NOT FULL.       */
/*                                                              */
        if (! (SSTS & 0x02))    /* if space in FIFO */
        {
          DREG = *dp++;         /* write byte to FIFO, bump ptr */
          length--;             /* decrement byte count */
        }
      }
      else
      {
/*                                                              */
/*      Read a byte from the FIFO if the FIFO is NOT EMPTY.     */
/*                                                              */
        if (! (SSTS & 0x01))    /* if space in FIFO */
        {
          *dp++ = DREG;         /* read byte to FIFO, bump ptr */
```

```
[ FMIEX.C  89-Feb-15  17:51 ]                        89-Feb-15  17:52  Page: 7

          length--;              /* decrement byte count */
        }
      }
    }
    else                      /* an interrupt is pending */
    {                         /* ... check type */
      if (INTS & 0x08)        /* if SVC REQ intr */
      {
        INTS = 0x08;          /* reset service required */
        return (SERVICE_REQUIRED);      /* exit early */
      }
      else if (INTS)          /* if other intr */
      {
        return (ERROR_INTR);   /* bus release, reset, SPC error intr */
      }
      else if (SERR & 0xc0)    /* read parity error ? */
      {
        return (PARITY_ERROR);
      }
    }                         /* ... process later */
  }
/*                                                                    */
/*     All bytes (length) in data stream have been transferred.       */
/*     Check for command complete interrupt after all data sent.      */
/*                                                                    */
  while (! (INTS & 0x10)) ;        /* wait for cmd complete */
  INTS = 0x10;                     /* reset cmd complete intr */
/*                                                                    */
/*     If target has not changed phase after sending all bytes        */
/*     then we should pad the transfer to let the target continue     */
/*     to the next phase.                                             */
/*                                                                    */
  if (((PCTL & 0x07) | 0x80) == (PSNS & 0x87)) /* new phase ? */
  {                         /* same phase */
    TEMP = 0;               /* do pad transfer, pad with 0's for write */
    SCMD = 0x85;            /* start programmed transfer PAD out */
/*                                                                    */
/*     The completion of the padding transfer is indicated by the     */
/*     command complete intr and the service required intr (since      */
/*     the target will normally change phase at the end of the transfer)*/
/*                                                                    */
    while ((INTS & 0x18) != 0x18) ;  /* wait for pad to complete */
    INTS = 0x18;               /* reset intr's */
    return (OKPAD);
  }
  else                         /* target has gone to next phase */
    return (OK);               /* transfer completed normally */
}


/*********************************************************************/
/*     SEND COMMAND                                                  */
/*     Send a SCSI command to the target                             */
/*     Assume: TCH, TCM, TCL regs = 0                                */
/*                                                                   */
/*     Entry:  cp - pointer to SCSI command stream                   */
/*             length - length of the command, 6, 10, or 12 bytes    */
```

```
[ FMIEX.C  89-Feb-15  17:51 ]                    89-Feb-15  17:53  Page: 8

/*      Exit:  > 0 - transferred all bytes in list              */
/*             < 0 - transfer terminated early                  */
/**********************************************************************/

int     send_command(cp, length)
unsigned char   *cp;            /* pointer to command stream */
int             length;         /* length of command stream */
{
  PCTL = 0x02;          /* indicate command phase */
/*                                                              */
/*      Start transfer                                          */
/*                                                              */
  return (transfer_data(cp, length, READ));
}


/**********************************************************************/
/*      READ STATUS IN                                          */
/*      Read the 1 byte status code from the target.           */
/*                                                              */
/*      Entry: sp - pointer to status byte                      */
/*      Exit:  > 0 successful read                              */
/*             < 0 unsuccessful read                            */
/**********************************************************************/

int     status_in(sp)
unsigned char   *sp;            /* pointer to status byte */
{
  PCTL = 0x03;                  /* indicate status phase */
  return (transfer_data(sp, 1, READ));
 }


/**********************************************************************/
/*      SEND MESSAGE OUT                                         */
/*      Send a 1 byte message to the target.                    */
/*      When the SPC is the INITIATOR, it will automatically     */
/*      negate the ATN signal when the message byte is sent, conforming */
/*      to the SCSI protocol.                                   */
/*                                                              */
/*      Entry: mp - pointer to message byte                     */
/*      Exit:  > 0 successful read                              */
/*             < 0 unsuccessful read                            */
/**********************************************************************/

int     message_out(mp)
unsigned char   *mp;
{
  PCTL = 0x06;                  /* indicate message phase */
  return (transfer_data(mp, 1, WRITE));
}


/**********************************************************************/
/*      READ MESSAGE IN                                         */
/*      Read a 1 byte message from the target                   */
/*      When the SPC is the INITIATOR, it will automatically     */
/*      hold the ACK line active on the last byte of the message. */
/*      This is to allow the host CPU to examine the message and */
```

```
/*      reject it, if necessary, via the SCSI protocol's message       */
/*      reject sequence.                                               */
/*                                                                     */
/*      Entry:  mp - pointer to message byte                           */
/*      Exit:   > 0 successful read                                    */
/*              < 0 unsuccessful read                                  */
/**********************************************************************/

int     message_in(mp)
unsigned char    *mp;
{
  int   rv;

  PCTL = 0x06;                  /* indicate message phase */
  rv = transfer_data(mp, 1, WRITE);     /* save return value */
  if (rv > 0)                   /* if message read successfully */
  {
    SCMD = 0xc0;                /* manually negate the ACK signal */
    INTS = 0x10;                /* reset cmd complete intr */
  }
  return (rv);
}


/**********************************************************************/
/*      READ SCSI DATA                                                 */
/*      Read up to 256 MBytes from the target device.                  */
/*                                                                     */
/*      Entry:  mp - pointer to byte stream                            */
/*              length - number of bytes to read                       */
/**********************************************************************/

int     data_in(mp, length)
unsigned char    *mp;
unsigned long    length;
{
  PCTL = 0x01;           /* indicate data in phase */
  return (transfer_data(mp, length, READ));
}


/**********************************************************************/
/*      WRITE SCSI DATA                                                */
/*      Write up to 256 MBytes to the target device.                   */
/*                                                                     */
/*      Entry:  mp - pointer to byte stream                            */
/*              length - number of bytes to write                      */
/**********************************************************************/

int     data_out(mp,length)
unsigned char    *mp;
unsigned long    length;
{
  PCTL = 0x00;           /* indicate data out phase */
  return (transfer_data(mp, length, WRITE));
}


/**********************************************************************/
```

```
[ FMIEX.C  89-Feb-15  17:51 ]                    89-Feb-15  17:53  Page: 10

/*      DECODE SCSI BUS PHASE                                          */
/*      After selection, read target's requested SCSI bus phase       */
/*      and go to the appropriate handler, continue calling this      */
/*      routine until the COMMAND COMPLETE message is sent from the    */
/*      target.                                                        */
/*                                                                     */
/*      Exit:   > 0 successful operation                              */
/*              = 0 no phase requested (REQ signal not active)        */
/*              < 0 unsuccessful operation                            */
/***********************************************************************/

int    decode_phase()
{
  switch (PSNS & 0x87)                  /* read phase sense reg */
  {                                     /* REQ bit (0x80) must be active */
    case 0x80:
      return (data_out(dataptr, datalength));
      break;

    case 0x81:
      return (data_in(dataptr, datalength));
      break;

    case 0x82:
      return (send_command(cmdptr, cmdlength));
      break;

    case 0x83:
      return (status_in(&status));
      break;

    case 0x84:                          /* undefined SCSI phases */
    case 0x85:                          /* ... should never see these */
      return (ILLEGAL_PHASE);

    case 0x86:
      return (message_out(&msgout));
      break;

    case 0x87:
      return (message_in(&msgin));
      break;

    default:
      return (NO_PHASE_REQUESTED);      /* REQ bit is not active */
      break;
  }
}
/***********************************************************************/
/*      DMA TRANSFER DATA TO/FROM SCSI                                 */
/*      Read or write a stream of bytes to the SCSI bus using DMA      */
/*      and check for the following conditions:                       */
/*      1) # of bytes transferred == # of bytes requested - normal     */
/*      2) # of bytes transferred > # of bytes requested - pad         */
/*      3) # of bytes transferred < # of bytes requested - phase change */
/*                                                                     */
```

```
/*      Entry:  dp - pointer to list of bytes                */
/*              length - number of bytes in list             */
/*              type - READ or WRITE                         */
/*      Exit:   > 0 - transferred all bytes in list          */
/*              < 0 - transfer terminated early              */
/*                                                           */
/*      Note: If the SPC is interrupt driven along with using DMA,  */
/*            the code below becomes even smaller since it is not   */
/*            necessary to test the INTS register within a loop.    */
/*            In fact, the overhead to start a data transfer in     */
/*            the SPC takes only 3 steps:                           */
/*                                                           */
/*            1) Write desired phase to PCTL register        */
/*            2) Write 1 to 3 bytes to the transfer counters, TCH/M/L */
/*            3) Write the DMA transfer code to SCMD register (0x80)  */
/*                                                           */
/*********************************************************************/


int     dma_transfer_data(dp, length, type)
unsigned char   *dp;
unsigned long   length;
int             type;           /* transfer type READ or WRITE */
{
  setup_dma(dp, length, type);  /* set up the DMA controller */
  TCH = length >> 16;           /* high byte of transfer count  */
  TCM = (length >> 8) & 0xff;   /* middle byte                  */
  TCL = length & 0xff;          /* low byte                     */
  SCMD = 0x80;                  /* start DMA transfer */
  while (! INTS) ;              /* wait for an interrupt */
  if (INTS & 0x10)              /* if cmd complete intr */
    return (TRUE);              /* ... done */
  return (FALSE);               /* handle other interrupt later */
}


/*********************************************************************/
/*                                                           */
/*********************************************************************/
```

Appendix D

SPC DRIVER EXAMPLES IN 8086 ASSEMBLY LANGUAGE

The following code is a group of routines, written in 8086 Assembly Language, that demonstrate the essential elements necessary for the implementation of a SCSI driver using Fujitsu's family of SCSI controllers. These routines make certain assumptions about the hardware interface, but are software compatible with all the Fujitsu SCSI controllers.

These routines use short (16-bit) pointers to keep the code relatively simple and limit the size of the transfer buffers to 64K bytes (due to the 8086 family's segmentation limitation). Even though the transfer routines and the SPC will take up to a 24-bit (28-bit for the MB87033B) transfer length and allow for transfers up to 16M bytes, the 24-bit size cannot be accomodated without re-writing the transfer routines to support segmented (20-bit) or 80386 extended (32-bit) pointers.

This code shows the programming and operation of the major functions of the Fujitsu family of SCSI controllers. It is not intended to be a tutorial for SCSI protocol or to show the construction of a driver for an SCSI host adapter.

This code was tested for syntax errors with the SMALL model and the following assemblers:

Borland TASM 1.0   Microsoft MASM 5.1.

For this example the controller is memory mapped somewhere in the 1MB address space of the 8086. This example assumes that the controller will be used in a polled environment (not interrupt driven) using programmed I/O (no DMA). Using the device in this mode requires much more code than an interrupt-driven/DMA environment, but the code will be less dependent on system hardware. At the end of this example is a re-write of the data transfer routine using DMA transfers instead of programmed I/O; the code is considerably smaller and simpler.

For detailed information on the SCSI protocol see the ANSI SCSI Standard noted in this book's Acknowledgements.

```
;************************************************************;
;                                                          ;
;              For information on Fujistu's SCSI controllers ;
;              contact:                                    ;
;                                                          ;
;              Fujitsu Microelectronics, Inc.             ;
;              3545 North First Street                    ;
;              San Jose, CA.95134-1804                    ;
;              (408) 922-9000                             ;
;                                                          ;
;              or your local Fujitsu representative.      ;
;                                                          ;
;                                                          ;
;************************************************************;
;                                                          ;
;                                                          ;
;              Copyright (C) 1990 Fujitsu Microelectronics Inc. ;
;              Copyright (C) 1990 Galbo and Associates, Inc. ;
;                                                          ;
;                                                          ;
;                                                          ;
;************************************************************
```

```
                          .model small
                          .code


;  ********************************************************************** ;
;         equates                                                        ;
;  ********************************************************************** ;
;
;
;         SPC memory mapped register addresses

BDID    equ     <byte ptr es:[bx+0]>    ; bus ID
SCTL    equ     <byte ptr es:[bx+1]>    ; SPC control
SCMD    equ     <byte ptr es:[bx+2]>    ; SPC command
TMOD    equ     <byte ptr es:[bx+3]>    ; transfer mode
INTS    equ     <byte ptr es:[bx+4]>    ; interrupt sense
PSNS    equ     <byte ptr es:[bx+5]>    ; phase sense
SDGC    equ     <byte ptr es:[bx+5]>    ; SPC diagnostic control
SSTS    equ     <byte ptr es:[bx+6]>    ; SPC status
SERR    equ     <byte ptr es:[bx+7]>    ; SPC error status
PCTL    equ     <byte ptr es:[bx+8]>    ; phase control
MBC     equ     <byte ptr es:[bx+9]>    ; modified byte counter
DREG    equ     <byte ptr es:[bx+10]>   ; data register (FIFO)
TEMP    equ     <byte ptr es:[bx+11]>   ; temp register
TCH     equ     <byte ptr es:[bx+12]>   ; transfer counter high
TCM     equ     <byte ptr es:[bx+13]>   ; transfer counter middle
TCL     equ     <byte ptr es:[bx+14]>   ; transfer counter low
EXBF    equ     <byte ptr es:[bx+15]>   ; external buffer register


SPC_OFFSET      = 1ff0h                 ; assume SPC is memory mapped
SPC_SEGMENT     = 0dc00h                ; at this address (seg:ofs)
;
;         Data transfer mode
;
READ                    = 0     ; read mode for data transfer routines
WRITE                   = 1     ; write mode for data transfer routines
;
;
SCSI    time-out values
;


SELECTION_TIMEOUT       = 4400  ; 275 msec. @ 8MHz clock
BUS_DELAY               = 4     ; 1200 nsec. @ 8MHz clock
;
;         Selection return values
;
SELECTED                = 100   ; target successfully selected
LOST_ARBITRATION        = -100  ; lost control of SCSI bus to another
                                        INITIATOR
TIMEOUT                 = -101  ; selected target did not respond
ERROR_INTR              = -102  ; hardware error occured during selection
;
```

```
;       Data transfer return values
;
OK                         = 200   ; transferred all bytes without error
OKPAD                      = 201   ; transferred all bytes plus padding
SERVICE_REQUIRED           = -200  ; early phase change, didn't transfer all
PARITY_ERROR               = -201  ; parity error during transfer
;
;       Phase decoder return values
;
NO_PHASE_REQUESTED         = 0     ; target's REQ signal negated
ILLEGAL_PHASE              = -300  ; target requesting undefined phase
;*********************************************************************************;
;         constants                                                              ;
;                                                                                ;
    *********************************************************************************
                           .data                  ; data area
Addr2ID                    db      1, 2, 4, 8, 16, 32, 64, 128
SPC_Pointer                label   dword
SPC_Ofs                    dw      SPC_OFFSET
SPC_Seg                    dw      SPC_SEGMENT


;*****************************************************************         ;
;         global variables                                                ;
;                                                                         ;
    *****************************************************************
                           .data?                 ; unitialize data area
@datalength                label   dword          ; length of transfer for DATA
                                                    IN/OUT phase
@datalength_lo             dw      0
@datalength_hi             dw      0
@dataptr                   dw      0              ; pointer to byte buffer for DATA
                                   IN/OUT
@cmdlength                 dw      0                 ; length of command block
@cmdblk                    db      12 dup (0)        ; command block, max = 12
@msgout                    db      0              ; message out byte
@msgin                     db      0              ; message in byte
@status                    db      0              ; status in byte

;*****************************************************************          ;
;         external routines                                                ;
;                                                                          ;
    *****************************************************************
                           .code
                           extrn   Setup_DMA:near     ; setup system's DMA controller
```

```
;*******************************************************************;
;                                                                  ;
;         INITIALIZE SPC                                           ;
;         Initialize the Fujitsu SPC                               ;
;                                                                  ;
;         Entry: BYTE @ [bp+4] = initiator's SCSI address          ;
;                                                                  ;
;         Exit:  void;                                             ;
;                                                                  ;
;*******************************************************************


InitSPC_record     struc
                   dw      ?                       ; bp
                   dw      ?                       ; ip - return address
InitAddr           db      ?                       ; initiator's SCSI address
InitSPC_record     ends

InitSPC            proc    near
                   push    bp
                   mov     bp,sp
                   les     bx,SPC_Pointer     ; point to SPC
                   mov     SCTL,0c0h          ; reset SPC
                   mov     al,[bp].InitAddr ; get initiator address
                   mov     BDID,al            ; write initiator's addr into Reg
                   mov     TMOD,0             ; clear reg
                   mov     SCTL,01ah          ; enable arbitration, parity
                                              ; ... and reselection
                   mov     SDGC,0             ; clear diagnostics reg
                   pop     bp
                   ret
InitSPC            endp
```

```
;******************************************************************************;
;       SELECT TARGET DEVICE                                                   ;
;       Select a target device on the SCSI bus with ATN line asserted.         ;
;       Check if the target responds to the ATN line with the message          ;
;       out phase. If so, send an IDENTIFY message to the target.              ;
;                                                                              ;
;       Entry: BYTE @ [bp+4] = target SCSI address,  0..7                      ;
;              BYTE @ [bp+6] = target SCSI logical unit number, 0..7           ;
;                                                                              ;
;       Exit:  AX = status message                                            ;
;******************************************************************************;


Select_record      struc
                   dw      ?                       ; bp
                   dw      ?                       ; ip - return address
TargAddr           db      ?,?                     ; target address
TargLUN            db      ?,?                     ; target LUN
Select_record      ends

Select             proc    near
                   push    bp
                   mov     bp,sp
                   les     bx,SPC_Pointer          ; point to SPC
                   mov     PCTL,0                  ; phase control = out indicates
                           ;                       ... selection phase
                   mov     al,BDID                 ; get initiator's SCSI ID,1..128
                   push    bx                      ; save SPC ptr
                   xor     bh,bh
                   mov     bl,[bp].TargAddr        ; get target SCSI address, 0..7
                   or      al,Addr2ID[bx]          ; convert to SCSI ID, 1..128
                           ;                       ...OR with initiator's ID
                           ;                       ...(for reselection, see spec.)
                   pop     bx                      ; [es:bx] -> SPC
                   mov     TEMP,al                 ; put arbitration ID's in temp reg
                   mov     TCH,high(SELECTION_TIMEOUT) ; load selection time-out
                   mov     TCM,low(SELECTION_TIMEOUT) ; ... value
                   mov     TCL,BUS_DELAY           ; load bus free delay time-out
                   mov     SCTL,060h               ; set ATN line, select with attention
                   mov     SCTL,010h               ; start selection operation
SelectWaitIntr:
                   cmp     INTS,0                  ; any intr bit set?
                    jne    SelectIntr              ; yes
                   test    SSTS,020h               ; no, select operation still
                                                     pending?
                                                   ;
                    ... check for lost arbitration
                    jz     SelectWaitIntr          ; still pending
                   mov     ax,LOST_ARBITRATION     ; we've lost the arbitration
                   jmp     SelectExit
```

```
SelectIntr:
                test    INTS,10h         ; command complete intr?
                 jz     SelectTimeout    ; no, check time-out
                mov     al,PSNS          ; yes, read phase
                and     al,087h          ; check REQ & phase bits
                cmp     al,086h          ; target requesting msg out?
                 jne    SelectNoMsg      ; no, skip msg out phase
                mov     al,0c0h          ; yes, send IDENTIFY message
                                         ;... with disconnect/reselect bits
                or      al,[bp].TargLUN  ; ... and target LUN
                mov     @msgout,al       ; save in msg out byte
                xor     ah,ah            ; clear upper
                push    ax               ; send AX message to target
                call    Message_Out      ; send message
                pop     cx               ; remove parameter from stack
SelectNoMsg:
                jmp     SelectOK
SelectTimeout:
                test    INTS,04h         ; time-out intr occured?
                 jz     SelectOtherIntr  ; no, unexpected interrupt
                mov     ax,TIMEOUT       ; return time-out error
                jmp                      SelectExit
SelectOtherIntr:
                mov     ax,ERROR_INTR    ; return error
                jmp     SelectExit
SelectOK:
                mov     ax,SELECTED      ; successful selection
SelectExit:
                pop     bp
                ret
Select           endp
```

```
;***********************************************************************;
;     TRANSFER DATA TO/FROM SCSI BUS                                    ;
;     General data transfer for all data transfer phases.              ;
;     Read or write a stream of bytes to/from the SCSI bus and check   ;
;     for the following conditions:                                    ;
;                                                                       ;
;     1) # of bytes requested == # of bytes transferred - normal       ;
;     2) # of bytes requested > # of bytes transferred - pad           ;
;     3) # of bytes requested < # of bytes transferred - phase change  ;
;                                                                       ;
;     This routine, and the SPC,  will accept a 24-bit number as a      ;
;     transfer length, allowing up to 16M bytes to be read or          ;
;     written to the SCSI device in one data phase transaction.        ;
;                                                                       ;
;     Entry:    WORD @ [bp+4] - pointer to list of bytes               ;
;               LONG @ [bp+6] - length - number of bytes in list       ;
;               BYTE @ [bp10] - transfer type - READ=0 or WRITE=1      ;
;                                                                       ;
;     Exit:     AX - error status                                       ;
;               AX > 0 - transferred all bytes in list                 ;
;               AX < 0 - transfer terminated early                     ;
;***********************************************************************;


Transfer_record struc
                dw      ?           ;           bp
                dw      ?           ;           ip
data_ptr        dw      ?           ;           ptr to byte to transfer
length_lo       dw      ?           ;           LSW length of transfer
length_hi       dw      ?           ;           MSW length of transfer
direction       dw      ?           ;           direction, READ=0, WRITE=1
Transfer_record ends

Transfer_Data   proc    near
                push    bp
                mov     bp,sp
                cld                             ; auto increment di,si
                mov     si,[bp].data_ptr    ;       ; point to stream of bytes
                mov     di,si                   ; di also, for read operation
                les     bx,SPC_Pointer          ; point to SPC
                mov     al,byte ptr [bp].length_hi ; get length MSW
                mov     TCH,al                  ; load counter high
                mov     ax,[bp].length_lo       ; get length MSW
                mov     TCM,ah                  ; load counter mid
                mov     TCL,al                  ; load counter low
                mov     SCMD,084h               ; do programmed i/o transfer
XferCmdWait:
                mov     al,SSTS                 ;read status, wait for transfer
                and     al,0foh                 ; ... operation to start
                cmp     al,0b0h                 ; connected as init and
                                                ; ... transfer in progress bit set?
                jne     XferCmdWait             ; no, wait for SPC to start
```

```
XferLoop:
                cmp     INTS,0              ; intr occured?
                   jne  XferCheckIntr      ; yes
                cmp     [bp].direction,WRITE ; writing?
                   jne  Reading            ; no, reading
Writing:
                test    SSTS,02h           ; fifo not full?
                   jne  XferLoop           ; no wait, fifo is full
                lodsb                       ; read byte, inc si
                mov     DREG,al            ; write byte to fifo
                jmp     XferDec            ; decrement and check count
Reading:
                test    SSTS,1             ; fifo not empty?
                   jne  XferLoop           ; no, wait for byte
                mov     al,DREG            ; get byte
                stosb                       ; write byte, inc di
                jmp     XferDec            ; decrement/check count
XferCheckIntr:
                test    INTS,08h           ; service required intr?
                   je   TestErrIntr  ; no
                mov     INTS,08h           ; yes, clear it
                mov     ax,SERVICE_REQUIRED    ; exit with error
                jmp     XferExit
TestErrIntr:
                cmp     INTS,0             ; any more intr pending?
                   je   TestParityErr  ; no
                mov     ax,ERROR_INTR      ; yes, exit with error
                jmp     XferExit
TestParityErr:
                test    SERR,0c0h          ; parity error?
                   je   XferLoop           ; no, wait for bytes
                mov     ax,PARITY_ERROR  ; yes, exit with error
                jmp     XferExit
XferDec:
                sub     [bp].length_lo,1     ; decrement count
                sbb     [bp].length_hi,0     ; 32-bit count
                mov     ax,[bp].length_lo    ; get length
                or      ax,[bp].length_hi    ; =0?
                   jne  XferLoop           ;    no, continue
```

```
XferDone:
                test    INTS,010h       ; command complete intr?
            je  XferDone                ; no, wait
                mov     INTS,010h       ; yes, reset intr
                mov     al,PCTL         ; read phase control
                and     al,7            ; get bus phase bits
                or      al,080h         ; add REQ bit
                mov     dl,PSNS         ; read phase sense reg
                and     al,087h         ; mask phase bits & REQ
                cmp     al,dl           ; are we in new phase?
                mov     ax,OK           ; assume good status
            jne XferExit                ; jmp if in new phase
                mov     TEMP,0          ; no, load temp with padding value
                mov     SCTL,085h       ; do padding transfer
                                        ;...to cause target to go to
                                        ; ... next phase
XferPad:
                mov     al,INTS
                and     al,018h         ; wait for cmd complete & svc req
                cmp     al,018h
            jne XferPad                 ; no, wait for pad to finish
                mov     INTS,18h        ; reset intrs
                mov     ax,OKPAD        ; return good with PAD status
XferExit:
                pop     di
                pop     si
                pop     bp
                ret
Transfer_Data   endp
```

```
;*************************************************************************;
;     SEND COMMAND                                                       ;
;     Send a SCSI command block to the target device.                    ;
;     Assume TCH, TCM and TCL registers = 0                              ;
;                                                                        ;
;     Entry:     WORD @ [bp+4] - pointer to SCSI command block           ;
;                WORD @ [bp+6] - length of command block, 6, 10, 12 bytes ;
;                                                                        ;
;     Exit:      AX  - transfer status                                   ;
;                > 0 - transferred all bytes in list                     ;
;                < 0 - transfer terminated early, error                  ;
;*************************************************************************;


Select_record     struc
                  dw      ?            ; bp
                  dw      ?            ; ip
cmd_ptr           dw      ?            ; ptr to cmd bytes
cmd_length        dw      ?            ; length of cmd
Select_record     ends

Send_Command      proc    near
                  push    bp
                  mov     bp,sp
                  les     bx,SPC_Pointer    ; point to SPC
                  mov     PCTL,02h          ; set command out phase
                  mov     ax,WRITE          ; write to target for transfer
                  push    ax                ; put parameters on stack
                  xor     ax,ax
                  push    ax                ; MSW of length = 0
                  push    [bp].cmd_length   ; LSW length of cmd
                  push    [bp].cmd_ptr      ; ptr to cmd bytes
                  call    Transfer_Data     ; do SCSI transfer
                  mov     sp,bp             ; AX has the transfer status
                  pop     bp
                  ret
Send_Command      endp
```

```
;********************************************************************* ;
;        READ SCSI STATUS                                             ;
;        Read the 1 byte status code from the target                  ;
;                                                                     ;
;        Entry:  WORD @ [bp+4] - pointer to byte to hold SCSI status  ;
;                                                                     ;
;        Exit:   AX - transfer status                                 ;
;                > 0 - transferred SCSI status to pointer location    ;
;                < 0 - transfer terminated early, error               ;
;********************************************************************* ;


Status_record      struc
                   dw     ?                ; bp
                   dw     ?                ; ip
status_ptr         dw     ?                ; ptr to status byte
Status_record      ends

Status_In          proc   near
                   push   bp
                   mov    bp,sp
                   les    bx,SPC_Pointer   ; point to SPC
                   mov    PCTL,03h         ; set phase to status in
                   mov    ax,READ          ; read mode
                   push   ax
                   xor    ax,ax
                   push   ax               ; MSW of transfer length
                   inc    ax               ; LSW of length = 1 byte
                   push   ax
                   push   [bp].status_ptr  ; pointer to status byte
                   call   Transfer_Data    ; read 1 byte from SCSI target
                   mov    sp,bp            ; AX = result code
                   pop    bp
                   ret
Status_In          endp
```

```
*********************************************************************** ;
;                                                                      ;
;      SEND MESSAGE OUT                                                 ;
;      Send a 1 byte message the the target device.                    ;
;      When the SPC is in the INITIATOR mode, it will automatically     ;
;      negate the ATN signal after the message byte has been           ;
;      successfully sent to the target device, this is in comformance   ;
;      with the SCSI spec. (See spec. for further details)             ;
;                                                                      ;
;      Entry:   WORD @ [bp+4] - pointer to message byte to send        ;
;                                                                      ;
;      Exit:    AX - transfer status                                   ;
;               > 0 - transferred message byte to target device        ;
;               < 0 - transfer terminated early, error                 ;
;                                                                      ;
*********************************************************************** ;


Message_Out_rec    struc
                   dw      ?              ; bp
                   dw      ?              ; ip
msg_out_ptr        dw      ?              ; ptr to message out byte
Message_Out_rec    ends

Message_Out        proc    near
                   push    bp
                   mov     bp,sp
                   les     bx,SPC_Pointer     ; point to SPC
                   mov     PCTL,06h           ; set desired phase to message out
                   mov     ax,WRITE           ; send byte to SCSI bus
                   push    ax                 ; param's on stack
                   xor     ax,ax
                   push    ax                 ; MSW of transfer count
                   inc     ax                 ; LSW = 1 byte transfer
                   push    ax
                   push    [bp].msg_out_ptr   ; pointer to message byte to send
                   call    Transfer_Data      ; send it
                   mov     sp,bp              ; AX has transfer status
                   pop     bp
                   ret
Message_Out        endp
```

```
;************************************************************************ ;
;      READ MESSAGE IN                                                  ;
;      Read a 1 byte message from the SCSI target device.              ;
;      When the SPC is in the INITIATOR mode it will automatically     ;
;      hold the ACK line active on the last byte of the message        ;
;      received from the target device. This is to allow the           ;
;      INITIATOR to interpret the message and accept or, if            ;
;      necessary,reject it according to the SCSI protocol's message    ;
;      reject sequence. (See spec. for further details)                ;
;                                                                       ;
;      Entry:  WORD @ [bp+4] - pointer to address to hold message byte ;
;                                                                       ;
;      Exit:   AX - transfer status                                    ;
;              > 0 - transferred SCSI message to pointer location      ;
;              < 0 - transfer terminated early, error;                 ;
;************************************************************************ ;
                                                                        ;

Message_In_rec    struc
                  dw     ?              ; bp
                  dw     ?              ; ip
msg_in_ptr        dw     ?              ; ptr to message in byte address
Message_In_recends

Message_Inprocnear
                  push   bp
                  mov    bp,sp
                  les    bx,SPC_Pointer     ; point to SPC
                  mov    PCTL,06h           ; set desired phase to message in
                  mov    ax,READ            ; read byte from device
                  pus    hax
                  xor    ax,ax              ; MSW of transfer length
                  push   ax
                  inc    ax                 ; LSW of length = 1 byte
                  push   ax
                  push   [bp].msg_in_ptr    ; ptr to message byte
                  call   Transfer_Data      ; read message
                  add    sp,6               ; remove param's from stack
                  or     ax,ax              ; if < 0 then error
                   jl    MIError            ; error
                  les    bx,SPC_Pointer     ; no error, point to SPC
                  mov    SCMD,0c0h          ; manually negate the ACK signal
                  mov    INTS,010h          ; reset command complete intr
MIError:
                  pop    bp
                  ret
Message_In        endp
```

```
;*********************************************************************;
;                                                                     ;
;          READ DATA STREAM FROM SCSI DEVICE                          ;
;          Read up to 16M bytes from the target device.               ;
;                                                                     ;
;       Entry: WORD @ [bp+4] - pointer to data buffer                 ;
;              LONG @ [bp+6] - length of transfer (24-bit)            ;
;                                                                     ;
;       Exit:  AX - transfer status                                   ;
;              > 0 - read byte from SCSI device                       ;
;              < 0 - transfer terminated early, error                 ;
;*********************************************************************;


Data_In_record    struc
                  dw      ?              ; bp
                  dw      ?              ; ip
data_in_ptr       dw      ?              ; ptr to byte to transfer
data_in_len_lo    dw      ?              ; length of transfer
data_in_len_hi    dw      ?
Data_In_record    ends

Data_In           proc    near
                  push    bp
                  mov     bp,sp
                  les     bx,SPC_Pointer     ; point to SPC
                  mov     PCTL,01h           ; desired phase = data in
                  mov     ax,READ            ; read bytes from target device
                  push    ax
                  push    [bp].data_in_len_hi; MSW of length
                  push    [bp].data_in_len_lo; LSW of length
                  push    [bp].data_in_ptr   ; pointer to receive buffer
                  call    Transfer_Data      ; read bytes
                  mov     sp,bp              ; AX has result code
                  pop     bp
                  ret
Data_In           endp
```

```
****************************************************************  ;
;                                                                ;
;        WRITE DATA STREAM TO SCSI DEVICE                        ;
;        Write up to 16M bytes to the target device.            ;
;                                                                ;
;        Entry: WORD @ [bp+4] - pointer to data buffer           ;
;               LONG @ [bp+6] - length of transfer (24-bit)     ;
;                                                                ;
;        Exit:  AX - transfer status                             ;
;               > 0 - wrote bytes to SCSI device                 ;
;               < 0 - transfer terminated early, error           ;
****************************************************************  ;


Data_Out_record    struc
                   dw     ?              ; bp
                   dw     ?              ; ip
data_out_ptr       dw     ?              ; ptr to byte to transfer
data_out_len_lo    dw     ?              ; LSW length of transfer
data_out_len_hi    dw     ?              ; MSW
Data_Out_record    ends

Data_Out           proc   near
                   push   bp
movbp, sp
                   les    bx,SPC_Pointer      ; point to SPC
                   mov    PCTL,0              ; set desired phase to data out
                   mov    ax,WRITE            ; write bytes to target device
                   push   ax
                   push   [bp].data_out_len_hi ; MSW of length
                   push   [bp].data_out_len_lo ; LSW of length
                   push   [bp].data_out_ptr; address of bytes to send
                   call   Transfer_Data       ; send bytes to target
                   mov    sp,bp               ; AX has result code
                   pop    bp
                   ret
Data_Out           endp
```

```
;**********************************************************************  ;
;                                                                       ;
;          DECODE SCSI BUS PHASE                                        ;
;          After selection, read target's requested SCSI bus phase      ;
;          and go to the appropriate handler, continue calling this     ;
;          routine until the COMMAND COMPLETE message is sent from the   ;
;          target, indicating the end of the SCSI operation.            ;
;                                                                       ;
;          Entry: void                                                  ;
;                                                                       ;
;          Exit:  > 0 successful operation                              ;
;                 = 0 no phase requested (REQ signal not active)         ;
;                 < 0 unsuccessful operation                            ;
;**********************************************************************  ;


Decode_Phase      proc   near
                  les    bx,SPC_Pointer    ; point to SPC
                  mov    al,PSNS           ; read phase sense
                  and    al,087h           ; mask REQ + phase
                  sub    al,080h           ; subtract bias
                  cmp    al,7              ; decode 0..7
                   jbe   DPA
                  jmp    NoPhaseReq
DPA:
                  mov    bl,al             ; make index into table
                  xor    bh,bh             ; 16-bit
                  shl    bx,1              ; * 2 = jump table ptr
                  jmp    cs:JmpTable[bx]   ; go to routine

JmpTable          label word
                  dw     p_data_out        ; target requesting data out phase
                  dw     p_data_in         ; target requesting data in phase
                  dw     p_send_command    ; target requesting command phase
                  dw     p_status_in       ; target requesting status phase
                  dw     p_illegal         ; reserved
                  dw     p_illegal         ; reserved
                  dw     p_message_out     ; target requesting msg out phase
                  dw     p_message_in      ; target requesting msg in phase

p_data_out:                                ; send data to target device
                  push   @datalength_hi    ; MSW number of bytes to send
                  push   @datalength_lo    ; LSW
                  push   @dataptr          ; ptr to bytes to send
                  call   Data_Out          ; write bytes
                  add    sp,6              ; remove stack parameters
                  jmp    DecodeDone        ; return with AX = transfer status
```

```
p_data_in:                              ; receive data from target device
            push    @datalength_hi      ; MSW number of bytes to receive
            push    @datalength_lo      ; LSW
            push    @dataptr            ; ptr to byte buffer
            call    Data_In             ; read bytes
            add     sp,6                ; remove stack parameters
            jmp     DecodeDone          ; AX = transfer status


p_send_command:                         ; send SCSI command block to target
            push    @cmdlength          ; number of bytes in cmd blk
            mov     ax,offset @cmdblk;  ptr to cmd blk
            push    ax                  ; stack it
            call    Send_Command        ; send bytes
            add     sp,6                ; remove stack param's
            jmp     DecodeDone          ; AX = status

p_status_in:                            ; read SCSI status from target
            mov     ax,offset @status   ; ptr to status bytes
            push    ax                  ; stack it
            call    Status_In           ; read status byte
            pop     cx                  ; remove stack param's
            jmp     DecodeDone          ; AX = status


p_illegal:                              ; undefined/reserved SCSI phases
            mov     ax,ILLEGAL_PHASE    ; AX = error
            jmp     DecodeDone


p_message_out:                          ; send message to target
            mov     ax,offset @msgout   ; ptr to msg byte
            push    ax                  ; stack it
            call    Message_Out         ; send it
            pop     cx                  ; remove param's
            jmp     DecodeDone          ; AX = status

p_message_in:                           ; read message from target
            mov     ax,offset @msgin    ; ptr to msg byte
            push    ax                  ; stack it
            call    Message_In          ; read it
            pop     cx                  ; remove param's
            jmp     DecodeDone          ; AX = status


NoPhaseReq:
            xor     ax,ax               ; target not requesting, REQ
                                        negated
DecodeDone:
            ret                         ; return to caller, AX=transfer
                                        status
Decode_Phaseendp
```

```
*********************************************************************  ;
;                                                                     ;
;       MANUALLY TRANSFER DATA TO/FROM SCSI BUS                       ;
;       Read or write a stream of bytes to/from the SCSI bus and check ;
;       for completion.                                               ;
;                                                                     ;
;       This example illustrates the use of the manual transfer mode  ;
;       of the SPC. This mode is useful for "spoon-feeding" eac byte to ;
;       a target device, this could be helpful when debugging         ;
;       SCSI software step-by-step or testing the behavior of a SCSI  ;
;       peripheral under certain conditions.                          ;
;                                                                     ;
;       This mode of operation does not use the transfer counter of   ;
;       the SPC. The transfer size is limited only by the size of the ;
;       transfer length parameter passed to this routine.             ;
;                                                                     ;
;       Entry:   WORD @ [bp+4] - pointer to list of bytes             ;
;                LONG @ [bp+6] - length - number of bytes in list     ;
;                BYTE @ [bp10] - transfer type - READ=0 or WRITE=1    ;
;                                                                     ;
;       Exit:    AX - error status                                    ;
;                AX > 0 - transferred all bytes in list               ;
;                AX < 0 - transfer terminated early                   ;
;                                                                     ;
*********************************************************************  ;


Manual_Xfer_rec          struc
                         dw        ?     ; bp
                         dw        ?     ; ip
Man_data_ptr             dw        ?     ; ptr to byte to transfer
Man_length_lo            dw        ?     ; length of transfer, up to 4G bytes
Man_length_hi            dw        ?     ; ... 32-bits
Man_direction            dw        ?     ; direction, READ=0, WRITE=1
Manual_Xfer_rec          ends

Man_Xfer_Data            proc      near
                         push      bp
                         mov       bp,sp
                         cld                      ; auto increment di,si
                         mov       si,[bp].data_ptr      ; point to stream of bytes
                         mov       di,si          ; di also, for read operation
                         les       bx,SPC_Pointer; point to SPC
ManXfer:
                         cmp       [bp].Man_direction,READ ; reading ?
                         je        ManRead        ; yes
```

```
ManWrite:
                test      PSNS,80h        ; wait for REQ asserted
                jz        ManWrite        ; not yet
                lodsb                     ; read byte from buffer, inc si
                mov       TEMP,al         ; load byte into temp register
                mov       SCMD,0e0h       ; assert ACK
MWNoReq:
                test      PSNS,80h        ; wait for REQ negated
                                          ; ... indicating byte accepted
                jnz       MWNoReq         ; not yet
                mov       SCMD,0c0h       ; negate ACK
                jmp       ManDec          ; decrement count
ManRead:
                test      PSNS,80h        ; wait for REQ asserted
                jz        ManRead         ; not yet
                mov       SCMD,0e0h       ; assert ACK
MRNoReq:
                test      PSNS,80h        ; wait for REQ negated
                                          ; ... indicating byte sent
                jnz       MRNoReq         ; not yet
                mov       al,TEMP         ; read byte from temp
                stosb                     ; write to buffer, inc di
                mov       SCMD,0c0h       ; negate ACK
ManDec:
                sub       [bp].Man_length_lo,1;    decrement count
                sbb       [bp].Man_length_hi,0;    32-bit count
                mov       ax,[bp].Man_length_lo    ; get length
                or        ax,[bp].Man_length_hi    ; =0?
                jne       ManXfer         ; not done
ManXferExit:
                mov       ax,OK
                pop       bp
                ret
Man_Xfer_Data   endp
```

```
****************************************************************************** ;
;                                                                             ;
;     DMA TRANSFER DATA TO/FROM SCSI BUS                                      ;
;     Read or write a stream of bytes to the SCSI bus using DMA               ;
;     and check for the following conditions:                                 ;
;                                                                             ;
;     1) # of bytes requested == # of bytes transferred - normal             ;
;     2) # of bytes requested > # of bytes transferred - pad                 ;
;     3) # of bytes requested < # of bytes transferred - phase change ;      ;
;                                                                             ;
;     Entry:   WORD @ [bp+4] - pointer to list of bytes                      ;
;              LONG @ [bp+6] - length - number of bytes in list              ;
;              BYTE @ [bp10] - transfer type - READ=0 or WRITE=1             ;
;                                                                             ;
;     Exit:    AX - error status                                             ;
;              AX > 0 - transferred all bytes in list                        ;
;              AX < 0 - transfer terminated early                            ;
;                                                                             ;
;     Note: If the SPC is interrupt driven along with using DMA,             ;
;              the code below becomes even smaller since it is not           ;
;              necessary to test the INTS register within a loop.            ;
;              In fact, the overhead to start a data transfer in             ;
;              the SPC takes only 3 steps                                    ;
;                                                                             ;
;              1) Write desired phase to PCTL register                       ;
;              2) Write 1 to 3 bytes to the transfer counters, TCH/M/L       ;
;              3) Write the DMA transfer cmd to SCMD register (0x80)         ;
****************************************************************************** ;


DMA_Xfer_record        struc
                       dw        ?        ; bp
                       dw        ?        ; ip
DMA_data_ptr           dw        ?        ; ptr to byte to transfer
DMA_length_lo          dw        ?        ; LSW length of transfer
DMA_length_hi          dw        ?        ; MSW length of transfer
DMA_direction          dw        ?        ; direction, READ=0, WRITE=1
DMA_Xfer_record        ends

DMA_Transfer_Data      proc      near
                       push      bp
                       mov       bp,sp
                       push      [bp].DMA_direction    ;get direction
                       push      [bp].DMA_length_hi    ; ... length
                       push      [bp].DMA_length_lo    ; ...
                       push      [bp].DMA_data_ptr     ; ... and address
```

```
                  call    Setup_DMA       ;set up the system's DMA controller
                  mov     sp,bp           ;remove stack param's
                  les     bx,SPC_Pointer; point to SPC
                  mov     al,byte ptr [bp].DMA_length_hi ;MSW of transfer size
                  mov     TCH,al          ; store in counter high
                  mov     ax,[bp].DMA_length_lo ; LSW of transfer size
                  mov     TCM,ah          ; store in counter mid
                  mov     TCL,al          ; store in counter low
                  mov     SCTL,080h       ; start DMA transfer
NoIntr:
                  cmp     INTS,0          ; wait for intr, signaling
                                          ;... the end of the DMA transfer
                  je      NoIntr          ; no intr yet
                  test    INTS,010h       ; cmd complete intr?
                  je      NoCmdCmp        ; no, transfer error
                  mov     ax,OK           ; transfer successful
                  jmp     DMADone
NoCmdCmp:
                  mov     ax,ERROR_INTR   ; transfer didn't complete properly
                  jmp     DMADone
DMADone:
                  pop     bp
                  ret
DMA_Transfer_Data endp

                  end
```

Appendix E

CONTROL SEQUENCE
FOR SPC DRIVER

The following examples show the essential elements necessary for the creation of a SCSI software driver using Fujitsu's family of SCSI controllers. Flowcharts are provided to outline the overall sequence of operation. Code that is dependent on the operating environment, such as error processing, exception handling and the operating system interface, are not shown for the sake of brevity and clarity. This example assumes that the SCSI controller is accessible via memory-mapped I/O and is controlled by an 8086 family processor. This code will operate on any of the Fujitsu SCSI controllers.

Initialize Controller

```
INITADDR   EQU     7

INITIALIZE:
      MOV    SCTL, OCOH         ; Reset controller
      MOV    BDID, INITADDR     ; Load INIT's SCSI addr, 0..7
      MOV    TMOD, 0            ; ASYNC I/O
      MOV    SDGC, 0            ; Diagnostic mode off
      MOV SCTL, 01AH            ; Relese reset with Arbitration on,
      RET                       ; Parity Check on, Reselect on,
                                ; H/W Interrupt off
```

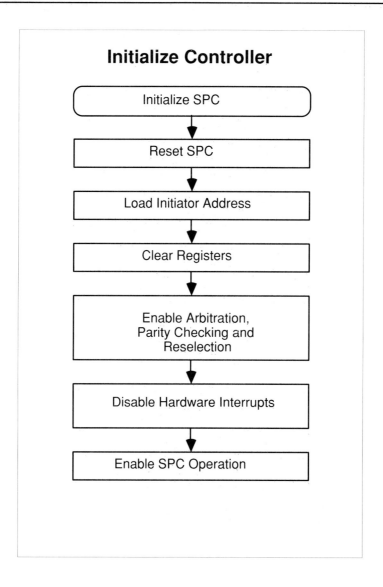

Arbitrate and Select Phase

```
; ENTRY:        BL = TARGET BUS ID (1,2,4,8,16,32,64,128)
;               BH = TARGET LUN
;

STD    EQU      4400                   ; 275 msec
BFD    EQU      4                      ; 1200 nsec

       MOV      PCTL,00H               ; Indicate selection phase,I/O = 0
       OR       BL,BDID               ; 'OR' in Initiator Bus ID
                                       ; ... So Target can reselect
       MOV      TEMP,BL               ; Set Target & Init bus ID
                                       ; ... during selection
       MOV      TCH,HIGH(STD)         ; Set MSB of sel timeout value
       MOV      TCH,LOW(STD)          ; Set LSB of sel timeout value
       MOV      TCL,BFD               ; Set bus settle + bus free delay
       MOV      SCMD,60H              ; Assert ATN signal
       MOV      SCMD,10H              ; Start ARB & Selection sequence
WAIT:
       CMP      INTS,0                ; Intr occur ?
       JNZ      INTR                  ; Yes
       TEST     SSTS,20H              ; Operation in progress ?
       JNZ      WAIT                  ; Yes
LOSTARB:                              ; No, lost Arbitration
 ... process lost arbitration
```

Arbitrate and Select Phase (continued)

```
INTR:
      TEST   INTS,10H          ; Selection successful ?
      JNZ    CONNECTED         ; Yes, continue
      TEST   INTS,04H          ; Target, timeout error ?
      JNZ    TIMEOUT           ; Yes, process
      JMP    OTHER             ; Process error
CONNECTED:
      CALL   CHECKMSGOUT       ; Check for MSG OUT Phase in order
                               ; ... to send Identify MSG
      JC     NOIDENT
      MOV    AH,BH             ; Load desired Target LUN
      OR     AH,0C0H           ; Send Identify, with support for
                               ; ... Disconnection & Reselection
      CALL   MSGOUT            ; Send message
NOIDENT:
      RET                      ; Target successfully selected

OTHER:
  ... process unexpected condition
  ... bus reset or SPC hardware error
```

Arbitrate and Select Phase

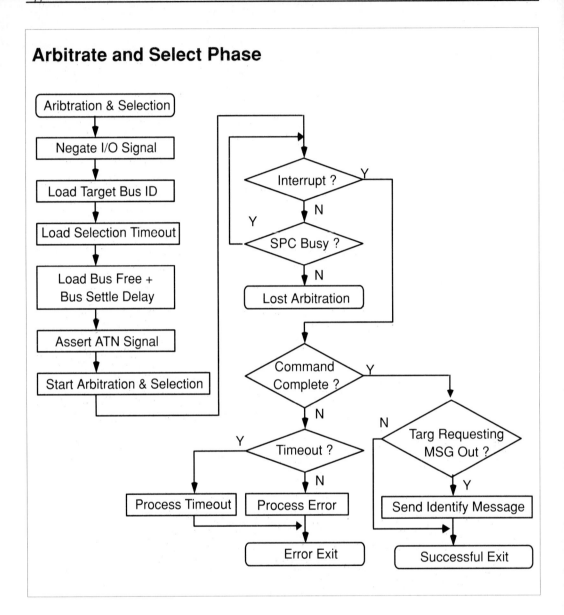

Command Phase

```
; ENTRY:        [ES:SE] ?> SCSI Command
;               CL = Command Length - 6,10 or 12
;               TCH, TCM, TCL = 0

SENDCOMMAND: MOV   TCL,CL       ; Load transfer count
             MOV   PCTL,02H     ; Command Phase
             MOV   SCMD,84H     ; Program transfer
             MOV   AL,0F0H      ; Wait for SPC command to begin
SYNC:        AND   AL,SSTS      ; Check Init & Busy bit
             CMP   AL,0B0H      ; Ready ?
             JNE   SYNC         ; No, Wait
             TEST  SSTS,02H     ; FIFO Full?
             JNE   COUT         ; Yes, wait
COUT:        LODS  BYTE PTR ES:[SI]Read byte, inc ptr
             MOV   DREG,AL      ; Send byte to SCSI
             DEC   CL           ; Count done?
             JNZ   COUT         ; No
             CMP   INTS,0       ; Intr Occur ?
             JZ    CWAIT        ; No, wait
             TEST  INTS,10H     ; Command completed ?
CWAIT:       JZ    CERR         ; No, process error
             MOV   INTS,10H     ; Reset CMD complete Intr
             RET                ; Finished




CERR:
 ...process unexpected condition
    ...bus reset, disconnect or SPC hardware error
```

Command Phase

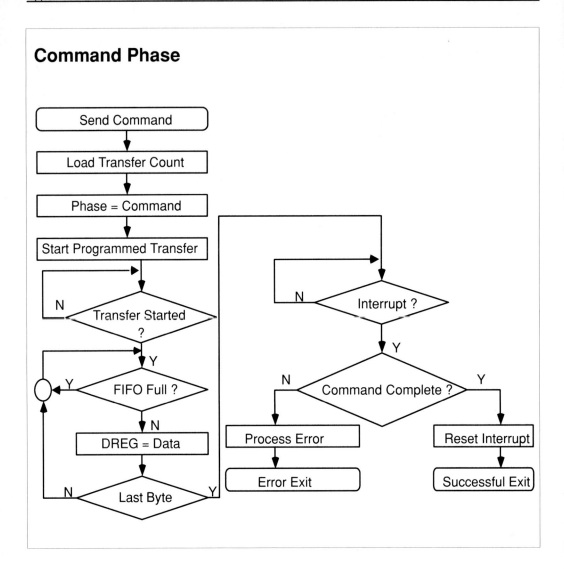

Message Out Phase

```
; ENTRY:       AH = Message Byte
;              TCH, TCM, TCL, = 0
;              ATN Signal Is Asserted

MSGOUT:
        MOV    TCL,1              ; Transfer 1 byte
        MOV    PCTL,06H           ; Specify MSG OUT phase
        MOV    SCMD,84H           ; Program transfer
SYNC:
        MOV    AL,0F1H            ; Wait for SPC command to begin
        AND    AL,SSTS            ; Check Init & Busy bit
        CMP    AL,0B1H            ; Ready and FIFO empty ?
        JNE    SYNC               ; No, wait
        MOV    DREG,AH            ; Send byte & automatically
                                  ; ... negate ATN signal
MOWAIT:
        CMP    INTS,0             ; Intr ?
        JZ     MOWAIT             ; Not yet
        TEST   INTS,10H           ; Command completed ?
        JZ     MERR               ; No, process error
        MOV    INTS,10H           ; Reset CMD complete Intr
        RET                       ; Finished
MERR:
 ...process unexpected condition
 ...bus reset, disconnect or SPC hardware error
```

Message Out Phase

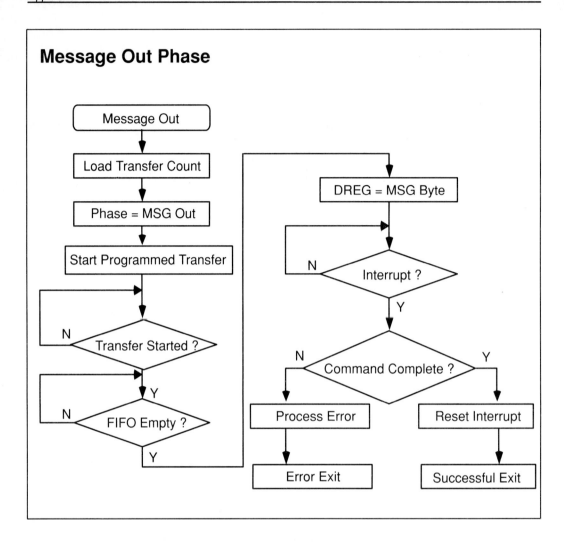

Data In Phase

```
; ENTRY:                   BX = Byte Count
;                          [ES:DI] = Data Buffer Pointer
; Must handle 3 conditions:
; 1) Target Xfers exact byte count requested
; 2) Target Xfers more bytes than requested (Pad Input)
; 3) Target Xfers less bytes than requested (Phase Change)

DATAIN:
    CLD                         ; Clear direction flag
    MOV     TCM,BH              ; Load count, 0..65535
    MOV     TCL,BL
    MOV     PCTL,01H            ; Data In Phase
    MOV     SCMD,84H            ; Programmed transfer
SYNC:
    MOV     AL,0F0H             ; Wait for SPC command to begin
    AND     AL,SSTS             ; Check Init & Busy bit
    CMP     AL,0B0H             ; Ready ?
    JNE     SYNC                ; No, wait
DILOOP:
    CMP     INTS,0              ; Any Intrs ?
    JNE     DISVC               ; Yes, process
    TEST    SSTS,01H            ; FIFO empty ?
    JNZ     DILOOP              ; Yes, wait
    MOV     AL,DREG             ; Read byte
    STOS    BYTE PTR [ES:DI]    ; Store & inc ptr
    DEC     BX                  ; Done ?
    JNE     DILOOP
```

Data In Phase (continued)

```
DICC:
      TEST    INTS,10H
      JZ      DICC
      MOV     INTS,10H; SPC Command complete ?
      MOV     AL,87H  ; No, wait
      AND     AL,PSNS ; Reset Intr
      CMP     AL,81H  ; Target still in Data-In phase ?
      JNE     DIEXIT  ; Read phase sense register
DIPAD:                ; Req + Data-In Phase ?
      MOV     SCMD,85H; No, exit normally (exact transfer)
DICCSR:               ; Target has more, pad input
      TEST    INTS,18H; Programmed xfer pad (long xfer)
      JZ      DICCSR
      MOV     INTS,18H; Command complete + service required intr ?
DIEXIT:               ; No, wait for pad to finish
      RET             ; Reset Intr's
DISVC:
      TEST    INTS,08H; Done
      JZ      DIERROR
      MOV     INTS,08H; Service req Intr (Phase Change) ?
      TEST    SERR,0C0H No, process error Intr
      JNZ     DIERROR ; Yes, xfer halted (short xfer)
 ... process phase change parity error ?
                      ; Yes
DIERROR:              ; No, short transfer
 ...process unexpected condition
 ...bus reset, disconnect, parity or SPC
hardware error
```

Data In Phase

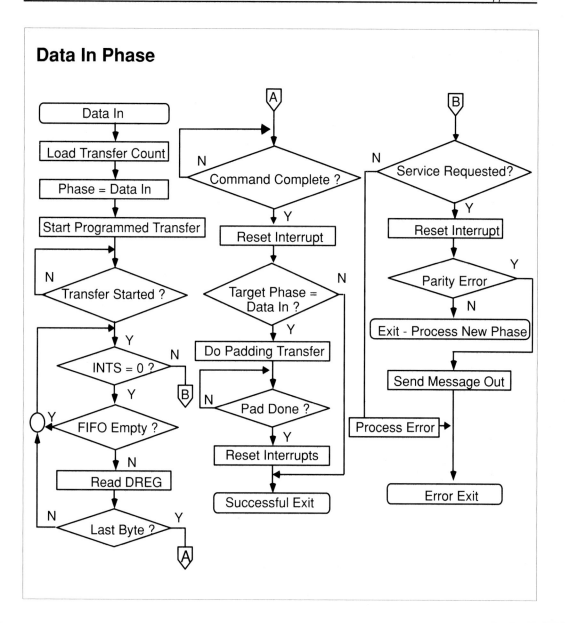

Data Out Phase

```
; ENTRY:        BX = Transfer Count
;               [ES:SI] = Data Buffer Address

DMADATAOUT:
        CALL    SETDMA              ; Set up DMA controller
        MOV     TCM,BH              ; Load transfer count
        MOV     TCL,BL
        MOV     PCTL,00H            ; Set Data Out phase
        MOV     SCMD,80H            ; DMA transfer
DMAOUTWAIT:
        CMP     INTS,0              ; Wait for DMA to complete
        JE      DMAOUTWAI
        TEST    T                   ; Command complete Intr ?
        JZ      INTS,10H            ; Process unexpected interrupt
        MOV     PUI                 ; Reset Intr
        RET     INTS,10H            ; Exit
```

Data Out Phase (continued)

```
DOCC:
      TEST INTS,10H   ; SPC Command complete ?
      JZ   DOCC       ; No, wait
      MOV  INTS,10H   ; Reset Intr
      MOV  AL,87H     ; Target still in Data-Out phase ?
      AND  AL,PSNS    ; Read phase sense register
      CMP  AL,80H     ; Req + Data-In Phase ?
      JNE  DOEXIT     ; No, exit normally (exact transfer)
DOPAD:                ; Target has more, pad output
      MOV  TEMP,0     ; Send 0's
      MOV  SCMD,85H   ; Programmed transfer pad
DOCCSR:
      TEST INTS,18H   ; Command complete + service required Intr ?
      JZ   DOCCSR     ; No, wait for pad to finish
      MOV  INTS,18H   ; Reset Intr's
DOEXIT:
      RET             ; Done
DOSVC:
      TEST INTS,08H   ; Service Req Intr (phase change) ?
      JZ   DOERROR    ; No, process error Intr
      MOV  INTS,08H   ; Yes, xfer halted (short xfer)
 ...process phase change
DOERROR:
 ...process unexpected condition
 ...bus reset, disconnect or SPC hardware error
```

Data Out Phase

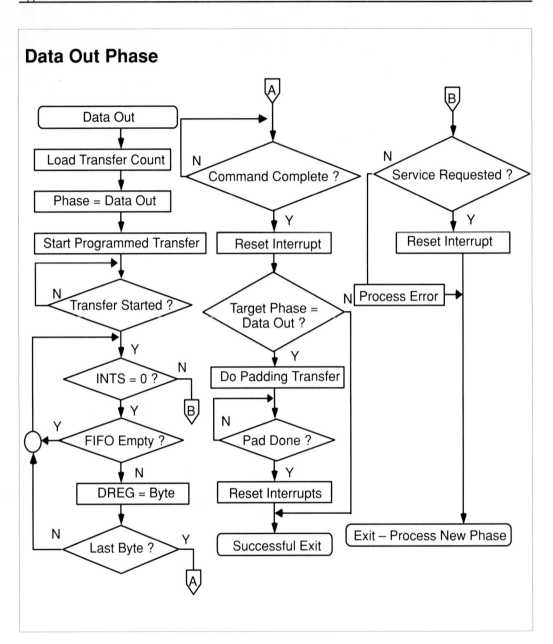

Status Phase

```
; ENTRY:      TCH, TCM, TCL = 0
;
STATUSIN:
      MOV     TCL,1              ; Xfer 1 byte
      MOV     PCTL,03H           ; Status Phase
      MOV     SCMD,84H           ; Programmed transfer
SYNC:
      MOV     AL,0F1H            ; Wait for SPC command to begin
      AND     AL,SSTS            ; Check Init, Busy bit & Empty bit
      CMP     AL,0B0H            ; Ready and FIFO not empty ?
      JNE     SYNC               ; No, wait
      MOV     AL,DREG            ; Read status byte
SWAIT:
      CMP     INTS,0             ; Intr ?
      JZ      SWAIT              ; No
      TEST    INTS,10H           ; Command completed ?
      JZ      SERR               ; No, process error
      MOV     INTS,10H           ; Reset CMD complete Intr
      RET                        ; Finished
SERR:
 ...process unexpected condition
 ...bus reset, disconnect or SPC hardware error
```

Status Phase

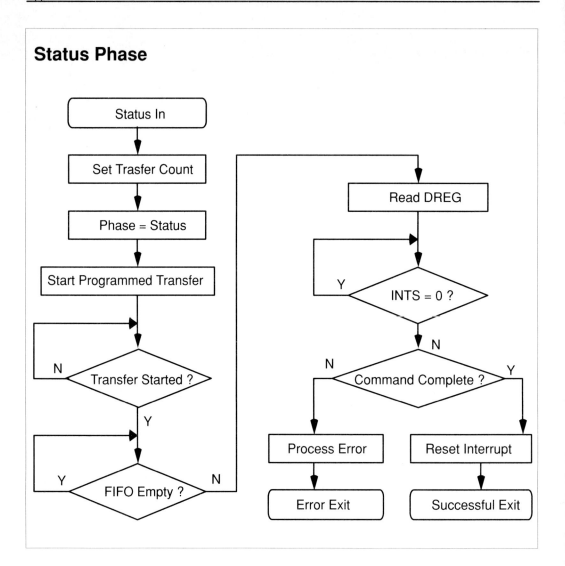

Message In Phase

```
; ENTRY:    TCH, TCM, TCL = 0
;
MGSIN:
      MOV    TCL,1         ; Read 1 byte
      MOV    PCTL,07H      ; Message In phase
      MOV    SCMD,84H      ; Programmed transfer
SYNC:
      MOV    AL,0F1H       ; Wait for SPC command to begin
      AND    AL,SSTS       ; Check Init & Busy bit
      CMP    AL,0B0H       ; Ready and FIFO not empty ?
      JNE    SYNC          ; No, wait
      MOV    AL,DREG       ; Read message byte & automatically hold
                           ; ...ACK active for possible message reject
MIWAIT:
      CMP    INTS,0        ; Intr ?
      JZ     MIWAIT        ; No
      TEST   INTS,10H      ; Command completed ?
      JZ     MIERR         ; No, process error
      TEST   SERR,080H     ; MSG parity error ?
      MOV    AH,09H        ; Parity err code
      JNZ    MSGEJECT      ; Yes, send MSG parity err message
      CALL   PROCESSMS     ; Perform message action
      MOV    G             ; MSG reject code
      JC     AH,07H        ; Not valid MSG, reject it
MIEXIT       MSGREJECT
      MOV                  ; Negate ACK
      MOV    SCMD,C0H      ; Reset CMD complete Intr
      RET    INTS,10H      ; Finished
```

Message In Phase (cont.)

```
MSGREJECT:
      MOV     SCMD,30H      ; Assert ATN, notify target that
                           ; ...last MSG is rejected
      MOV     SCMD,C0H      ; Negate ACK
      MOV     INTS,10H      ; Reset CMD complete Intr
      CALL    CHECMSGOU     ; See if target supports Message Out
      JNE     T             ; No, exit
      CALL    MIEXIT        ; Send MSG
      JMP     MSGOUT        ; Done
MIERR:        MIEXIT
 ...process unexpected condition
 ...bus reset, disconnect or SPC hard-
ware error
```

Message In Phase

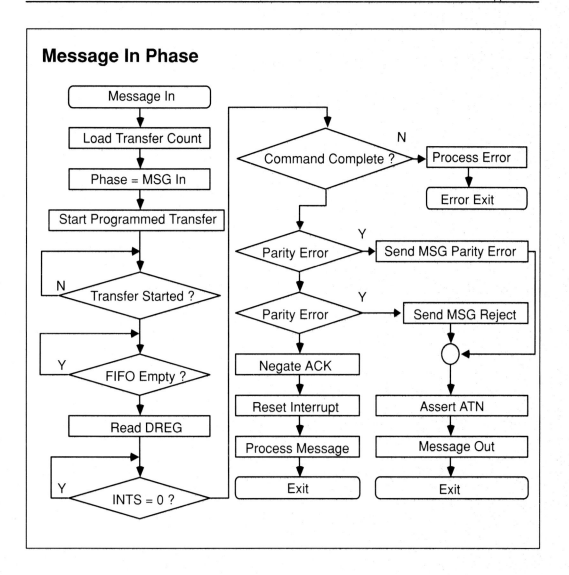

Phase Decoder

```
PHASEDECODE:
        MOV    BL,PSNS              ; Read phase sense registger
        TEST   BL,80H               ; Req asserted ?
        JZ     PHASEDECODE          ; No, wait
        AND    BL,07H               ; Mask out SCSI phase bits
        XOR    BH,BH
        SHL    BX,1                 ; *2
        JMP    CS:PHASETABLE[BX]; Go to phase processing routine

PHASETABLE:
        DW     DATAOUT              ; 0 = Data Out Phase
        DW     DATAIN               ; 1 = Data In Phase
        DW     SENDCOMMAND          ; 2 = Send Command Phase
        DW     STATUSIN             ; 3 = Status Phase
        DW     PHASEDECODE          ; 4 = Reserved
        DW     PHASEDECODE          ; 5 = Reserved
        DW     MSGOUT               ; 6 = Message Out Phase
        DW     MSGIN                ; 7 = Message In Phase
```

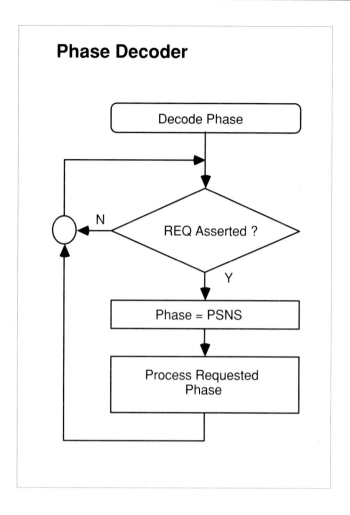

Phase Decoder

Decode Phase

REQ Asserted ?

N

Y

Phase = PSNS

Process Requested Phase

Glossary

SCSI TERMS

As with most advances in computer technology, SCSI brings new terminology to the area of system design. Terms directly related to SCSI are defined in this section.

Term	Definition
ANSI	American National Standards Institute.
ANSI X3.131	ANSI document number for SCSI specification.
Asynchronous Mode	SCSI operating mode where data transfers between INITIATOR and TARGET occurs at discrete rates without regard to specific amounts of time.
Basic SCSI	SCSI product that does not support ARBITRATION.
Bus Arbitration	In a SCSI system, the ability of both INITIATORS and TARGETS to compete and gain control of the SCSI bus for data transmissions.
Bus Free Phase	SCSI bus is idle.
Command Descriptor Block (CDB)	Series of bytes used to define and initiate a SCSI command.
Command Phase	SCSI-bus phase in which INITIATOR is sending a CDB to TARGET.
Daisy-Chained	A method of electrically connecting multiple devices together so all devices use a common set of command/data transfer signals.
Data Phase	SCSI-bus phase which encompasses intertransfer of data between INITIATOR and TARGET.

Term	Definition
Direct Memory Access (DMA)	Method of data transfer to main memory without use of the CPU.
Full SCSI	SCSI product that supports ARBITRATION and the SELECT/DISCONNECT/RESELECT options.
Handshake	Control signals that initiate an asynchronous data transfer between two devices. A handshake is required for each byte transferred and no specific response time is required for either the INITIATOR or the TARGET.
Host Adapter	Usually a plug-in board that performs the host bus-to-SCSI bus communication.
Initiator	SCSI device that is capable of beginning a data transfer operation. Usually, the INITIATOR is the host computer; however, in full SCSI systems, the TARGET can also serve as the INITIATOR.
Intelligent Interface	Any interface (like SCSI) which can execute a high-level protocol and a supporting set of commands.
Mandatory Command	SCSI command that must be supported by the products to remain compatible with the ANSI specifications.
Message Phase	SCSI-bus phase in which the INITIATOR and TARGET exchange information regarding recent transfers of data.
Non-arbitrating	A non-arbitrating SCSI configuration is made up of a single INITIATOR and one or more TARGETS. The INITIATOR is the bus master and the TARGETS are slaves. RESELECTION is not supported since the reselection process requires the TARGETS to arbitrate for the bus. In this basic SCSI configuration, the INITIATOR selects a TARGET and remains connected to the TARGET until the transfer is complete

Term	*Definition*
Optional Command	SCSI command which may or may not be implemented in a SCSI product; the absence of such a command does not affect compatibility.
Reconnect/Disconnect/Reselect	Ability of SCSI device to DISCONNECT from the SCSI bus before completion of certain commands and RESELECT the INITIATOR at a later time.
Reselection Phase	SCSI-bus phase where a device has won Arbitration and a connection between an INITIATOR and a TARGET is re-established after going through disconnection.
Reserved	Command code or byte in SCSI protocol reserved for a future function. The use of reserved bytes violates the requirements for SCSI compatibility.
SCSI ID	A one-of-eight code used to address a device connected to the SCSI bus.
Status Phase	SCSI-bus phase in which the TARGET sends status information to the INITIATOR.
Synchronous	SCSI method of transferring data from INITIATOR to TARGET (or vice-versa) in a specified time interval. In synchronous mode, a data transfer rate of 5.0 megabytes per second is possible.
Target	Any SCSI device capable of receiving commands or data from another SCSI device.
Vendor Unique	SCSI command codes which are undefined.
X3T9.2	The ANSI number designation for the small computer systems interface committee.

Index

A

A0 to A3, 59

ABORT, 26, 27, 34

American National Standard, A–1

ANSI, 2

Arbitration and selection sequence control block, 54

Arbitration delay, A–1

Arbitration enable, 66

Arbitration fail, 191

Arbitration IDs, 42, 43

ARBITRATION phase, 16, 63, 66, 72, 74, 76
  non–arbitrating device, 16
  SCSI ID, 17

Assertion period, A–1

Asychronous, REQ/ACK handshake, 20, 21

Asynchronous bus conditions, 22
  ATTENTION condition, 22
  RESET condition, 22

Asynchronous data transfer, 20

Asynchronous handshake, 22

ATTENTION condition, 22

Attention condition interrupt, 148, 205

Attention detect, 137, 191

B

BDID register, 90, 98

BIOS, B–1

Burst transfers, 191

Bus clear delay, A–1

Bus configurations, 3

Bus device identifier register, 63

BUS DEVICE RESET, 28, 34

Bus free delay, A–2

Bus free interrupt enable, 113

BUS FREE phase, 16, 44, 76

Bus phase control block, 54

Bus phase descriptions, 15

Bus Phases, 15
  DATA TRANSFER, 15

Bus release command, 69, 72, 76

Bus set delay, A–2

Bus settle delay, A–1, A–2

Bus signals, 8
  ACK (ACKNOWLEDGE), 10
  ATN (ATTENTION), 10
  BSY (BUSY), 9
  C/D (CONTROL DATA), 10
  DATA BUS, 9
  DB0–DB7, DBP, 9
  I/O (INPUT/OUTPUT), 10

O

P

R

S